LETHAL PROVOCATION

LETHAL
PROVOCATION

THE CONSTANTINE MURDERS AND THE
POLITICS OF FRENCH ALGERIA

JOSHUA COLE

CORNELL UNIVERSITY PRESS

Ithaca and London

First published 2019 by Cornell University Press

Library of Congress Cataloging-in-Publication Data

Names: Cole, Joshua, 1961– author.
Title: Lethal provocation : the Constantine murders and
    the politics of French Algeria / Joshua Cole.
Description: Ithaca : Cornell University Press, 2019. |
    Includes bibliographical references and index.
Identifiers: LCCN 2018053417 (print) | LCCN
    2018053804 (ebook) | ISBN 9781501739439 (pdf) |
    ISBN 9781501739446 (epub/mobi) |
    ISBN 9781501739415 (cloth)
Subjects: LCSH: Jews—Algeria—Constantine—History. |
    Riots—Algeria—Constantine—History—20th century. |
    Ethnic conflict—Algeria—Constantine—History—20th
    century. | Constantine (Algeria)—Ethnic relations. |
    Constantine (Algeria) —History—20th century. |
    France—Politics and government—1914–1940.
Classification: LCC DS135.A3 (ebook) | LCC DS135.A3
    C64 2019 (print) | DDC 305.892/40655—dc23
LC record available at https://lccn.loc.gov/2018053417

CONTENTS

A gallery of figures appears between parts 2 and 3.

Acknowledgments

This book could not have been written without help. I thank my colleagues in the history department at the University of Michigan, especially Kathleen Canning, Juan Cole, Geoff Eley, Dena Goodman, Jean Hébrard, Mary Kelley, Deborah Dash Moore, Sonya Rose, and Jeffrey Veidlinger. In addition to the history department, three other units at the university provided financial assistance and time away from teaching: the Institute for the Humanities, the Frankel Center for Judaic Studies, and the Eisenberg Institute for Historical Studies. UM's Undergraduate Research Opportunity Program provided me with two excellent research assistants, Lalita Clozel and Nisreen Khokhar, and the Office of Research offered me a subvention to cover publication costs. In France, I was generously hosted by the École des hautes études en sciences sociales in Paris. In Algeria, I was warmly received by the University of Algiers, Bouzareah, and the Centre d'études maghrébines in Oran. At the Archives nationales d'outre-mer in Aix-en-Provence, André Brochier guided me through the documentation on the Department of Constantine. Shrewd suggestions from Emily Andrew at Cornell University Press made an overlong manuscript shorter—and better.

Writers want a room of their own, but before they get there they need to engage with others. The book was shaped by conversations with Aida Bamia, Laure Blévis, Thierry Bonzon, Raphaëlle Branche, François Brunet, Caroline Campbell, Omar Carlier, J. P. Daughton, Jean-Luc Einaudi, Julien Fromage, Jonathan Glasser, Jane Goodman, Emily Gottreich, Nancy Green, Jim House, Eric Jennings, Samuel Kalman, Charles Keith, Lisa Leff, Patricia Lorcin, Neil MacMaster, James McDougall, Maud Mandel, Claire Marynower, John Merriman, M'hamed Oualdi, Robert Parks, Kevin Passmore, Jean-Louis Planche, Miranda Pollard, Eve Troutt Powell, Mary Louise Roberts, Sophie Roberts, Claudio Saunt, Bryant Simon, Miranda Spieler, Sarah Abrevaya Stein, Judith Surkis, Sylvie Thénault, and Martin Thomas.

I am especially indebted to colleagues who read the work in manuscript. Ethan Katz fielded more than one anxious phone call, offered wise advice, and generously shared his own research. Joan Scott and Daniel Sherman read a very early draft and saw what was of value. Benjamin Brower and Julia Clancy-Smith gave me the benefit of their deep knowledge of North Africa. Malika Rahal hosted me in Rouen and was a patient sounding board for my arguments. Todd Shepard, as always, was a valued reader. James McDougall stepped up at a moment when I had no right to make demands. Jennifer Sessions provided me with photos of an archival dossier that I missed in Paris. Daniel Williford took time off from his dissertation research to photograph Mohamed El Maadi's service record and double-checked the transliteration of Arabic words and names. Ken Garner helped to prepare the manuscript for publication with meticulous care. All these friends and colleagues read drafts of chapters and offered comments. Responsibility for the arguments and any errors contained in this book are mine alone.

Portions of chapter 4 were published previously in "Constantine before the Riots of August 1934: Civil Status, Anti-Semitism, and the Politics of Assimilation in Interwar French Algeria," *Journal of North African Studies* 17, no. 5 (December 2012): 839–61. Portions of chapter 10 appeared in "Anti-Semitism and the Colonial Situation in Interwar Algeria: The Anti-Jewish Riots in Constantine, August 1934," in *The French Colonial Mind*, ed. Martin Thomas (Omaha: University of Nebraska Press, 2011), 2:77–111.

Every book also has a local history, and this one was familial. Lucas and Ruby met the demands that this project made on their lives with a freely expressed mix of cheerfulness and pointed critique. My parents, Susan and Brock, moved into our house as I finished the manuscript, and this cohabitation brought sustenance of an unexpected kind. My partner, Kate Tremel, takes what is heavy and makes it light.

NOTE ON TRANSLITERATION

All translations from French or Arabic into English are my own. Following a custom that has developed in English-language historiography, I have transliterated Maghribi Arabic words according to a simplified system based on the recommendations of the *International Journal of Middle East Studies*, without full diacritics or vowel markings. I use an apostrophe (') to indicate hamza only when it is in the middle of a word, and an opening single quotation mark (') for 'ayn when it is at the beginning or middle of the word. To avoid confusion in referring to documents from the colonial period and more recent historical work, I have used the Gallicized form of Arabic proper names that are commonly encountered in the literature. Place names are given in the form used during the colonial period in Algeria, followed by the current postindependence name of the locale in parentheses at first mention.

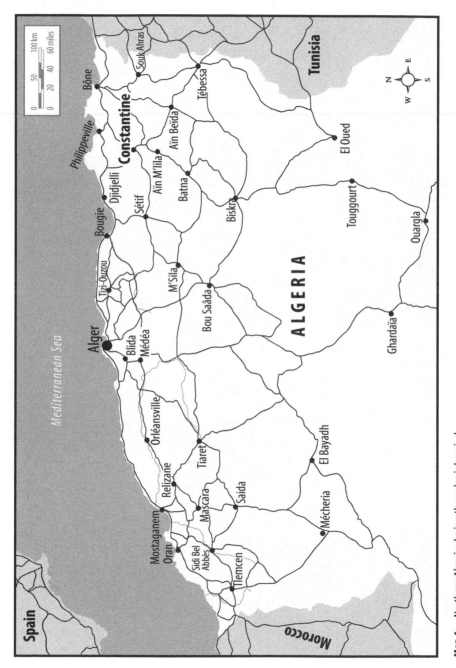

MAP 1. Northern Algeria during the colonial period.
Map by Mike Bechthold.

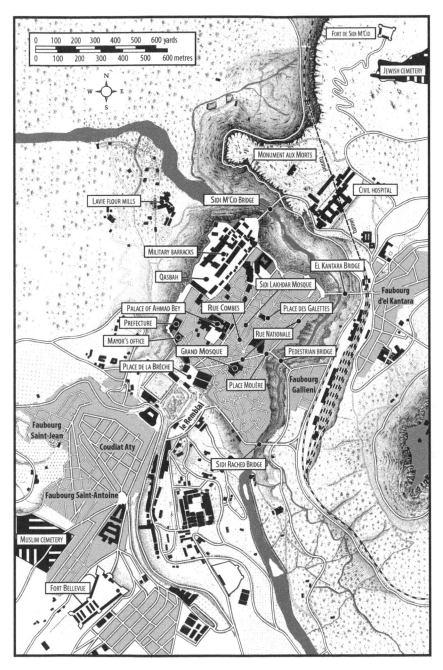

MAP 2. The city of Constantine in 1934, with major landmarks and neighborhoods.
Map by Mike Bechthold.

Introduction

One might tell the story like this. Over three days in August 1934, an outburst of violence in a medium-size French city left twenty-eight people dead. Everybody who participated possessed French nationality. The ground on which they walked was French territory. The municipal institutions that struggled to contain the events of that weekend were French institutions, and the civil laws that reigned in the city were French laws. The soldiers brought in to reestablish order were French soldiers, commanded by French officers, and the police who lost control of the city during the hours of street fighting, looting, and murder were French police. The accused murderers were French, as were the judges that later condemned them. The victims were French, and so were the families and neighbors that mourned them. The officials who sought to avoid responsibility were French, and the local journalists who wrote about the riot in lurid terms were as French as the writers for the Parisian dailies who reported the same events.

Told in this fashion, this story points to something peculiar about the term "French." Even if every use of the word has at least some claim to accuracy, the story sounds different when more details are added. The "French" city where the violence took place was Constantine in eastern Algeria. Algeria had been a part of the Ottoman Empire for four centuries before French armies invaded in 1830. The land became French civil territory in 1848, and legislation across the nineteenth century gave a form of French nationality to the colony's diverse inhabitants. The Jews of Algeria—a small but diverse minority that included Berber Jews whose presence in North Africa preceded the arrival of Islam and descendants of Iberian Jews exiled from Spain in 1492—were excluded from French citizenship until 1870. In that year the newly created Third Republic promulgated the Crémieux decree, granting full citizenship to nearly all Jews in Algeria, with the exception of a tiny Jewish population in territory still under military rule. The majority population of Muslims in Algeria, also a heterogeneous group, were excluded from full citizenship for almost the entire colonial period (1830–1962), but their possession of a degraded form of French nationality was implied by decree as early as 1834, and formally recognized in law in 1865. An 1889 law revised the nationality code to make it easier for settlers who came from elsewhere to become French citizens, so long as they were not Muslim. The distinction between nationality and citizenship necessitated a new word to refer to the colonized peoples of Algeria who were not French citizens: they were sometimes referred to in official documents as "French subjects." The colloquial term, however, was *indigènes* ("natives").[1]

With these facts, one might tell the story differently. The 1934 riots began on a Friday evening when a drunken Jewish man named Elie Khalifa insulted several Muslim men as they prepared for their prayers at a mosque in the ancient walled city of Constantine. The streets nearby connected to a Jewish neighborhood with several synagogues and many Jewish-owned businesses and homes. The dispute led to a larger confrontation between Muslims and Jews later that night, in the course of which a Muslim man was shot in the stomach. Crowds armed with sticks and knives besieged several buildings where Jewish families lived, until early the next morning, when soldiers finally succeeded in clearing the streets. The following day witnessed a tense standoff between Muslims and Jews in the city, while local leaders—elected and religious—attempted to calm the population after hastily convened meetings with the authorities.

On Sunday morning, August 5, the violence began again after false rumors spread that a popular Muslim elected official had been assassinated by Jews. Angry people, massed in crowds, attacked many homes and businesses in Constantine's Jewish quarter. Sixteen Jews were murdered in three locations alone—in two apartments and an office that rioters invaded. Others were killed in the streets nearby. Several Jews were also killed in attacks in other towns in the region, bringing the total number of Jewish deaths to twenty-five. Three Muslims also died. The man who was shot on Friday evening died in hospital twenty days later, on August 23. A Muslim man who was shot on Sunday shortly before midday died in the street before hundreds of onlookers; and a Muslim boy who was shot in the stomach during a disturbance in the nearby town of Aïn Beïda died on Tuesday, August 7. He was only twelve years old. During roughly six hours of rioting in Constantine on August 5, the police and the military garrison—which included both Jews and Muslims within their ranks—seemed to have ceded control of the city to angry crowds. The local and national press emphasized the passivity of the authorities, precipitating a crisis within the colonial administration, which was forced to explain its failure to either predict or to contain the outbreak of violence.[2]

This version of the story also has issues. First, there is a missing term: as in the first narrative, I managed to tell a story about something that happened in Algeria without using the word "Algerian." Is that because the terms I did use—"Muslim" and "Jewish"—carry their own explanatory weight? Given that the riots began with an argument at a mosque between an inebriated Jewish man and Muslim men preparing to pray on a Friday evening, it is clearly impossible to tell the story without using the words "Jewish" and "Muslim." Nevertheless, invoking these terms seems to drive the story inevitably toward its violent conclusion, as if such occurrences were already scripted and needed no further explanation.

This is in part due to the tragic history of Muslims and Jews in the Middle East and North Africa in the twentieth century. Six years after the events described above, the Jews of Algeria—about 140,000 people—had their French citizenship revoked by the Vichy regime, the government that came to power in France after the German invasion in 1940. This act relegated Algeria's Jews back to the "native" status they had shared with Muslims after the French conquest in 1830.[3] The Vichy government enacted its own antisemitic policies during the Second World War, eventually deporting over 75,000 Jews to Nazi extermination camps in Poland. Only 2,567 survived.[4] Jews who remained in French Algeria during the war escaped deportation, but it took the Free French authorities nearly a year after Allied troops landed in Africa to restore their citizenship in 1943. When the Fourth Republic was founded after the war, Algeria's Jews were welcomed as full members of the French nation, but the possibility that Algeria's Muslims would find a place alongside them seemed increasingly remote after nationalist violence broke out in Sétif on VE Day (May 8, 1945). When police fired on nationalist demonstrators, marchers and their supporters responded by attacking and killing 102 Europeans in the surrounding streets and nearby countryside. Following these murders, the French authorities responded with a brutal collective repression that killed thousands of people in the region.[5]

In the wake of these traumatic events, a determined Algerian nationalist movement challenged French sovereignty in North Africa, culminating in a war for independence that lasted from 1954 to 1962.[6] The position of Algeria's Jewish citizens became untenable at the end of this war, though some Jews supported the cause of independence from France.[7] After the establishment of independent Algeria in 1962, the French colonial settler population migrated en masse to France, and the vast majority of Algerian Jews came with them.[8] This migration of Jews from Algeria had some similarities with migrations to Israel by Jews from elsewhere in the Middle East and North Africa after 1948. In 1962, however, only about 10 percent of Algeria's Jews chose to go to Israel, preferring instead to remake their lives in France, the country that had granted them citizenship in 1870.[9] By the end of the twentieth century there were virtually no Jews living in Algeria.

Invoking this history to explain the Constantine riots of 1934 obscures as much as it illuminates: this is not a story about Algerian or Arab nationalism, or pan-Islamism, or Zionism in North Africa. None of these movements are irrelevant to this history, but none are more important than another adjective that was also absent from the second account of the riots, that peculiar word "French." As we will see, the violence in Constantine broke out largely because of the possibility that both Muslims and Jews might be *included* in the French polity on equal terms. This bears repeating—the riots took on their contemporary meaning in the context of a debate about *reforming* the colonial system, not ending it. Although a small nationalist movement was active in the diaspora of Algerian laborers working in France in the 1920s, there was no mass-based nationalist movement in Algeria until several years after the riots took place. Virtually everybody in Constantine in 1934 assumed that the French empire would continue to exist for the foreseeable future. The drama of Algeria's subsequent history makes it hard to reconstruct the particular dynamic of social and political relations in French Algeria before the rupture between Muslims and Jews took place. The problem for the historian in recounting the story of Constantine in 1934 is that words like "Muslim," "Jewish," "Algerian," and "French" are both necessary and too resonant. Their constant threat is that they "make sense," but too much of it. This problem is at the heart of this book.

Parts 1 and 2, accordingly, examine the ways that the preceding century of colonial settlement recast relations between Muslims, Jews, and "Europeans" in Algeria. From the French invasion in 1830 until the Constantine riots of 1934 and beyond, citizenship in French Algeria was an unsettled question. French sovereignty created many obstacles to political participation for Algeria's Muslims, even as it offered citizenship for Algeria's Jews, but this did not prevent the Muslim majority from attempting to shape the social world they lived in and its future. Algeria's Jews came to welcome the opportunity that full citizenship offered them, while many of Algeria's Muslim leaders sought a similar form of belonging that was commensurate with the preservation of their culture and religion. The violence of 1934, as we will see, emerged precisely because of the many dissonant ways that the people of this North African city found the term "French" to resonate with the meanings of "Jewish" and "Muslim."

The second half of this book tells an even darker story. Uncertainty about the boundaries of citizenship left the population of Constantine vulnerable to acts of provocation, defined here as menacing mobilizations of difference in the furtherance of political goals. At the heart of the cycle of provocation and reaction that produced the riots of August 1934, a small group of agitators committed multiple acts of murder with the goal of intentionally escalating the horror of the event with spectacular acts of brutality. By the end of this book, I will present evidence that at least eighteen and perhaps as many as twenty of the twenty-five Jews who died on August 5, 1934, were killed by a relatively small and organized group. The local police were themselves convinced that this was the case and said so publicly until their investigation was shut down and taken over by their superiors. Eventually, the police came to believe that one of the primary agitators responsible for the murders was a soldier in the French army named Mohamed El Maadi, although they never made this information public.

If this is true—and this book will argue that it is—our understanding of what happened in Constantine in 1934 will have to be revised. This was not simply, as some historians have suggested, a "classic pogrom."[10] Certain aspects of the initial outburst on August 3 invite such a comparison, but the perpetrators of the majority of the August 5 murders had more complicated goals. Mohamed El Maadi was no ordinary local conspirator. He is a notorious figure in the history of political extremism in France, well known to the French police in the late 1930s as a member of a violent terrorist organization, the Comité secret d'action révolutionnaire (CSAR), that unleashed a campaign of assassination and bombings in France in 1937–1938. This right-wing network, known in the contemporary press as the Cagoule (the Hooded Cloak), brought together militants from nationalist leagues in France who sought authoritarian or fascist solutions to the political crises of the 1930s. El Maadi was arrested in 1937 and detained for ten months for his connections to this group. During the Second World War, El Maadi became an enthusiastic supporter of French collaboration with the Nazis and a propagandist for Vichy's antisemitic campaigns. After working with the Gestapo in Paris, El Maadi finished the war as a captain in the SS, the commander—and primary recruiter—of a North African Brigade of Algerians who fought alongside German troops against the French resistance in the weeks after the D-Day invasion.[11]

Given his subsequent history, it is important to recognize at the outset that El Maadi's antisemitism was linked to his embrace of an extreme form of French nationalism that was also viciously anti-Jewish. His engagement in 1934 was not an expression of a specifically "Muslim" antisemitism or Arab nationalism that had affinities with National Socialism. El Maadi gravitated toward extreme French nationalism while serving as a career officer in the French colonial army in Morocco. Sometime in the early 1930s, he became involved with a group of militants from a right-wing league—the Action française—who advocated violent attacks on the Third Republic and leftist politicians. His participation in the murders of August 1934 marked an important step in his political evolution toward extremist nationalism and, ultimately, a form of fascism with deep roots in the history of French colonialism.

Because Mohamed El Maadi's participation in the Constantine riots remained unknown to most people, contemporaries blamed the city's Muslim population as a whole for the murders that took place on August 5. This was El Maadi's goal. He and his conspirators assumed that the riots would drive Muslims in Algeria to forge a bond with French extremists by encouraging a shared hatred of Jews. The Vichy regime gave him an unexpected further opportunity to push for this alliance by advocating for a "Eurafrican" form of fascism that would connect the "superior races" of North Africa and Europe. El Maadi's provocations in 1934 and his later engagement as a foot soldier for Vichy and the Nazis were failures—his dream of a "Eurafrican" fascist alliance found few supporters. Nevertheless, the murders that El Maadi helped to organize in Constantine terrorized Algerian Jews, and permanently tainted any discussion of political reform in 1930s Algeria. The chances for such reform were never good and would almost certainly have failed even if the riots had never taken place. The murders in Constantine nevertheless narrowed the room for maneuver that political leaders on all sides possessed and gave a powerful argument to those who favored force in pursuit of their goals.

During the Constantine riots, El Maadi was on the streets as a uniformed officer in a French regiment, the Third Zouaves. No evidence found so far connects him to the violence of Friday, August 3, but multiple sources point to his involvement in the attacks of Sunday, August 5, including a police report that identified him as "one of the agitators who provoked the 'pogroms' of Constantine."[12] Military documents place El Maadi at the home of Makhlouf Attali, one of three sites in the same neighborhood where multiple murders took place. His commanding officer's report mentioned El Maadi, and his name appeared later on a list of injured soldiers, with a note on the injury—a bullet wound to the hand—and the time and location, the Attali home. El Maadi also testified for the prosecution in the February 1936 trial of those accused in the Attali case. In his testimony, El Maadi described the bloody scene in the apartment at the moment the soldiers first entered the door, and his account was instrumental in convicting those charged with the murders.

No mention of El Maadi's name appeared in the official report produced by the investigating commission appointed by the governor-general of Algeria, although many of the documents that allow me to tell this story were included in the papers collected by the commission. These documents make clear that the local police initially hoped to charge a small group of suspects with multiple murders at a relatively small number of locations in the same neighborhood. When this theory was leaked to the press, the governor-general's office in Algiers intervened to prevent the conspiracy thesis from being confirmed. After the governor-general asserted control over the investigation, the local police in Constantine came up with a separate list of perpetrators for every site where murders took place, a move that effectively dispensed with any reference to conspiracies that could tie the murders together. These separate lists formed the basis for the trials that took place in July 1935 and February 1936. Each of the arrested men was charged with murders that occurred at single location, even in cases where they had confessed to being involved with murders in more than one place. The official report—never released to the public—blamed the violence on the religious fanaticism of Algeria's Muslim population.

This book, then, is a story of a murder mystery and its cover-up—wrapped in a social history of political violence in colonial Algeria. Both parts of the story are indispensable. The evidence for the social history of political violence is plentiful and detailed. The evidence for the murder mystery is more fragmentary. Putting them together requires the patient reconstruction of events whose connections might seem at first obscure. Nevertheless, the murder mystery—the story of Mohamed El Maadi's role in the killing— needs the accompanying social and political history for its full significance to be understood, since it is key to establishing his motives. Finally, the fact that powerful members of French Algeria's settler establishment apparently knew about El Maadi's involvement and conspired to conceal it after the fact reveals the ferocity with which that establishment defended the strict boundaries that separated "French" from "native" and "Muslim" from "Jew" in colonial Algeria.

Untangling the threads of this story requires a multipronged approach that begins with an appreciation of the broader history of France and North Africa in the Mediterranean world. Rather than emphasizing the colonial encounter as a repeated enactment of conflict between an unchanging "traditional" society confronted by the modernizing force of Europe, I emphasize a long history of population movements and cultural exchange in a region of the globe that was often defined as much by its connections with other places as it was by its territorial integrity. Close attention to the interaction of different peoples in North Africa makes it possible to tell the story of "French" colonial reforms and French-Algerian political experiments as "Algerian" stories—that is, as interventions and attempts to describe a future for French Algeria that were shaped by the involvement of Algerian people, and not simply as failures on the part of the French. Next, I propose to tell the history of the riot in Constantine and its aftermath as if it were a "French" story— that is, a story that poses questions about the nation-state whose institutions and laws were so dramatically thrown into relief by the violence on that August weekend. The fact that this riot occurred in Algeria, the fact that the violence occurred between Muslim Algerians and Jewish Algerians, has long led people to think of this riot, when they thought of it at all, as a relatively banal event, easily explained as a resurgence of precolonial atavistic hatreds between two peoples whose violent conflicts predated the settlement of Europeans in North Africa. At least two books on antisemitism in France in the 1930s have been written without mentioning the riot at all, despite the fact that, when measured by the number of deaths, this was the deadliest anti-Jewish event to take place on "French" soil in peacetime in modern history.[13]

This silence, however regrettable, is less astonishing than it might first appear. An extraordinary amount of work went into the construction of this moment as an "Algerian" event rather than a "French" one. For the local political establishment in Constantine, this work was more important than anything else—more important than commemorating the dead, more important than finding justice for the families of victims, and more important than remedying the inequities of the colonial system that were implicated in the explosion of hatred that killed twenty-eight people. Because of this work, it is just as hard for historians to talk about the riots in Constantine today as it was for contemporaries in the 1930s. The violence took place in an Algerian city that now seems far from "France." Jews no longer live there. The Algerians who do face their own challenges with the violent history of decolonization in the twentieth century. The political complexities of the

French empire's fragility in the interwar years—and its failed efforts to imagine a world in which Muslims and Jews could be simultaneously "Algerian" and "French"—have been understandably overshadowed by the dramatic events that took place in the decades that followed. This is the story of a terrible event that unfolded in the harsh glare of imagined futures that never arrived.

PART 1

Algerian Histories of Empire

CHAPTER 1

Constantine in North African History

Constantine sits on a plateau in the Atlas Mountains in eastern Algeria, perched precariously on the edge of a deep gorge that bounds the central city on nearly three sides. The gorge skirts the old city from south to north, then makes an abrupt ninety-degree turn to the northwest, forming the apex of a rocky promontory on which the city's oldest settlements were built. At the bottom of the limestone canyon runs the river Rhumel, flowing in a labyrinth of rocky rapids and cascades. In photographs of Constantine from early in the twentieth century, one sees a line of modest buildings ranged across the gorge's outer lip, directly above a sheer rock face that falls away from the town with vertiginous indifference.

The city has long been a dense transfer point for people, goods, and cultures. Several nearby valleys connect the fertile but seasonally arid plains of the interior with the Mediterranean coast, eighty kilometers to the north. This geographical location made Constantine an important hub in a North African trading network that linked the trans-Saharan caravan routes in the south to the wider Mediterranean world beyond.[1] During the period of Ottoman rule in Algeria (1519–1830), merchants in Constantine traded grains, livestock, dates, charcoal, salt, and oils, but one could also find rustic and fine wool, elaborately embroidered clothing, gold and silver jewelry, perfumes, ostrich feathers, and luxuriously decorated swords and pistols. Many of these goods came from distant sources: Turkish textiles from

Constantinople, rugs from Persia, mocha coffee from Yemen, and Syrian silk. The monthly caravan to and from Tunis, which ferried many of these products, regularly included two to three hundred mules.[2]

Long-distance commerce and migration—both voluntary and involuntary—played a role in diversifying the populations of Algeria.[3] Islam arrived in the seventh century with the arrival of Arabs from the Middle East, and these populations eventually intermarried with local Berber groups, who adopted the new religion. Muslim Andalusians who fled Spain after the end of the Reconquista in 1492 settled in many North African cities, bringing with them a distinctive and perhaps elitist sensibility, as well as different modes of dress and speech that persisted among their descendants well into the colonial period. Later called "Moors" (*Maures*) by the French, the descendants of these Iberian migrants were concentrated above all in the cities of the Moroccan and Algerian coast and the near hinterland. Slavery, the most involuntary form of migration, had also left its imprint on urban populations in Algeria. The capture and sale of sub-Saharan Africans as slaves continued throughout the Ottoman period and into the era of the French conquest after 1830.[4] Both male and female captives were brought from sub-Saharan regions to Ottoman Algeria to work, sometimes as domestic servants in the homes of urban elites, but also as forced laborers. Some were freed through manumission, and both Algiers and Constantine probably had populations of around a thousand sub-Saharan Africans in the early nineteenth century. Christian slaves—most often taken from ships or in raids on Mediterranean shores and islands—were numerous in Algerian coastal cities in the seventeenth and eighteenth century but probably less often encountered in inland Constantine.[5]

Adding to the diverse mix of urban populations was the presence of North African Jews.[6] The Jews of this part of the world were the result of at least three major instances of Jewish mobility. So-called Berber Jews were present even before the migration of Arabs to North Africa from the Middle East, having moved westward from the eastern Mediterranean in antiquity. A wave of Iberian Jews expelled from Spain during the fifteenth century settled in North African cities, bringing with them their distinct cultural traditions. These migrations were followed in the seventeenth and eighteenth centuries by the arrival of Spanish, Portuguese, French, and Italian-speaking Jewish traders associated with the expansion of Mediterranean trade—many of these families also traced their roots to Iberian Jews forced out of Spain earlier.[7] Migrations of Sephardic Jews to North African cities introduced a cleavage between two Jewish populations. North Africa's Berber Jews, poorer and isolated from traditions of Jewish learning, had long experience of living in a Muslim society. Sephardic Jews from Spain, on the other hand, were wealthier, more literate, and possessed a culture shaped by living as a Jewish minority in a Christian realm.[8] The Jews of North Africa were never more than 1–2 percent of the population, but their concentration in cities gave them a visibility and presence that went beyond their numbers.

Constantine thus bore the imprint of population movements in the region over many centuries, and this diversity was an indicator of the multiple connections that the ancient city had with a wider world. With its mix of prosperity and poverty, power and dependency, and a population marked by differences of social rank, occupation, religion, and place of origin, the city was both dynamic and in tension with itself. There are very few reliable sources on the numbers of people residing in Constantine at the moment of the French conquest, but one source from a local *qa'id* (district governor) from 1832 suggests that there were 5,025 Turkish and Kouloughli (formed through the marriage of a Turkish official with a woman from a local family) households, 6,000 Moorish families, and 1,000 Jewish families.[9] These figures are almost certainly inflated, as they imply an unlikely total of around 39,000 inhabitants. The proportions nevertheless give an indication of the relative weight of the different populations in the city, and its distinctiveness when compared with the surrounding region, which would have seen no Turks or Moors and very few Jewish households. A more reasonable estimate might be 25,000 inhabitants on the eve of the French conquest, amounting to more than 80 percent of the urban population of the province as a whole.[10]

By the 1830s, Constantine had about sixteen hundred residential buildings, five hundred workshops and retail businesses, and four principal mosques, corresponding roughly to the city's four principal quarters (*harat*). There were numerous smaller mosques in each neighborhood. The city had four gates, but three were quite close together on the southwestern wall that looked out over the road to Algiers. The fourth gate opened onto the gorge to the east, giving way to an ancient Roman bridge that had been rebuilt by Salah Bey in the late eighteenth century. Inside the city walls, the streets were narrow, often only five paces in width, with frequent turns and impasses. Most of the buildings had a ground floor and two stories above, with little external decoration, apart from a few grilled openings. Of the four quarters, the Qasbah (*qasba*) to the north was the most clearly distinguished from the rest of the city, and its enclosed walls contained a mosque, shops, barracks for troops, and private homes. Tabiyya, divided into Tabiyya al-Kabira (Greater Tabiyya) and Tabiyya al-Barrani (Tabiyya of Foreigners), lay just below the Qasbah along the western wall, abutting the palace of the bey. To the southeast was a residential quarter, Bab al-Jabiyya. In the northeast, suspended over the lip of the gorge above the bridge, was another residential neighborhood, al-Qantara, which also held the Jewish quarter. In the late eighteenth century, during the construction of the Mosque of Salah Bey, an older Jewish neighborhood alongside the Qasbah in the northern quadrant of the city had been cleared by expelling the families who lived there. These expelled households were resettled alongside Jews from other parts of the city into the narrow streets alongside the ravine walls above the al-Qantara (El Kantara) bridge. This was the neighborhood that became the scene of the first conflicts on August 3–5, 1934, in the streets adjacent to a market square known during the French colonial period as the place des Galettes.

At the center of Constantine, where the four major quarters converged, was the largest of the town's markets, the Suq al-Tujjar, which served as a kind of hub for several smaller streets containing the town's many artisans. These crucial contributors to urban society were organized distinctly by trade: a list put together by a nineteenth-century French observer identified discrete areas of the market devoted to saddle makers, shoemakers, goldsmiths, textile sellers, embroiderers, blacksmiths, rug weavers, sieve makers, coopers, carpenters, mixers of medicinal herbs and creams, and manufacturers of parchment.[11] Muslims had a near monopoly on many professions, including weaving, shoemaking, vegetable sellers, grain and tobacco sales, as well as the sale of milk, butter, and honey. They also dominated the leather trade, including tanning, saddle and harness making, basket weaving, the lumber trades, ironmongery, and hardware. On the other hand, Jews owned the majority of the city's textile establishments, and most of the city's tailors were Jewish as well. Nearly all the goldsmiths and jewelers in Constantine were Jewish.[12] Languages spoken in the market in the early nineteenth century would have included Turkish, multiple Arabic dialects, Berber dialects from Kabylia, the Awras (Aurès) Mountains, and the M'Zab, as well as the Judeo-Arabic spoken by the city's Jewish population, and the occasional phrase of Italian, French, Spanish, or Maltese.

The French conquest of Algeria had its origins in a diplomatic row over a debt that the revolutionary Jacobin government had incurred between 1793 and 1798 to facilitate the importation of North African wheat to France. Negotiations over the debt were a source of tension for years, and Algerian demands for high interest payments on the debt forced the issue in the 1820s, leading to war between France and Algeria in the summer of 1830. When French armies invaded and overran the Ottoman capital in Algiers, the government of Hussein Dey was forced to capitulate. A charismatic leader of a venerated family, 'Abd al-Qadir, organized a determined resistance by setting up a state in central Algeria that continued until his surrender in 1847. In the east, the reigning bey of Constantine, Ahmad ibn Muhammad (Ahmad Bey), fought alongside Hussein Dey in 1830 and witnessed his defeat. After the fall of Algiers, Ahmad Bey took it upon himself to organize resistance to the French from his walled stronghold in the city of Constantine.[13] He defeated a first attempt to dislodge him from his citadel in 1836, but in October 1837 the French captured the fortified city after a second bitter siege.

Many of Constantine's inhabitants fled during and after the battle, and the French army savagely sacked their homes. The violence against the civilian population was especially merciless, and French soldiers were given free rein to rob, kill, and rape. In the aftermath, soldiers improvised a public market where they haggled and traded the spoils among themselves. The population of the city was reduced to poverty, and the situation was no better in the surrounding countryside. Ahmad Bey had ordered the destruction of food stores to prevent them from falling into the hands of the French siege troops. When cholera—part of a global pandemic in the 1830s—raced through the region in the aftermath of the French military campaign, the population was already weakened by malnutrition. Many of those who survived the pitiless combination of famine, disease, and military defeat were driven to abandon their homes and lands in search of sustenance elsewhere.[14]

Malek Bennabi, an Algerian historian and philosopher who was born in Constantine in 1905, recalled in his memoirs the mythic status of these events in the collective memory of the city. Among his earliest memories were the stories of an elderly female relative, Hadja Baya, who died at the age of one hundred when he was four. At the moment of the French siege in 1837, Hadja Baya and her family joined a panicked procession of households who fled to the ravine with their daughters, seeking to escape the French soldiers who breached the city's defenses.

> Once the city was taken, the families of Constantine had no other goal but to save their honor, above all the families that had young girls. They were forced to evacuate them toward the side of the river Rhummel where today stands the Kaouki mills and high above, the suspension bridge. While the French entered through the breach in the wall, the young women and their families departed their city using ropes [to descend into the ravine]. For some, the ropes gave way, and the virgins were precipitated into the abyss.
>
> Hadja Baya lived through this tragedy. Her father and her mother, pushing her through the streets of a city in disarray, drove her to the edge of the precipice, as Abraham had driven in ancient times his son Ismail for the propitiatory sacrifice on the altar of God. This time, my

relative was to be immolated on the altar of a destroyed fatherland in order to save the honor of a Muslim family. But my relative escaped this terrible fate: the rope along whose length she descended did not part. And with her family she was able to find refuge in Tunis, then in Mecca, before her return to Algeria several years later, having married and having children. She is dead, but the memory of this tragic episode that I have just recounted survived her.[15]

Bennabi's anecdote moved rapidly between an almost mythological evocation of a lost world under assault by a foreign force and a matter-of-fact mention of the futures that came with it—the mills of Kaouki and the suspension bridge at Sidi M'Cid (built in 1912 and until 1929 the tallest suspension bridge in the world). The anecdote played on the theme of violation at several levels: the private anguish of Constantine's households over the rape of their daughters; the penetration of the city's spaces by the French army at "la Brèche" (the breach); and finally the destroyed "fatherland" itself, depicted as an imaginary altar for a purifying act of sacrifice made necessary by this crescendo of humiliations. At the same time, however, he emphasized that Hadja Baya's family did not emigrate forever. After the birth of her children, Hadja Baya returned to Constantine to raise her family. Most members of Bennabi's parents' families also remained, unwilling to break their ties with relatives despite their worsening economic position. Many others did the same, having no choice but to find a way to live within the new circumstances of French control.[16]

In October 1839, the French authorities called upon the city's leading personalities to organize a ceremonial welcome for a visit by the French crown prince, the duc d'Orléans.[17] Since the fall of Constantine two years before, few Europeans had visited, leaving the city largely an Algerian space. Many had returned to their homes, though some had sold their property at bargain prices and moved to areas outside French control. On the morning of the prince's arrival, the population exited the city in a gesture of reluctant ritual obedience, assembling themselves on the slopes outside the walls. Contemporary sources noted the order of this massive (male) spectacle, a physical enactment of the city's idealized social and political hierarchy according to the vision of its own inhabitants. Arranged at the front of the crowd, at the lowest point on the slopes, came the corps of religious and judicial scholars, the ulama, accompanied by the highest-ranking religious figure in the city, the *shaykh al-Islam*, Muhammad bin al-Fakkun. A mufti (interpreter of Islamic law) accompanied the *shaykh*, bearing with him the French colors. Next were assembled the city's municipal officials, headed by a *qa'id*.

Following them came a much larger assemblage of some two thousand city dwellers, organized into corporate bodies by trade and profession, each led by its most senior member. After this large number of people came a fourth body, the men of the city's Jewish population. At the very end came the city's military garrison, organized into two groups: first, the French troops, followed by the *goums*, recent Algerian recruits.

Taken as a whole, the procession revealed that the city's corporate structure had survived the military defeat. Historian Isabelle Grangaud's account of the event emphasized that the arrangement of the city's body politic on the slopes leading up to the city displayed the indispensable nature of its three organizing principles: religious, administrative, and professional. The separation of Constantine's Jews from these orderly categories of social and political life was significant, but their presence in the ceremony nevertheless illustrated an essential form of belonging, a recognition of their place in a complex and heterogeneous urban social environment. Grangaud pointed out that the placement of the Jewish men, after the town's trade organizations but before the foreign troops, underlined their status as a protected non-Muslim people—the *dhimmi*—in Ottoman law, and acknowledged their position within the city's economy. They were separate, but they also belonged, in a fundamental way, to the city's population.

Grangaud also insisted, however, that the apparent clarity of this social vision hid an important truth: this urban society was not static. Like the category of *indigène* that the colonial government imposed on the population, the spectacle of Constantine's social order at this crucial moment in its history displayed a unity that was both required by the circumstances *and* constructed precisely because of them. Tensions within the social order—between Turks, Kouloughli, and Arabs, between Muslims and Jews, between military elites and the commercial classes, between members of families with ties to the Ottoman regime and those who had less to lose from regime change, between landowners and the laborers they depended on, between those who produced for local consumption and those whose business interests were wrapped up in long-distance trade—all of this was held in suspension during the ceremony that brought the town's population out onto the slopes for the inspection of the crown prince.

Before the French conquest, then, North African society was already in motion in multiple ways. The Algerian economy was already connected, for better or worse, with wider cycles of Mediterranean trade. Algeria's fertile agriculture regularly produced a surplus, and Algeria was frequently a net exporter of food. The culture of North African cities bore the imprint of centuries of population movement and exchange with Europe, the Middle East, and sub-Saharan Africa. Much more than a "traditional" society encountering the allegedly "modernizing" force of European colonialism, Algeria was already embedded in a densely connected and rapidly changing Mediterranean world. In the coming decades, the lines of potential fracture within the city would be recast as the political and social order was transformed under the conditions of colonial rule.

CHAPTER 2

"Native," "Jewish," and "European"

In the middle decades of the nineteenth century, the French government established a civil regime in Algeria with new institutions of local governance that consolidated the power of colonial settlers. Military authorities were replaced with administrators and—eventually—elected officials who represented the growing European population in Algeria in the French parliament.[1] The transfer of rural land and urban property from Algerian to French hands began while Algeria was still under French military authority in the years 1830–1848, and continued as the population of European settlers grew. In the process, Algeria's economy and society were irrevocably transformed, with destructive consequences for the population. Kamel Kateb, a historical demographer, estimated that 75,000 Algerian soldiers died fighting the French during the period 1830–1875, a figure that must be considered in juxtaposition to his estimate of 825,000 total deaths attributable to war and pacification. Add to this the 800,000 deaths in 1867–1868 caused by a famine that followed French land reforms, and the total figure for Algerian deaths directly or indirectly caused by the conquest approaches 1.6 million over four and a half decades.[2]

Constantine's experience under the French paralleled the story of Algeria as a whole, although the region saw proportionately fewer settlers in rural areas and a slower and less thorough replacement of local customs with French institutions than in the departments of Algiers or Oran.[3] As a result, the social and cultural authority of elite Muslim families was less diminished in Constantine than in other Algerian cities across the nineteenth century. By 1900, central Algiers and Oran, with their active ports, increasingly took on a European aspect. In Constantine, physical changes to the city were more gradual. Only one major construction project disturbed the city before 1840: the clearing of five hectares of the Qasbah to make room for a French military garrison.[4]

Observing the extent to which the city seemed to have resumed its normal life after the defeat, the French governor-general of Algeria, Thomas-Robert Bugeaud, commented in 1840 that Constantine "is an Arab city . . . we must conserve its type and its character."[5] In fact, one-third of local property in Constantine was already owned by Europeans when he said this, but the image of Constantine as "an Arab city" persisted, and defending it became a part of French policy in the region, in part because such a posture allowed the French to claim that they were safeguarding the interests of Algerians under their authority. Bugeaud decreed that Europeans could reside in the old city only if given special authorization, and he ordered that a new European quarter be constructed outside the city walls. Unlike in Algiers or in Oran, the military did not move against Constantine's religious establishment, and the mosques of the city were not disestablished. For Bugeaud, such an attitude was required by the city's strategic value and the region's economic importance—it was necessary to work with local elites in order to consolidate French control. Over the decades that followed, however, Bugeaud's decision to "conserve" Constantine as "an Arab city" resulted in the confinement of the Algerian population in the oldest neighborhoods, while European settlers developed new residential quarters on the slopes below the walled gates.

By the end of the nineteenth century, the hole in the city's fortified wall—la Brèche—that allowed French troops to enter the city during the siege of 1837 had been expanded into a large public square. The surrounding buildings contained the administrative and cultural heart of the settler establishment: the city hall, the Palais de Justice, the post office, and the municipal theater. Over time the three main transversal streets of old Constantine inside the wall were widened and renamed—the rue Damrémont, the rue Caraman / rue de France, and the rue Nationale (later the rue Georges Clémenceau)—but many of the winding narrow side streets retained their older character. By the beginning of the twentieth century, the central artery of the rue de France was lined with French-style apartment buildings that flanked a newly constructed cathedral.

The poorest of Constantine's Muslim inhabitants, especially those more recently arrived from the countryside, lived in the Remblai on the southern edge of the city, outside the old wall, adjacent to the shrine of the marabout (*murabit*) Sidi Rached, and just down the slope from the place de la Brèche. The improvised structures in the Remblai were built on the rubble produced by the leveling of an adjacent hill, Coudiat Aty (Koudiat Aty), to make way for a new residential quarter. (In French, *remblai* refers to a pile of earth or gravel that one might use to level a road or fill a hole.) Because the structures in the Remblai were seen as temporary, the quarter appears in some maps from the first half of the twentieth century as an empty space looped by intersecting paths, labeled simply "Arab Village." In the years after the conquest, the streets of the Jewish quarter within the city walls were also renamed. The incongruously named "rue Grand"—a narrow winding street that traced a semicircle around the heart of the nineteenth-century Jewish neighborhood—emerged sinuously out of the more appropriately labeled "rue Vieux"—the old artery of the al-Qantara quarter. As the city developed in the nineteenth century, the rue de France became a thriving center of Jewish-owned businesses.

The newer "European" districts that were built outside the limits of the old town's walls were Bellevue, Coudiat Aty, the faubourgs Saint-Jean and Saint-Antoine on the left bank of the river, and Mansoura, the faubourg Gallieni, and Sidi-Mabrouk on the right bank. A working-class neighborhood, called the faubourg d'el Kantara by the French, occupied the land directly across the gorge from the old neighborhood of al-Qantara (El Kantara) in the central city, connected by the bridge of the same name. The faubourg d'el Kantara housed many of the laborers who worked at the nearby railroad yard and gasworks. The use of the French term *faubourg* (outer neighborhood or suburb) to describe these newer communities outside the city gates imposed a comforting metropolitan vision of urban development on the growing colonial city. This incongruous word nevertheless could not hide the underlying layers of social exclusion that were being built into the city's physical spaces.

These changes to the city were accompanied by the transfer of urban and rural property from Algerian to French hands in the department as a whole.[6] The earliest investors came from the French military, as officers formed private companies in the 1830s to accumulate valuable agricultural land. This process created a vested interest on the ground in favor of settlement even before the arrival of colonists. As the number of settlers increased in the 1840s, the military regime passed a series of *ordonnances* that imposed French property law on Algerian territories so as to free up land for new arrivals. The authorities declared that the customary rights enjoyed by Algerian nomadic groups gave them access to more land than they actually needed, and through a process known as *cantonnement*, the French subdivided tribal lands (*'arsh*) and forced local populations to settle on a portion of their former territories. The French regime granted the rest, invariably the most fertile land, to colonial settlers for growing cash crops.

The resulting crisis hit farmers and pastoralists among the Algerian population equally. The combination of an expanded regime of individual private property with the reintegration of the Algerian economy into international markets had a devastating effect on rural Algerians. In good years, peasants suffered from low prices for goods they had to sell. In bad years, they suffered from higher prices for goods they needed to buy. They lost rights to land that had formerly been available during times of scarcity, and lacking collateral, they could borrow only enough to guarantee a state of permanent indebtedness, which in turn pressured communities to sell even more land.[7] This cycle persisted into the twentieth century and was an important part of the background to the outbreak of violence in 1934. The combination of a global economic crisis during the Depression with poor crop yields in Algeria during the early 1930s drove many from rural areas in the region into Constantine itself in search of employment, while those who remained on the land petitioned their Muslim representatives for assistance from the administration.[8]

Historians have rightly characterized French policy after the conquest as a "land grab" of massive proportions.[9] Nevertheless, the French state's hope that settlement would create a reliable rural middle class of European property owners was never realized. Although the announced goal was to encourage settlement by farmers who would occupy the land themselves, in practice it was easier to grant concessions to large-scale absentee landowners and speculators. This was especially the case in the department of Constantine, where large estates—known to the French as *grande colonisation*—took root early, and small-scale settlement never penetrated as far into the countryside as it did in western Algeria. In Algeria as a whole, there were over 109,000 European settlers by 1848, but only 15,000 of these settled in rural areas.[10] The western city of Oran quickly took on the appearance of a quasi-European city, with a total population of nearly 22,500 in 1847, of which over 15,000 were recent colonial arrivals, largely from Spain, Italy, Malta, or France. In the city of Constantine, on the other hand, the total population was over 20,800 in 1847, though the number of Europeans was much smaller, at just over 1,900.[11]

The conversion of tribal lands to plantations for export crops such as grain, tobacco, or grapes for wine production revealed a new kind of vulnerability for rural Algerians when the price of wheat at home soared to levels approaching what one would pay in Europe. Reserve silos were emptied for sale abroad, and people were driven to consume even their seed for the next year. When exacerbated by drought in the 1860s, this situation could only have one outcome, and much of Algeria was experiencing famine by 1867–1868. Another consequence was the revolt in Kabylia in 1871, a major insurrection whose defeat marked the beginning of the end of organized resistance to colonization in the nineteenth century.[12] Even before this event, at least 20 percent of the department of Constantine had died of hunger. This generalized figure, which comes from the official statistics based on declarations of death, is almost certainly too low, owing to the underreporting of deaths of children and women. Certain areas were particularly hard hit by hunger: three districts, the cities of Constantine, Aïn Beïda, and Tébessa, accounted for more than half the deaths from starvation.[13] Those who remained survived by eating semi-toxic roots.

These political and material changes were made possible by a new legal structure that determined the rights and obligations of Algeria's peoples under French rule. The foundation of this colonial civic order was the status of the "native." When Algeria was annexed to France by the *ordonnance royale* of February 24, 1834, the populations of Algeria were multilingual and heterogeneous, divided into categories that included Arabs, Turks, Berbers, Muslims, Jews, town dwellers, and rural inhabitants, as well as groupings that depended on complex relations of kinship. The 1834 *ordonnance* amalgamated these peoples together indiscriminately into a group labeled *indigènes* (indigenous, native-born). This label flattened out the diversity produced by centuries of population movements in North Africa; simultaneously, it provided a means to distinguish those who were already present in North Africa from the latest arrivals from Europe in ways that emphasized the newcomers' apparent uniqueness. It drew attention to what Algerians did not share with Europeans and relegated their laws and culture to the realm of the primitive and the backward.

The 1834 *ordonnance* implied a form of French nationality for the group labeled *indigènes* by making the land they lived on subject to French sovereignty, but simultaneously denied all "indigenous" Algerians—both Muslims and Jews—the full rights of citizenship.[14] The juridical status of Algerian *indigènes* was thus inferior to that of other French people, and the conquered peoples of Algeria in practice came to occupy an intermediary position as "subjects" rather than "citizens," a distinction that left them ambiguously between those who were "foreign" and those who were treated as "French."[15] Within this intermediary space, Algerian *indigènes* lived in accordance with Islamic or Jewish laws regarding marriage and inheritance, but this very "privilege" also became a justification for excluding them from the full rights enjoyed by citizens under French law. Under the 1834 legislation, both Islam and the Judaism practiced in Algeria were seen as incompatible with the prescriptions of the French Civil Code. The exclusion of Islam was straightforward in legal terms, because no Muslims had ever possessed French citizenship. The exclusion of Algerian Jews was more anomalous, however, since Jews living in metropolitan France had been granted full citizenship during the French Revolution in 1791. The conquest of Algeria drew attention to the fact that there were two kinds of Jews living under French law—those in France who were citizens, and those in colonial territories, who remained subjects of French law without citizenship.[16] Algeria's Jews were a small minority, but the absolute number was large enough to draw the attention both of Jewish community leaders in France and of the government itself.

Understanding how Algeria's Jews became the subject of official concern in Paris requires a look at the larger story of Jewish emancipation in France in the nineteenth century. French Jews were granted civil rights during the French Revolution, a period of intense and at times violent debate about citizenship and national sovereignty. After 1791, Jews were no longer subject to special laws regarding residency, professional choices, or economic activity, and could—at least in principle—pursue a different kind of life as free individuals who were members of the nation. In practice, social and political integration happened slowly. Before the mid-nineteenth century, few French Jews entered political life, the state bureaucracy, or the military without converting to Christianity.[17] At the same time, the association of Jewish emancipation with the polarizing events of the French Revolution meant that powerful counterrevolutionary political traditions were marked by an easily awakened anti-Jewish prejudice. Defenders of the monarchy or conservative Catholics outraged by revolutionary attacks on the church were quick to see the new freedoms enjoyed by Jews as a sign of a degraded society.

From the perspective of Jews in France, the end of legal discrimination offered both opportunities and dangers. Some worried that emancipation might threaten the cohesiveness and distinctiveness of Jewish communities in a rapidly evolving society. Even considering the very gradual nature of Jewish assimilation, emancipation created questions about the institutions that had preserved Jewish community life in earlier periods—the rabbinical courts, schools, and charitable organizations that supported Jewish life in France. What could justify their communitarian focus in an era of civic equality? Napoléon answered this question after the Revolution by creating a centralized structure for administering to French Jews: the Jewish Central Consistory, founded in Paris in 1808. The Central Consistory oversaw a network of regional consistories that administered to local Jewish congregations and tied them publicly to the state. Since comparable centralized bodies linked the French state to Catholic and Protestant populations, Jewish distinctiveness was henceforth simply one of the forms of religious difference that had official recognition.[18] Napoléon's innovation solved the problem of French Jews' relationship to the state but did little to mitigate the latent antisemitism that persisted in French society as a whole.

In 1845, King Louis-Philippe signed a law placing Algerian Jewish communities on a more equal footing with Jews in metropolitan France, by duplicating in Algeria the network of consistories set up in France by Napoléon. Louis-Philippe's law proposed that new consistories be established in Algiers, Oran, and Constantine, and that respected Jews from France be appointed to the new leadership positions in these cities. As in metropolitan France, the consistories in Algeria facilitated the inclusion of Jews into the polity, while also serving a disciplinary function by subjecting Jews to state authority.[19] They policed the activities of local Jewish organizations, kept an eye on the material well-being and social integration of Jewish populations, and acted as intermediaries between Algerian Jewish communities and the French state. While they were decidedly "modernizing" in their impact as new institutions that facilitated the integration of a formerly despised population into French society, in French Algeria this process of integration took place against the background of the continued exclusion of Muslim colonial subjects, who were equally despised, and whose religion was afforded no equivalent form of recognition.

Historians are not in agreement about the extent to which the new consistories should be seen as willing accomplices of France's colonial civilizing mission in Algeria. On the one hand, the Algerian consistories were an expression of the need to establish control over Algeria's urban populations, and these initiatives, supported as much by pragmatists among the military as by the defenders of assimilation, were linked to the larger goals of colonial expansion. They were also an important precedent for the eventual decision to grant citizenship to Algeria's Jews in 1870.[20] On the other hand, the Algerian consistories can be distinguished from the French colonial project because their essentially humanitarian and educational measures were targeted at a specific population, and their overall goals were different from those of France's imperial nation-state.[21] This is a disagreement that hinges less on the activities of the consistories than on definitions of colonialism, however, and whatever one thinks of the consistories' humanitarian projects, they have to be considered within the context of France's efforts to exert its authority over all of Algeria's diverse populations. Humanitarian intentions did not preclude a concern with political authority and an extension of state power over the Algerian population.

Algeria itself first became French civil territory—as opposed to an area of military operations—in 1848, during a brief period of republican government before the establishment of Napoléon III's Second Empire in 1852. Within this territory, Algeria's Muslim and Jewish populations remained *indigènes* or "native" in law until 1870.[22] A significant change to this arrangement came in 1865, however, when a new law granted a limited right for certain *indigènes* to apply for the status of "naturalized" citizens, so long as they surrendered their rights to live in accordance with Jewish or Islamic customary laws.[23] The law of 1865, in other words, allowed indigenous Algerian Muslims and Jews to become full French citizens, but only if they agreed to abide by the French Civil Code. Since the Civil Code differed from Islamic regulations regarding marriage and inheritance, most Algerian Muslims viewed such naturalization as an implicit renunciation of their religious beliefs. Between 1865 and 1940, only about twenty-five Algerian Muslims a year undertook to become naturalized citizens under the terms of the 1865 law, amounting to about two thousand individuals in all.[24] Almost all these naturalized French Muslim Algerians were male heirs from a select francophone elite, many of whom were educated in France. Significantly, Algerian Jews seemed equally reticent about the opportunity provided by the 1865 law. According to Charles Ageron, only 142 Jewish men took the opportunity to become French citizens between 1865 and 1869, out of a total population of approximately 38,000 Jews living in Algeria.[25]

In 1870, the French defeat in the Franco-Prussian War produced a constitutional crisis that resulted in the creation of the Third Republic out of the wreckage of the Second Empire. Amid the chaos of the defeat and the siege of Paris by Prussian troops, French lawmakers promulgated a bundle of decrees that defined the place of Algeria in the new constitution. Central to this effort was the reinforcement of Algeria as a part of French civil territory, with its populations subject to French laws. The 1870 decrees, pushed through by the emergency powers of the new minister of justice, Adolphe Crémieux, awarded Algeria six parliamentary representatives for the settler population (they had only four in 1848) and established the office of the governor-general as the chief executive authority in Algeria. The decrees also subjected all Algerian Muslims living in a circumscribed "zone of colonization" to French civil authority. This area was eventually divided into three departments, each named after its capital city: Oran, Algiers, and Constantine. A large, lightly populated region in the south, the Algerian Sahara, remained under military jurisdiction during the Third Republic, referred to in official documents as the "Southern Territories."

Crémieux's decree of October 24, 1870, granted French citizenship to all Algerian Jews who lived in the three departments of Algeria's civil territory, thus completing a process of legal assimilation that had begun with the establishment of the Jewish consistories in 1845.[26] The only Jews who remained *indigènes* were those who lived in the last remaining zone of military authority in the south. The Crémieux decree posed the new definition of Jewish citizenship in these terms: "The indigenous Jews [*israélites indigènes*] of the departments of Algeria are declared French citizens: as a consequence, their real status and their personal status will be, in accordance with the present decree, governed by French law: all rights that they have enjoyed up to this day remain inviolable."[27] The first clause of this sentence is an unusual one in French colonial law in that the word "indigenous" and the word "citizens" apply to the same group of Algerian people. The Crémieux decree granted the Jews of the three Algerian departments the enjoyment of all the rights and obligations possessed by other French citizens under the Civil Code. At the same time, the decree removed Algeria's Jews from the jurisdiction of rabbinic courts and placed them under French civil law, whether they had asked for this or not. The Crémieux decree upended the lives of Algeria's Jews, especially the families of artisans and shopkeepers whose children now had access to education and professional careers that had been unimaginable to their parents' generation. Many of Algeria's Jews accepted this opportunity for civic belonging by embracing the republican doctrine of assimilation offered to them as citizens and as members of society.[28]

In the years that followed, the Third Republic codified the inferior juridical status of the remaining (largely Muslim) subject population in the 1881 Code de l'indigénat, creating a list of crimes specific to this portion of the Algerian population.[29] This severe code prohibited Muslims from meeting in groups or traveling without official permission, and punished "disrespectful" acts with sanctions that included the sequestration of property, fines, and imprisonment. The Third Republic's legislation prior to 1914 thus created a situation where the majority of Algerians were technically "French," but also "native," without citizenship and subject to a harsh juridical regime and severe fiscal and economic inequalities, while another native group—Algeria's Jews—became French citizens with the same rights as all other non-native French people. As Muslim elites began to organize themselves and call for reform of the Republic's treatment of its colonial subjects, they increasingly focused on a call for a form of full citizenship that would allow them to preserve the personal legal status granted to them as Muslims. Overt calls for national independence came much later, in the years just prior to the outbreak of the Second World War.

With the Muslim population's civil status defined by the Code de l'indigénat and the 1865 law that permitted naturalization to those who accepted the Civil Code, and the citizenship of almost all of Algeria's Jews established by the Crémieux decree of 1870, there remained a third question: how would the Republic treat settlers in Algeria who came from somewhere other than France? Many settlers in the last third of the nineteenth century were from Spain, Italy, Malta, or elsewhere, and they and their children could become citizens only through a process of naturalization that was open only to adults.[30] The government encouraged settlement by Europeans, but it also worried about the growing number of foreigners in Algeria. Parliament found a remedy with a measure included in the nationality law of 1889, which expanded the rights of people born to foreign parents on French territory including French Algeria. The law's overall motivation was explicitly nationalist, and it made it easier for migrants to become French citizens through naturalization. These measures were meant to facilitate military recruitment, especially in France's border regions where migrants sometimes did not bother to naturalize. Under the old law, French women who married foreigners lost their nationality permanently, and sons of foreign-born residents could avoid military service. The 1889 law allowed women who married foreigners to keep their citizenship and pass it to their children through filiation, making it easier for children who were the product of such marriages to become citizens. Insofar as it explicitly excepted Muslims from its revised provisions for naturalization, however, the 1889 law was also a response to the Crémieux decree's generous provisions toward Algerian Jews.[31]

In Algeria, the 1889 law had an immediate effect on the composition of the settler population. The proportion of foreigners declined, and the law greatly eased the assimilation of foreign nationals who settled in Algeria, so long as they came from a recognizably European background. Note that although the law's overall thrust explicitly denied an ethnic or racial element to national identity by being relatively open to migrants from elsewhere in Europe, its application in French Algeria hardened the increasingly racial or ethnic identification of the "European" settler community, since non-European arrivals could not benefit from the same easing of restrictions. A Muslim Moroccan or Tunisian who entered Algeria to live remained an *indigène* and had no recourse to the benefits of the 1889 law. Muslim Algerians, meanwhile, remained skeptical of the naturalization measures that were available to them through the earlier 1865 law, because of its apparent conflict with their religious beliefs. As very few became French citizens, they passed their native status to their children.[32]

The creation of the *indigène* or "native" as a legal category that eventually encompassed many but not all the diverse populations residing in Algeria in 1830 was thus much more than a simple necessity born of the facts of violent conquest. It was a *relative* category whose meaning was constructed, step by step, in opposition to other evolving definitions of "Frenchness" and "Europeanness," and in response to changing circumstances within colonial society. In civil law—though not, of course, within their lived experience—the *indigènes* in Algeria suffered from a kind of existential homelessness, living on French sovereign territory but possessing only a denatured form of nationality that was not even explicitly named until 1865, when the *sénatus consulte* of Napoléon III declared that the natives of Algeria were French. Historian Laure Blévis has suggested that in this sense, the Algerian *indigène* was a "new category of foreigner," with even fewer rights than people from other countries.[33] Italians and Spaniards could take advantage of the 1889 law and become naturalized French citizens upon arrival. The native Algerian, on the other hand, was in principle expected to assimilate in place, if at all, and no courtesies were extended to Muslims from elsewhere who crossed the frontier in French Algeria. The "native" was a category that made sense only in a world where "Europeans" moved about while everybody else stayed still.

This vision of the world, and the relationships it contained, necessarily produced a similar reimagining of Algerian spaces, as the distinction between "native" and "European" was imposed on different neighborhoods in Algerian cities, and as territories in the countryside were inscribed into a new political and administrative order that determined how such spaces were to be governed.[34] This reordering of space in Algeria has a complex history, however, that was produced by movements of people within the colonial situation in Algeria, and France's shifting political regimes across the nineteenth century. During the Second Republic (1848–1852), the French state used the balance of population between settlers and indigenous peoples to subdivide the Algerian countryside into distinct districts that it called "civil territories," "Arab territories," and "mixed territories." This early plan for the division of territories favored the growing settler population and left areas with few settlers under military authority.

The imperial regime of Napoléon III (1852–1870)—a self-described Arabophile—sought to limit the settlers' independent power by bringing, and thus co-opting, the Arab aristocracy into the administration. He allowed Arab elites to participate in local assemblies, known as *jamma'at* after a traditional council of male adults that had long been a part of North African society.[35] As the settler population increased in size, however, any pretense at preserving autonomous "Arab territories" was dispensed with, and the *jamma'at* were increasingly marginalized, surviving only in a severely curtailed fashion. The structure of the "mixed territories" (*communes mixtes*), meanwhile, was laid out in the law of 1863 that established the registration of all landed property. The *communes mixtes* were governed by a single French administrator who acted as both mayor and judge, in association with lesser French officials and a few cooperative notables from the Muslim population.

Towns where the European population was over 10 percent were designated "towns exercising full rights under French law" (*communes de plein exercice*) and given the standard French institutions of municipal governance, including an elected town council and a mayor. These institutions nevertheless operated in an environment very different from that of their counterparts in mainland France. The *communes de plein exercice* were allowed to support themselves financially by annexing neighboring villages of Muslim colonial subjects as taxpayers. This meant that their territory was much larger than towns in France with comparable numbers of electors—by 1880 an estimated one-third of the 176 *communes de plein exercice* in Algeria possessed a territory of over 10,000 hectares, while in France the average size of a commune was only 1,643 hectares. In the smaller *communes de plein exercice* a few dozen European voters could represent thousands of Muslim taxpayers. In 1884, the Third Republic's revision of the law on municipalities contained a measure that was applied to the Algerian *communes de plein exercice* only: each of these Algerian communes would appoint up to six Muslim colonial subjects to sit on the municipal council, chosen presumably from compliant elite families who cooperated with the authorities. The number of these Muslim councilors would never exceed one-fourth of the total, and except for a brief window between 1876 and 1884, they were not permitted to participate in the election of mayors.[36]

This situation meant that severe fiscal inequities were built into the colonial situation in Algeria, on top of the onerous legal discriminations of the Code de l'indigénat. By 1908, Algerian colonial subjects—of whom all but a few thousand were Muslim—constituted roughly 90 percent of the population of Algeria, but the amount of land left in their hands meant that their combined economic activity accounted for only about 20 percent of the colony's gross domestic product. In spite of this, this native majority paid 70 percent of the direct taxes collected by the government and 45 percent of the total taxes collected. This last statistic—that 90 percent of the population paid only 45 percent of the total taxes collected—was often cited by the settler political establishment as evidence that Algerian colonial subjects paid fewer taxes proportionate to their number in the total population. This number was misleading, however, as it did not take into account the fact that 80 percent of the colony's GDP had been taken over by settlers who amounted to less than 15 percent of the total population. Of course, not being able to vote meant that the vast majority of the Algerian population had no say over how these tax revenues were spent.[37]

Establishing the fact of "indigeneity" was both an essential condition of colonial rule in French Algeria and an act of willful oversimplification that had profound material consequences for those who found themselves relegated to this category. For Muslim Algerians, native status simultaneously recognized a profoundly felt religious identity but also isolated them from France's republican institutions and relegated them to a kind of homelessness in their own land. This native civil status subjected Muslim Algerians to a cruel and discriminatory legal code and made them vulnerable to fiscal exploitation by municipalities that profited from the taxes that Muslims paid without the benefit of political representation. Seeking redress for these inequities required acting—at least in part—in the name of religion, because the exclusion had been made on religious grounds. For Jewish Algerians, on the other hand, the fact that they were granted citizenship after 1870 allowed them to embrace the Republic, but the taint of their earlier native status persisted in the eyes of many European settlers in Algeria, who resented the fact that this formerly subject population could now participate in politics and economic life on equal terms. The great irony of French colonialism in Algeria lay in the way that the secular republic's civil regime made the question of political reform inseparable from the question of religious identity. Whether one supported more or fewer rights for Algeria's Muslims and Jews, politics and religion were permanently linked.

CHAPTER 3

The Crucible of Local Politics

The growth of a large European minority in French Algeria during the nineteenth century was accompanied by the development of particularly complex local political relationships. In the 1901 census, European settlers were almost 13 percent of the total population— over 600,000 out of 4.7 million people. By this time, however, settlement had fallen to only a few thousand a year, and the settlers' proportion of the total population would not change much in the twentieth century.[1] The population of settlers in cities was higher: in 1911, 32 percent of Constantine's population were of European origin, just over 14 percent were Jewish, and nearly 54 percent were Algerian Muslims, out of a total population of 65,193. These proportions remained roughly similar over the next decades, though the total population grew considerably, rising to 101,526 in the 1931 census. French settlers came mostly from the southern Mediterranean coast, poorer regions in the Alps, and from eastern France along the German border, where the loss of Alsace and Lorraine after the Franco-Prussian War caused many to emigrate. The next largest group was Spanish immigrants, who tended to settle in rural areas, above all in the department of Oran, often without becoming naturalized citizens. Italians and Maltese were more numerous in the department of Constantine, where they constituted a significant portion of the fishermen, dockworkers, masons, and market gardeners who helped make up the region's growing urban population.[2]

Historian Charles-Robert Ageron noted that already by the years 1895–1900, the expression "the Algerian people" had come to refer exclusively to the "European" population, which itself was self-conscious about the distinction between those of French origin and those "naturalized French" who had come from elsewhere, especially Spain, Italy, and Malta. After the passage of the 1889 law on nationality, the number of naturalized French citizens increased rapidly, and those of French origin began to refer to the new arrivals who opted for naturalization as the "neo-French" in order to draw attention to the potential danger of growing numbers of French citizens whose loyalties were suspect. Concerns about foreign invasion dissipated over time, however, and by the first decade of the twentieth century, the number of "Europeans" born in Algeria exceeded the number who had migrated from elsewhere for the first time.

Inevitably, distinctions between Europeans, Muslims, and Jews shaped the politics of local communities in French Algeria. Throughout the Third Republic (1870–1940), a few settler clans in each city dominated the assemblies that served as the focus of political life. These loose coalitions were led by a small number of powerful figures who often accumulated multiple elected offices, at the national level in parliament as well as in local assemblies at the municipal and departmental levels. A seat in parliament allowed Algerian politicians to forge strong connections with decision makers in Paris, and these levers of power were backed up by the patronage networks that greased the wheels of business and power in Algerian cities. These networks were often familial: Jean Ernest Mercier, the mayor of Constantine from 1884 to 1887, was the father of Ernest Mercier, who advised Prime Minister Raymond Poincaré on petroleum issues in 1923 and became the director of the Compagnie française des pétroles (later Total) in 1924. Gaston Thomson, a parliamentary deputy from Constantine who served as the minister of commerce and industry during the early months of the First World War, held his parliamentary seat for fifty-five years, from 1877 until his death in 1932, the longest tenure on record in the French National Assembly. He was reelected for the last time only eight days before his death. Thomson was a defender of legislation that reinforced France's colonies, especially in Cochinchina, where his brother Charles served as governor-general from 1882 to 1886. The sense of political impregnability that came with membership in these political clans was on display in the reputation for high living that the Algerian parliamentary delegation enjoyed among Parisian political circles: they were known for their luxury town houses, large domestic staffs, and sumptuous dinners accompanied by "excellent liqueurs and exquisite cigars."[3]

The department of Constantine's parliamentary delegation was shaped by enduring rivalries, above all that between the Cuttoli brothers, Paul and Jules, and Émile Morinaud, the long-serving mayor of Constantine who was also deputy in parliament from 1898 to 1902 and again from 1919 to 1942. Paul Cuttoli, the deputy from Constantine from 1906 to 1919, senator from 1920 to 1941, and mayor of Philippeville (Skikda) from 1929 until his death in 1949, began his career on the municipal council of Constantine, where Morinaud and he competed for support from within the settler community in the 1890s. In 1896, Morinaud challenged Paul Cuttoli for the mayor's seat on an anti-Jewish platform and won. After 1906, Paul Cuttoli and Morinaud settled their differences and entered into a truce that lasted thirty years, until their agreement fell apart in the bitter election that brought the Popular Front to power in 1936.[4] Cuttoli's brother Jules also served in parliament from Constantine from 1928 to 1936. In general, these leading members of Constantine's settler political clans belonged to parliamentary groups close to the anticlerical republican center. For these figures, however, ideology often meant less than maintaining their patronage networks and protecting French Algeria's privileges in budgetary and spending matters.

Elected officials with a national profile such as Morinaud or the Cuttoli brothers understood that maintaining their authority meant keeping in close touch with local notables from the business world or the professions. Common membership on the municipal or departmental councils, or a seat on the *délégations financières algériennes*, created bonds between the leading personalities of colonial society.[5] Marc-François Lavie founded Constantine's commercial flour mill on the banks of the Rhumel in 1837, the year the French took the city. His grandson, Marcel Lavie, sat on the *délégations financières* in the years after the First World War. Accompanying him was Édouard Gueit, managing director of the Usines Lavie, which by the early decades of the twentieth century had expanded from its original flour operation to include an olive processing plant and a dam on the Rhumel that became the source of hydroelectric power for the region. Alongside Mercier and Gueit on the *délégations financières* was Louis Morel, the proprietor of Constantine's daily newspaper, *La Dépêche de Constantine*, a part of the support network for the Cuttoli brothers in parliament—Paul Cuttoli was the paper's political director. That such a narrow elite might have their hands on the levers of local political and economic power was not at all unusual in Third Republic France, but this concentration was magnified in the settler colony of Algeria, where the majority population of Muslim colonial subjects paid a disproportionate share of taxes but were excluded from political life by their secondary "indigenous" status.

Muslims in French Algeria could not help but confront the power of their "indigeneity" in their dealings with the authorities, and they did so by insisting on the continued relevance of their customs, their religious beliefs, and their political and social structures. By the first years of the twentieth century, these efforts were led by a group of men who came from prosperous families that had accommodated themselves to the colonial order. Many of these men, known as the Young Algerians—a reference to the reformist "Young Turks" within the Ottoman Empire—were French-speaking products of colonial schools, and their program was essentially assimilationist, seeking greater representation of Muslim Algerians in French institutions without necessarily giving up the personal status as Muslims granted them by the 1865 law or demanding outright citizenship. As one of their leading figures, Si M'hamed Ben Rahal (Muhammad bin Rahal al-Nadrumi), cautiously stated in 1903: "Our French compatriots are free to claim for themselves the rights of citizens. As for us, we are French subjects, and we desire to remain French subjects. If we claim a place within [French] assemblies, that is only because within the French constitution, whoever is not represented has no defenders."[6]

Ben Rahal's desire to remain "subjects" rather than becoming "citizens" amounted to an acknowledgment that few Algerian Muslims would accept the implicit abandonment of their faith that naturalization seemed to imply. The Young Algerians hoped that in the absence of legal reforms, Muslim civic associations would foster a greater incorporation of Algerian colonial subjects into French society. Their emphasis on education led them to found a wide array of circles, clubs, musical societies, and literary discussion groups in all the larger Algerian cities. These organizations became vehicles for new forms of sociability among young men and contained within them the seeds of future political activism.[7] A key priority of these groups was to attain official recognition of the role played by Algerian Muslims in the French military. In 1908 a delegation of Young Algerians visited Prime Minister Georges Clemenceau in order to convince him that Algerian colonial subjects who served in the army should receive full civil and political rights. In 1912, a group from the Arab section of the *délégations financières* traveled to Paris to hand a message personally to Prime Minister Raymond Poincaré. This document, later known as the Young Algerian Manifesto, supported the conscription of Algerian Muslims into the French army. They demanded, however, that this show of patriotic sacrifice be met with reforms that addressed the inequities of the colonial system. They called for terms of service that were equal to those of French citizens, reducing the period of conscription to two years and setting the minimum age for military service at twenty-one instead of eighteen. Beyond these changes in military procedures, the Young Algerians also called for reform of the Code de l'indigénat, "serious and sufficient" political representation for Algerian Muslims in Algeria and in the metropole, increased social spending, and a more just division of taxes. The First World War intervened before the Young Algerians could pursue these demands further, and no serious discussion of Muslim civil status in Algeria came until after the war.[8]

In this constellation of shifting perceptions of status and political rights, Algeria's Jews remained a special case. Many settlers of French origin saw the Crémieux decree of 1870 as an illegitimate form of naturalization, an ill-conceived law that was forced on Algerians by politicians in Paris, most notably by Adolphe Crémieux, who was himself Jewish. Opponents of the Crémieux decree seized on the insurrection in Kabylie in 1871 as proof that Muslim Algerians would not tolerate the assimilation of Algeria's Jewish population, but historians have traced El Mokrani's (Muhammad al-Hajj al-Muqrani) revolt to the French state's refusal to reimburse his family for expenditures to alleviate the famine of the 1860s. In Ageron's words, the effect of the Crémieux decree on the Muslim majority in Algeria was "null."[9] In the long term, the decree fostered what would later be perceived as divergent social and cultural paths under French colonialism for two populations that had long lived together. The decree's immediate impact on Muslim Algerians, however, was minimal.

At the same time, granting the vote to Jews transformed the electoral calculus in Algeria's cities. Jews were less than 2 percent of the population, but Jewish voters were a significant proportion of the total electorate in some cities, as Muslim Algerians could not vote, and many "European" new arrivals had not been naturalized. Jews constituted 15 percent of the voters in the department of Oran, and they were over 50 percent of voters in the major western city of Tlemcen. By the 1890s, in some smaller towns such as Aïn Beïda (department of Constantine), Nedroma (Oran), or Bou Saada (Algiers) where there were few "European" settlers, the percentage of Jewish voters was between 50 and 80 percent.[10] Such circumstances provided the context for the eruption of an anti-Jewish backlash in the 1890s as a new cohort of politicians coming from the settler community tried to shoulder their way into elected office by attacking the power of Jewish electors in Algerian towns and cities.

The eruption of this powerful wave of anti-Jewish agitation in French Algeria coincided with the most spectacular crisis of antisemitism in modern French history, the Dreyfus affair of 1894–1906. Part of the European-wide backlash against Jewish emancipation that marked electoral politics in many countries during the last decades of the nineteenth century, this scandal demonstrated the extent to which older forms of religious antisemitism had been reinvigorated and made relevant to modernity by the emergence of mass society and the politics of nationalism. The affair began when Alfred Dreyfus, a captain on the army's general staff who happened to be Jewish, was wrongly accused of treason and sentenced to solitary confinement in a prison colony off the coast of French Guiana. The affair unleashed popular expressions of anti-Jewish hatred, and Jews in both France and French Algeria were deeply disturbed to discover the extent to which their presence in public life was still the object of fury.[11] The Dreyfus affair became a cause célèbre for the defenders of individual rights under the secular Third Republic, and he was eventually pardoned in 1899. Before the pardon, however, Anti-Dreyfusards organized marches and burned members of the Dreyfus family in effigy, decrying the alleged influence of Jews in French society and the economy. Although it was common at the time to claim that the Dreyfus affair was primarily a Parisian story, historians have now made clear that the Dreyfus case penetrated deep into the French countryside, where rural people "read about it, talked about it, joked about it, fought about it."[12]

Throughout metropolitan France, the Dreyfus affair became an effective recruiting tool for activists who rallied conservative Catholics, monarchists, defenders of the army, and nationalists at a moment when older political formations on the right in France were still suspicious of universal manhood suffrage. These militants found that they could use a highly charged language about the essential foreignness of Jews in France to drum up support for a new right-wing populism that was capable of taking votes from the left. Anti-Jewish politicians found that their message resonated with laborers and small shopkeepers who felt victimized by the concentration of economic power that accompanied industrial development during these decades, and that it was not hard to convince voters that there was a connection between these changes and the emancipation of French Jews. At the same time, conservatives could also use the language of antisemitism to attack what they did not like about French republicanism—in particular its commitment to secularism and the separation of church and state.

Unlike the traditional conservatism of France's aristocratic elites, however, the new reactionary antisemitism was well versed in the propaganda opportunities offered by the modern press. In pamphlets, illustrated broadsheets, and political speeches, anti-Jewish agitators took advantage of the spread of literacy and cheap newsprint to reach a wide audience. Anti-Dreyfusard organizations that formed during the 1890s, such as Charles Maurras's Action française, became a permanent presence in the French political landscape, eventually shaping the generation of French nationalists who rallied to the collaborationist and antisemitic Vichy regime during the Second World War.[13] These organizations represented a line in French political thought that had never accepted the French Revolution, the Declaration of the Rights of Man, or the principles of a secular Republic in France, but their reactionary views were now propagated to a broader voting public. What these militants all had in common was the realization that talk about Jews—still just a tiny minority in France—could be effectively harnessed to attack the foundations of the Republic in an age of mass politics.

In Algeria, anti-Jewish rhetoric was never the sole property of political extremists, and it was just as likely to come from the left wing of the political spectrum as the right.[14] A moderate republican group known as the Opportunists consolidated their control of the municipal councils in French Algeria in the 1870s and 1880s, often by combining the support of local landowners and commercial elites with alliances of convenience with Jewish voters. When the so-called Radical Republicans challenged the Opportunists in the 1880s and 1890s, the Radicals in French Algeria found anti-Jewish rhetoric to be their most potent electoral tool, especially when it could be combined with a populist anticapitalism of a vaguely left-wing tint. Antisemitic appeals thus became frequent among rival groups within the settler political establishment as they competed for the profitable patronage networks that came with control of municipal budgets. Vote buying and other forms of corruption often accompanied the demagogic posturing of anti-Jewish candidates.[15] The financial and budgetary power of local French Algerian politicians depended, as we have seen, on their ability to collect taxes from Muslim colonial subjects who could not vote. Getting elected, however, meant either forming a coalition with the bloc of Jewish voters in Algerian cities, or loudly running against them on an anti-Jewish platform.

The first anti-Jewish league in Algeria was founded in Miliana in July 1871, mere months after the signing of the Crémieux decree. Others followed, most notably in Tlemcen in 1885, after several years of intermittent unrest in this western Algerian city. Similar groups appeared in other colonial towns following the publication of Édouard Drumont's incendiary polemic *La France juive* in 1886. Drumont's newspaper, *La Libre Parole*, circulated in both France and French Algeria, and when the Dreyfus affair catapulted Drumont to the status of a celebrity, he ran for a seat in parliament in Algiers—and won. In Oran, Drumont's disciples Jean Pouzet and Paul Bidaine became influential propagandists for anti-Jewish politics, and Fernand Grégoire's left-wing Ligue socialiste antijuive prepared the way for the election in 1898 of Max Régis, the editor of *L'Anti-Juif d'Alger*, as mayor of Algiers in 1898.[16] Régis's election came on the heels of prolonged unrest and periodic attacks on Jews in the French Algerian capital. In January 1898 a crowd in Algiers ransacked and looted Jewish neighborhoods over a period of three days, apparently with the approval of local civil and military authorities.[17] Throughout the many anti-Jewish protests in France and French Algeria during the Dreyfus affair, these incidents in Algiers were the only ones with fatal consequences, leading to the deaths of two Jewish men.[18]

The anti-Jewish militants in Algiers found a counterpart in Constantine in the figure of Émile Morinaud, who was elected mayor in 1896 and deputy in the French parliament in 1898, at the height of the Dreyfus affair. He and his colleagues within the Radical Party—a left-of-center Republican group— had correctly predicted that they could use anti-Jewish rhetoric to mount a challenge to the more conservative Opportunist republican majority that was in control of the city's political establishment. Not coincidentally, Morinaud was also the editor of a regional newspaper, Le Républicain de Constantine, that became the voice of the Radical Republicans in Constantine. He led a constant battle with the Opportunist newspaper, L'Indépendant, which supported the rival network of Constantine's representative in parliament, Gaston Thomson. Thomson and his allies had cultivated Jewish voters in the department, and Morinaud's paper fueled his campaign against the Opportunists with a relentless barrage of anti-Jewish articles. A telegram from Elie Narboni, a lawyer and leader within Constantine's Jewish community, to the minister of the interior and the minister of justice reported that the region's antisemitic newspapers had accused the Jews of the city of murdering children and using their blood to make cakes. Their central campaign promise was to make the Jews "bite the dust."[19]

These tactics worked, and when Morinaud was elected mayor, he used his office to attack the Jewish population of the city. He tried to keep Jewish pupils from registering at public schools, and attempted to exclude Jews from the city's programs of public assistance. In 1902, however, he lost his parliamentary seat as the Dreyfus affair subsided and his anti-Jewish polemics were no longer enough to stitch together a majority of local electors. In consolidating his local power base after this loss, Morinaud did a remarkable about-face. He formed a political alliance with local Jewish political leaders in Constantine, eventually forming a close connection with none other than the same Elie Narboni, who helped Morinaud organize his municipal electoral campaigns after 1904.[20] That Narboni and other Jewish leaders in Constantine found such an alliance expedient indicates how vulnerable they felt themselves to be from anti-Jewish militancy, but it was also a part of a larger pattern of conservatism among the leaders of Constantine's Jewish consistory. Morinaud's shrewd but cruel electoral calculations betrayed the essential cynicism that lay behind the anti-Jewish agitation of Algerian politicians.[21] They also demonstrated that the extraordinarily raucous debate that accompanied the Dreyfus case in Algeria was never really about the circumstances of Alfred Dreyfus's arrest and conviction.[22]

In his memoirs, Morinaud attributed his anti-Jewish awakening to the municipal elections of 1888, when the mayor's seat had been left open after the retirement of the incumbent, Ernest Mercier. Morinaud, already well known for the outspoken editorials he published in his newspaper, hoped to use his popularity among the shopkeepers and small businesses owners in the city to win the election. His opponent, Pierre Casanova, had the support of more prosperous business owners and Gaston Thomson's political coalition, which included many Jewish voters. Morinaud recounted his optimism before the vote and his bitterness after the results were known:

> We did not take into account the Jewish mass, manipulated by the Isaac family, M. Stora and other influential members of the Consistory and the Jewish Charitable Office [Bureau de bienfaisance israélite].
>
> The polls had hardly opened when we saw the Jews brought in squads to the City Hall. Exiting the Jewish quarter, they crossed the Place du Palais, took the rue Morès, which led to the old City Hall located where the current one now stands, passing by the printer's office of the *Indépendant* where they had received their miraculous *manna* and came out under the guidance of their leaders [*courtiers*] to go to deposit in the ballot box the bulletin that had been given to them.
>
> We watched this odious carousel from the balcony of our Club that looked out on the printer's office. Our indignation grew. At two o'clock in the afternoon, I could no longer contain myself. I ran down the stairs of the Club and stood in front of the door of the printer. It was crowded with Jewish voters. I began to shout at one of the Jewish leaders who came out with a gang of voters. I told him to stop this shameful traffic. He responded to me crudely. I took him by the collar and shook him strongly. He fell backwards while the proprietor of the print shop tried to close the door. The police arrived, under the orders of our opponents. I was taken to the station, where under pretext of an investigation I was held for two hours. . . . During that time the last of the herds of Jewish electors had voted in mass for Casanova's list. . . . The radicals had the great majority of French voters behind us, but we had been beaten by the vote of the Jewish bloc against us.[23]

Morinaud's anecdote contained all the elements of his future career: his deep understanding of the push and pull of local politics, his assumption that Jews should be understood above all in collective terms (as a "bloc" or "mass," who move in "squads," "gangs," or "herds"), and that they were to be distinguished from the true "French" who had apparently voted in his favor. His description of the movement of Jews invoked a kind of invasion of the "European" spaces of the city, as he described the way that these men emerged from the "Jewish quarter" and walked through the squares and open streets that stood as the symbolic reminders of the way that the French had taken over the city's spaces and replaced its vision of the future with their own. The Jews' acting as a collectivity was proof of the illegitimacy of their vote, and of their citizenship itself, which had been bestowed upon them by a Jew, Adolphe Crémieux.[24] In recounting this example of "Jewish provocation"—which after all was simply a description of a particularly well-organized get-out-the-vote effort—Morinaud reminded his readers that Gaston Thomson, the patron of his opponent Pierre Casanova, was married to Henriette Peigné-Crémieux, Adolphe Crémieux's granddaughter. He attributed Casanova's victory to this fact alone, which he claimed had made Thomson "a kind of demigod in the Jewish quarter."[25] The marriages in the Crémieux/Peigné/Thomson families could have been seen as a sign of successful assimilation, but Morinaud drew the opposite conclusion: they had the rights of French citizens, but they were still Jews, and it was as Jews that their exercise of power would be judged.

In the late nineteenth century, there appears to have been little convergence between moments of anti-Jewish agitation by the settler population in Algeria and incidents of conflict between Muslims and Jews in Constantine. In 1875 and again in 1888 Algerian Muslim riflemen of the Constantine garrison came to blows with individual Jews in Constantine, leading to incidents in which soldiers seeking revenge ran through the Jewish quarter beating passersby. These tensions had their origins in the streets and in the *cafés maures* near the Jewish quarter where men met to drink, and led the local authorities to admonish the Jewish consistory for being unable to control the members of their community.[26] The available evidence suggests, however, that Algeria's Muslim colonial subjects did not participate in the anti-Dreyfusard disturbances of the 1890s in significant numbers.

At the same time, however, it is also clear that Muslims in Algeria observed the debates about Jewish citizenship as well as the demographic shifts in the Algerian population from their own perspective. Few were inspired by the virulent antisemitism of anti-Dreyfusard militants—which was not aimed at Muslims but rather at other voters—but Muslim Algerians also knew and

understood the ways that difference and political exclusion worked in colonial society. There is evidence that they, too, were troubled by the divergence
between Algeria's Jewish citizens and Muslim subjects as they reflected on
their own challenges. Malek Bennabi, the Algerian philosopher and shrewd
observer of Muslim society in his home city of Constantine, wrote in his
biography of the changes that his parents' generation had witnessed in the
years before and after his birth in 1905. In his memoirs, he noted that the Jews
of the city served as a marker of these transformations:

> In the streets of Constantine where in the past one saw only turbans,
> *burnous* and embroidered flannel, all of that began to disappear. And
> the boutiques where one manufactured different articles . . . closed one
> after another. One only saw European clothes or discarded rags [*fripe-
> rie*] from Marseille. The urban landscape transformed itself on all sides.
> The arrival of more and more Europeans and the massive Frenchifica-
> tion [*francisation*] of the Jews gave a new face to the city, with its new
> population, its cafés, its own commerce on the newly expanded streets,
> like the rue Caraman, with its banks, its restaurants, its electricity, and
> its shop windows. The life of the "native" [*indigène*] was in retreat and
> took refuge in the alleys and dead-ends of Sidi Rached.[27]

Bennabi's description of the changes that the city had undergone in the late
nineteenth century was a list of visual cues, moving outward from the adorned
bodies of people in the street to the content of the shops and the landscape
of the new neighborhoods. The differences in the appearance of the city's
Jews—and the way that these changes were perceived by Bennabi himself—
were simply one item among many, but the "massive Frenchification" that
he mentions is the detail that reveals the power of the processes that were
under way. However the Jews may have experienced these changes—and it
was not easy for them either[28]—it was impossible for Bennabi to imagine
their "Frenchification" as anything but the opposite of the "retreat" that the
Muslim majority felt their own culture had undergone as a result of their corresponding "nativization." In Bennabi's formulation, the story of Algeria's
Jews after 1870 was the counterexample that allowed him to name the homelessness of the Muslim colonial subject in a newly Frenchified Algeria. This
connection—between an awareness of what Muslims in Algeria had lost and
what Algeria's Jews had gained under the French—did occasionally produce
moments of tensions between Muslims and Jews in Constantine, but it never
translated into the development of a mass-based Muslim anti-Jewish political
movement that shared the ideological vision of settler antisemites. As we
will see, there were moments after the riots of 1934 when certain Muslim

politicians were tempted by the possibility that their supporters could be gal-
vanized by an anti-Jewish message, but attempts by anti-Jewish Europeans to
provoke Muslims into violence against their Jewish neighbors usually did not
work. Throughout these decades, Algeria's Muslims understood that their
Jewish neighbors were being attacked by European antisemites for what they
had in common with Muslims, as the despised bearers of a precolonial North
African culture.

By the end of the nineteenth century, then, relations between Muslims
and Jews in Algeria had been transformed by seven decades of French rule
and settlement. In the Ottoman period, Muslims and Jews belonged in fundamental ways to the city, though their status was marked as legally different, and they occupied different quarters. On the eve of the First World War,
a new class of "Europeans" governed in Algeria, maintaining their power
through cynical electoral calculations that played Muslims and Jews off one
another. After 1870, Muslims remained excluded from citizenship, and were
subject to onerous fiscal obligations and an oppressive penal code. The seizure of land, the establishment of a new property regime, and the creation
of new forms of civil administration imitated French institutions, while also
allowing the colonial regime to protect itself from the majority population
of Muslims that it sought to subjugate. The Jews of Constantine became
citizens after 1870, but this declaration of belonging had been accompanied
by a curse. The dynamic of local politics in French Algeria invited Jews to
participate in local governance and simultaneously nurtured a vicious antipathy against them, as organized political groups among the settler population
realized that they could use anti-Jewish animus as a stepping-stone to political power. In the crucible of France's colonial situation, antisemitism and
discrimination against Muslims became inextricably entangled.

PART 2

Colonial Society in Motion

Chapter 4

The Postwar Moment

Constantine's Monument to the Fallen from the First World War stands on a narrow promontory on the opposite side of the gorge from the old city, high above the tumbling cascades of the Rhumel river and the Plain of Hamma far below. The monument, designed by the Constantine architect Marcel Dumoulin, consists of a freestanding arch, with four columns per side, topped by an imposing winged statue, the *Victory of Cirta*, recalling the Winged Victory of Samothrace in the Louvre in Paris. Inside the monument is a bronze plaque that lists in alphabetical order the names of 844 soldiers from Constantine who died between 1914 and 1918. The first stone was laid on November 18, 1918. The original intention was to complete the structure in time for the 1930 centennial celebrations of the conquest of Algeria. In fact, the official inauguration of the monument would not take place until November 2, 1934, three months after the riots in Constantine.

Mayor Émile Morinaud took credit for the monument's construction. The alphabetical list of the dead made no distinction of religion and contained both Muslims and Jewish names alongside the Italian, Spanish, Corsican, German, and French family names of the European settler population. Given the extent to which Morinaud's career depended on perpetuating and reinforcing the ethnic and social differences that fractured Constantine's population, this somber commemorative plaque is probably the only nondenominational mixed list ever to be associated with the mayor's name. At the moment of the monument's founding, even Morinaud was briefly forced to nod toward a capacious definition of national identity, open at its edges, recognizing the sacrifices made by all residents of the city.

The participation of Algerians in the French war effort between 1914 and 1918 gave new urgency to debates about incorporating the Muslim majority in Algeria into the French polity.[1] The movement of people during the war years and their service to France forced the government to confront the contradictions inherent in a Republican empire that had separate laws for colonial subjects and citizens. French government officials could not ignore the fact that colonial subjects could and did cross borders and that they were coming to metropolitan France to live, work, and fight for their country.[2] Would their status as "indigenous colonial subjects" move with them? Or did confronting this reality mean that the status itself would evolve? Adding to the urgency of these questions were the many claims for self-determination made by colonized peoples throughout Africa and the Middle East as a result of the territorial negotiations that were a part of post–First World War treaty arrangements.[3] The fact that this discussion took place in France as well as in Algeria and other parts of the empire created a much broader audience for discussions of colonial reform.

There were already ten thousand Algerians living in France in 1914, including at least two thousand in Paris alone and probably about the same number in Marseille, part of a growing population of colonial laborers working in industry and in port cities.[4] A law of July 15, 1914, gave Algerians the right to emigrate to France, just in time to support the mobilization effort at the war's outbreak that August.[5] These laborers often faced difficult circumstances. French employers complained about Algerian workers, claiming that they were unskilled, that they would not work during Ramadan, and that they posed a sexual danger to French women.[6] Desperate need during a national crisis prevailed over prejudice, however: seventy-nine thousand Algerians were mobilized to work in French industry and agriculture during the war years, alongside some fifty thousand Indochinese, thirty-six thousand Moroccans, eighteen thousand Tunisians, and forty-five hundred Malagasy.[7]

In the first two years of the war, labor recruitment efforts were carried out in an ad hoc fashion by different ministries, but in 1916 the government set up a Service d'organisation des travailleurs coloniaux (SOTC), which coordinated the recruitment of colonial workers with representatives of business and organized labor.[8] For the remainder of the war, these colonial workers were treated as part of what was an essentially militarized body.

Algerian laborers were transported separately from civilian populations, and billeted in segregated barracks alongside men from West Africa, Madagascar, Indochina, and China. Exceptions were made for some workers who were recruited from Kabylia, who were at times placed under the same conditions as French civilian laborers.[9]

Algeria also contributed directly to the French military's inexhaustible need for soldiers. The French army had half a million casualties within the first five months of the war, and by the end 1.3 million French soldiers were dead. In the face of these catastrophic losses, military recruitment from the empire became essential. In all, approximately 173,000 Muslim Algerians served in the French army between 1914 and 1918. Of these, 2,750 were reservists called back into service when the war broke out, 83,000 were draftees, and 87,000 were volunteers. Of these Algerian soldiers, 25,000 died.[10] When voluntary enlistments declined as the war dragged on, the army demanded an intensification of conscription efforts, which fell especially heavily on rural Algerian populations.[11]

In December 1915, Georges Clemenceau and Georges Leygues—both future prime ministers—wrote a letter to Prime Minister Aristide Briand stating that the participation of Algerians in the war effort necessitated reforms of Algeria's civil status laws. The letter, made public in January 1916, recalled many of the reforms supported by the Young Algerians in 1912. It asked for "naturalization" of Algerian Muslims without prejudice to their religious status, an increase in the number of Muslim electors, the appointment of Muslim representatives on a national council of Muslim affairs, and reform of Algeria's tax and property laws.[12] The letter caused a firestorm of protest from the settler population in Algeria, reawakening the secessionist undercurrent that had been dormant since the Dreyfus affair. Governor-General Charles Lutaud took exception to the proposal and argued until the last year of the war that Algerian laborers in France should be subject to the Code de l'indigénat, so as not to set a dangerous precedent by treating them as if they qualified for equal treatment under French civil law.[13] A chorus of voices in parliament took the opposite view, demanding that the National Assembly recognize the contributions of Muslims by awarding them citizenship, or at least making naturalization easier.[14] Clemenceau became prime minister in November 1917, at the same moment that the League of the Rights of Man took up the cause, and demanded citizenship for Algerians who had fought in the French army.[15] Understanding that the war's end would bring pressure to resolve this question, Clemenceau appointed a moderate figure known for his cautious support of reform, Charles Jonnart, to the office of governor-general in January 1918.

Jonnart's original plan was to explore offering citizenship to all veterans, but the proposal he brought before the National Assembly was significantly watered down. The Jonnart Law, promulgated on February 4, 1919, contained no naturalization for combat veterans. It maintained the personal status for Muslims that had been used to exclude them from citizenship under the 1865 law. Jonnart's innovation was to grant a circumscribed right to vote in local elections to roughly 425,000 Algerian colonial subjects, amounting to about 43 percent of the adult male population. Prior to the First World War, the number of "native" electors was only 57,044 for all of Algeria. The new electors would no longer be subject to the Code de l'indigénat and could vote for members of the approximately one thousand *jamma'at* (village councils) that existed in both the *communes mixtes* and the *communes de plein exercice*. In 281 larger Algerian *communes de plein exercice*, these electors could also vote for Muslim members of municipal councils, and these Muslim councilors could, in turn, participate in the election of mayors. A smaller group among them—approaching one hundred thousand—were also able run for office in the departmental assemblies (*conseils généraux*) of the three departments of Algiers, Oran, and Constantine.[16] Qualifying for this new status of "elector" were veterans of the French army, landowners, business owners and industrialists, civil servants, recipients of French decorations, members of local chambers of commerce and agriculture, and graduates of elementary schools. Most significantly, however, the Jonnart Law contained no provision that would allow Muslim colonial subjects to vote or run for office in the French National Assembly—settler opposition forced Jonnart to take parliamentary representation for Algerian Muslims off the table.

Jonnart's compromise, which produced only a degraded form of second-class citizenship for Algerian colonial subjects, pleased nobody. The primary novelties were an increase in the number of Muslim members on municipal councils and in departmental assemblies and the participation of Muslim councilors in mayoral elections, but these innovations were so constrained that their ability to exert much influence was curtailed from the start. The settler political establishment was shocked at the mere idea of self-representation for Muslim colonial subjects, no matter how circumscribed, and they demanded that the state restore the disciplinary powers of the Code de l'indigénat and put an end to the conscription of Muslims in the military (this last was to prevent the creation of new electors). Algerian veterans and their political representatives, on the other hand, were frustrated by their continued inability to vote or run for office in parliament and by the lack of any provision that would make full citizenship compatible with Muslim "personal status."

In fact, the Jonnart Law's requirements for naturalizing Algerian colonial subjects were even more restrictive than the 1865 law. Candidates for naturalization had to be at least twenty-five years of age, unmarried or monogamous, with no previous criminal convictions, and had to satisfy at least one of the following criteria: military service, literacy in French, ownership of property, possessor of an elected office, service in the civil administration, recipient of a French decoration, or born to a father who possessed citizenship. Even if a candidate satisfied these requirements, the new law left the final decision to the administration, which could deny citizenship to anybody if the candidate was judged to have not fully embraced French customs and ways of life.[17] This principle of administrative discretion was built into the application of the new electoral procedures as well. Although the governor-general's office expressed its desire to "reproduce common [i.e., French] law in municipal matters," it reserved the right to make "the inevitable exceptions required by the social state of our subjects."[18] These exceptions included a suspension of the principle of a secret vote and no guarantee that all voting would take place on the same day. Such measures made it clear that the administration would use all means at its disposal to prevent the new electors from meddling with the balance of forces that preserved settler dominance of local politics.

Observing the situation in Algeria at the end of the war, the administration found much to confirm its fears. Security had been tight since a largely leaderless insurrection in the Aurès Mountains south of Constantine in November 1916 had led to the murder of an administrator and a sub-prefect in Batna.[19] The revolt began as a protest against conscription, and an investigation concluded that "we demanded an effort of national defense that was too intense and too precipitous from a region that was too primitive, having hardly any contact with colonization."[20] The logic of this kind of social explanation was not merely a criticism of the wartime recruitment policy—it was also a justification for not granting more rights to Algerians in the postwar era. In the eyes of the colonial administration, the natives of Algeria remained unfit for citizenship.

By the end of the war, then, the authorities saw military recruitment through a different lens. Rather than celebrating the sacrifices that Algerians made for France, they feared that the return of demobilized veterans and conscripted laborers who had become familiar with the culture of Europe would destabilize Algerian society. In many ways, these fears were justified. Muslim veterans resented the expectation that they would simply take up their former occupations after four years of military service, and they found many opportunities to express their frustration, sometimes accusing those who stayed behind—especially those who occupied positions of authority—of having profited from the war. Others hoped to obtain posts within the colonial bureaucracy or to be granted concessions of land. Such aspirations were almost inevitably disappointed, and it was in this context that Algerian veterans began to realize the limits to what the Jonnart Law offered them, as well as the narrow but still significant opportunities it afforded them to make their voices and aspirations heard.[21]

These frustrations and fears provided the context for the first electoral campaigns that followed the Jonnart Law. Algerian candidates and the new electors debated among themselves the proper position to take, given the opportunities they now possessed to capture the new constituency that had been brought into Algerian political life.[22] A faction under the leadership of the ophthalmologist and naturalized citizen Dr. Belkacem Benthami initially took a cautious approach, accepting the strict limits to the reforms and avoiding any form of direct confrontation with the colonial authorities. Benthami soon faced an outspoken opponent, however: Emir Khaled, a former French military officer who announced much more ambitious goals, including full citizenship and parliamentary representation for Algeria's Muslims.

Emir Khaled (1875–1936), born Khalid bin Hashimi bin Hajj 'Abd al-Qadir, was the grandson of the famous nineteenth-century Algerian military leader 'Abd al-Qadir. He was born in Syria and attended a French school in Algiers before going on to attend the Lycée Louis-le-Grand in Paris and the French military academy in Saint-Cyr. Upon completion of his military studies, Khaled refused to apply for naturalization—because many would have seen him as repudiating Islam—but he nevertheless served in the French army in Morocco and Algeria between 1897 and 1908, becoming a captain in 1905. During these years, he came into contact with the Young Algerian movement, and became a vocal supporter for greater participation of Algerians in French political life. His political activities led him to leave the army, but he reenlisted in 1914 and served in the war for two years before a bout of tuberculosis brought him back to Algeria.

In the political opening that followed the war, Khaled wrote a letter in 1919 to the U.S. president Woodrow Wilson asking that Algeria be allowed to become a founding member of the League of Nations in the coming year. At the same time, he campaigned as a representative of Algeria's Muslims under the provisions of the Jonnart Law and was elected to the municipal council in Algiers in 1919, and in 1920 to the délégations financières and to the departmental assembly for Algiers.[23] Khaled's first goal was parliamentary representation for Muslim Algerians, but he also called for the suppression of the Code de l'indigénat, a transfer of authority over local budgets to the *jamma'at* or village councils, an equitable participation of Algerian Muslims in the distribution of lands for settlement, a system of competitive exams or elections for the appointment of *qada* (village chiefs under the colonial system), and infrastructural development in communities that had been neglected by the colonial administration.[24]

In Algeria's cities, Khaled's program immediately captured public attention. Two prewar newspapers associated with the Young Algerian movement, *L'Islam* and *Rachidi*, published by Saddek Denden and Hamou Hadj Amar respectively, merged their operations, appearing after March 7, 1919, as *L'Ikdam*.[25] With articles in both French and Arabic, *L'Ikdam* became the house paper for Khaled's political movement. Although it had a limited print run, individual issues of *L'Ikdam* were passed from hand to hand, reaching a considerable number of people. The governor-general's Bureau of Native Affairs took note of its embrace of Khaled's program and monitored it closely, labeling *L'Ikdam* "the instrument for the defense of Muslim political and economic interests in North Africa" and condemning its "combative spirit."[26] This tendency on the part of the administration to see any form of political discussion among Muslims as a symptom of disloyal opposition remained virtually constant throughout the interwar decades, drastically limiting the ability of even the most moderate of Muslim political leaders to find interlocutors within the administration. By 1923, frustrated with his inability to gain support among France's political elites for his reforms, Khaled withdrew from politics and left Algeria, shutting down *L'Ikdam* as he did so.

Historians disagree about the significance of Khaled's movement. John Ruedy sees him largely as an assimilationist, a champion of the greater integration of Algerians into the French polity.[27] Mahfoud Kaddache and Nadya Bouzar Kasbadji emphasize his oppositional stance, his famous letter to President Wilson, and see him as an important precursor of the Algerian nationalist movement that would eventually lead to independence in 1962.[28] Lizabeth Zack, meanwhile, has suggested that Khaled's emphasis on a Muslim identity as the common heritage of Algerians made him an important precursor to Algeria's movements of political Islam in the latter decades of the twentieth century.[29] Perhaps the important takeaway is that in the early 1920s there was no necessary contradiction between any of these positions, in spite of appearances. Khaled could embody any and all of these aspirations in a political field that had not yet crystallized as a set of clear choices or alternatives. Within the hybrid form of restricted political participation set up by the Jonnart Law, Khaled could be at one moment a champion of an inclusive vision of the French Republic, a devout Muslim believer, and even a kind of Algerian nationalist without necessary contradiction. Muslims who entered political life in the aftermath of his movement had no choice but to work within the institutions of the Jonnart Law, but they took from his example a sense of the broad range of positions that might possibly be used to mobilize Algeria's colonial subjects politically in the postwar decades.

What were the effects of the Jonnart Law on relations between Muslims and Jews in Algeria? There were some reports of tensions in the western Algerian city of Tlemcen, where several Jews were brought up on charges of violence against Muslims, but there were also reports of educated Muslims and Jews forming an electoral alliance in order to support a challenge to an incumbent majority in Oran.[30] In Constantine, the municipal council became the target of renewed antisemitic agitation, even as Muslim council members were seated for the first time by virtue of the Jonnart Law. Mayor Émile Morinaud, who in 1919 regained the seat in parliament that he had lost in 1902, had come out strongly against the Jonnart Law, seeking to present himself as the true ally of Algeria's Muslims. Such paternalism fooled nobody, however. All sides understood that Morinaud and his political allies would not support any expansion of the electorate that would threaten their hold over local politics. Lacking any other weapon with which to challenge Morinaud, the mayor's local political opponents resorted to antisemitism. Pointing to his long-standing alliance with Jewish council members, they tried to portray him as an agent of Jewish manipulation. Morinaud's Jewish allies reacted indignantly to these attacks, and Morinaud did not back away from them, in spite of the fact that many of his ostensible supporters among the settler population were increasingly open about their strong antisemitic views.

Unfortunately for the region's social peace, this attention to the place of Jewish officials within municipal government coincided with the passage of the law of July 29, 1920, which reestablished many of the disciplinary powers associated with the harshly punitive Code de l'indigénat. The 1920 law attempted to appease the anger felt by Algeria's settler elite over the Jonnart Law by perpetuating the prewar penal code that gave local authorities the right to punish any colonial subject found guilty of violating the code's list of crimes, which included mundane acts of disrespect toward French authority, public statements critical of the government, and violations of the laws regarding permission to travel.[31] The months before and after the passage of the 1920 law thus witnessed a potentially toxic mix of increasing visibility of both Muslim and Jewish elected officials, growing defensiveness on the part of a fearful settler establishment, and a reassertion of the colonial government's right to apply the harshest forms of legal coercion against a Muslim population with few rights. Predictably, several localized incidents of tension between Muslims and settlers or between Muslims and Jews were recorded in more than one town in the department of Constantine during the summer of 1920.[32]

In 1921, however, a concerted campaign by French antisemites to provoke the Muslim residents of Constantine into violence against the city's Jews failed to have any effect. Beginning in February, a local antisemitic newspaper called *La Tribune* began publishing regular attacks on local Jewish leaders and Jewish organizations. Once again, the galvanizing issue in the campaign had to do with the question of urban space and patterns of sociability between populations conceived as properly endogamous and distinct from one another. *La Tribune*'s campaign began after a group of young Jewish men seated at a café with an actress became involved in a dispute with other customers. Recounting the incident, the paper complained that Jews no longer knew their place, and it developed this theme persistently in a subsequent series of articles. The prefect published a rebuttal when *La Tribune* criticized the work of a local society for Jewish war orphans, but when challenged by local Jewish leaders to prohibit such attacks, he defended the paper's right to publish its invective. The matter became more serious during the summer of 1921, after a local Jewish gymnastics club participated in a ceremony at the Tomb of the Unknown Soldier at the Arc de Triomphe in Paris, alongside the department's parliamentary delegation. *La Tribune* responded with attacks on the club and its director, and the prefect told Jewish elected officials that he had received a letter from the editors containing an overt threat: the Jews of Constantine should look out for their lives because *"les indigènes"* were ready to intervene in the dispute.[33]

A group of men from the European population sacked the hall used by the Jewish gymnastics club and destroyed their equipment on June 11. The next day, adolescent supporters of the club and Jewish military veterans responded by attacking *La Tribune*'s printer, breaking the windows and throwing bins of movable type onto the street.[34] Police reports claimed that four hundred people were present that morning in protests at both the home of *La Tribune*'s coeditor, Amalfitano, and at the printer.[35] The next day, angry Jewish men cornered Amalfitano's partner Ernest Lanxade in a hotel after recognizing him in a café. To prevent any attacks of vengeance from antisemitic groups, the police and soldiers blocked the entrances to the Jewish quarter. A crowd of some four thousand onlookers gathered in the streets, some of them shouting anti-Jewish slogans.

After these events, Jewish leaders in Constantine concluded that the prefecture and the police had turned against the city's Jews. They complained of arbitrary arrests of young Jewish people who sought to move through the city, and when they met with the prefect, he told them that "taking the side of the Jews" in this dispute would "allow the Arabs to believe that the French were nothing and would destroy French power in Algeria."[36] Bitterly disappointed by the prefect's attitude, the Jewish elected officials offered their collective resignation. Over the next week, fights and disputes in the streets and on the terraces of the city's cafés became a daily occurrence, but only Jews were arrested after these disturbances. At one point, shots were fired, and one ricochet struck the chief of departmental security in the thigh.[37] For the next two days the police and military barricaded the center of the city, preventing any movement by Constantine's residents.

In the end, the tensions dissipated because Mayor Morinaud refused to go along with the prefect and the police in blaming the Jews for the situation. He published an interview in the Parisian daily Le Matin that reasserted his support for the Jewish elected officials who had offered to resign.[38] Morinaud emphasized that the responsibility for the violence lay with the antisemitic editors of La Tribune, and that it was only natural that the Jewish population of Constantine, which included many war veterans, would respond as they had to such provocations.[39] Following his intervention, the violence subsided, though La Tribune continued to publish.

What can one conclude from this brief look at incidents of antisemitism in 1920–1921? Most obvious was the overarching importance of the war as a force that shaped the ways in which individuals and groups within the polity viewed their relation to the larger community. The controversy over the Jewish effort to raise money for war orphans reveals the extent to which the war offered new opportunities for different groups to make their own highly localized and contested claims for civic belonging. Given that one of the precipitating incidents involved the presence of a Jewish gymnastics club at a public ceremony at the Tomb of the Unknown Soldier in Paris, and that military veterans were repeatedly mentioned as participating in the gatherings of Jews on public streets in Constantine during this week of troubles, the links that existed between military service, public and collective gestures of national belonging, and masculine forms of public identity were demonstrably clear. Participation in sports had been heavily emphasized as a necessary part of postwar national regeneration, particularly during the run-up to the Paris Olympics of 1924, and the participation of Jewish young men in the gymnastics club was seen both by Jewish families and their antisemitic opponents as having a larger political context. The references to sport, and the repeated mention of combat veterans, lent weight to the claims made by the Jewish elected officials about their place within the community. These references to more broadly shared forms of nationalist sentiment also made it less likely that outside observers—and even the city's residents themselves—would interpret the events through the lens of local political contests.

Second, the lines of fracture were essentially between two groups within the Algerian electorate who already possessed full citizenship rights: that is, between Jews and antisemites among the European population. Except for the threat made by Amalfitano and Lanxade that was conveyed to the Jewish elected officials by the prefect, there was no mention of Constantine's majority population of Muslim colonial subjects in this dispute, beyond vague references in several police reports that the *indigènes* were "troubled" by the events. That certain members of the administration feared some sort of response from Constantine's Muslim population, however, was never in doubt.

Third, one sees again the importance of contested visions of gender, ethno-religious identity, and public space in these encounters. Presumptions about socializing in groups that included both men and women were clearly an issue, and these concerns were overlaid onto assumptions about the ways that the colonial city was geographically segregated according to religion and civil status. In the 1890s, Émile Morinaud voiced his dismay at the way Jewish voters streamed out of "their" neighborhood in the central city to place their bulletins in the urn during the municipal elections. In the 1920s, anti-Jewish animus among the European population focused on the presence of Jews on the terraces of Constantine's cafés in the European quarter.[40] These spaces were above all associated with the European population and its forms of sociability—the freedom and leisure of middle-class consumers, and the casual mixing of men and women in public. Circulating freely within such spaces was a marker of one's acceptance of the changes that the city had undergone, and of one's affiliation in a shifting social landscape. These spaces were not only racially coded; they were marked by conceptions of historical and social progress that the French presence had allegedly brought to Algeria. From the point of view of the city's anti-Jewish militants, these spatial and temporal boundaries were violated by the presence of people who were tainted with the status of *indigène*, whether Muslim or Jewish. The police reinforced the power of these urban boundaries with their response to moments of disorder. For the authorities, the very presence of ethnically mixed populations in public spaces during moments of tension was to be avoided, and their goal at all times was to enforce a territorial notion of the town's geography whereby each population mapped easily onto a specific district that could be contained and made orderly by virtue of its homogeneity. This tactic, already clearly established in the summer of 1921, would be followed repeatedly by Constantine's police in the years to come. Their failure to do this on August 5, 1934, was seen at the time as a contributing cause of the riot.

Jewish civic leaders in Constantine reacted to the very present threat of settler antisemitism in the 1920s by embracing a more visible role in the city's patriotic organizations and in associations associated with public welfare. Jewish leaders in Constantine had long been concerned with the poor quality of housing in the traditional Jewish residential quarter. They were also concerned about the inadequacy of primary instruction in both religious and academic subjects for Jewish children. Taking advantage of the opportunities offered by parliament's passage of the Ribot and Loucheur laws in 1922 and 1928—laws designed to increase the availability of low-cost housing throughout France—Jewish elected officials in Constantine sought to encourage the movement of poorer Jewish families from the traditional Jewish quarter into newly constructed state-subsidized buildings (*habitations bon marché*, or HBM) on the city's modern periphery.

The Public Office of HBM in Constantine was directed by two prominent leaders within the Jewish community: Henri Lellouche, a member of the departmental assembly, and Maurice Laloum, a municipal councilor and judge in the Tribunal de commerce. Many Jewish families were initially reluctant to leave the older neighborhood in the center of town for the HBM, but by December 1930 the demands for places in the newly constructed apartments far outstripped the supply, with more than four hundred applications for sixty-three apartments.[41] As these families moved into their new homes, the Cité Lellouche in Sidi-Mabrouk, the Cité Laloum in Bellevue, and the Cité Gaillard near the civil hospital on the right bank of the gorge became focal points for newer Jewish neighborhoods outside the old city's walls. That this movement did not develop earlier is a powerful reminder of how long it took Jews to take advantage of the changes in civil status brought about by the Crémieux decree. The fact that it occurred at all, however, points to the growing self-confidence and material resources of the Jewish community leadership in Constantine during the years after the First World War. During these same years, Rabbi Maurice Eisenbeth (who served as the grand rabbi in Constantine before moving to the same position in Algiers) and Émile Barkatz, who had succeeded Elie Narboni as the president of the Jewish Consistory in Constantine, founded a new departmental federation of Jewish religious associations. One of the federation's initial projects was to support the work of a newly founded Hebrew school in Constantine, the École Etz Haïm, which aimed to encourage both religious teaching and to promote an awareness of Jewish history in the region.[42]

In the eyes of the Jewish leadership in Constantine there was no contradiction between the explicitly Jewish mission of the École Etz Haïm and the assimilationist housing program that aimed to increase their presence in other areas beyond the city's center. The Jewish leadership embraced a modernist vision of Jewish identity that strongly identified with the protections offered to Jews by the republican state and saw no inconsistency in their self-awareness as a Jewish minority and their place as citizens in the French nation.[43] Nevertheless, this renewed civic activity on the part of Constantine's Jews took place against the background of an increasingly intense expression of antisemitism elsewhere in France and Europe, and this widely held French antipathy toward Jews had an echo among Constantine's settler population.

Historians are divided as to the main causes of renewed French antisemitism during the interwar years. Jacob Katz and Pierre Birnbaum have argued that the virulence of French antisemitism prior to the Second World War was a long-simmering reaction to the success of Jewish assimilation in France over many decades, and as much a backlash against the Republic that offered Jews civic equality as it was a movement against French Jews themselves.[44] Birnbaum, in particular, has highlighted a continuity that stretches from the late nineteenth-century crisis of the Dreyfus affair to the anti-Jewish policies of the Vichy regime, a strain of "political antisemitism" that focused above all on the illegitimacy of "state Jews" who had taken advantage of emancipation to launch political or administrative careers within the elected assemblies and bureaucratic offices of the Third Republic.[45] Vicki Caron and Ralph Schor, on the other hand, have emphasized short-term factors such as the Depression and the influx of Jewish refugees from Central and Eastern Europe after 1933 as the central motivators of a virulent antisemitism from elements within the middle class who connected Jews to a threatening vision of a capitalist society committed to free markets.[46] Gérard Noiriel, meanwhile, has suggested an interpretation that combines elements of both arguments, suggesting that antisemitism in France—always latent—became most virulent at moments when it was conflated with xenophobia.[47] A few historians, including Eugen Weber and Stephen Schuker, have emphasized the extent to which antisemitism in France may have been a reaction to the involvement of Jews in left-wing politics during these years.[48]

Deciding which of these overlapping interpretations is correct is not likely to be solved by going back to the sources, as examples can be found for all these arguments over both the short and long term. Describing anti-Jewish sentiment as latent in France is simply another way of saying that questions of difference have always been the vehicle by which notions of citizenship and belonging have been hammered out in the public realm, and one would expect the hammering to become more urgent at moments of crisis. Whether the issue is the status of colonial subjects, the place of religious minorities, or the play of gendered relations in the spaces of diversely populated cities, moments of abrupt transition or rupture—such as mobilization in 1914, demobilization in 1918, or the political and economic crises of the 1930s—became moments for questioning the relative power of difference to determine the boundaries of national belonging in France and French Algeria. For our purposes, therefore, the point is not really to choose between the interpretations of historians of antisemitism in France—which are probably compatible with one another in any case—but to look at the ways that this dynamic worked itself out at the local level in Constantine. The next two chapters will lay out this story in two parts. The first task—covered in chapter 5—is to explore the ways that the institutions and habits of local governance in Constantine were challenged by the appearance of new political movements in the interwar years. The second—the subject of chapter 6—is to explore how the people of Constantine experienced these challenges at street level in the years leading up to the riots of 1934.

CHAPTER 5

French Algeria's Dual Fracture

The years between 1928 and 1936 produced a
seismic shift in local politics in Algeria. In France as a whole, political life
was disrupted by a growing polarization between left and right as the French
Communist Party squared off against right-wing leagues that sought to imi-
tate Mussolini's Fascists and Hitler's National Socialists. In Algeria, the political establishment was further challenged by the emergence of a newly
energized movement of Algerian Muslim elected officials under the terms
of the Jonnart Law. These Algerian political figures were cautious in comparison with the Algerian nationalists who appeared on the scene later, but
they nevertheless tried to take advantage of this opportunity to represent
Algeria's Muslims. Their presence complicated the calculus of all political
groups in French Algeria, for even if the leverage of Muslim elected officials
remained limited, their novelty made them an unpredictable force, potentially disruptive, but also a tempting ally under the right circumstances. The
anti-Jewish riots of August 3–5, 1934, in Constantine occurred in the midst
of this realignment and shaped its eventual outcome.

It is tempting to see the shift in local politics that preceded the riots of 1934
as being driven by a hardening of ethnic, religious, and racial boundaries—
that is, by a deepening divide that was conceived in both religious and ethno-
racial terms. As we will see, this is the explanation that was given at the time
by the authorities after the riots occurred. There are good reasons, however,

to suppose that the opposite was the case. The riots resulted at least in part from political experiments with alliances that crossed the ethnic and religious divisions of colonial society, even as they rejected others. The political establishment in Constantine, long dominated by a mayor who had begun his career as a strident antisemite, maintained its hold on city hall by cultivating a relationship with Jewish leaders. When republican politicians in Paris proposed new legislation that would extend to Algerian Muslims more of the benefits of citizenship, the delicate balance within local politics was called into question. Some supporters of the settler establishment in Algeria gravitated toward right-wing political movements that defended the colonial order, attacked the Republic, and increasingly blamed Jews for what they saw as a weak foreign policy and a fragile economy. The most prominent of these right-wing leagues in Constantine was the Croix de feu, a veterans' organization that admitted Jewish veterans in its early years but which increasingly became an incubator for anti-Jewish militancy. When this complicated situation led to violence, as it did in Constantine on August 3–5, 1934, the boundaries that separated different groups from each other certainly hardened, but this is better understood as the *result* of the dynamic that characterized political life during these years rather than its *cause*.

Understanding this dynamic is made doubly difficult by the fact that Constantine and Algeria as a whole stood at the intersection of two axes of political turmoil during the interwar years: unrest in North Africa and the Middle East after the First World War that would lead to the development of strong nationalist movements in the coming decades, and the parallel European catastrophes of the Bolshevik Revolution and extremist political movements led by Benito Mussolini and Adolf Hitler in Italy and Germany. Both these axes of political conflict threatened the French Republic. In the long term, it was the former cleavage—between defenders of the French imperial regime and supporters of Algerian, Moroccan, and Tunisian independence— that would do the most to shape the future of North Africa in the coming decades. In the short term, however, it was the confrontation between the French Third Republic and extremisms of the right and the left that did the most to shape the particular history of the Constantine riots in the summer of 1934.

The appearance of Fascist and National Socialist movements in Italy and Germany created an atmosphere of crisis and domestic political polarization in France, and this atmosphere was intensified in the crucible of Algerian politics. Historian Kevin Passmore memorably described this polarization as the result of a "dual fracture"—simultaneous lines of conflict on both the left and the right.[1] On the one hand, the Russian Revolution and the growth of the French Communist Party after 1920 drove a wedge between an activist left supported by trade unions and more moderate republicans who were struggling to reset the economy and international relations after the First World War. At the same time, a second split opened up between centrists seeking political stability and various authoritarian nationalists, xenophobes, and fascist sympathizers on the far right who sought to undermine the institutions of the French Republic.[2] This "dual fracture" lay behind the whipsaw-like movements of political realignment in France in the 1930s, which saw the nation stagger from an apparent threat of a right-wing coup in February 1934 to a leftist parliamentary majority in 1936, only to end the decade with the formation of a right-wing collaborationist and antisemitic government under the Nazi occupation after 1940.

Right-wing leagues rioted in Paris on February 6, 1934, because they believed that members of the parliamentary majority were covering up a financial scandal engineered by a Jewish fraudster that implicated high-ranking members of the government.[3] The spark for their anger was the firing of the prefect of police in Paris, Jean Chiappe, who was widely admired on the right for his energetic anticommunism and his apparent sympathy for right-wing causes. Thousands of extremists—including street brawlers, university students, and militants from political leagues such as the Action française, the Jeunesses patriotes, and the Croix de feu—fought with police on the place de la Concorde and in several other neighborhoods of the capital. During several hours of pitched battles, sixteen people died. The riots of February 1934 created a political crisis for the Third Republic and resulted in Prime Minister Édouard Daladier's resignation the next day. This show of force nevertheless failed to provoke the coup that many rightists were looking for and instead generated a strong reaction—a Popular Front coalition of the left and center that brought Léon Blum to power in April 1936, the first time a Jew and a socialist had been elected to the office of prime minister. Blum's Popular Front government banned the right-wing leagues and embarked on ambitious economic reforms, but ultimately failed to overcome the twin crises provoked by Hitler's international aggression and the economic catastrophe of the Depression.

In French Algeria, the triangulation of political relationships produced by the colonial situation led to a different but no less intense trajectory during these tumultuous years. The local political establishment run by Algerian settler elites had long had a disproportionate voice in national politics because of their overrepresentation in parliament. They nevertheless moved toward a more conflicted relationship with the government in Paris in the 1930s as they struggled to contain the challenges posed by the participation of Muslim elected officials in local politics. The right-wing political organizations that were so disruptive in metropolitan France were even stronger in Algeria, and the left was correspondingly weaker. In the pivotal election of May 1936, when the Popular Front came to power in metropolitan France, the department of Constantine moved in the opposite direction—opponents of the Popular Front took two of the department's three parliamentary seats in 1936, and the extremist right-wing leagues saw their membership peak in Algeria during this same period.[4] This realignment was the result of a breakdown in the local coalitions that had governed politics in Constantine since the turn of the century.

In the early 1930s, these coalitions were still intact. Paul and Jules Cuttoli (senator and deputy in parliament, respectively), the industrialist Marcel Lavie, the newspaper publisher Louis Morel, and Mayor Émile Morinaud held on to their elected seats on the departmental Conseil général, where they rubbed shoulders with leading members of Constantine's professional community, including two future mayors, Pierre Liagre (a medical doctor who was mayor from 1935 to 1938) and Joseph Durieu de Leyritz (a lawyer and mayor from 1938 to 1939). Morinaud's son, Jean, a lawyer and newspaper owner in the nearby town of Djidjelli (Jijel), also served on the Conseil général, along with the brothers Jules and Eugène Valle (both lawyers—Jules would later become a senator in the Fourth Republic). The head of the Constantine bar, Étienne Muracciole, also sat on the departmental assembly, where he defended the colonial order and repudiated critics of the local establishment with a dismissive condescension that could only come from a sense of comfortable impregnability. Muracciole's colleague, Albert Rédarès, a lawyer and publisher of another local paper, *La Brèche*, also sat on the municipal and departmental councils, where he led an independent group that had thrown its lot in with Morinaud in the late 1920s, in the name of a conciliation between rival groups.[5] Both Muracciole and Rédarès later played leading roles in the most significant of the murder trials that resulted from the riots of 1934.[6]

The Jewish political presence in Constantine in the early 1930s was led by Henri Lellouche, the only Jewish elected official to have a seat on the Conseil général of the department. Lellouche, a veteran of the First World War with conservative political instincts, was president of the Jewish Consistory in Constantine at the time of the riots. He also presided over the Cultuelle israélite, a religious association that oversaw local Jewish charitable and educational activities.[7] If Jews were not well represented at the departmental level, they made up for it by their presence on Constantine's municipal council, where Lellouche also had a seat alongside Émile Barkatz (who also served as deputy mayor), Maurice Laloum (a judge at the Tribunal de commerce), Adolphe Sultan (a lawyer), Benjamin Zaoui (a businessman), and Simon Tobiana (also a lawyer).[8] The presence of these men meant that six out of thirty-four seats on the municipal council were held by Jewish representatives, although the Jewish population was less than 12 percent of the city's residents. In all, twenty-three municipal councilors "with French status" (*au titre français*) represented the 49 percent of Constantine's population who had full citizenship, including both Jews and those listed in the census as "European." They served alongside eleven Algerian Muslim municipal councilors "with native status" (*au titre indigène*) who represented the remaining 51 percent of the population, including the relatively few colonial subjects who were allowed to vote under the Jonnart Law, as well as the much larger nonvoting population.

The presence of Muslim elected officials alongside the leading personalities of settler society and representatives of Constantine's Jewish community complicated the way that the "dual fracture" of the interwar years played out within the colonial situation. The terms of the Jonnart Law ensured that the electoral system was rigged against Muslim officials, limiting the number of seats that they could hold in any assembly, and making it impossible for them to assemble a majority position on any matter of importance. At the same time, however, their very presence, and the nature of their evolving demands, destabilized an already uncertain political landscape.

Muslim elected officials realized that their only hope was to organize themselves into political associations whose greater public profile might give them a larger collective voice. The first attempt to provide a unified body resulted in a Federation of Muslim Elected Officials (Fédération des élus musulmans) in 1927. Members of the prewar generation of Young Algerians were active in this group, including Belkacem Benthami, an ophthalmologist from Algiers, and Moussa Benchenouf, a medical doctor from Constantine. These early leaders of the federation were from the educated elite of Gallicized francophones. They defended the religious commitments of Muslims without explicitly challenging the colonial order with claims of an Algerian identity that was independent of French domination.[9] As historian Salah el Din el Zein el Tayeb put it, "Nationalist terms such as *wataniyya* (patriotism) and *qawmiyya* (nationalism) were not part of the vocabulary of the Young Algerians."[10]

Efforts to maintain the unity of this first federation faltered, however. The Bureau of Native Affairs in Algiers attributed these difficulties to divisions between Arabs and Berbers in different regions of Algeria and to a split between French-educated elites and others with a more traditional outlook.[11]

Such divisions played a role, but an additional reason for the failure was simply that, under the terms of the Jonnart Law, most Muslim elected officials were locally based, and their concerns were better served by regional bodies whose networks facilitated relations both with their voting constituents and with the local mayors and administrators in the *communes de plein exercice* and the *communes mixtes*. Subsequent efforts to organize Muslim elected officials on a regional basis were more successful, and ultimately separate federations emerged in each of the three Algerian departments of Oran, Algiers, and Constantine.

Of the three departmental federations, the Fédération des élus musulmans de Constantine (FEMC) was by far the most active. Its outspoken leader, Mohamed Salah Bendjelloul, was the most prominent politically active Muslim official in Algeria in the 1930s.[12] Although historians sometimes include Bendjelloul as part of the Young Algerian movement, he was more ambitious than the preceding generation of assimilationist politicians. He was also more willing to challenge the status quo, and at times even eager to confront the representatives of the colonial establishment with the potential power of his constituency of Muslim colonial subjects. Whereas the Young Algerians of the 1920s often emphasized their acceptance of the French language and focused on gathering support from the educated Muslim elite, Bendjelloul gave speeches in Algerian dialectal Arabic as well as in French and developed a more populist program. He called for a more just system of taxation and advocated an extension of full political citizenship to Algerian Muslims without relinquishing their personal religious status. This call for full political rights for all Muslim Algerians meant that Bendjelloul spoke not only to the relatively small number of Muslim voters under the Jonnart Law, but also to the majority population of Muslim colonial subjects.

The Third Republic had always rejected full citizenship for Algerian Muslims on the grounds that the Civil Code applied to all citizens without distinction. Since Islam's civil prescriptions in matters of marriage, inheritance, and family law differed from the French Civil Code, Algerians could not simultaneously be good Muslims and French citizens. Bendjelloul and his colleagues at the Fédération were well aware, however, that the French principle of legal universality was a conceit that had been violated before. Alsace and Lorraine, which had been a part of Germany between 1871 and 1919, had been allowed to retain the state organization of Catholic, Protestant, and Jewish religious life that they had enjoyed under German rule when the two departments were reabsorbed into France after the First World War. In the rest of France, the 1905 law on the separation of church and state had outlawed such arrangements, but this law was not seen as an obstacle to reintegrating the two formerly German provinces. This exception had been debated in the francophone Algerian press in the 1920s, and Algerian assimilationists were indignant that religion was still used to exclude Muslims from full citizenship in French Algeria, while the formerly German provinces were allowed to persist with their own idiosyncratic religious institutions.[13] In their mind, the continued exclusion of Muslims from full citizenship on religious grounds masked the essentially exclusionary and undemocratic character of French policy in Algeria. Even more frustrating for members of Bendjelloul's Fédération was the fact that informal supervision of Algeria's Islamic institutions was a routine part of the colonial prefectures' administrative responsibilities, even though such supervision contravened the spirit of the 1905 law on the separation of church and state.[14]

The FEMC's program has led historians to treat Mohamed Bendjelloul and his colleagues as transitional figures in the history of Algerian politics, falling somewhere between the reformist modernizers of the Young Algerian movement and the more militant nationalists who emerged in the late 1930s and after the Second World War.[15] Within Algeria, Bendjelloul is sometimes remembered as the leader of a generation of elite and prosperous Muslim politicians whose concern with their own status within the colonial order prevented them from effectively confronting the inequities of French Algeria.[16] Historian Julien Fromage countered this essentially negative portrait, suggesting that Bendjelloul's Fédération succeeded in embodying a kind of "anti-colonial reformism on a legal basis"—an oppositional movement of Algerians that attempted to use the institutional structures of the Jonnart Law and the Third Republic to transform the nature of France's relationship to Algeria.[17] This formulation is a useful one, precisely because it embodies the contradictions of the Third Republic's paradoxical arrangements on civil status in Algeria. It was not always apparent—either to the members of Bendjelloul's Fédération or to their opponents—how they could carry through their proposal to expand the voting rights of Muslims while at the same time remaining within a legal framework that structured its exclusions around religious difference. Most of the time, Bendjelloul went out of his way to demonstrate that his movement was nothing more than a loyal opposition. Local authorities in Algeria remained deeply skeptical of his motives and looked upon him and his colleagues at the Fédération as potentially disloyal subjects of the French imperial state. The public statements of FEMC members were closely watched by the administration in Algeria. In the eyes of the prefecture in Constantine, Bendjelloul's political platform was indistinguishable from nationalism because it depended on a potential constituency of Algerian Muslims. This misapprehension probably hastened the development of a more radical and truly nationalist movement in Algeria after the late 1930s by making it harder for Bendjelloul to find support for his reformist program.

Bendjelloul's career embodied the contradictions that he faced between the apparent promise offered by the possibility of French citizenship and his desire to recognize and preserve the distinctiveness of Algerian society and culture. He was born in 1893 to a Constantine family of magistrates and administrators that was no longer as wealthy as it had been, but which had been prominent in the city since the last decades of the Ottoman period. Educated both in Arabic and at Constantine's French lycée, he received a degree from the medical school in Algiers and went to work as a doctor in the colonial service in 1924. First elected to the municipal council of Herbillon (now Chetaibi), a fishing village west of Bône where he began his medical practice, Bendjelloul was elected to the Conseil général of the Department of Constantine in 1931.[18] In 1932, he became the president of the FEMC, while continuing to practice medicine from an office at his family residence on the rue Chabron in Constantine, appropriately located between the French lycée and the madrasa—that is, between the most important French and Islamic schools in the city. In 1935 he was elected to the *délégations financières*, and in June 1936 he presided over the Muslim Congress that supported the Popular Front government's effort to extend parliamentary representation to Algeria's Muslim population for the first time. These efforts failed, but after the Second World War, Bendjelloul continued to promote reform, serving as a senator from 1946 to 1948 and as a deputy in parliament from 1951 to 1955 under the Fourth Republic.

Bendjelloul was related by marriage to the Ben Badis family, one of Constantine's most prominent households.[19] The Ben Badis family traced their lineage to a Berber dynasty of the tenth century, and they maintained their elite status through the colonial period by virtue of the respect they enjoyed from the city's residents and by using the opportunities offered by the new French regime. Muhammad Mustafa Ben Badis held a seat on the Conseil général of the department, and was elected to the *délégations financières* in 1923, enjoying a reputation in the French administration as a loyal servant. His younger son, Mouloud Ben Badis, was a French-educated lawyer who served on the city's municipal council. Muhammad Ben Badis's older son, 'Abd al-Hamid Ben Badis, received a classic Islamic education in Constantine and at the Zaytuna mosque in Tunis. By the 1930s, 'Abd al-Hamid Ben Badis had become the most esteemed Algerian Islamic scholar of his generation. Publishing and speaking in public only in Arabic, 'Abd al-Hamid Ben Badis founded the Association of Algerian Muslim Ulama in Constantine in 1931, a group of religious teachers that sought to demonstrate Islam's relevance in the modern world.[20] Teaching from a humble mosque in the center of old Constantine—the same mosque where the initial dispute before the riots of August 1934 occurred—'Abd al-Hamid Ben Badis was the only Muslim personality in Constantine whose fame and moral authority matched that of Mohamed Bendjelloul in the 1930s. The activities of the two men were in different realms—Ben Badis was a religious figure who sought to insulate himself from French political institutions, while Bendjelloul explicitly sought a role in electoral politics—but they were sometimes forced to reckon with one another in ways that were not always easy, by virtue of their larger-than-life reputations and their differing conceptions of the relationship between political activity and religious faith.[21]

Other members of the FEMC shared a general background similar to that of Bendjelloul, as members of well-connected Algerian families who had received both Muslim and French educations and were active participants in the associational life of their communities. Bendjelloul's predecessor as president of the FEMC, Chérif Sisbane, was a lawyer from Batna who was president of the "Arab" section of the *délégations financières*. Chérif Benhabylès was a *qadi* (judge) and a notary who was president of the *jamma'a* of Douar Dehemcha in the *commune mixte* of Takitount. Inducted into the Legion of Honor in 1927, Benhabylès became a senator in the Fourth Republic, like Mohamed Bendjelloul, as a member of the second electoral college reserved for Algerian colonial subjects. Mohammed Zerkine, also a member of Constantine's municipal council, was a surgeon-dentist who was active in the Club Sportif Constantinois. Omar Bentchicou, a prosperous tobacco manufacturer whose factory lay just across the gorge from the old city of Constantine, was a member of the chamber of commerce. Mohamed Lakhdar Dahel, Mahmoud Benyacoub, and Hassen Benkhallaf, who all served as vice presidents of the FEMC, were landowners based in Guelma, Bône, and Djidjelli, respectively. Finally, Mouloud Ben Badis held a seat on the municipal council, continuing his family's close association with the colonial administration for another generation, even as his brother worked to reclaim a specifically Islamic basis for Algerian culture. Bendjelloul himself succeeded Mouloud Ben Badis's father, Mohamed Mustapha Ben Badis, on the *délégations financières* in December 1934. The most famous of Bendjelloul's associates in later years was Ferhat Abbas, a pharmacist based in Sétif. During and after the Second World War, Abbas became an important figure in the Algerian nationalist movement as the founder of the Democratic Union of the Algerian Manifesto (UDMA) in 1946 and as the first president of the Provisional Government of the Algerian Republic in 1958, during the war for independence. This line of progression, from the Ben Badis family, through Bendjelloul and the members of the Fédération, to Ferhat Abbas's post–Second World War career, encapsulates a powerful narrative of Algerian history in the twentieth century, one that seems to capture a consistent movement of both religious and political awakening. One should be careful of assuming, however, that everybody understood or accepted the destination of this movement in the years before the Second World War.

Bendjelloul's program was completely compatible with the modernizing rhetoric of the Third Republic, which he never repudiated. While his political engagement was premised on public displays of loyalty, he also insisted on his ability to represent a new Muslim constituency within the Republic. He did not resort to nationalist rhetoric, and his most visible goal before 1934 was to become more of an insider: he led a public campaign to be named a representative of Algeria's Muslims on the Interministerial Commission on Muslim Affairs (CIAM), a government body with high visibility.[22] This commission, which oversaw the practice of Islam and the organization of mosques, as well as Islamic education and the Arabic press, had been created in 1911 but had never sought input from independent representatives of France's Muslim colonial subjects.

Bendjelloul presented himself as the French government's most important Algerian Muslim interlocutor while also propagating a more populist message in public meetings in the towns and villages of the Constantine region. These rallies disturbed local administrators, who feared any signs of collective action by Algeria's Muslim population. When Bendjelloul encountered resistance from local officials, he was willing to jump over the administrative hierarchy in Algeria and address the central government's ministries in Paris directly. In August 1932, he helped to organize a tax strike in Ain M'Lila, a small agricultural commune about forty kilometers south of Constantine. This campaign brought him wide popularity throughout the department, and he set off ripples of concern throughout the colonial bureaucracy when he sent a telegram directly to the prime minister, the minister of the interior, and to Senator Maurice Viollette about the abuses that accompanied the collection of taxes in Ain M'Lila.[23] Bendjelloul called for an end to these abuses and proposed a new plan where taxpayers in economic difficulty might schedule their payments over a longer period. In all its dimensions, Bendjelloul's leadership of the FEMC paralleled the efforts of Constantine's Jewish elected officials to represent their own community within the existing institutions of French Algeria. Whereas Constantine's Jewish leaders found some protection for their constituents through alliances with other political groups, Bendjelloul and his Fédération faced an uphill struggle for recognition and few offers of cooperation.

Bendjelloul's political effectiveness depended on his ability to represent the interests of Muslim colonial subjects while also finding productive political relationships with other groups in the polity of French Algeria. The problem was that these tasks often worked at cross-purposes. French officials saw Bendjelloul's cultivation of a broader constituency among the population of colonial subjects as disruptive and demagogic. If he became too close to French politicians, on the other hand, he risked being seen as too conciliatory by his supporters. The image of the fawning and corrupt "Béni-oui-oui"— Muslim "yes-men" in office who sold out other Algerians by currying favor with their superiors—was a common motif in Algerian popular culture and the object of much derision during these years.[24] In many ways, then, Bendjelloul's position was an impossible one. His assimilationist project could work only if the FEMC could prove to representatives of the colonial state that being Muslim was compatible with being fully French. Through no fault of his own, he was forced to defend this challenging position at a moment when extreme political polarization and a lack of consensus about national priorities made "Frenchness" itself a moving target that was difficult to hit.

In such a situation, there was no obvious choice for Muslim politicians like Mohamed Bendjelloul in their search for the alliances they needed to serve their constituency. Could the Fédération find allies on the left? This was certainly something the administration feared. Police spies counted fifty Muslim colonial subjects among the seven hundred people attending a meeting in Constantine sponsored by the local section of the Socialist Party on December 8, 1930.[25] Cause enough for concern, perhaps, but this paled in comparison with the demonstrations in February 1934 in Algiers, when Muslims made up as much as 40–50 percent of the crowds who marched through Algiers singing the "Internationale" and shouting "Long Live the Soviets!"[26] Bendjelloul and his colleagues at the FEMC rejected such radicalism, preferring to project an image of bourgeois respectability. Many of his supporters within the FEMC were property owners who feared Communist rhetoric about overturning France's social order. For this reason, Bendjelloul and the Fédération worked hard to distance themselves from the small number of active Communist organizers. They acknowledged that Communists and Socialists in France supported a partial extension of citizenship to Muslims, but it made little sense for Bendjelloul to attach his political future to left-wing politicians in Paris who were the bitter opponents of those politicians he encountered every day at the town hall or the prefecture in Constantine.

Could Bendjelloul therefore find allies in the besieged center? Here the story was similar. Maurice Viollette, a Radical Republican senator and a former governor-general of Algeria, proposed a law in 1931 that would create parliamentary representatives for some twenty-five thousand Muslim electors. Viollette was in contact with Bendjelloul and was a potential ally for the FEMC in parliament. For Viollette's parliamentary colleagues who represented "European" voters in Algerian circumscriptions, however, the thought of cooperating with Bendjelloul and the FEMC was anathema. Given the power of the settler lobby in parliament, the Viollette proposal was a nonstarter. It was taken up by the Popular Front government of Léon Blum in 1936 but was defeated in the Senate and never brought to the floor of the National Assembly. Among the loudest of those opposed to the Viollette proposal was Émile Morinaud, parliamentary deputy and mayor of Constantine.

Without allies on the left or in the independent center, could Bendjelloul and the FEMC find support on the right? Here the story is also complicated, because different right-wing movements rose to the forefront of local politics in Algerian cities in the interwar years, and local circumstances mattered as much as ideology in determining their success or failure. A few Paris-based right-wing leagues such as the Action française or the Jeunesses patriotes attempted to expand their operations in Algeria in the 1920s, but they made little headway because their mix of elitism, monarchism, and antirepublicanism gave them little traction among the settler population.[27] Organizations that put their anti-Jewish beliefs front and center found a more immediate response among French settlers who resented the Crémieux decree, but here, too, there was no pattern that emerged for Algeria as a whole, and local particularities seemed to drive the evolution of these groups.

In Oran, the largest city in western Algeria, Jules Molle was elected mayor in 1921 and became the best known of a group of politicians who reinvigorated an anti-Jewish electoral platform in Algeria in the 1920s, imitating the strategies used during the Dreyfus affair. Molle's political movement, the Unions Latines (UL), dominated Oran's politics until his death in 1931, and was supported by Molle's own paper, *Le Petit Oranais*, which carried a swastika on its front page for years. The ideology of the UL blended racial theories of civilization with a revisionist history that attributed the successes of the settler colony to the particular blend of Spanish, Italian, and French peoples that colonized Algeria in the nineteenth century. The result of this mixing was a new racial fusion that UL members spoke of proudly as *algérianité*. Their hatred of Algeria's Jews went hand in hand with the contempt that they felt toward the Arab and Berber cultures of Muslim North Africa.[28] For this reason, Molle and the Unions Latines never seriously attempted to create bridges between their own cadres and the new cohort of Muslim politicians that became active in Algeria in the 1920s as a result of the Jonnart Law.

Molle's toxic xenophobia—he was not above republishing articles by Nazis Joseph Goebbels and Alfred Rosenberg—was partly a product of Oran's unique demographic situation. Among a population of 158,000 in 1932, Oran's non-Jewish "European" citizens constituted almost exactly 50 percent of the total, about the same percentage of "European" citizens that lived in Algiers, and much more than the 34 percent of the population that were "European" citizens in Constantine. Jewish citizens constituted about 10 percent of the population in Oran, a larger proportion than in Algiers (7 percent) but not as large as in Constantine (about 12 percent). What made Oran different was a large percentage of foreigners of European origin—a group that included Spaniards, Italians, Anglo-Maltese, and a smattering of others. This group amounted to nearly 20 percent of the population in 1932, a remarkable 29,436 people out of a total population of 158,000.[29]

Thus, although Oran's population had a similar proportion of "European" voting citizens when compared to Algiers, it "felt" much more European to the residents moving through its streets on a day-to-day basis. This was true whether compared to the larger Algiers (total population 246,061) or the smaller Constantine (total population 99,595). In Oran, the Muslim population did not reach even 20 percent of the whole, and even after the Jonnart Law allowed some of these Muslim residents to vote, European elected officials had little to fear from the appearance of a new cohort of Muslim officeholders. Because all adult male Jews could vote, however, even their relatively small numbers made them vulnerable to Molle's opportunistic antisemitism, since the Jewish population was just large enough to constitute a visible presence but not large enough to prevent others from assembling a majority on the municipal council without them. A similar calculus, though less pronounced, favored the chances of anti-Jewish demagogues in Algiers, where the Jewish population was even smaller in proportion, at just over 7 percent of the total.

Constantine, on the other hand, had a proportionately larger Jewish population and a significantly smaller population of non-Jewish European voters. Muslims made up fully one-half of the city's population, and the 12 percent of the population that was Jewish constituted an impressive 25 percent of the non-Muslim voting public—and of course non-Muslim citizens were the only voters in parliamentary elections, even after the Jonnart Law. These proportions produced a very different kind of electoral calculation for Constantine's political dynasties. As we have seen, Émile Morinaud relied on alliances with Jewish elected officials to maintain his hold on city hall and his parliamentary seat after 1902, and in the early 1920s he did not repudiate these alliances even in the face of anti-Jewish agitation. These alliances held firm until the early 1930s, when Morinaud's majority on the municipal council was challenged by the rise of the anti-Jewish right in Constantine.

The most important right-wing organization to make its presence felt in Constantine was the Croix de feu, a veterans' organization founded in 1927 by Maurice d'Hartoy with funding from a wealthy perfume manufacturer, François Coty, who had long underwritten right-wing groups. Coty replaced the ineffectual d'Hartoy with Colonel François de La Rocque as president in early 1930, and membership in the Croix de feu began to grow rapidly. The Croix de feu's size distinguished it from other right-wing leagues, none of which ever approached anything resembling a mass movement. Initially restricted to combat veterans from the First World War, the Croix de feu soon added new classes of membership including women, veterans who had not served at the front (*briscards*), and men too young to have served in the war (the so-called *volontaires nationaux*). By the mid-1930s, the Croix de feu was the largest right-wing group in France, with as many as half a million active adherents and sections throughout metropolitan France and Algeria.[30] Dissolved by order of the government in 1936 as a threat to public order, along with the other major right-wing leagues, the Croix de feu reconstituted itself as a political party, the Parti social français (PSF), which claimed three million members by 1938.

Before its dissolution, the Croix de feu was organized along paramilitary lines, with authority emanating from the party's president and executive council through regional federations and local sections organized by neighborhood. Local sections were supposed to be able to call out their members for a show of force at a moment's notice. Their readiness to demonstrate publicly, often in uniform, led to a reputation for belligerence. Their willingness to embrace violence as a political tool was widely understood as a threat to their political opponents on the left. These activities led many contemporary observers to assume that the Croix de feu was a vehicle for a specifically French form of fascism. This fear became particularly acute during the right-wing riots in Paris on February 6, 1934, when the Croix de feu participated in a mass march on parliament that seemed to presage a coup attempt. Police surveillance reports on the organization make clear that the February 1934 crisis was a turning point in the evolution of the Croix de feu. Recruitment soared in the aftermath, and de La Rocque's group became a mass movement to be reckoned with.

Historians disagree about the Croix de feu's relationship to fascism.[31] The fact that the later Vichy government that collaborated with the Nazis borrowed the Croix de feu slogan "*Travail, Famille, Patrie*"—Labor, Family, Fatherland—indicates at least an ideological affinity with the most extreme forms of authoritarian nationalism, even if the fascist character of Vichy itself remains subject to debate. The Croix de feu's embrace of an aggressive hyper-masculinity in its public propaganda also shows parallels with the highly gendered propaganda of Italian Fascists or German National Socialists.[32] Others point out that the Croix de feu's leadership never seriously attempted to use its mass movement to seize power, even when at least a portion of its membership seemed to desire it.[33] Colonel de La Rocque himself appears to have become more cautious in his political views over time, more committed to legal forms of opposition, perhaps because he feared that his organization might actually precipitate the disorder that he claimed to oppose.[34] It is safe to say, however, that by the time of the Popular Front victory of April 1936, the organization attracted a large number of people both in metropolitan France and in Algeria who did not hide their antisemitism, their skepticism about parliamentary government, their militarism, or their admiration for the extreme nationalism and anticommunism of Mussolini and Hitler. This was as true in Constantine as it was in metropolitan France.

The first Croix de feu sections were created in Algeria in 1930, but prior to the February 1934 crisis there was little indication that the organization would develop into a vehicle for a new authoritarian sensibility in Algeria. Colonel de La Rocque visited Algeria himself in February 1931, in the run-up to a general congress of the Croix de feu's Algerian members in June of that year. Four hundred members attended the meeting in Algiers, representing a total of some three thousand members in Algeria organized into separate federations in Algiers, Constantine, and Oran.[35] The sections in the department of Constantine would eventually become the most active in Algeria, but their period of greatest influence came *after* the riots of August 1934. It also appears that the group paid little attention to the possibility of a political alliance with Muslim politicians until the riots convinced local Croix de feu leaders that they might be able to use the antisemitism of their European members as a lure to attract Muslim colonial subjects to their cause. In spite of their best efforts, this tactic largely failed.

Between 1930 and 1932, in fact, the local section of the Croix de feu in Constantine was far from the militant organization that it would become later. Its leadership was cautious and sought good relationships with local authorities. During its earliest years, it was led by a retired officer, Paul Levas, who emphasized the apolitical nature of the Croix de feu's engagement, and discouraged members from participating in overtly partisan behavior. This apolitical stance was in fact a part of the Croix de feu's public face on the national stage, since de La Rocque insisted that the veterans in his organization remain above the fray in a society contaminated by a corrupt political system. In Constantine, Levas parroted the official line: the group was open to veterans from all social classes and of all confessions. In point of fact, however, Croix de feu members were almost all from the city's middle class of professionals, businessmen, and government functionaries. Strikingly, several Jewish veterans appear to have been active during the period of Levas's leadership. Lucien Bensimon, a lawyer in Constantine, took a leading role in the early years as a member of the local section's executive board.[36] One Muslim name, Mahdi, is mentioned during this period as serving as a treasurer for the Constantine section of the Croix de feu, but there is no evidence of a concerted effort to recruit Muslim colonial subjects in these early years.[37]

Paul Levas's most significant act as leader of the Constantine section was to oppose Mayor Morinaud's plans to reward several prominent political allies with the Legion of Honor during the July 1930 centennial celebration of the Algerian conquest. The episode is worth recounting in detail for what it reveals about an emerging right-wing sensibility that had not yet broken completely with the local political leadership. In preparation for the centennial, Morinaud nominated three candidates for the Legion of Honor, all elected officials with seats on the departmental Conseil général. Of the three, only the decorated veteran Jules Valle was a member of the Croix de feu. Henri Lellouche, the Jewish political leader, was a veteran but had not served at the front. Étienne Muracciole, the prominent lawyer, had not served in the war at all. In the end, only Jules Valle was left off the list when the Ministry of the Interior published the names of the honorees. The Croix de feu protested, and one member from Constantine sent a telegram to the ministry saying that if Étienne Muracciole were to receive the award, then the members of the Croix de feu would renounce their own medals, and publicly hang an effigy of the cross of the Legion of Honor, draped in black crepe, from a lamppost in the place de la Brèche. Four uniformed members of organization would stand guard over this effigy for twenty-four hours while a cortège marched through the streets bearing signs saying "Long Live Doctor Armistice!"[38] Levas apologized for the provocative letter, and in the end, Morinaud got his way. The awards were given to Muracciole and Lellouche, and Levas's leadership of the Croix de feu section in Constantine was significantly weakened.

In the spring of 1932, Levas's leadership again came under severe strain when Stanislas Devaud, a local member of the Croix de feu, announced his intention to challenge Jules Cuttoli for his seat in parliament, one of three seats representing the department of Constantine. Devaud, a lycée philosophy professor who had lost a leg in the First World War, was a municipal councilor in Constantine and one of the Croix de feu's most outspoken local members. Levas attempted to enforce the rule on political neutrality and was initially supported in this by the leadership in Paris, who temporarily suspended the membership of all the sections in the department during Devaud's campaign. The rank and file overwhelmingly supported Devaud, however, and Levas resigned in June 1932. He was replaced by a much more militant—and anti-Jewish—retired lieutenant colonel named Gros.[39] Cuttoli defeated Devaud in the election, but only by 820 votes out of 9,000. This narrow victory served as a warning to both Morinaud's and Cuttoli's political networks—they could no longer depend on their traditional coalitions and patronage to maintain their political positions. Morinaud, whose dominance of city politics in the early 1930s still depended on an alliance with Jewish municipal councilors, took notice. By the end of 1933, the Croix de feu claimed seven thousand members in North Africa, including Morocco and Tunisia, with two thousand members in the department of Constantine alone. After the February 6, 1934, riots in Paris, the Algerian sections of the Croix de feu reported that they were gaining forty to forty-five new members a day.[40]

The new president of the Constantine section, Lieutenant Colonel Gros, and the vice president, Dr. Gaston Guigon, stacked the section's executive committee with a group of veterans representing the city's respectable middle classes, including doctors, lawyers, engineers, pharmacists, bank employees, and no fewer than five secondary school professors, colleagues of the indefatigable Stanislas Devaud. According to the police reports, the group had twelve meetings between April 1934 and July 1935, with attendance ranging from 200 to 1,000, with most of these gatherings attended by between 450 and 600 people. The section itself was subdivided into eleven neighborhood groups, and each group was further subdivided into smaller *dizaines* (tens) and *mains* (hands) of five men each, each with its own leader and liaison officer. The structure of the organization reflected the group's desire to call up teams of armed men in the event of a left-wing insurrection.

The Croix de feu eventually sought Muslim recruits, though this does not seem to have been a priority until the 1934 riots in Constantine revealed the possibility of using antisemitism as a tool both to threaten Jews and attract new members. There were precedents for this kind of cooperation: Solidarité française, also funded by François Coty, and the Jeunesses patriotes, a right-wing student group funded by the champagne producer Pierre Taittinger, recruited Algerian laborers working in France as foot soldiers for street protests in the early 1930s. A former colonial officer organized the recruits into paramilitary brigades. Some of these North Africans were present during the demonstrations of February 6, 1934, in Paris that ended in pitched battles between the leagues and the police. Gali Meziane, a metalworker from Algiers, was among those killed on February 6, and 150 people attended his funeral at the Paris mosque.[41]

Historians have been unimaginative in speculating why Algerians may have been attracted to these right-wing groups, suggesting condescendingly that these individuals were "lumpenproletarians" who were easily bought off with cash, cigarettes, clothing, and anti-Jewish propaganda.[42] Although no one should dismiss the possibility that money mattered for Algerian laborers living in precarious and vulnerable circumstances, it is also possible that they saw these forms of political engagement as a way of proving that they belonged to the society in which they lived and worked. Facing discrimination in housing and employment, many of them would have discovered, as did Bendjelloul in Constantine, that "Frenchness" was a moving target that was hard to hit. Within the milieu of the far right, of course, anti-Jewish sentiments were a strong part of what it meant to be "French." Some Algerians may well have been attracted to the kind of belonging offered to them by such a milieu, because it was precisely this kind of belonging that had previously been denied to them in French Algeria.

The sections of the Croix de feu in Algeria never supported colonial reforms that would have granted more rights to Algerian Muslims, but in the mid-1930s some sections appeared to see an advantage in the pressure that they could bring to bear on local politicians by presenting a united front with at least a portion of the Muslim population. Even if some sections were open to this possibility, however, the national organization kept close tabs on the recruitment of Algerian colonial subjects. The national leaders demanded that new Muslim members be approved by the Croix de feu's executive council in Paris, while local sections were allowed to vet new "European" members themselves. These rules ensured that the membership of Algerian colonial subjects in the Croix de feu was largely associated with Muslim notables who had served in the French army, an arrangement that brought colonial subjects into the organization without upsetting the social and racial hierarchies of Algerian colonial society. Under these circumstances, Muslim membership in the Algerian sections of the Croix de feu peaked at about

4 percent of those attending regular meetings in 1936–1937 before falling off rapidly to nearly zero after that period. But if the recruitment of Muslims in Algeria as a whole remained relatively insignificant, the level of participation in Constantine may have been higher; one historian has suggested that as many as 8 percent of the members regularly attending meetings of the Croix de feu in Constantine were Muslim during the months just before and after the legislative elections of 1936.[43]

Note, however, that these figures for Muslim recruitment are for the period *after* the anti-Jewish riots of August 1934, when tensions between Muslims and Jews were at their highest levels. During the crucial period of the group's expansion *before* the riots, there is little evidence that the Croix de feu in Constantine was actively recruiting Muslims to its cause. In fact, when the local Croix de feu members in Constantine first made their presence felt in public affairs in the early 1930s, they largely ignored the Muslim majority and behaved like any other local opposition group that was anxious to gain access to the sources of patronage and public spending that came with political power. They quarreled with Mayor Morinaud about the Legion of Honor and made no effort to recruit Muslims during Stanislas Devaud's failed parliamentary campaign in 1932. They claimed in their propaganda to welcome all veterans who had served at the front "without distinction of class, origin, confession, or rank," but made no explicit appeals to Muslim soldiers. In 1932 and 1933, the police reports in Constantine state that about forty people regularly attended the group's meetings, but only occasionally mentioned Muslim names in their list of members. The exception, a gathering of three hundred people on November 10, 1933, included a mention of ten *"indigènes"* who were in attendance—an indication of the relative lack of interest in the group among Constantine's Muslim veterans.[44] Some 850 people attended the Croix de feu lecture and discussion led by Gros and Devaud on December 6, 1933, but the police report paid more attention to the members of Constantine's political elite who were present (Pierre Liagre, then the first deputy mayor, Brigadier General Bru, several members of the municipal council, and the chief prosecutor of the criminal court) and did not mention a single Muslim attendee. During the first half of 1934, Muslim colonial subjects continued to play little role in the Croix de feu in Constantine, although the overall numbers were increasing rapidly, and more women began to participate.

The fact that local sections of the Croix de feu sought to recruit Muslims in the aftermath of the riots points to the ways that the riots helped to crystallize an emerging set of political boundaries that were more fluid before the riots occurred. In France as a whole, the right-wing violence in Paris in

February 1934 was a galvanizing moment in the evolution of the "dual frac-ture" in national politics, accentuating extremism on the right and forcing Socialists, Communists, and centrist republicans to overcome their mutual repugnance in order to create an antifascist coalition in the Popular Front. In Algeria, on the other hand, the Constantine riots of August 1934 were more important than the Paris violence of the previous February in forcing open a set of political cleavages that conformed more or less explicitly to ethno-religious lines. Before the Constantine riots, Jews could belong to the Croix de feu, and the veterans group was more interested in recruiting a base among the city's middle classes than it was in attracting Muslim supporters. After the riots, local sections of the Croix de feu opportunistically sought to use anti-Jewish platforms as a lever to form alliances with members of Mo-hamed Bendjelloul's Fédération. Such an alliance probably helped to elect a Croix de feu mayor in Sétif in October 1934. Bendjelloul himself repudiated any cooperation with the Croix de feu, however, and there is no direct line to be traced between the growth of the Croix de feu as a social and political movement in Constantine in the early 1930s and the violence that burst forth in the city on August 3–5, 1934. Provocation and incitement by local resi-dents played their role, but these acts of provocation only worked because the tissue of social relations between Muslims and Jews had become progres-sively more frayed since the end of the First World War. To understand this process, we need to return to the streets of Constantine.

CHAPTER 6

Provocation, Difference, and Public Space

With hindsight, it is relatively easy to come up with a plausible list of factors that contributed to the increase of tensions between Muslims and Jews in Constantine in the years after the First World War. Such a list might include the growing visibility of Muslim and Jewish community leaders and the alliance between Jewish municipal councilors and Mayor Morinaud at a moment when the latter and his allies were opposing a new cohort of Muslim politicians. These political circumstances were accompanied by shifts in the city's population as Jews began to move out of their traditional quarter to newly constructed housing in other residential areas. To these local circumstances, one might add a growing awareness in Algeria of conflict between Arabs and Jews elsewhere: most importantly in Palestine, where tensions erupted again in 1928 and culminated in attacks on Jews in Jerusalem in August 1929. These attacks and the subsequent repression by the British police led to hundreds of deaths and injuries and were reported in the North African press, causing the authorities to worry about local repercussions.[1] Finally, the late 1920s saw the emergence of a new kind of right-wing extremism in French and French-Algerian politics, as authoritarian and fascist groups imitated both the rhetoric and the street violence of Mussolini's blackshirts as well as the Nazi Party's aggressive attacks on Jews.

These local, national, and international circumstances form a necessary part of any account that seeks to explain the larger context of the Constantine riots of 1934, but they carry with them a danger. Most obviously, they loom larger in hindsight than they did to historical actors at the time. Neither local political alliances nor the changes in the city's residential patterns were seen as leading inexorably to an explosion of violence between Muslims and Jews in Constantine, except perhaps by a few provocateurs from the settler population who periodically—and mostly unsuccessfully—hoped to incite conflict between Muslims and Jews. Second, the inherent plausibility of this list of explanatory factors ultimately relies on an unstated assumption that violence between Muslims and Jews was an ever-present possibility, only awaiting a proverbial "spark" that was beyond anybody's ability to control or predict. The fact that provocation was both frequent and almost always unsuccessful is evidence enough that such an assumption would be misguided. The fact that provocation succeeded in August 1934, on the other hand, suggests that we ignore these circumstances at our peril. The challenge for historians is to find a way to present these circumstances as part of the social environment that made this violence possible without assuming that it was either inevitable or foreordained.

In the 1920s, provocation emerged as the name for a special kind of political and social problem in colonial Algeria. Of course, provocation itself— a form of verbal or physical attack that is designed to draw attention to perceived differences in such a way as to heighten or elevate the sense of conflict between them—was not new. What was new was the conjuncture between ideas about ethno-religious difference and a sense of vulnerability connected to the perception of accelerating change within colonial society. The reform of French Algeria's electoral system created an atmosphere of urgency about the need for political institutions that could transcend the colony's divided society. At the same time the very limited ambition of the proposed reforms made it clear that these very same divisions would remain as the foundation of the existing political system. Some groups understood that this sense of urgency served their purposes well, and they did everything that they could to elevate the temperature of political debate by demonizing their opponents. Even those who sought calmer forms of political discourse, however, found themselves drawn into the fray. In this context, any attempt to speak out loud about the political interests that separated "Europeans" from "natives" or Muslims from Jews was immediately susceptible to being labeled a provocation by one's neighbors or political opponents, even if such speech was invited by the dynamic of reform and the possibility of political evolution.

As a result, provocation became a kind of currency in political speech on both the left and the right during the interwar years. When elected officials spoke behind closed doors to their supporters, referring to political interests in terms of ethno-religious identities could be a virtue, a sign of plainspokenness, and a willingness to confront the "real" conflicts that underlay society. Making similar claims in the public space defined by the French Republic's political institutions, however, opened one up to a charge of defending particular communities at the expense of the nation. In such an environment, extreme forms of nationalism possessed an unrivaled advantage, since their point of departure was that the "nation" was congruent only with the particular form of identity that mattered most to them—their own. In interwar French Algeria, a portion of the European settler population increasingly rallied to groups such as the authoritarian Croix de feu or Jacques Doriot's Parti populaire français that mimicked the fascist political parties in Italy and Germany. For the Algerian followers of such groups, the primary short-term goal was to undo the Crémieux decree and remove Algerian Jews from the electoral rolls. They were also opposed to granting parliamentary representation to Algeria's Muslims, but by the mid-1930s some of these groups were willing to make overtures to the Muslim majority if it would help them to isolate Algeria's Jews. For these groups, provocations—invocations of difference for political gain—were part of their political vernacular.

Within the city of Constantine itself, however, there is little evidence that right-wing groups such as the Croix de feu were working to recruit Muslims to their cause before August 1934, probably because the growing strength of Mohamed Bendjelloul's movement made them fear political activity by the Muslim majority population in Algeria. At the same time, however, the cohort of Muslim politicians who operated under the conditions imposed by the Jonnart Law felt the full force of its paradoxes as they sought to appeal to their constituents: only Muslims could vote for them, but if they acted on behalf of Muslims they were accused of disloyalty, sectionalism, or even—ironically—of nationalism. The terms of their political participation doomed them to continual accusations of provocation, and thus to repeated but disbelieved protestations of their loyalty to the Republic, and to France.

Other provocations came from cynically organized political groups who clearly hoped to profit from fear and violence. Their members put up political posters, plastered handmade stickers onto city walls, gave inflammatory speeches at public meetings, and published articles in ephemeral newspapers. At the other end of this spectrum of provocations were the personal affronts that frequently arose from the most banal kinds of interactions on the street, in the market, or on the stairs of apartment buildings. An exchange of insults, a sudden elevation of voices, an altercation that may or may not have led to blows, a denunciation to the local police, the sending of anonymous threats, or even the repetition of an unfounded rumor—all might be perceived as acts of provocation by virtue of the way they drew attention to lines of conflict or social division, and by their ability to raise the temperature of social interaction, and thus invite further provocations in turn. By the mid-1930s, this sense of "justifiable" provocation—and the justifications were endlessly repeated—would come to characterize almost all political discourse in France and French Algeria.

The riots in August 1934 were directly linked to this history of escalating provocations, but one must be careful in telling this story. The line from provocation to murder was not direct. Although one can and should attribute real responsibility to provocateurs who deliberately incited hatred of Jews in the antisemitic press or by posting images on walls, it is also true that such crude provocations did not always produce the effects desired by the people who performed them. A provocation can only be successful when the ground has been well prepared—and telling that story requires a patient reconstruction of local interactions over time. In the case of August 1934, the background to provocation was a discontinuous process, not necessarily directed from above or from below. Perhaps the best way to describe it is to say that the interactions that led to violence unfolded with all the contingency of every other kind of human activity—an argument here, a misunderstanding there, a dispute between a market seller and a client who had done business with each other many times before, an insult exchanged between men who drank at the same café every day, an altercation between neighbors who kept track of one another's comings and goings. Individual incidents such as these can never be said to have "caused" the riots, but cumulatively they provided the background to a moment when the lines of fracture invoked by a provocative act suddenly conformed to the very real divisions of a local community in distress.

Prior to the First World War, the police records from Constantine note occasional disputes between Jewish shopkeepers in the markets and impoverished men—labeled as "indigènes"—coming from the countryside to sell used clothing and shoes. Established shopkeepers guarded their market spaces with a watchful eye and resented improvised displays on the street that crowded their customers. This policing of space led to occasional expressions of contempt for the poorer sellers whose desperate circumstances led them to pocket their meager gains and leave the market without making purchases of their own. These disputes were frequent enough to generate a trace in the archives, but they were essentially about distinctions of class, socioeconomic status, and the separation between urban and rural populations. They did not lead to anything more serious than a momentary disruption of the market's routines. It is possible that the memory of these conflicts survived into the interwar period when economic crisis brought more desperate people to the city looking for work and subsistence. It is also true that these disputes seemed significant only in retrospect. The prewar reports were patiently gathered after the riots of 1934 and compiled in dossiers labeled "Antisemitism." This is how, after the fact, lines of fracture can seem to align in predestined ways.

More serious were troubles occasioned by visits of Muslim soldiers from the military garrison to cafés and brothels in or near the Jewish quarter. These reached a crisis point in the months before the First World War. In February 1914 local authorities posted seventy-two soldiers at three locations in the Jewish quarter—place Négrier, rue Thiers, and the place des Galettes—after brawls broke out between Muslim soldiers and Jewish men who resented them passing through their streets while on leave. The fighting was frequent enough that the military prohibited soldiers from entering the Jewish quarter, though the authorities appear to have later settled for a simple prohibition against Muslim soldiers entering the neighborhood's cabarets and brothels. The commanding officer protested to the prefect when Jews in the city tried to regulate the movement of soldiers: "It is difficult to accept that a part of the population of Constantine, which enjoys all the rights of French citizens, should have the privilege of transforming a portion of the public thoroughfares into a forbidden zone."[2] The statement betrayed the complex mix of assumptions built into the triangulation between Frenchness on the one hand and the status of Muslims and Jews in Algeria on the other. Muslims in French uniform were subject to a wide range of serious discriminations within the military, but the officer saw no contradiction in citing their circulation in Constantine's streets as he defended the liberty of the city's public thoroughfares. At the same time, he repackaged the defensive gestures of a few Jewish men as a provocation asserted by the Jewish community as a whole. In each case, the paradox was a familiar one: claims made *by* Jews could only be seen as claims made *in the name of* Jews, thus violating the fundamental invisibility that was a part of the religious group's social contract with Frenchness. Muslims in the French military, on the other hand, could serve as the vehicle for a defense of fundamental liberties even as their inferior civil status remained unmentioned.

When tensions between Muslims and Jews flared again in the late 1920s, this older pattern involving Algerian Muslims, occasionally in uniform, and Jewish men who felt obligated to protect their neighborhood seems to have been remembered. In late December 1928, only a month after the first reports of tension in Jerusalem began to circulate in Algeria, three Muslim men brought a complaint against five Jewish young men who had beaten them up the night before as they passed by the rue de France in Constantine's Jewish quarter.[3] The police initially regarded it as an isolated incident, but became more concerned a week later when a similar situation occurred, this time involving 'Abd al-Hamid Ben Badis, the prominent Islamic scholar and member of the notable local family. He had been returning home with an associate when they were accosted by a group of Jewish men returning from a party sponsored by a workers' aid society. Ben Badis took refuge in the offices of a Muslim charity, but his colleague was badly beaten. Police interviews with witnesses revealed that the attack was not premeditated and that the aggressors had no idea who Ben Badis was. The prefect was worried enough, though, to call a meeting with Henri Lellouche, the Jewish member of the departmental assembly, and Rabbi Maurice Eisenbeth, then the chief rabbi of Constantine (he would later hold the same post in Algiers). These Jewish leaders assured him that they would not amplify the affair among their constituency and called for the men who had beaten Ben Badis and his associate to be punished. The prefect did not meet with Muslim leaders or with anybody from the Fédération des élus, but he noted that the mufti of Constantine had called for calm after the incident. In the aftermath of these conversations, the Office of Muslim Affairs in Algiers reported to the governor-general that earlier incidents where Jews had attacked Muslims had not resulted in charges "because of the intercession of the town's Jewish elected officials."[4]

The attack on Ben Badis was followed by eighteen months in which relations between Jews and Muslims deteriorated. Police reports documented thirty-one incidents of Jews convicted of violent acts against Muslims between late 1928 and June 1930. Taken individually, they appear to have been isolated incidents of hostility between men meeting one another by chance on the street. The perpetrators were often described as drunk or known for their disorderly behavior.[5] During these months, the Jewish leadership's relationship with the police became more confrontational.

The police reports of these incidents seem at first glance to be empty of political content. All that was necessary for such a report to be filed under "Antisemitism" was for a dispute to take place in the presence of a Jewish person. They often involved alcohol, dominoes, cards, cafés, or prostitutes. Others were clearly driven by tensions between groups of adolescents who aggressively defended "their" streets from outsiders. In at least one case, dated January 5, 1929, the theme of increased tension between Muslims and Jews was written into the narrative in order to distract attention from the more prosaic reasons that lay behind the dispute. The case involved a Muslim police inspector, Mohamed Bouam, and two brothers from a Jewish family who accosted him either on the landing or in the street in front of 11 rue Sérigny, a narrow byway in the center of the old city. Bouam claimed that he was in the rue Sérigny "gathering information on the recent incidents between natives and Israelites" when he was accosted by the two brothers who told him to leave the neighborhood. When he identified himself as a police officer, they grabbed him by the throat and beat him, taking away his service revolver. Bouam's call for help drew reinforcements from the police station in the nearby rue de France, and the two Jewish men were arrested. The brothers, Lucien and Simon Drai, claimed they had returned home to find a Muslim man they did not recognize on the landing of their building. Suspecting a thief, they were forced to disarm him when the man drew his revolver, but they said they had not beaten him. Two witnesses—"one, a native, and the other a young Israelite girl"—gave statements saying that they had seen the brothers strike the inspector.

To these two contrasting stories from Inspector Bouam and the Drai brothers, the report added a third, coming from another police officer who lived in the same building, Agent Atlani. (Atlani was a common Jewish surname in Algeria.) Atlani had been on duty the night before, but when he came home, the owner of the building—a woman named Fatima Hattat—told him that members of the Drai family had beaten her as well as Inspector Bouam. Atlani also reported that Mohamed Bouam visited Fatima Hattat "almost every day." The police commissioner who authored the report thought the event significant enough to send a copy to the governor-general, noting "in this affair, everybody wants to hide the truth." In his view, the dispute began as an argument between the Drai family and Fatima Hattat, described as a "woman of ill repute" (*femme de moeurs légères*) whose "assignations" with Mohamed Bouam dishonored the household. When Inspector Bouam intervened, the Drai brothers turned their anger onto him as well.

For our purposes the "facts" of the matter are less important than the terms of the dispute and the glimpse that the story offers of the complicated interactions that were a part of daily life in the old city during these years. The cast of characters is suggestive: a Muslim woman who was also a landlord, a Jewish family living as tenants in her house, a Muslim police inspector who may or may not have been carrying on an affair with the landlord, and his colleague, a Jewish police inspector who was also a neighbor, communicating information separately to his superior. We might also note the importance of the disagreement over the site of the dispute: for the Drai brothers, the dispute took place "on the landing," the very threshold of their home. For Mohamed Bouam it took place "in the street," the domain of his authority as a police inspector. The dispute itself had nothing to do with being Jewish or Muslim and arose from the banal circumstances of people living at close quarters in a densely populated heterogeneous neighborhood. The commissioner's report identified nobody by religion, except the young "Israelite" witness. Only a familiarity with the names of the individuals involved and the fact that the report was filed under "Antisemitism" allow a reader to discern the different identities that were at stake in this confrontation. If there was anything at stake here, it is not so much the meaning of what it meant to be "Muslim" or "Jewish" but rather that ever-absent term "French." For it is in fact the "Frenchness" of the scene that allowed both Bouam and Atlanti to be colleagues in the police, and it is through the changes in the city under the French that Fatima Hattat could become the landlord of the Drai family and of the police officer Atlanti.

Inevitably, given the assault on the police inspector before witnesses, the Drai brothers were found guilty. Lucien Drai was sentenced to fifteen days in prison and a 200 franc fine; his brother Simon was sentenced to eight days in prison and a 100 franc fine. Another family member, Rahim Drai, was fined 25 francs, and the family was also forced to pay 300 francs in damages to Fatima Hattat and 600 in damages to Bouam. Others took notice as well: on January 7, two days after the dispute, En-Nadjah published an article on "the aggressions committed by Israelites on diverse natives [indigènes] of the locality," drawing a connection between the latest incident and the earlier attack on Ben Badis.[6]

In succeeding weeks, police reports on other minor incidents continued to pile up, each more banal than the last. It is hard to avoid the impression that if there had not been the initial incident involving Ben Badis, all this would have passed unnoticed. The accumulation of disparate incidents was experienced as an escalation, however, and the reports began to take on a more ominous tone when it came to assessing the long-term consequences of these disputes. On January 12, another incident was recorded: Fredj Nakache, a Jewish jeweler, became drunk at a café maure and struck a "native sergeant" playing dominoes at the next table. Nakache was jailed for two months, and the police commissioner confidently announced that this case "had no correlation with those events that have taken place recently between natives and israelites." He added, however, that "the natives believe such acts occur too frequently," and warned "if this continues serious incidents could result."[7]

Over the next few weeks, reports of similar disputes continued to accumulate, and there is some indication that the tension was spreading to other communities. By mid-April 1929, the mayor of Châteaudun-du-Rhumel (Chelghoum Laïd), a small town to the south of Constantine, declared his intention to prohibit the carrying of sticks, clubs, and iron bars in the streets, and banned gatherings of more than four persons, saying such restrictions were necessary to prevent a *"nefra"* or a *"rixe."*[8] On April 28, when a twenty-two-year-old Jewish blacksmith was charged for a second time with assault on a Muslim, in this case a sixteen-year old youth, the prefect called on the prosecutor to demand a harsh sentence "to make an example of him" because "aggressions committed by Israelites against natives are becoming too frequent and risk degenerating into severe troubles if severe sentences are not handed down in affairs of this nature."[9] One month later (May 28), the central police commissioner reported to the prefect that a shoving match between Jewish boys and a Muslim boy ended up with the latter being taken to the hospital after striking his head on a stone. The fight caused "a great effervescence" in the neighborhood until people realized that the injuries were not serious.

In early August 1929 a flurry of reports prompted yet more communication between the prefect's office and Jewish community leaders. On August 6, two Jewish teenagers ran through the place Négrier holding a large branch by the ends, sweeping people off their feet. A Muslim man in his sixties was injured as he fell, and then beaten as he tried to escape. He provided a medical certificate: incapacity to work for twelve days.[10] The same day, two Algerian Muslims were accosted by a group of Jewish men in a bar. Léon Boucara, having already spent six days in jail for beating a Muslim man, struck a Muslim man with a carafe, causing "12 days incapacity to work."[11] On August 7, an eight-year-old Muslim boy was climbing a wall with other boys when an eight-year-old Jewish girl intentionally caused him to fall two meters and suffer serious injury as a result. On August 9, a Jewish girl visited a grocery owned by Boussadi Youcef to buy an egg. She returned ten minutes later to exchange it, complaining that the egg was bad. When the grocer refused, the girl's brother visited the grocery and after a short discussion struck him several times in the face with his fists. These events produced yet another letter from the prefect's office to a Jewish community leader—in this case to Émile Barkatz, first aide to Mayor Morinaud—urging him to "use [his] prestige in the Jewish community [*en milieu israélite*] in order to prevent any regrettable excitation and any excessive exaltation of racial sentiment."[12] The prefect reported the ongoing tensions to the governor-general's office and received a strangely mixed response. "These events . . . should not in any way be taken as serious, nor is there any reason to see here a clear manifestation of racial antagonism." At the same time, he demanded that the prosecutors call for severe punishments in order to send a message to the community.[13]

Only three days later, however, a further incident indicated the extent to which these banal events were taking on more political significance. A Muslim lawyer and elected member of the municipal council, Belkacem Benhabylès, wrote to the prefect on August 26, 1929, about a public dispute with a Jewish policeman and Émile Barkatz, a Jewish elected official who was also deputy mayor. Benhabylès had been sitting on the terrace of the Brasserie de l'Étoile in the center of town when he saw a crowd gather around a police agent who was berating—and possibly beating—a young man from the countryside who was attempting to guide a heavily loaded mule across the square. Benhabylès approached the agent, identified by name as Nakache, to ask what the problem was, only to be rebuked and brushed off with a rude comment: "It's none of your business, your presence here is useless." Benhabylès noted at this moment that Barkatz was also passing through the area, and he asked Nakache to accompany him to Barkatz in order to appeal to a third party. To Benhabylès's surprise, however, Barkatz simply said, "Nakache, fulfill your duties with all necessary independence, it's all the same to me!" Benhabylès described how Barkatz walked off, "persuaded that he had fulfilled his own duties with 'indépendance.'" Benhabylès's letter continued, playing with multiple allusions to "indépendance"—Nakaches's, Barkatz's, and his own. Claiming that Nakache had been fired and rehired multiple times by the police force, and that he had a long criminal record before coming to his current position, Benhabylès threatened to bring suit against the police agent in court, revealing Nakache's history of violence before public opinion. He concluded by saying "Mr. Second Deputy Mayor wants to teach us a lesson about 'indépendance'—well, we thank him, we will know what to do with it."[14]

The police records of these incidents are probably selective both in the choice of incidents that were recorded and in the responsibility they assign for the incidents they describe. The dossiers on incidents of conflict between Muslims and Jews between 1928 and 1934 that now can be found in the archives were assembled after the 1934 riots under the authority of Police Commissioner René Miquel, who took office in 1930 as the situation began to deteriorate. Miquel was well known for his affinities with the anti-Jewish and nationalist right wing in the city, and he later boasted about his efforts to increase the "French element" among the police force and to lessen their reliance on Jewish and Muslim officers.[15] With these circumstances in mind, it is also worth noting that after the riots the police authorities had some interest in suggesting that the Jews of Constantine brought trouble on themselves. After the death of twenty-five Jews on August 5, 1934, many people questioned the failure of the police either to anticipate or to put a stop to antisemitic violence, and a tactic of blaming Jews for "provoking" Muslim anger could help to deflect this criticism.

It is possible, then, that the dossiers compiled after August 1934 were selective in their inclusion of more incidents that could be blamed on Jewish provocation. It is also possible that the authorities simply believed that Jews, as the minority population in the city, had more of a responsibility to restrain their behavior. In September 1930, the prefect was concerned enough about the possibility of Jewish provocation that he wrote a letter to Rabbi Maurice Eisenbeth asking for him to intervene to prevent further deterioration of relations between Muslims and Jews.[16] Because it may have suited the police to attribute any increase in anti-Jewish activity to provocative acts by Jews in the old city—and their repeated letters to Jewish community leaders seems to indicate that this was their belief—one should not take these reports as necessarily representative of the many different kinds of encounters between Muslims and Jews in Constantine. At the same time, however, it is unlikely that these incidents were simply invented. Given the bureaucratic habits of Constantine's police commissioners, who seemed to spend a good part of many days signing typed reports of minor altercations on the street, any manipulation of the documents was probably subtler, involving the framing of witness statements, or a lack of follow-up if the investigation might embarrass powerful local notables. In spite of the likelihood of anti-Jewish bias within the police reporting, therefore, it seems reasonable to accept that these records show an increase in the number of violent encounters between Muslims and Jews in Constantine in the months after the attack on Ben Badis in December 1928.

Between September 1931 and the spring of 1933, when antisemitism flared again within the city, fewer incidents between Muslims and Jews are reported in the police records. Nevertheless, a pattern seems to have been set, and two parallel developments seem to have perpetuated this already tense atmosphere: a marked deterioration in the relationship between Constantine's Jewish leadership and its police force, and an unrelated but nevertheless significant increase in the intensity of political activity by local Muslim elected officials. The already fragile relationship between Jews and the police worsened as some of the more outspoken and aggressive local figures who were active in street-level community self-defense activities found themselves subject to prosecution by the police. In January 1932, a controversy erupted when the police arrested Ruben Aouizerat—also known as "Cabassou"—following a brawl that occurred in the rue de France. The local police had attempted to arrest a young man who was drunk and causing trouble, and Aouizerat led a crowd that intervened to stop the arrest. Aouizerat, known as the "prefect of the rue de France," enjoyed a street reputation as a charismatic figure, and he also helped to organize voters during municipal elections. After the brawl in January 1932, he was charged with "rebellion" and imprisoned, and the affair became linked in the minds of the local Jewish leadership with the firing of several Jewish police officers by Commissioner Miquel later that spring. Finding themselves isolated within the city and unsure of the protection that they could expect from an increasingly hostile police force, the Jewish leadership of Constantine wrote a petition to Mayor Morinaud and the prefect in June 1932, calling for the replacement of René Miquel.[17] The letter bore 143 signatures from among the most prominent Jewish residents of the town. The archives do not contain any response from Morinaud, but the antisemitic Miquel was still in office as police commissioner during the riots of August 1934.

These stories about violence between Jews and Muslims in Constantine seem so particular, so rooted in local circumstance that one might hesitate to look for more general conclusions. One might equally ask, however, if it is really possible to understand the exclusions of the French Republic without taking such local stories into account. Their details demonstrate the ways that French Algeria's fatal combination of legal discrimination and the political opening offered to Muslims by the Jonnart Law raised the temperature of social interactions in a turbulent period. The colonial city had developed according to the exclusionary logic that underpinned the French Algerian civic order in the nineteenth century, and the postwar electoral reforms forced the city's residents to reconsider the significance of these exclusions for the spaces they moved through every day. The terraces of European-style cafés, the colonial city's segregated residential spaces, the gymnasiums used by athletic clubs, the pools used by water polo teams, the printing offices and the pages of the local press became the flashpoints of conflict in the interwar years—and in each of these spaces, the issue for both Muslim colonial subjects and Jewish citizens was how to confront the forms of inclusion and exclusion that had been built into the spaces of their daily lives.

CHAPTER 7

Rehearsals for Crisis

The riots of August 1934 in Constantine were not inevitable, but there were precedents. Tensions between antisemitic settlers, Muslims, and Jews nearly boiled over in May 1933 as disputes in the streets converged with a moment of political volatility. In 1933, as in 1934, there was a close affinity between conflict in public spaces and the repeated failure of Mohamed Bendjelloul's political movement to find support for expanding political rights for Muslims. These failures were all the more frustrating because they followed the July 1931 political opening that came from Senator Maurice Viollette's proposal to grant full citizenship and parliamentary representation to a small elite of Algerian Muslim colonial subjects. Viollette was a former governor-general of Algeria who publicized the need for reform in a book he published the same year titled *Will Algeria Survive?*[1] His parliamentary colleagues from Algeria angrily rejected his proposal, but Bendjelloul and the members of his Fédération saw the Viollette proposal as a welcome opportunity to change the nature of the debate about electoral reform. In 1933, as in 1934, the atmosphere in the streets became venomous during the weeks that Bendjelloul's efforts attained their greatest publicity—but the police behaved differently in 1933. When conflict seemed imminent in 1933, the police shut down the city and blockaded the Jewish neighborhood, and violence was avoided. In 1934, the police failed to do this, and twenty-eight people died. The riots of 1934, in other words, were a performance that came after a full dress rehearsal. Some of the actors, at least, had plenty of time to learn their lines.

Bendjelloul did not appear to seek violence, and the evidence suggests that he had no interest in making it more likely before August 1934. At the same time, he understood that his program could not succeed without a level of political intensity that would shake up the city and the department of Constantine as a whole. To accomplish this, Bendjelloul pursued a two-pronged approach, simultaneously expanding his popularity among Muslim colonial subjects while also going over the heads of local officials who were his primary opponents. Accordingly, Bendjelloul designed his campaign with two audiences in mind. The first was the small group of reform-minded politicians in Paris, including Maurice Viollette himself. The second audience was the much larger number of Algerian Muslims who would be his base in future elections if his program for reforms succeeded. In both cases, Bendjelloul sought to parlay his connections with the one into greater standing with the other. He sought to convince French politicians such as Viollette that he was the only presentable republican face among the various strands of politically active Algerian Muslims, while also telling his potential electorate in Algeria that only he had the necessary connections in Paris to counteract the most powerful opponents of reform, the well-entrenched local settler establishment. Fulfilling these tasks simultaneously required Bendjelloul's presence both in Paris and in Constantine, and between May 1932, when he became president of the Fédération des élus musulmans, and the riots of August 1934, he made several trips back and forth, stitching together in his own person the political relationships that shaped Algerian politics in the interwar period. In Constantine, Bendjelloul placed himself at the center of a network of civic action groups, some of which took on an increasingly public and political profile.[2] In 1933, he sided with Ben Badis when the French government tried to prohibit members of the Association of Algerian Muslim Ulama from speaking in Algeria's mosques. In Paris, on the other hand, Bendjelloul sought an audience with France's most powerful political figures—repeatedly contacting and addressing letters to the prime minister and the Ministry of the Interior to discuss issues of importance to Algeria's Muslims.

This habit of going straight to the top began in August 1932, during the tax strike in Aïn M'lila, when he published a telegram addressed to Prime Minister Édouard Herriot, Interior Minister Camille Chautemps, and Senator Viollette about the "brutalities, torture, beatings, insults, whippings, imprisonment, forced labor, exposure to sun, seizure of clothing worn by taxpayers, seizure of women's jewelry, tools and last supplies of food" during the collection of taxes in that region.[3] This leapfrogging over the administration's hierarchies made Bendjelloul an enemy to all officials in Algeria, including the mayor's office in Constantine, the prefect, and Governor-General Jules Carde. Following the publication of Bendjelloul's telegram, the governor-general called upon the prefect of Constantine to discipline Muslim elected officials who supported him, writing that "we must put an end to Bendjelloul's activities."[4] In the following months, Bendjelloul and the FEMC were subjected to intense surveillance.

The administration felt that the worsening international situation made it impossible to envisage any potentially destabilizing reforms of the electoral system. Bendjelloul's campaign to draw the attention of Parisian political figures in the spring of 1933 climaxed in the midst of a changing political environment in Algeria as the population began to react to major events in Europe. The prolonged political crisis in Germany that culminated in Hitler's accession to power on January 30 encouraged the spread of rumors about the imminent arrival of Jewish refugees.[5] In March, an antifascist demonstration in Constantine led by a young Jewish man led to a whisper campaign that the city's Jews were in favor of war with Germany.[6] In April the police recorded talk of a boycott of the Job cigarette company by Constantine's colonial subjects, following a rumor that they intended to fire their Muslim employees in order to hire Jewish refugees. Soon after, rumors spread that a M. Levy, the owner of a grain mill, was about to fire fifty Muslim employees.

The next month, a new antisemitic newspaper appeared in Constantine, *L'Éclair*, published by a local troublemaker named Henry Lautier. Born in Batna in 1904, Lautier founded his first newspaper in Constantine in 1928, but it failed after only a few editions. He tried to join the right-wing league, Action française, but was kicked out for "indiscipline." After two short stints in prison for fraud and passing bad checks, and further convictions for fighting and cutting wood in state-owned forests, he found his true calling as a rabble-rousing antisemite and publisher.[7] *L'Éclair* first appeared in May 1933 and irregularly thereafter. In the fall of 1933 Lautier founded an anti-Jewish "Ligue d'action latine" to "defend Latin intellectual traditions and customs" and attempted to make this association official by filing the necessary paperwork, but the prefecture soon determined that Lautier had lied about the members of the league's executive committee and that it existed in name only. Lautier's antisemitism was neither original nor imaginative—the headline on December 2, 1933, was "Jews Masters of the World"—but the appearance of the paper understandably unnerved the Jewish population of the city. Lautier was beaten up at least four times between May and September, and he was convicted of libel in November for his published attacks on a local lawyer. He also found some support in the ranks of the police department—Commissioner René Miquel forwarded to the prefect a sympathetic report by an inspector that noted Lautier's "intelligent, agreeable, and educated conversation."[8] The director of departmental security noted that few Muslims in the city appeared to be interested in Lautier's paper, but *L'Éclair's* first appearance coincided with a rash of antisemitic activity by young people from the European population who scrawled slogans supporting Hitler and swastikas on the walls of Jewish shops.[9] Lautier exacerbated the tension by hiring young Muslim boys to sell his paper on the streets, leading to altercations where the papers were seized by angry passersby and torn to shreds. In this uncertain atmosphere, tensions between Muslims and Jews on Constantine's streets remained palpable.

While the city sought to make sense of these local and international developments, Bendjelloul launched a very public campaign in May 1933 to be seated as a member of the government's Interministerial Commission for Muslim Affairs (CIAM). CIAM had been created in 1911, and although a debate about Muslim representation had begun in 1915, the right of Muslim "councilors" to sit on the commission was not granted until a decree of 1931.[10] After that, the government in Paris appointed five Muslim clerics to the commission, which deliberated and made recommendations relating to Muslim education, the use of Arabic in schools, and the regulation of the Arabic press. The designated Muslim representatives, handpicked by the colonial administration for their reliability, were not well received by other Muslim leaders or the by wider Muslim public in Algeria. Since taking over the presidency of the FEMC in May 1932, Bendjelloul sought to use this issue as a centerpiece in his efforts to rally support for his electoral federation in the Constantine region.

On May 11, Bendjelloul left for Paris and Dreux, accompanied by several other Muslim elected officials, to attend a jubilee in honor of Maurice Viollette in his home district. On his return to Constantine, on May 20, he was greeted in triumph by members of the FEMC with a reception at the train station, an offering of floral wreaths, and a ceremonial *thé d'honneur* designed to display public recognition of the status that he claimed, that of the leader of a Muslim delegation to the highest levels of power in France. Immediately after his return, Bendjelloul and the journalist Rabah Zenati announced a speaking tour of the department to tell their electorate about their trip to Paris and to demand that Bendjelloul be seated as a member of CIAM.[11] His failure to achieve this goal by the summer of 1934 was a huge disappointment for Bendjelloul's constituency in Constantine and contributed to the anger that manifested itself in the riots of August 1934.

As Bendjelloul and his colleagues prepared for the speaking tour in May–June 1933, events in Constantine threatened to overwhelm the local authorities. On May 23, after a water polo match between a Jewish team and a team made up of Europeans, a fight between two individuals identified only as Kalifa and Berger (a Jewish man and a European respectively) led to the arrest of four people. A mixed crowd of about 150 people gathered before the police station, and several were injured as fights broke out in the crowd. Two hours later, another European, named Dumont, was beaten by a group of young Jewish men, and the brawl threatened to become general when another group of young Jews fought with railway workers from the faubourg d'el Kantara. This encounter occurred near a work site that provided both sides with abundant projectiles, and the police reported that the Muslim laborers at the work site took the side of the railway workers against the Jewish adolescents.[12] The police closed the cafés in the affected neighborhoods in order to prevent any recurring violence, but that evening a young Jewish boy was attacked by a group of Muslim men, who beat him about the head and arms with sticks.

The following day saw Constantine once more preoccupied by rumors of all sorts: the police reports mentioned whispers about the formation of a committee to undertake a new campaign against the city's Jews, and plans for violent reprisals against Jews were also recorded. The worst was a rumor about plans to explode a truck filled with gasoline on the rue de France, a large commercial street that ran through the center of the old city. That night groups of people circulated excitedly in the streets, and at midnight a poster was hung on the wall outside a Jewish barbershop in El Kantara with an inscription in French: "Long Live Hitler—Down with the Jews—Cursed Race."[13]

On the day after the brawl at the water polo match, May 24, Bendjelloul received a letter claiming to be from a Jewish man named "Allouche." The letter insulted the Muslim elected official in the most vulgar language and openly threatened violence by Jews against Muslims:

> To the *bicot* [offensive derogatory term for "Arab" derived from the word for "goat"] Bendjelloul, General Councilor. You have ruled as master thanks to the French but today we are strong and we can tell you that we piss on you and on all Arabs put together. We Jews are not afraid of you and one day soon you will hear from us, we'll burn your house and break your face, you pile of *bicots*, dirty race, we're waiting for you with the French whose ass we piss on in the same way, and you can get together with them, nothing will stop us, we want to be the masters of the country, we shit on your mosque.

Down with the *bicots*
Down with the French
Long live the Jews
A group of Jews who shits on all of you
One more time
Down with the *bicots*
Down with the French
Long live the Jews.
For the Committee, ALLOUCHE,
See you soon, dirty race.[14]

The letter was almost certainly a provocation by an antisemitic group or individual seeking to sow dissent between Constantine's Jews and Muslims by invoking themes of sexual domination, bodily impurity, and religious profanation in the most shocking of ways. Most revealing is the chant that concluded the letter: "Down with the *bicots*, down with the French, long live the Jews." The implicit distinction between Jews and the French, and the blanket condemnation of France itself, would have been a highly unusual position for any Jewish resident of Constantine during these years, and is the strongest indication that the letter was written by an antisemitic provocateur from the settler population. It is also likely that Bendjelloul understood this. He does not seem to have mentioned this letter anywhere else, though its existence in the police files indicates that he took it seriously enough to provide it to them.

The police compiled further evidence of organized anti-Jewish activity coming from members of the European population the same week, but also noted that Muslim colonial subjects were becoming involved in these disputes. On the evening of May 24, a Jewish man reported that a crowd of people marched aggressively through the rue Caraman in the old Jewish quarter shouting antisemitic slogans. When they encountered a group of police agents, they shouted: "The cops are our servants, even the police commissioner!"[15] On May 25, a group described as "young people"—in other words, not identified as either "Muslim" or "native"—ran through the Cité Laloum, one of the newly constructed apartment complexes on Constantine's outskirts where Jews had moved in the preceding years, shouting "Down with the Jews, Long Live Hitler!" That night a crowd estimated at three hundred people attempted to enter the rue de France, where the police stopped them. The next day, police reports indicated that a group of Jewish men attacked and beat two Muslim men in the old city. Following this incident, rumors spread quickly throughout the city that a struggle between Muslims and

Jews had broken out and that one of the two Muslim victims had died. Large groups of Muslims, estimated by the police to be close to a thousand people, responded by descending on the Jewish quarter armed with clubs. The police intervened and pushed the crowd back up the rue Caraman to the rue de France. At the corner of these two streets the police erected a barrier to keep the disputing groups of men apart. Salah Améziane, a Muslim municipal councilor and FEMC member, contributed to the effort to calm the crowd. While this group dispersed, another crowd of Muslims and Europeans gathered in front of the Cinéma Cirta, known to be owned by a Jew. Stones were thrown, glass was broken, and several shouts of "À bas les juifs!" (Down with the Jews!) were heard. A passerby in a car had his windshield broken, and the police arrested two men after breaking up the crowd. Late that night, between 11:00 and 11:30 p.m., two groups of Muslims marched through the faubourg d'el Kantara and in the *quartier réservé* (neighborhood with legal brothels) crying: "Long live France! Down with the Jews!" They did not resist when the police intervened to disperse them. The next day, however, the police feared the worst. For the first time, the police felt that a portion of the Muslim population had turned against the Jews, and they reported rumors that May 27 had been named as the day for undertaking "a violent action against the Jewish quarter."[16] On that day, noted the police reports, fifteen purchases of revolvers were made by Jews.

In this tense atmosphere, one can understand the nervousness felt by Constantine's Jews at Bendjelloul's decision to go ahead with his speaking tour of the department, a move that was designed to drum up support for his planned return trip to Paris in June. The tour began on May 27, the very day around which so many rumors were swirling, with a lecture before four hundred followers in Batna. Bendjelloul continued his bid for the attention of the Muslim population on May 30 with a lecture at the Cercle d'Union in Constantine attended by two hundred "elected officials, notables, tradesmen, and railway workers." These appearances were followed by speeches in Souk Ahras (June 1: "one thousand listeners"), Djidjelli (June 2: "400 *indigènes*"), Bougie (Béjaïa, also June 2), Saint-Arnaud (El-Eulma, June 4, "300 *indigènes*"), and Sétif (June 4). Eventually his run of speaking engagements included stopovers in Canrobert (Oum el Bouaghi), Aïn-Beïda, Sédrata, Montesquieu (M'daourouch), Bône (Annaba), El-Kseur, Sidi-Aich, Akbou, Bordj Bou Arréridj, and Châteaudun-du-Rhumel.[17] The police reports on these speeches indicate that they followed a similar format: Bendjelloul recounted (in French or in Arabic, depending on the context) the story of his encounter with France's most prominent political leaders and the support they offered for reforming Algeria's electoral laws during his participation in Viollette's jubilee in Dreux. Most troubling to the colonial administrators, Bendjelloul reported an encounter with a French senator who advised the Muslim leader that "a wet-nurse only gives suck to her infant when he demands it."[18] Bendjelloul seemed to welcome the strange familial metaphor, which stressed the closeness of the relationship that bound Algeria to France even as it perpetuated patronizing and infantilizing stereotypes about North African society in relation to French civilization. Nowhere in any of the reports on this speaking tour, however, did the police mention Bendjelloul making antisemitic appeals.

In spite of the apocalyptic rumors and the potentially provocative political campaign mounted by Bendjelloul during the same week, nothing dramatic happened on May 27, 1933. The police intervened quickly when crowds began to form and barred anybody from entering the Jewish neighborhood. Over the next few days, while Bendjelloul continued his tour, other Muslim elected officials worked alongside Jewish leaders in the city to calm their respective constituencies. On May 30, the mufti of Constantine engaged a public crier to announce a lecture at the Great Mosque on the rue Nationale. Three hundred people responded to the call, and the mufti used the occasion to call on Muslims in the city to maintain a skeptical attitude toward the many circulating rumors. He counseled them to remain calm and to avoid gathering in groups, especially in the central neighborhoods. He noted that Jewish leaders had advised their own community to do the same.

At the end of the month, as the city began to return to a more normal routine, Bourette, the chief of departmental security, summarized the lessons that the authorities in Constantine felt they had learned from the agitation of the spring of 1933:

- The antisemitic movement in the city had no obvious or unified leadership.
- The incidents emerged from accidental, chance encounters and in each case had their origins in an act that engendered reprisals.
- The foreign population was not involved (the Italian surnames of some settler antisemites had been the subject of some concern, but Bourette reported that the individuals were from naturalized families of long residence).
- The Muslim population as a whole did not get involved until two Muslims were injured in attacks on them by Jews.
- The relative restraint of the Muslim population was due to the effective leadership of the Muslim notables who called for calm.

- The calm of the city had been only momentarily disturbed, and the police were effective in their interventions, especially in barring access to the Jewish quarter.
- The five days of disturbances had been prolonged by "storytellers" (*raconteurs*) who circulated unceasingly in the city's streets, "distorting and amplifying the most insignificant incidents, and failing that, inventing them completely."[19]

He concluded his report by saying that there was no reason to think that these tensions were completely dissipated, and that it was impossible to predict whether this agitation would recur in the near future. Notably absent from this list of conclusions was the disturbing evidence that the accumulation of incidents between Muslims and Jews in the preceding years had created a situation that was ripe for manipulation by provocateurs. For the first time in the interwar years, the disturbances of May 1933 had witnessed an evolution from demonstrations by anti-Jewish groups among the settler population to open violence between groups that saw themselves as defending the interests of "Muslims" and "Jews." There is no evidence that Bendjelloul's political campaign explicitly aired the grievances of his constituency in these terms, but the convergence of his political activities with a worsening climate in the city clearly made it easier for individuals to find multiple targets for their growing frustrations.

The threats of explosive violence dissipated rapidly after the police interventions of May 27, and Bendjelloul's campaign to be seated on CIAM ended in anticlimactic failure the next month. In June, he led a delegation of Muslim elected officials to Paris, ostensibly to meet with members of the government and to press for official recognition of the Fédération as the legitimate representatives of Algeria's Muslim population. Expecting a public relations coup, Bendjelloul was instead humiliated when the ministers refused to meet with him—he was left waiting in the anteroom of their offices before being told that he would not be granted an audience. He returned to Constantine in July with his prestige tarnished. Bendjelloul and his associates initially provoked a mass resignation of Muslim elected officials in Algeria to protest the government's treatment of the delegation, but the effort was mostly symbolic. After an intervention by Senator Paul Cuttoli, the FEMC's resignations were withdrawn, and the president of the Fédération des élus de Constantine worked to shore up his support through local appearances throughout the department.[20] In the ensuing months, he reestablished his authority among the members of the Fédération, and he used its General

Assembly on November 20, 1933, to voice his strong support for Maurice Viollette's proposal to grant parliamentary representation for Algeria's Muslim colonial subjects.[21]

Having helped to create the space where Muslim elected officials could act in the public realm, the French colonial administration could think of no other way to limit their public participation than to aim at the figure of Bendjelloul himself. The prefect asked the Office of Departmental Security to prepare a report on Bendjelloul's medical practice, hoping to find incriminating information about the neglect of his patients.[22] This monitoring of Bendjelloul's professional life was accompanied by an intensive surveillance of his political activities. Local sub-prefects throughout the department of Constantine compiled lists of his associates in every town, noting carefully the sites where meetings took place, especially the *cafés maures*. In such cases, the prefecture found its authority subverted, as the licensing of the *cafés maures* was considered a valuable patronage tool by the administration, and they often awarded titles to such cafés to Algerian Muslims who had been in the military as a form of compensation for loyal service.[23] When the sub-prefect of Philippeville discovered that Bendjelloul's principal lieutenant in the city was a grocer named Belkacem Abada, and that Abada's brother Ahcène ran a *café maure* licensed to their mother, the widow of a former *cavalier de la sous-prefecture*, the sub-prefect recommended closing the café as a warning to others. The reason: Bendjelloul was considering inviting Belkacem Abada to accompany him to Paris as a part of a new delegation to meet with members of the government.[24] There was clearly more than one way to foreclose the emergence of a Muslim public sphere in Algeria.

Following the FEMC general assembly in November 1933, Bendjelloul's public campaign for government recognition suddenly went quiet. In early December, he took several trips to Algiers, ostensibly to support the candidature of several officials running for office, but his political adversaries began to whisper that his silence had been bought by the governor-general in exchange for some unknown favor.[25] Records of conversations between police informants and members of Bendjelloul's circle indicate that the Fédération may have experienced disagreements over the correct strategy to undertake during these weeks. Some appear to have felt that they had no choice but to wait patiently for a change of government. Having been rebuffed by officials in Paris, there was no use in continuing to demand recognition of Bendjelloul's leadership until a more favorable government was in place. Others feared that assuming a low profile would damage their standing with their Muslim constituency, who had come to expect more confrontational representatives.[26]

The Parisian authorities took their cues from Governor-General Jules Carde's office in Algiers, and it was Carde's opposition to Bendjelloul that prevented the latter from getting a hearing from either the CIAM or Interior Minister Camille Chautemps during his visit to Paris in June 1933. Chautemps retained his post as interior minister under Albert Sarraut's government of October 1933, and Chautemps himself became the head of government after another ministerial shuffle in November. Given the unlikelihood that Chautemps would change his mind about meeting with him during these months, Bendjelloul may well have sought some sort of understanding with the governor-general's office in late 1933 and early 1934. But the fall of the Chautemps government in the midst of the Stavisky affair at the end of January 1934, and the eruption of right-wing violence on February 6, led to the formation of a new government by Gaston Doumergue. This change of faces at the top opened up new possibilities for Bendjelloul and the Fédération. By March his colleagues at the FEMC and he were once more talking about forming a new delegation of Muslim elected officials to seek a meeting with representatives of the new government in Paris.

The changing political circumstances apparently put some pressure on the governor-general's office as well. In late February 1934, Carde announced the creation of a special commission for the "study of improvements that could be made in the material and moral situation of Native Populations," and he corresponded with the prefect of Constantine about choosing Muslim notables to sit on it. This decision was clearly an attempt to defuse Bendjelloul's initiative by establishing a body that could act as the voice of Algeria's colonial subjects in deliberations about reform without being under the control of either Bendjelloul or the Fédération. At least one exchange of letters between Carde and the prefect of Constantine spoke of the need to recruit candidates for such seats who were not part of Bendjelloul's entourage. At the same time, however, the governor-general took steps to co-opt Bendjelloul by offering him a seat as well.[27] Sensing a trap, Bendjelloul refused to join the commission. After the humiliation of the previous summer, it was important to him that any such recognition come in the form of an official recognition of the Fédération as a whole rather than a reward for himself as an individual.

Bendjelloul nevertheless persisted in the hope that a workable agreement could be reached with the new government after the third week of March 1934, when the Chamber of Deputies' Committee on the Colonies appointed Jean Montigny, a deputy from the Sarthe, to look into the need for a possible investigation into social and political unrest in Algerian cities. As soon as word arrived of the parliament's actions, Bendjelloul sent a warm telegram to the president of the Committee on the Colonies, thanking him for the National Assembly's interest in the cause of "native Algerians" and their evident desire "to listen to their representatives." The telegram also begged the deputy to ignore the parliamentary delegation from Algeria who exaggerated the extent of Bendjelloul's quarrel with the governor-general's office and stated that "all misunderstandings have entirely dissipated."[28] This parliamentary initiative sparked a new attempt by the FEMC to create a delegation of officials who would meet with Montigny to press their case for a reform of the electoral laws.[29]

Through its routine surveillance procedures, the prefect intercepted Bendjelloul's telegram and forwarded it to Governor-General Carde's office. It is likely that Carde contacted Montigny, who in any case had no interest in serving as a sounding board for Bendjelloul's political claims. Montigny immediately denied that he had any intention of meeting with representatives of Algeria's Muslims, and claimed instead that he would simply pay a courtesy visit with the Governor-General in Algiers as he returned from a fact-finding trip to Morocco.[30] Bendjelloul and his supporters at the FEMC were dismayed by Montigny's backpedaling but decided to insist on a meeting with him during his stopover in Algiers. Warned by the prefect of Constantine of Bendjelloul's intentions, Carde was able to intercede, and when Bendjelloul wrote him asking for a meeting with the parliamentary deputy, Carde's office was able to report that Montigny had already left town.[31]

This repeated failure to gain a hearing from Parisian political figures evidently encouraged Bendjelloul to take a more public and oppositional stand once more.[32] The opening salvo of his renewed activity came in a letter to the prefect of Constantine, dated April 3, 1934. Written in the form of a *"cahier des doléances"* (list of grievances), the letter contained twenty-two numbered paragraphs, enumerating both the larger social and economic injustices faced by Bendjelloul's constituency, and the political injustices perpetrated against the Fédération and its members by the colonial administration since the failed attempt to meet with the authorities in Paris the previous summer.[33] The first numbered paragraph sought to portray the FEMC as the agent of modernity in Algeria, arguing that the administration's hostility toward land reform defied all reason: "It would be logical to move with the times and to adapt [agricultural practices] to the era in which we live." The letter protested against the brutality of tax collection, which was often accompanied by forced labor, threats of imprisonment, and the seizure of goods. The letter also highlighted the severe effects of the administration's habit of removing water from reservoirs set aside for the use of *indigènes* and complained about the practice of using charity as patronage and of allowing settlers to encroach on lands previously deemed to be open to common use. The bulk of the letter, however, focused on the relentless harassment of Bendjelloul's own organization by the administration, the proliferation of fines and minor charges against the members of the Fédération for petty violations, the confiscation of hunting permits from those who spoke out at public meetings, the closing of *cafés maures* used as meeting places, and the corruption of the electoral process.

Once again, Bendjelloul's renewed campaign in the spring of 1934 took place against the background of an increasingly polarized political atmosphere. The local factions in Constantine once more attempted to take advantage of events happening elsewhere in France and Europe in order to increase their leverage and profile at home. The violent clashes between militant right-wing leagues and the police in Paris on February 6 had briefly threatened the stability of the national government and elicited a strong reaction among leftist organizations who feared a fascist coup. In the months that followed, the Croix de feu section in Constantine attempted to capitalize on the disappointment of those who hoped that the right might topple the government in Paris by staging more frequent public meetings and attempting to increase their membership.

The political left in France also stepped up its organizational activities following the violence of February 6, and this was also true of local political groups on the left in Constantine. Local representatives of the Ligue des droits de l'homme (LDH), the Socialist Party (SFIO), the Confédération générale du travail (CGT, France's largest labor federation), and the Communist Party (PCF), along with other smaller groups such as the Association internationale contre l'antisémitisme, met on March 16 in Constantine at the Maison de l'Ouvrier to found a new pan-leftist association, the Vigilance Committee for the Defense of Public Liberties. According to the police reports, about seventy people were present at this meeting. They signed a resolution calling for the dissolution of all armed paramilitary groups and the presentation of a unified "entente" among all the members of the left in order to oppose the forces of dictatorship in France.[34] A few of Constantine's more prominent Jewish citizens were involved in this effort, including Adolphe Sultan, a lawyer, member of the municipal council, and the president of the local section of the League of the Rights of Man.

There is little evidence that shows a significant participation of Algerian Muslims in leftist political movements—or indeed, any political movement other than that led by Bendjelloul—during this crucial period before the riots of August 1934. In spite of the colonial administration's eagerness to connect pan-Islamist movements abroad with the threat of international communism, there are relatively few reports of organized activity by Communists that reveal more than a token level of participation by Muslim colonial subjects. The most active recruiter for the Communist Party in Constantine was Lucien Sportisse, a teacher in the city since the 1920s, who was also Jewish. When Sportisse had attempted to organize a sports club affiliated with the Communist Party in the faubourg d'el Kantara on August 31, 1933, the police reported that only seventeen young people attended the meeting, "14 israelites and 3 Muslims, aged 17 to 23 years." Those attending received a sheet of paper with the words of the "Internationale," and Sportisse talked of the need to organize the unemployed in Constantine. The police report noted that the three Muslims in attendance "wore berets, in an evident attempt to not be noticed."[35]

Bendjelloul did not neglect the possibility of allies on the left, but this was less to mobilize his supporters than it was to search for interlocutors who could support his program for electoral reform. When Jules Moch, a Socialist deputy from the Drôme, passed through the department on a trip to investigate the calls for reform in Algeria, Bendjelloul took the opportunity to meet with him. He escorted Moch to Bône in the company of a large entourage of the Fédération's most active members. While in Bône, the Fédération presented Moch with a dossier of their political claims, which the Socialist deputy accepted, claiming that he would work toward their political success in parliament. That evening Moch spoke before a mixed audience at the Municipal Theater in Bône, saying "the investigation that I have undertaken in Algeria revealed to me that French justice has two different standards here, following the race of the accused."[36]

Given the extent to which organized political groups in Constantine were mobilizing in an atmosphere of mutual antagonism, while Bendjelloul seemed to be reaching out to other oppositional forces in the region, it is not surprising that the authorities reacted with concern when Bendjelloul appeared together at a rally with 'Abd al-Hamid Ben Badis on May 16, 1934. This meeting was the last significant public gathering of Muslim leaders before the riots of August 3–5. Bendjelloul and Ben Badis orchestrated the rally carefully to show both their respect for the Third Republic and their displeasure with the ways the government solicited the opinions of Algerian Muslims on the Interministerial Commission on Muslim Affairs. On May 15 the FEMC sent a telegram to Prime Minister Doumergue, signed by a group that included a wounded war veteran, a landowner, and a shoemaker.[37] Bendjelloul was disappointed the next day, however, when three of the eleven Muslim municipal councilors in Constantine refused to sign the telegram, and a fourth could not be reached. According to the police report, this lack of unanimity in the FEMC led Bendjelloul to call for a public meeting on May 16 in the hopes that a wide turnout would show the depth of his support among the population.

The public meeting had originally been planned for an indoor location at the Cercle de l'Union, an auditorium that could hold a thousand people. By 9 a.m., however, so many people had gathered in front of the hall that the organizers moved the gathering to an outdoor location across the gorge in the woods of Mansourah, near the faubourg d'el Kantara. This site, a natural amphitheater known as "Les Pins" or *la cuvette* (the basin) in French (*boutouil* in Arabic), thus came to be associated with Bendjelloul's new style of mobilization on behalf of Algerian Muslims and their demands for political inclusion. Bendjelloul expressed some concern about the move, worrying that provocateurs might mix with the crowd as they made their way across the bridge to the clearing at Les Pins.[38] Urging the assembled people to maintain a peaceful demeanor, Bendjelloul accompanied them across the bridge. The police estimated the crowd to be between twenty-five hundred and three thousand. Other estimates were even higher.[39] This meeting, only eleven weeks before the August riots, was among the largest public gatherings Bendjelloul had ever organized—and the site, Les Pins, would also play a role in the disturbances of August 5.

At Les Pins, Bendjelloul and the members of his federation improvised a podium, and Ben Badis spoke first, opening the meeting with a recitation of several verses from the Quran. The religious leader began with a reminder that Islam was affiliated with no political party. The government tolerated the activities of Ben Badis's Association of Muslim Clerics under the condition that they refrained from overtly political activities, and his statement served as a reminder of the association's essentially religious and cultural role. Perhaps just as important, the statement served as a public reminder to the audience that no one individual, including Bendjelloul himself, could claim to speak for the interests of all Muslims.[40] Ben Badis went on to attack the authority of CIAM, and stated that the commission's members had no legitimacy in any of the three main areas of their activity—overseeing Islamic religious practices, the teaching of the Quran, and the arabophone press. His argument here was perfectly consonant with the stated principles of the Third Republic: it was up to the Muslim population to designate their own qualified representatives. He reminded the audience that the mission of the Association of Muslim Clerics was an educational one, to teach religious principles and the Arabic language. Ben Badis protested vehemently against the closing of Muslim schools under the pretext that they had not observed newly imposed hygienic standards, and he noted bitterly the decision by the government to treat Arabic as a "foreign" language. This measure meant that the Arabic press in Algeria fell under the stricter censorship laws that pertained to foreign languages, allowing local administrators to ban issues of Arabic-language newspapers in Algeria arbitrarily. Ben Badis then gestured to the members of the FEMC and said, "It is through them that we make our complaints known to the Government. They are our spokesmen, and we count on them to protect our religious rights. We have confidence in the future, and we count on the wisdom of the Government to whom we remain faithful servants[;] let us hope that our liberties will always be safeguarded."[41]

When Bendjelloul himself took the podium, he repeated a similar attack on the legitimacy of the CIAM, going so far as to suggest that the "native delegates" seated on the commission had taken payments to ensure their docility. Like Ben Badis, he couched his critique in terms that were completely consonant with the republican values of representation and freedom of expression and suggested that the colonial administration had perverted these values by rigging the CIAM and excluding any Muslim representatives who might disagree with the governor-general's office. The result of this situation was that none of the five "native delegates" on the commission protested when Governor-General Carde banned Cheikh Tayeb El Okbi, an important member of the Association of Muslim Clerics, from preaching at mosques in Algeria, along with a list of fifteen other Muslim teachers. Bendjelloul's speech thus returned the favor that Ben Badis had bestowed on him by lending his support to the Fédération with his presence at the public meeting. Bendjelloul's support for El Okbi presented the possibility of a unified front of Muslim elected officials and religious leaders, who up to that point had been more cautious about positioning themselves in the political realm.

The meeting at Les Pins was closely watched by the colonial authorities, but for some weeks afterward there was a lull in Bendjelloul's activities. In all likelihood he was waiting for the fall to begin his campaign to be elected to the *délégations financières*, the highest elected position available to a Muslim political figure such as himself under the terms of the Jonnart Law. The election for the *délégations financières* was scheduled for January 1935, but Bendjelloul's preparations for his campaign were interrupted by the outbreak of violence between Muslims and Jews on the weekend of August 3–5, 1934. On the evening of August 4 and again during the day on August 5, Algerian Muslim colonial subjects attacked the businesses and homes of Constantine's Jewish population, and the police and military failed to implement the security measures that had prevented an outbreak of violence in the face of known provocations during the previous summer. The police also knew about the atmosphere of provocation in 1934. They either did not care, or they underestimated its potential effects. In the meantime, a group of conspirators working with Mohamed El Maadi of the Third Zouaves Regiment had apparently taken note of the repeated rehearsals for crisis. On the morning of August 5, they were ready.

FIGURE 1. View of Constantine taken from the faubourg d'el Kantara in the early twentieth century, showing the El Kantara bridge and the gorge cut by the Rhumel river.
Source: Chronicle / Alamy Stock Photo.

FIGURE 2. Rioters in Constantine on August 5, 1934. The site is the boulevard Berteaux near the place de la Brèche, in front of the Cinéma Nunez. The figure on the left, brandishing a knife, appears to be simultaneously inciting others and performing for the unknown photographer. The shadows of the figures on the left seem to indicate that the photo was taken sometime before noon, close to the moment that the Halimi household was invaded several streets away at about 11:30 a.m. Eight people were murdered in the Halimi apartment.
Source: Musée d'art et d'histoire du Judaïsme.

FIGURE 3. Fire in the Remblai, on the edge of the old city, August 5, 1934. The shantytown in the foreground stands in stark contrast to the newer apartment buildings of the European suburb of Coudiat Aty at the crest of the slope.
Source: Musée d'art et d'histoire du Judaïsme.

FIGURE 4. Attack on the autobus carrying Elie Guedj on the route de Sétif, place Lamorcière, Constantine, at approximately noon, August 5.
Source: Musée d'art et d'histoire du Judaïsme.

FIGURE 5. Soldiers on the rue des Zouaves in Constantine after the riot on August 5. The arched door on the left is the entrance to the building containing the homes of the Attali and Attal families, where five people were killed at around 1 p.m.
Source: Musée d'art et d'histoire du Judaïsme.

FIGURE 6. Dining room in the Attali apartment on the rue des Zouaves, after the riot of August 5.
Source: Musée d'art et d'histoire du Judaïsme.

FIGURE 7. Fire on the rue Nationale in the afternoon of August 5.
Source: Musée d'art et d'histoire du Judaïsme.

Figure 8. Soldiers accompanying Jewish victims of attacks to a first-aid station as European residents of Constantine look on, August 5.
Source: Musée d'art et d'histoire du Judaïsme.

Figure 9. Family members of victims among the coffins during the collective funeral at Constantine's Jewish cemetery, August 8, 1934.
Source: Musée d'art et d'histoire du Judaïsme.

FIGURE 10. Mohamed El Maadi at a restaurant on the rue de la Huchette in Paris's Latin Quarter during the German occupation, sometime in 1943 or 1944.
Source: Archives Nationales de France, Pierrefitte-sur-Seine, Z/6/593.

Part 3

A Riot in France

CHAPTER 8

Friday and Saturday, August 3–4, 1934

When did the events that led to the deaths of twenty-eight people in Constantine and several outlying towns between August 3 and 5, 1934, begin? Should one mention the shooting of Léon Mimoun on July 24? Late that evening, two men identified in the police reports as "natives" and "habitual criminals" were crossing the bridge across the gorge at Sidi M'Cid when they came upon a Jewish family—Maurice Halimi, his wife, and two children—taking the evening air. A quarrel broke out, and Derradji Bourenane pulled out a revolver and fired once, striking a passerby, Léon Mimoun, in the leg. Bourenane and his friend disappeared into the darkness, but the police tracked them down the next day. They confessed and led the police to the hidden revolver. The police charged Bourenane and his friend with attempted murder; and Jacques Cauro, the chief of the city's Police Mobile (the investigative unit of the local force), filed his report on the incident with the governor-general's office on Monday, July 30. Six days after that, at the height of the violence in Constantine, eight people would be murdered in the home of Maurice Halimi's brother, Alphonse.[1] Jacques Cauro would lead the investigation into their deaths.

Should one mention a poster plastered on the city walls by the Croix de feu the next day? The poster proclaimed the group's rejection of all political parties and called for supporters to rally to the right-wing organization:

FOR PUBLIC SAFETY

We demand:

The punishment of those responsible, no matter how high they are
The prohibition of secret societies and street violence
The separation of powers, and silence from political parties
The struggle against financial speculation and increases in the cost of
    living.

WE DO NOT BELIEVE

In deflation [of currency] without lower prices
In punishing the guilty without punishing those responsible
In a reform of the constitution that emerges from disorder.

THE NATION DEMANDS A TRUCE
IT WANTS PEACE
NOT FOR THE POLITICIANS
BUT IN SPITE OF THEM

French people, nothing separates you
Unite, Organize
Reject the freemasons, the corrupters, the party hacks.

Join the
POPULAR AND INDEPENDENT MOVEMENT
of the CROIX DE FEU![2]

The poster displayed the Croix de feu's conviction that the political system in
Algeria and France was irrevocably broken. It was a call for popular vengeance
against shadowy personalities pulling the strings behind the scenes in political and economic life. It did not mention France's Jewish population, but the
coded language about financial speculation and secret societies had been a
staple of the anti-Jewish press in France and Algeria since the Dreyfus affair
of the 1890s. This poster appeared on the walls of Constantine two days after
Jacques Cauro filed his report on the shooting of Léon Mimoun and two days
before the first outbreak of violence on Friday, August 3.

The dispute that was universally seen as the cause of the violence of
August 3–5, 1934, in Constantine differed little from earlier incidents except
for one thing: it happened at a mosque.[3] On Friday evening, August 3, a

Jewish member of the Third Zouave Regiment, Elie Khalifa, was walking to his home on the rue Combes after a few drinks in a café when he became involved in a dispute with several Muslim men who were readying themselves for the evening prayer. A tailor like his father before him, Khalifa was forty-five, a decorated soldier, and a family man, the father of five children.[4] He was an unlikely figure to become a flashpoint in an ethno-religious conflict between Muslims and Jews. He was born in 1889, the son of Messaoud Khalifat and Melki Oureida. Messaoud died in 1894 when Elie was five. Locals believed that Elie's mother lived with a Muslim man after her husband's death and had two more children who were raised as Muslims. Rumors in the neighborhood held that this Muslim man was Elie Khalifa's real father. Leading members of Constantine's Jewish community repeated these stories in the aftermath of the riots.[5] If true, this gossip about Khalifa points to a complicated neighborhood story involving masculine honor and community integrity in a family whose ties straddled the social boundaries that separated Muslims from Jews in the city.

Khalifa and his family were well known to the men who came every day to pray at the Sidi Lakhdar Mosque. To get to the front door of the Khalifas' apartment it was necessary to traverse a narrow passage and pass by a window of the mosque. When open, this window allowed people in the street to look into the room where men would wash themselves before prayers. On August 3, Khalifa confronted several men through the iron grill that separated the window from the street. The men in the mosque later said that he interrupted their ablutions by calling them savages and insulting their religion. "God curse your prophet, your religion, your notables and you all!" he reportedly shouted.[6] A man in the mosque, Ali ben Ahmed Bettiche, later reported that he was just leaving the chamber when he heard insults coming from the window: "God curse your religion, your mosque, your prayer, your Prophet!"

Khalifa's own version of the story was somewhat different. He left the barracks of the Third Zouave Regiment at 6 p.m., stopped by a tailor's shop in the rue des Zouaves, and then proceeded to the Bar Victor, where he drank with the bartender before meeting his wife and children for the walk to their apartment. As they passed the grill of the mosque, he noticed several naked men washing themselves. He quickly took his family home, and then returned to ask them to be more careful in displaying their nudity in front of his wife. According to him, one of the men called him a "dirty Jew" and said it was all the same to him what Khalifa thought about their actions. Khalifa stated that he replied "Dirty wog!" and returned to his home.[7]

A Jewish neighbor of Khalifa, Binhas Zerbib, gave another version of this encounter. Zerbib came home to the rue Combes at about 8:20 p.m. and met Khalifa in the street before their building. Asking him what he was doing there, Khalifa stated that "the natives are washing themselves and showing their sexual parts to our women." At that, one of the men inside the ablutions chamber spoke up, saying that "we are not in your house and we always wash ourselves here." Khalifa then became very angry and called the man a "dirty Arab." The man responded in kind, calling Khalifa a "dirty Jew."[8]

In a newspaper article about the incident the next day, La Dépêche de Constantine reported that Khalifa had entered the interior of the mosque.[9] This was untrue, but the rumor may have contributed later to public anger over his insults. Equally inflammatory were the reports that Khalifa had urinated on the wall of the mosque, though he denied having done so, and this was later supported by Binhas Zerbib. Muslim witnesses nevertheless later stated that they saw him urinating. Ahmed Bendjelloul, the khaim of the mosque, reported that he had come downstairs to the ablutions chamber in time to see Khalifa, whom he knew to be a neighbor, urinating through the open grill.[10] Mouloud ben Khodja Bentounsi, a milk merchant who had arrived late for the prayers, also reported Khalifa's words: "If you're not happy, I piss on you." The men in the ablutions chamber told Khalifa to leave and accused him of being drunk. He shouted back at them, "I am not drunk, I have my full intelligence, I am a military officer!"[11] Khalifa later insisted that he cursed them only after they had started it by cursing the Jews. He stated that he had had only four anisettes and was not drunk.[12]

Incensed by Khalifa's profanation of a sacred space, a group of angry men gathered in front of the mosque after he returned to his apartment. Ahmed Bendjelloul and the mufti Mouloud Benelmouhoub attempted to calm the growing crowd. Their efforts at first seemed successful, but by 9:30 p.m. a new group gathered in front of Khalifa's building, and somebody in the crowd threw a stone at a window. Khalifa's wife suddenly appeared, cursed the crowd down below, and slammed the shutters closed. One witness claimed that Khalifa himself threw three bricks down to the street below.[13] The crowd—now approaching fifty people—began to shout and throw more stones.[14] The mufti again came out of the mosque and tried to quiet the crowd, and three police agents attempted to enter the building to speak to Khalifa. Eventually, the police and the mufti managed to disperse the people who had gathered in the street.

Sometime between ten and eleven that evening, however, a much larger crowd of nearly two thousand people, armed with clubs, sticks, knives, and stones, came through the rue Vieux-Sidi-Moussa, the rue Bleue, and the rue Combes to the place des Galettes and the small place in front of the mosque.[15] The crowd's intention was ostensibly to move through the Jewish quarter, but they found their way blocked by the police, who were soon supported by two patrols of *tirailleurs algériens* that kept an eye on the neighborhood cafés and brothels every evening.[16] These patrols were small, however, only seven men in total, and the situation deteriorated rapidly. Meanwhile, people from the crowd seized and beat several unfortunate passersby, and debris rained down on the demonstrators' heads from the apartments above, including bricks and hot cinders swept from stoves. Shots were fired on the adjacent place des Galettes. The police reports stated that the gunfire came from inside the besieged apartment buildings. Witness statements later collected by Muslim elected officials claimed that Jewish police officers had fired on the crowd, naming two in particular—agents Elbaz and Drai. A third, Allouche, was named later, after he was hospitalized with injuries caused by a razor.[17] The mufti continued to try to calm the angry demonstrators, and he was also joined by the city's best-known Muslim notable and elected official, Mohamed Bendjelloul.[18]

Constantine's police chief, René Miquel, was in Algiers when the trouble began. Mayor Émile Morinaud was at his summer residence at Duquesne (Kaous) near Djidjelli, and Constantine's recently appointed prefect, Jean-Marie Laban, was on the other side of the Mediterranean in France. Such absences were no surprise in the first weeks of August, but the fact remains that the town's principal political and administrative leaders were all elsewhere when the trouble began, and the first decisions about how to contain the situation were made by their subordinates. With Miquel gone, Commissioner Lucien Fusero, the station chief of the second arrondissement (which included the Jewish quarter), assumed control of the city's police forces. Fusero later reported that when he heard of the growing disturbance on the place des Galettes, he went to see for himself, accompanied by several police agents.[19] Finding his forces quickly overwhelmed by a crowd "coming from the prostitutes' quarter," he asked for reinforcements, and soon a squad of twenty-five soldiers from the Third Zouaves Regiment arrived along with the secretary-general of the prefecture, Joseph Landel, and the director of the prefecture's office of departmental security, Henri Coquelin.[20] When Landel arrived by taxi in his prefect's uniform, his appearance was greeted by cries of "Vive la France!" coming from the demonstrators.[21] This significant indicator of the state of mind of at least some of the Muslim demonstrators was later downplayed in press reports and public accounts, though some Jewish commentators later noted these patriotic cries as proof of their belief that Muslims in the city were responding to an anti-Jewish sentiment that was widely shared by members of the European settler population in Constantine.[22]

After an hour or so, the police, soldiers, and civil authorities cleared the place des Galettes of demonstrators with the help of Bendjelloul and the mufti. Not until the additional squad of Zouaves arrived after 12 a.m., along with a detachment of gendarmes, did the troops succeed in clearing the rest of the old city. Several incidents occurred sometime after midnight, however, that would have significant repercussions later. Between 12 and 1 a.m., two European men, identified by an employee at the prefecture only as "Lanxade" and "Lauffenberger," came upon the body of an injured Muslim man at the place where the rue Caraman changed its name to the rue de France. Belkacem Boutarane was twenty years old and a resident of the Remblai. He had been shot in the stomach. Lanxade and Lauffenberger took him to receive medical attention, and news of his injury spread rapidly through the city. The precariousness of his condition in the coming days was an important aggravating factor driving the anger of Muslims in Constantine after the evening of August 3.

Assuming that the original report's use of surnames meant that these two individuals were already known to the prefecture, it is probable that "Lanxade" was Ernest Lanxade, the anti-Jewish troublemaker in Constantine who had been an editor of *La Tribune* in the early 1920s (see chapter 4) and whose new anti-Jewish paper, *Le Tam Tam*, had been appearing weekly in the city since 1927. "Lauffenberger" must have been Roger Joseph Lauffenberger, the proprietor of a photography studio in Constantine founded decades earlier by his father Georges Lauffenberger. Roger Joseph Lauffenberger was the photographer responsible for many of the most dramatic images that we now possess of the riots of August 5, 1934, including some of those reproduced in this book. If these speculations about the identity of these men are correct, it would be interesting to know what relation, if any, Lauffenberger had with this known anti-Jewish provocateur, and what exactly they were doing after midnight in the rue Caraman on August 3. Unfortunately, the deposition that is the source of the reference to Lanxade and Lauffenberger appears to have been mislaid or removed from the documents assembled by the investigating commission after the riots.[23]

The shooting of Belkacem Boutarane after midnight on the night of August 3–4 would hang over the city the next day as the leaders of the Muslim and Jewish communities struggled to prevent further violence. Their efforts were also made more difficult by a further incident on the evening of August 3 that involved Mohamed Bendjelloul, the city's most important Muslim political figure. While the police were still clearing the streets between the rue Combes and the place des Galettes, a Jewish man, Ruben Robert Halimi, sent his son Charles out to drop some letters in a postbox, unaware of what was happening only a few streets away. A group of men stopped Charles as he passed a café and beat him. An inspector from the Sûreté, Boudjema Gassab, arrested one of the attackers, Boufar Salah, and brought him to the police station on the place des Galettes. When the young Charles Halimi went home and told his father what had happened, Ruben Halimi immediately went to the police station to see the young man who had been arrested. Halimi asked Boufar Salah why he had participated in the beating of his son, and the young man said that he thought Charles was a *roumi* (dialect slang for "European"—literally, a "Christian"). Believing that there was nothing to be gained by pressing charges, Ruben Halimi asked the police to release the young man. By chance, Mohamed Bendjelloul was present in the police station when this exchange took place, and he praised Ruben Halimi for his generosity. A few minutes later, however, as Bendjelloul was attempting to clear the crowd from the place des Galettes, he and the arresting inspector Gassab had a violent exchange in front of the police station that resulted in Bendjelloul striking Gassab twice, bloodying his face. Later accounts differed as to the precise words that were exchanged between the two men. Bendjelloul claimed that Gassab called him a "liar" and "anti-French." Another witness claimed that Gassab told Bendjelloul that "your electors shouldn't be here."[24]

Secretary-General Landel and Constantine's general prosecutor Cura were both present in the street in front of the station as this unfolded, and they decided to arrest Bendjelloul, who was taken into custody by Fusero, the station chief. After a brief meeting at the place des Galettes police station with the prosecutor, the Muslim leader was charged with striking an officer. A trial date was set for late September, and Bendjelloul was released and escorted to his nearby home by Commissioner Jean Besse, chief of Constantine's third district station, and several gendarmes. The fact that the most prominent Muslim elected official in the region had been arrested and was facing charges of interfering with the police weighed heavily over the mood in Constantine in the coming weeks because of the inevitable association between Bendjelloul's energetic political campaign of the previous year and the outbreak of violence in the city.

On the evening of August 3, nineteen people were injured severely enough to seek medical treatment, and five were hospitalized. Three Jewish police agents were injured, two of them severely. Ferdinand Sebah had been stabbed, and David Allouche was hospitalized after being clubbed. Twelve injured Muslim demonstrators were taken to the police commissariat of the second arrondissement.[25] Belkacem Boutarane, the Muslim man who had been shot in the stomach, was hospitalized in serious condition, his intestine perforated in seventeen places. He would linger on the edge of death for nearly three more weeks before dying on August 23. At least two other Muslim men were injured by gunshot wounds that same evening.[26] Meanwhile, Léonce Bensimon, attacked and beaten on the place de la Brèche, was taken to a clinic with a broken arm, broken ribs, and contusions on his head.[27] He was the brother of Lucien Bensimon, the lawyer who was one of the few Jewish war veterans who belonged to the local section of the Croix de feu in Constantine. Six storefronts of Jewish-owned jewelry stores had their windows broken that Friday evening. The violence of Friday night was soon overshadowed by the tragedy that took place two days later, but it is important to recognize that the shooting of Boutarane, the beating of Bensimon, the attack on Jewish property, and the numerous injuries suffered by both Muslims and Jews had a galvanizing effect on two populations who had each begun to think of themselves as the aggrieved party in an ongoing dispute. The arrest of Bendjelloul only aggravated this already inflammatory situation.

A report from the local gendarmes congratulated their troops for preventing the spread of violence to the nearby neighborhood of Cité Lellouche in Sidi-Mabrouk, where many Jewish families who had moved out of the central city now lived.[28] Meanwhile, during the night of Friday to Saturday, groups of Jewish men in the Jewish quarter of the old city began to organize the defense of their neighborhood, and this became the occasion for arguments with soldiers stationed in the streets outside their homes. As Lucien Fusero returned to the police station on the place des Galettes after 3 a.m., he encountered a car with broken windows carrying an administrator, Catoni, from nearby Mila. The administrator reported that the roads from Sétif and Philippeville were beset with groups of men stopping cars and throwing stones.[29] News of Khalifa's insult to Constantine's Muslim residents had spread quickly to the surrounding region.

The handwritten notes from the prefect's office on the morning of Saturday, August 4, indicate that Secretary-General Landel did not yet fear the worst. At one point he jotted in his pad: "If things do not completely calm down (even though the current situation would allow us to think that this is the case) ensure the protection of: the gasworks, the electric works, the Schell depots and other gasoline storage tanks."[30] Requests for police protection came in from the city's banks, the gunpowder storage building, and the train station. Landel contacted the postal authorities and instructed them to cancel package deliveries and to ensure that only Jewish mail carriers delivered to the Jewish quarter, and only Arab carriers to the Arab quarter. That afternoon, Fusero ordered that all public buildings, *cafés maures*, and dance halls be closed, along with the terraces of the city's cafés.[31] These were normal procedures—a similar plan had been implemented in May 1933. The rules were simple: secure the city's infrastructure, prohibit public gatherings, limit the movements of people, and minimize opportunities for conflict.

Landel's notes also indicate his preoccupation with the distribution of available forces: he noted that he had eight patrols of six men each within the walls of the old city, five patrols of ten men each in Sidi-Mabrouk, four more patrols of ten in Bellevue, and a single unit of ten in El Kantara—a total 148 soldiers, supplemented by 52 police agents in "sensitive quarters" and patrols of gendarmes in Mansara and in Bellevue that had remained in place over the night of August 3–4.[32] Meanwhile, Fusero and Commissioner Besse of the third district arrested Elie Khalifa and had him brought to the commissariat to make a statement. Since nothing allowed the police to detain him, they released him to the military authorities.[33]

Sporadic eruptions of anger on the streets during the day on Saturday revealed that the city was still tense. At the same time, a flurry of meetings took place, bringing members of the local political establishment together with police and military leaders. Lucien Fusero remained in charge of the police—Central Commissioner René Miquel left Algiers at midday and did not arrive in Constantine until 10:30 p.m. The meetings of local officials began early on Saturday morning as a group of Jewish and Muslim notables met at the house of Adolphe Sultan, a lawyer, municipal councilor, and the president of the local section of the League of the Rights of Man. Benjamin Zaoui, Sultan's Jewish colleague on the municipal council, spoke with several of their Muslim counterparts, Salah Améziane, Ammar Hammouche, Hamouda Ben Charad, Chabane Touam, and Mohamed Zerkine, all members of Bendjelloul's FEMC. The documents reveal little about what was said, but the fact that this meeting took place at all demonstrates that the leaders of the various communities in Constantine were not retreating to their respective corners. On the contrary, they were talking among themselves, reaching out to one another, and searching for a way out of a crisis that appeared to be in nobody's interest.

Together this group made their way first to the town hall and then to the prefecture, where they met Fusero, Secretary-General Landel of the prefecture, Émile Barkatz, who was the acting mayor in Morinaud's absence, and several other members of the municipal council, including Eugène Bourceret, Jules Valle, and Alfred Dournon. Henri Lellouche, the only Jewish elected official on Constantine's departmental council, joined them after making the rounds of the city's synagogues that morning. Lellouche and the grand rabbi of Constantine, Sidi Fredj Halimi, called on the Jewish population to remain calm and avoid any provocation.[34] Mayor Morinaud telephoned from his summerhouse that morning, instructing Commissioner Fusero "to speak, in his name, to Muslim elected officials and native notables."[35] Fusero and Landel sent out word that they would convene a formal meeting between Jewish and Muslim elected officials in Landel's office at 11 a.m.[36] The same handwritten notes from the prefecture record that Fusero had already spoken to Lellouche and Barkatz, who both insisted that the Jewish population should remain in place in their quarter and not be evacuated.[37]

During the meeting at the prefecture, the assembled figures pledged to cooperate in spreading a message of social peace. There were moments of tension as well, as people acknowledged the depth of the divisions in the city. 'Abd al-Hamid Ben Badis recounted the story of being attacked by Jews several years previously and called on the Jewish leadership to prevent such aggressions. A Kabyle merchant, Yahia Ouahmed, pointed out that Jews were allowed to purchase firearms, because of their full citizenship rights, and he demanded that their arms be collected by the authorities. This was a reaction to the shooting of Belkacem Boutarane, who lay dying at the hospital.[38] It also revealed the extent to which the Muslim population viewed the prerogatives of Jewish citizenship as unjust privileges. After these tense exchanges, the midday meeting broke up amid pledges of cooperation and loud applause. The leaders of both communities agreed to meet again at five that afternoon at Adolphe Sultan's house with the mufti and the grand rabbi to organize a procession that would visit both the Jewish and native quarters together, with arms linked to show their mutual understanding to the population at large.

That afternoon, however, the elected officials were called once more to the prefecture, and the planned unity procession never took place. At the prefecture, the atmosphere was confused. General Kieffer, the commander of the local gendarmerie, met with acting mayor Barkatz and other municipal officials, including Henri Lellouche, while Bendjelloul and other Muslim elected officials and notables waited outside Landel's office. In the course of this conversation Kieffer stated that he did not have sufficient men on hand to secure the city, and it was agreed that they would ask for West African troops from Philippeville. After the riot, Lellouche accused Landel and Barkatz of "fatal imprudence" in discussing the lack of troops with General Kieffer in front of the assembled Muslim elected officials.[39]

The shortage in manpower was only relative—the *tirailleurs algériens* had been confined to barracks for fear that they would side with demonstrators against the Jewish population.[40] Fearing a further disturbance, Kieffer asked Landel for permission to post the *tirailleurs* in the streets and to distribute cartridges for their rifles. Landel refused, saying that the troops would be too easily provoked. In an earlier phone conversation, Paul Souchier, secretary-general of the governor-general's office in Algiers, had instructed Landel to be careful about inflammatory acts, and not to exaggerate the significance of Bendjelloul's arrest the night before.[41] A similar concern with avoiding escalation led Fusero to send Commissioner Besse to the hospital to check on the status of the Belkacem Boutarane, the man who had been shot in the stomach. Besse informed Fusero that Boutarane was not expected to live much longer, and Fusero warned him not to let the news get out if Boutarane died that night.[42] On the streets, the police were under orders to disarm men carrying clubs or other weapons, but not to arrest them unless they resisted.[43]

At 6 p.m. on Saturday, while the notables were meeting at the prefecture, a large number of people gathered at the central mosque on the rue Nationale to hear calls for calm from the mufti, Ben Badis, and Bendjelloul.[44] Henri Coquelin's report from the office of departmental security contained the most detailed account of what was said at this meeting because of his access to Arabic-speaking informants. Ben Badis spoke first, reciting several verses from the Quran, and thanking those in attendance for coming. He emphasized the need for calm and for safeguarding their dignity as Muslims who desired only to be respected in their faith and in their customs. According to Coquelin's report, Ben Badis acknowledged the depth of the injury that Muslims in Constantine felt they had suffered as a result of Jewish actions toward them, and the need to continue to work with the local authorities to address their legitimate complaints: "We have very often been provoked by the Jews, and my heart is as wounded as yours. We will bow down today for the last time. The delegation that met with the prefect was well received, and we have shared with him our expectations. The Jews cannot refuse to obey the instructions of their elected officials and notables, and we Muslims will prove to them, as well as to the high administration, our solidarity, and we will withdraw ourselves in the greatest calm."[45] He concluded by calling on believers to come to the mosque more often. Bendjelloul also spoke and repeated his understanding of the affront that Muslims felt after "having been several times provoked by the Jews [les Juifs], who profit from their status as citizens to deride the natives [les indigènes] at every opportunity." He mentioned other grievances—that there were too many cafés in the rue de France in central Constantine, that Jews were allowed to possess arms—and reported his hopes that the administration would remedy these affronts by decree: "We hope that the administration will understand the necessity of applying these measures energetically." He promised that the minutes of the meeting would be drawn up and sent to the prefect. What is most striking about both Ben Badis's and Bendjelloul's words are both their confidence in the local authorities and their willingness to express this publicly before their supporters.

That afternoon, an apparent misunderstanding caused a rumor to spread that Bendjelloul would address the city's residents at seven the next morning at the clearing in the woods known as Les Pins on the other side of the El Kantara bridge.[46] He had used the same spot eleven weeks earlier for the meeting of May 16 when he spoke to an assembled crowd of several thousand people about his failed struggle to be seated on the government's Interministerial Commission for Muslim Affairs. When Landel heard the plans for a meeting at Les Pins, he immediately prohibited it, obviously wishing to avoid any public gathering by Muslims that could be associated with a political message. Once the news of the meeting spread, however, there was little that he could do to prevent a crowd from gathering the next morning on the other side of the gorge.

During the night of August 4–5, the Constantine section of the International League against Racism and Antisemitism put up posters in French and Arabic calling for an end to racial struggle and hatred. Addressing the city's Muslims and Jews, the posters said,

> **Muslim Comrades**! . . . An individual showed a lack of self-control and respect for the Muslim faithful. This individual was drunk. . . . Let us say immediately that we declare our lack of solidarity with this individual. We are the first to demand that he be punished severely. This stupid incident must not degenerate into a racial struggle. . . .
>
> **Jewish Comrades!** Muslims and Jews have always lived side by side. Common interests unite us to them. We ask you to understand, from your side, how much the idiotic gesture of an isolated individual could shock the sentiments of our Muslim comrades. . . .
>
> **Comrades!** The gesture of a solitary individual, whatever it may be, must not reflect on the entire community! . . . Our association includes Muslims, Europeans, and Jews, all united in the same idea: THE STRUGGLE AGAINST RACIAL HATRED. . . .[47]

The poster was similar to others that had periodically gone up on the city walls in the year and a half since Hitler came to power. The fact that a poster with such a large amount of text could be printed up in sufficient numbers within twenty-four hours shows the presence of a group of quick-thinking activists, and their good relations with local printers.[48] Local supporters of the antifascist Popular Front (an alliance between the Socialist and Communist Parties) commonly used the presses run by Makhlouf Attali, a Jewish printer in Constantine, to produce their posters.[49] The next day, the home of Makhlouf Attali in the rue des Zouaves was one of those invaded by assassins. Five people from two families were killed in his apartment, including Attali's two children, Alexandre and Ausélia.

CHAPTER 9

Sunday, August 5, 1934

Early on the morning of August 5, Jewish and Muslim elected officials gathered in Constantine's old city on the rue Caraman to prepare for the funeral of Elie Narboni, the former president of the Jewish Consistory and an old ally of Mayor Émile Morinaud. In Morinaud's absence, acting mayor Émile Barkatz attended, along with Henri Lellouche and other leaders of Constantine's Jewish community. Mohamed Bendjelloul, Salah Améziane, and Touam Chabane, members of the Fédération des élus musulmans de Constantine, were also in attendance.[1] At 9 a.m., Narboni's funeral procession left the rue Caraman for the synagogue on place Négrier. After the service, the funeral proceeded to the Jewish cemetery on the far side of the gorge. General Kieffer, Constantine's military commander, paused to watch them pass as he went on a morning walk to gauge the city's atmosphere after two nights of tension.

At the moment the violence began, therefore, the most important leaders of Constantine's Jewish community were away from the city center, as were some of the local Muslim notables with whom they enjoyed the most cordial relations.[2] Busy paying their respects to their deceased colleague, these men were not immediately informed that Mohamed Bendjelloul's followers had begun to gather at Les Pins outside the faubourg d'el Kantara, also on the other side of the gorge from the old city. The police, meanwhile, were already on edge, as reports of small disturbances began to arrive during the

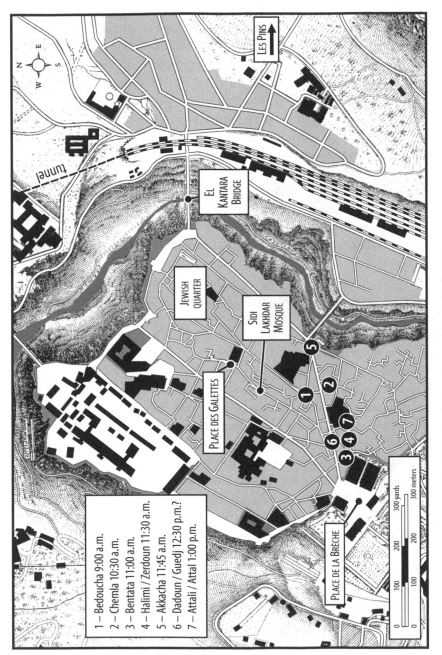

MAP 3. A map of the city showing murder sites and other locations associated with the riots. Map by Mike Bechthold.

1 – Bedoucha 9:00 a.m.
2 – Chemla 10:30 a.m.
3 – Bentata 11:00 a.m.
4 – Halimi / Zerdoun 11:30 a.m.
5 – Akkacha 11:45 a.m.
6 – Dadoun / Guedj 12:30 p.m.?
7 – Attali / Attal 1:00 p.m.

LES PINS

tunnel

EL KANTARA BRIDGE

JEWISH QUARTER

SIDI LAKHDAR MOSQUE

PLACE DES GALETTES

PLACE DE LA BRÈCHE

early hours of the morning. At 7:30 a group of taxi drivers "having fun" in front of the Palais de Justice on the place de la Brèche began to shout, attracting a large crowd who believed that something had happened between Muslims and Jews.[3] This square occupied a central and strategic site that connected the old walled city to the new residential neighborhoods constructed on the plain below. Informed of the disturbance by Lieutenant Fusero, Police Commissioner René Miquel sent one hundred Zouaves to clear the square. Between 8 and 9 a.m., these soldiers prevented the crowd from occupying the square, but allowed a small corridor for people to pass through to reach other neighborhoods in the city.[4]

At 8:30 a.m. Miquel was told about the growing crowd at Les Pins as people gathered there to hear Bendjelloul, unaware that the prefecture had prohibited the meeting the day before.[5] Miquel decided to go to Les Pins himself, but first he went to the place de la Brèche, where Fusero had set up a command post in front of the central post office. Miquel was looking for acting mayor Barkatz but found instead members of the mayor's staff in conversation with Lellouche. Together, they decided to call Mayor Morinaud, in spite of Barkatz's refusal to do so the day before. Reached by telephone, Morinaud agreed to leave his country house in Duquesne at once and make his way to Constantine. Miquel finally found Barkatz in the rue Caraman at the Narboni funeral, and together they went over the security plans for the day.

Miquel then proceeded through town and across the El Kantara bridge to Les Pins, where he met two Arabic-speaking police agents, Alliche and Abassi, whom he often assigned to attend the political meetings of Bendjelloul's FEMC. Arriving at the hillside amphitheater, Miquel saw a crowd of seven to eight hundred people waiting for Bendjelloul to speak. The majority of them, he claimed, were "shoeshine boys" (cireurs).[6] Miquel's report also noted several Communist trade unionists from the post office watching the crowd.[7] At about 9 a.m., an emissary from Bendjelloul arrived and announced that the meeting had been prohibited by the prefecture. The emissary also announced that ʿAbd al-Hamd Ben Badis had scheduled another meeting for three that afternoon at the Muslim cemetery. At this news, the assembled crowd milled about for some minutes before beginning the walk back across the bridge that led into the town center.[8] There they encountered a police barrier that prevented them from entering the city en masse. The agents allowed them to cross the bridge only in small groups, but the flow of people was nevertheless considerable.

A significant provocation appears to have occurred at this moment. As people made their way slowly across the bridge and reentered the old city, several individuals ran toward them from the direction of the madrasa, shouting that Bendjelloul had been assassinated.[9] For many witnesses, this was the crucial spark. Nearly all accounts emphasize that the rumor of Bendjelloul's assassination had a galvanizing effect on the crowds, and this false information appears to have been spread quickly: to the place de la Brèche, up and down the rue Nationale, and among the people streaming back across the El Kantara bridge after the aborted meeting in Les Pins. Those entering Constantine by the El Kantara bridge would have to pass by the Jewish quarter if they intended to proceed to the central commercial areas of the city. Police Commissioner Miquel himself would have retraced this path as he returned from Les Pins to his command post on the place de la Brèche. On his way he may have crossed paths with Salah Améziane and Touam Chabane, the Muslim elected officials returning home from the Narboni funeral along with other attendees.[10]

If anybody intended to provoke violence against the Jews of Constantine, intentionally spreading the false rumor of Bendjelloul's death would have been a good way to do it. Other witnesses believed that the precipitating event was not when the shouts reporting Bendjelloul's death reached the crowd crossing the El Kantara bridge, but slightly earlier, when a group of Jewish men apparently fired shots into a crowd in the neighborhood market around the place des Galettes. The report produced later by the investigating commission on the riot suggested that the rumor of Bendjelloul's assassination may have originated in a shout of "Death to Bendjelloul!" as these shots were fired.[11] Whatever the rumor's origins, it appears to have been rapidly disseminated. At approximately 10:15 a.m., a police agent named Selim Benmoussa reported that while posted in the rue Sidi Nemdil in what he referred to as the *"quartier indigène,"* he heard a group pass by shouting the following words: "Run! Doctor Bendjelloul has been killed by the Jews. Arm yourselves! We have to be done with them, it's the last day, it's a Holy War." Benmoussa reported that the men were all strangers to the city, and that they ran to join up with other assembling groups armed with knives and clubs.[12] If true, Benmoussa's report gives credence to the idea that the crowd's spontaneous anger was being reinforced by active provocateurs.

The gunshots that precipitated the violence on August 5 appear to have occurred following a series of escalating incidents that began earlier that morning as the market on the place des Galettes opened for business.[13] Between 7:30 and 8:00 a.m., a Jewish shoemaker arrived at his customary spot in the market, exchanging his usual joking insults with the Muslim vegetable sellers who were his neighbors in the square. Warned by bystanders to avoid any provocative gesture, he quieted down without protest. Between 8:00 and

8:30, as Jewish women began arriving at the market to buy vegetables for the day, one woman exclaimed, "What? There must be a war on, seeing that the price of vegetables is so high today!" Soon after, a Jewish man addressed the market sellers with what the police later reported as "an arrogant air" and found himself refused service. Unable to buy anything, he left angrily, while another Jewish man was more successful: saying "All the Arabs know me!" he was able to shop without trouble.

Shortly thereafter, at about 9 a.m., a Jewish woman named Reine Atlan was clubbed in the face by a man she did not know. She went immediately to the police station on the southeast edge of the place des Galettes to lodge a complaint, saying that she had done nothing to provoke the attack.[14] A witness heard her exclaim as she passed by, "These Kabyles live on our heads like fleas! There is no God—today I will kill a dozen Arabs with acid!"[15] Soon after, a second Jewish woman, Djohra Halimi, was struck with a club from behind.[16] The first witnesses to these incidents were not close to the corner of the square where the fighting broke out. They only saw Atlan after she was struck, and a few minutes later they saw a police agent carrying a wounded Muslim man into the police station, while another man with a bloodied face crossed the rue Henri Namia and entered the square shouting in anger. As he did so, witnesses heard shots coming from two different locations on the square: either from the windows of the third-floor hair salon that stood over the square or from a group of Jewish men who stood where the rue Henri Namia opened up onto it.[17] These men were well known in the market and were identified as the Zaoui brothers, sons of Amar Zaoui. Charles Zaoui, known as "Lieutenant" because of his rank in the army reserves, was seen holding a revolver.[18] It was shortly after these shots were fired that the rumor of Bendjelloul's death was transmitted to the crowd of people returning from Les Pins.

The rumors spread rapidly, often exaggerated for dramatic effect. By 9:20, Bendjelloul himself was at the place des Galettes, intervening in the dispute and trying to stop people from sacking Jewish-owned businesses.[19] At 9:30, the municipal councilor Salah Améziane, who had heard the reports as he returned from the Narboni funeral, came to Commissioner Miquel's command post in the place de la Brèche to ask if it was true that two Muslim men had been killed on the place des Galettes. Miquel sent Fusero to the police station there to investigate. By 9:45, news of conflict had brought a crowd of approximately two thousand to the place des Galettes neighborhood, making it hard to move through the narrow streets and the small market square that also contained the police station.[20] When Fusero arrived he saw Bendjelloul there, along with two other members of the Federation of Muslim Elected

Officials, Bendjelloul's brother Allaoua, a pharmacist, and Salah Améziane. In spite of their presence, large groups of angry men confronted smaller groups of Jewish men who clustered in the streets at the edge of the market throwing stones and bricks. As the sound of shots rang across the square, people began demanding that Jewish police officers stationed at the market be pulled off the street; Fusero called the Jewish agents from their posts and closed them in the station. When agent Drai, one of the Jewish police officers accused of firing his weapon the night before, tried to exit the station, he was brought down with a blow from a club. Caught in the melee, Fusero himself was struck in the abdomen by a large stone, fell to the ground, and was rescued by Bendjelloul, who cleared a space around him as the crowd rushed into the square and down the rue de France.[21]

The police were overwhelmed as the angry crowd set fire to a textile shop that looked out onto the square.[22] The first to burn was among the largest, the textile warehouse of the Société Tenoudji at number 11 rue Nationale. The presence of Muslim notables—Mohamed Bendjelloul, his brother Allaoua, Salah Améziane, and Touam Chabane—did little to halt the escalation.[23] This fighting on the place began sometime between 9:30 and 10:00 and continued for "more than an hour, with multiple shots being fired from houses of Israelites," according to a later report from Commissioner Besse.[24] Not until about 11:00 a.m. did soldiers from the Third Zouaves Regiment arrive, allowing Fusero and the police to construct barricades in the surrounding streets and to arrange for ambulances to carry away the wounded.[25] At least two soldiers were shot in the chest.

At the same time, the disorder was general throughout the streets that lay between the place des Galettes and the place de la Brèche. Multiple fires burned, and the pillage of Jewish-owned businesses left the streets littered with scattered debris and smoldering merchandise. At the prefecture, Barkatz took stock of the deteriorating situation and handed authority over to the sub-prefect, Joseph Landel.[26] Meanwhile, as Fusero organized an aid station for those injured in the fighting on the place des Galettes, several groups of 150–200 converged on Commissioner Miquel's position in the place de la Brèche. Miquel's report describes how he was knocked to the ground as he attempted to stop people from entering the square.[27] His men and he succeeded, nevertheless, in clearing the rue Nationale all the way to the madrasa on the place Molière, leaving Commissioner Besse responsible for the stretch of the street that fed into the place de la Brèche. At the far end of the rue Nationale, Fusero worked toward the madrasa from the opposite direction, having left the security of the place des Galettes in the hands of the soldiers who had come to reinforce the second district police station. It was during this attempt to clear the rue Nationale that Besse stumbled on the body of a Jewish man, later identified as Henri Guedj, age fifty. According to Besse's report, his throat had been slit.[28] Guedj was the first body to be discovered by the police. It was impossible to know exactly when he was killed, but later reports make it clear that Guedj was probably not the first person to die that morning.

According to the chronology that can be reconstructed from the police reports, the first person killed on Sunday morning was Abraham Bedoucha. He was returning home "around 9 am" when he was attacked near the intersection of the rue Rouaud and the rue Humbert, not far from the section of the rue Nationale that led from the place de la Brèche to the madrasa.[29] Bedoucha was clubbed on the head, stabbed in the ribs, and his throat was cut. Sometime later, near 10:30, as the Jewish businesses on the nearby rue Germon came to the attention of pillagers, a group of men broke into the office of a car messenger service. They found the owner, Lucien Ichoua Chemla, hiding in the back. His throat was also cut.[30] Another murder occurred shortly before 11:00, on the rue Béraud. Jacob Bentata, a watchmaker, was clubbed and stabbed in front of the door to his shop. His throat, too, was slashed. After Bentata's murder, his shop was ransacked, and a number of watches were taken from his display case.[31]

Abraham Bedoucha's death occurred almost simultaneously (sometime after 9:00 a.m.) with the escalation of rioting at the market several blocks away, and both its timing and location are difficult to account for if one assumes that the violence was largely a spontaneous reaction to the rumors of Bendjelloul's death or an angry response to reports of shots fired on the place des Galettes. Bedoucha was apparently killed before events spun out of control at the market, and before rumors of Bendjelloul's assassination began to spread. The murder of Lucien Chemla at the car messenger service at 10:30 and the deaths of Jacob Bentata—and probably that of Henri Guedj as well—around 11:00 all took place as the fighting and looting that began on the place des Galettes spread along the rue Nationale between the place Molière and the place de la Brèche. While this was happening, Commissioners Miquel, Besse, and Fusero were nearby working to clear the main thoroughfare of the rue Nationale as the pillaging of Jewish businesses continued throughout the neighborhood. Miquel's report noted that at this moment, "from all sides, by telephone, Jewish families called for troops" to protect them.[32]

At about 11:00 a.m., a unit of gendarmes stationed in the rue Nationale at place Molière heard gunshots coming from a building on the corner where the rue Perrégaux opened up onto the square. The officer in command,

Captain Boulant, ordered one of his men, Lucien Blanc, to identify who was firing and order them to stop. According to a statement made later, Blanc entered the building, where he found the family of Abraham Guedj. He instructed the family to refrain from shooting from their window, but Guedj assured them that he had not fired a gun. Blanc returned to the square, where multiple storefronts were thronged with rioters.[33] Sometime after, the gendarmes once again heard gunshots, and a Muslim man on the place Molière fell to the ground. Lachemi Akkacha, twenty-two years old, died immediately, and his body lay on the ground before hundreds of angry people.[34] Fusero was present in the square at that moment, and he had several men carry Akkacha's body to the wall of an adjacent store to prevent him from being burned in a bonfire of pillaged goods in the street.[35]

Later, the official account would state that Akkacha's death took place at 10:45 a.m. and was the final spark that infuriated the crowd and caused them to redouble their efforts to break into the homes of Jewish families.[36] Lucien Blanc's report, however, makes clear that it was already 11:00 when he and his men entered the Guedj apartment, and that Akkacha was killed only after they returned to the place Molière "around 12 o'clock."[37] By that time, the murders of Bedoucha, Chemla, Bentata, and Henri Guedj had already occurred. Fires were already burning at multiple businesses on the place Molière. It also appears that the first of the two most lethal home invasions that took place during the riot—the murders of the Halimi and Zerdoun families on the rue Abdallah Bey—was already taking place at the moment Akkacha was shot.

Sometime before Akkacha was killed—probably around 11:30—a group of people broke through the iron shutters protecting the Société Halimi & Ksentine, a wholesale textile business at number 12 rue Abdallah Bey, which ran between the rue Perrégaux and the rue Nationale close to the place de la Brèche. The Halimi business was also very close to the watch store where Jacob Bentata had been murdered only minutes before. Members of the crowd besieging the Halimi establishment believed that gunshots had been fired from the windows of the family's apartment above the business, although the surviving family members later denied that any shots were fired.[38] Eventually, a group of men succeeded in entering the store on the ground floor and breaking down the door that led to the family's private apartment above. Twelve people were hiding in the apartment. Alphonse Halimi and his wife, Fortunée, were with their two daughters, Mady and Jeanine, ages nine and six, and a son Roland, age ten. When the violence began to intensify earlier in the morning, the Halimis had sheltered the family of their concierge, Mouni Zerdoun, along with her daughter-in-law, Rosa, and Rosa's three children,

Jacqueline, age four, Huguette, age three, and Jacques, a three-month-old infant. There were also two domestic employees, Turkia Benmerabet and Rosette Benisti. As was common among middle-class Jewish households in Constantine, neither servant was Jewish.

Alphonse Halimi telephoned the police several times as the crowd gathered in the street before their store but was unable to get help. When the rioters broke through the door and entered the apartment, the two families and the servants rushed up a back staircase to an attic on the roof. The servants, Benmerabet and Benisti, were able to take young Roland Halimi and hide in a space between the wall and the roof beams. The rest of the Halimi and Zerdoun families faced the full anger of the men who caught them in the attic. Eight people were killed in the space of a few minutes. Alphonse Halimi, his wife, and their two daughters were clubbed, and their throats were cut. Mouni Zerdoun and her daughter-in-law Rosa Zerdoun, and Rosa's two daughters, were killed in the same fashion. The only survivors were the infant, Jacques Zerdoun, who lay unobserved in a cradle, the two servants, and ten-year-old Roland Halimi, who remained in their hiding place for six hours, separated from the bodies of eight Halimi and Zerdoun family members by a thin wall. Several of the killers returned more than once to the attic. Deeply traumatized, the boy and the servants remained in their hiding place even after soldiers arrived and removed the bodies to the hospital morgue. They did not emerge until after 5:00 p.m., when the smell of smoke forced them to leave their attic and climb down by the roof.[39]

Sometime after the Halimi and Zerdoun family members were killed in the rue Abdallah Bey, the Attali family home in the nearby rue des Zouaves was also invaded, probably shortly before 1 p.m. Earlier that morning, as the riot began, Makhlouf Attali, a well-known printer in Constantine, was returning home to his third-floor apartment at 6 rue des Zouaves with his sister Zaïra Zerbib, her husband Moise, and their three-year-old daughter. Moise and Zaïra were visiting Constantine from their home in Aïn Beïda. They heard the clamor of voices and saw smoke from the first fires of Jewish businesses. As they approached their door they saw a man club their neighbor, Joseph Salomon Attal, who lived on the second floor of the same building. The assailant ran away, and Makhlouf Attali and Moise Zerbib helped the injured Attal inside, aided by Attali's twenty-four-year-old daughter Ausélia, who came downstairs on hearing the noise. The group gathered together the family of Joseph Attal—his wife, Turkia, their two daughters, Rosine and Marie, and their son, Jacques—and made their way up to the Attali apartment on the third floor. Young Rosine Attal suffered from an infirmity and needed crutches to move about. Reaching the apartment, the group joined

Makhlouf Attali's wife, Zebida, and the other Attali children, Alexandre and Nathan. They barred the door as the noise on the street increased. Thirteen people in all had taken shelter in the apartment. From their balcony they looked for help but saw only crowds of rioters breaking doors and windows in the rue des Zouaves and the rue Béraud. Makhlouf called across the street from his balcony to a neighbor, Eugène Delaporte, and asked him to use his telephone to call his older sons and tell them to stay where they were, and not try to come home. Delaporte called the police several times for help as he watched the scene on the street become more and more violent.[40]

The press reports from the 1936 trial of the accused murderers of the Attali family suggested that the soldiers nearby on the rue Nationale were distracted by the need to extinguish the multiple fires that were burning in the neighborhood.[41] Nevertheless, Caporal Chef Émile Kottman of the Third Zouave Regiment mentioned seeing several members of the Attali family on the balcony of number 6, calling for help, at about 1:00 p.m. Kottman and his unit were quite close, attempting to prevent the pillaging of Jewish businesses where the rue Béraud intersected the rue des Zouaves. He tried to make his way to the door of the building, but too many people surrounded the entrance. He watched while several people reappeared on the balcony, including a middle-aged woman, and saw a man fire several shots from a revolver while the others threw "all sorts of projectiles on the pillagers."[42] It was at that moment, Kottman said, that members of the agitated crowd on the street "burst" into the building. After the shots were fired, the people on the balcony ran back into the apartment, and a few seconds later Makhlouf Attali and his wife appeared with two children "all covered with blood," crying for help, and retreating to the farthest corner of the balcony.

The surviving members of the Attali family later recounted what happened when the rioters burst into the apartment, and their story conforms well with Kottman's testimony with one exception: they all said that none of the people hiding in the apartment had fired a revolver from the balcony. This was confirmed by the neighbor across the narrow street, Eugène Delaporte, who watched the scene unfold from his window.[43] When the first men entered the apartment, Makhlouf Attali tried to speak with them. His daughter Ausélia stepped forward to beg for their lives, but the father and daughter were both clubbed and stabbed. Ausélia fell to the floor, but Makhlouf and his wife were able to run back to the balcony carrying Moise and Zaïra Zerbib's three-year-old daughter and were accompanied by the young boys. Several men rushed upon them. This is the scene that Kottman witnessed from the street. Joseph Attal was clubbed on the head, and he collapsed on the floor near the door. More men entered the apartment, storming from room to room.

On the street below, Kottman and other Zouaves were renewing their attempts to break through the crowd in front of the building's front door. They had been joined sometime before by Said Djemaa, a police officer from the commissariat who had been sent in response to a neighbor's telephone appeal for help.[44] Djemaa arrived in time to watch as several attackers on the balcony above slashed at Makhlouf Attali with knives as he sought to protect his family. During one of the multiple charges made by the soldiers, Djemaa succeeded in passing in front of the Zouaves and was able to enter the door giving onto the street. It took him some time to explore the building—he went first through the Attal apartment on the first floor before going upstairs to the roof and then coming back down. He was the first police agent to enter the Attali apartment while the attackers were still there, and the soldiers were still struggling with the large crowd near the entrance. He later testified:

> I saw about twenty rioters in the interior who were breaking wardrobes, and furniture, throwing themselves desperately on their victims. Passing by on my way to the balcony, I saw a body on the floor in the dining room, an old man. Arrived on the balcony, I saw M. Attali, covered in blood, standing to the right, protecting himself against his attackers, who numbered two or three, his arms covering his face. He had been wounded on his arms.
>
> On the other side of the balcony, there were four or five people, women, one of whom had her fingers cut off, covered in blood; an older woman was sitting on the ground, Madame Attali, I believe. The other women were also on the floor at the back of the balcony. A child of about three years was on the balcony behind the father, alone and I rescued her. A towel hanging from taut string had hidden the child. I took the child and went down with her to take her to the police station, but in the rue Nationale I met the son of Attali and I gave the child to him.[45]

The child that Djemaa rescued was the three-year-old daughter of Moise and Zaïra Zerbib. He was later credited by Marie Attal for having saved eight of the thirteen people who had sought safety in the apartment.[46] In his deposition, Djemaa recounted how he had threatened the rioters in the apartment with his revolver when he encountered them on the balcony. They said to him that if he fired at them he would meet the same fate as the people in the apartment. Speaking to them in Arabic, he replied: "I am here to prevent the deaths of these people. You will leave, if not I will shoot, even if I must die after I have emptied my weapon." The men did not respond and fled the apartment.

While this was going on, Kottman and two other soldiers managed to enter the building, but only after trying several more times to break through the angry crowd. In the hallway at the bottom of the stairwell, they encountered Caporal Chef Albert Juif and "two or three other soldiers" from Kottman's own regiment, the Third Zouaves. The presence of these soldiers in the hall is perplexing. Djemaa, the police agent who entered the building first, was later questioned and said that he did not encounter any soldiers on the inside of the building. In Kottman's narrative, it is clear that the murders were taking place at the moment he and his men entered the building after considerable difficulty. Who were these soldiers that he met in the stairwell, how had they gotten in, and how long had they been there?

Once in the building, Kottman raced up the stairs to the upper floors, followed by Caporal Juif and several other soldiers. While still on the stairs they encountered a group of four or five men attempting to flee, whom they clubbed with the butts of their rifles. Kottman's report stated that the men "fell to the ground and were no doubt carried away by their accomplices."[47] Caporal Juif went into the Attal apartment on the second floor and then descended to the street immediately, saying that he had not found anybody inside. Kottman ran to the third floor, finding the door broken, and entered the Attali apartment, which he described as "splattered with blood." Joseph Attal's lifeless body was found near the door. The bodies of Alexandre and Ausélia Attali lay where they had fallen, alongside Moise Zerbib, in the dining room. Makhlouf Attali and his wife were still on the balcony with Zaïra Zerbib and Turkia Attal, all severely injured in the attack. Zaïra, with a fractured skull, was still alive when the soldiers arrived but died three days later in Constantine's Hôpital Civil. Makhlouf survived his injuries, as did his wife Zebida. Joseph Attal's wife, Turkia, also survived, but her attackers cut off her left hand and several fingers on her right as they tried to remove her jewelry. The two boys, Jacques Attal and Nathan Attali, were also injured but survived, as did Rosine and Marie Attal.

Kottman and his men searched the apartment to verify that none of the killers were still present, and then tried to go back down the stairway until they were confronted with gunshots coming from below. Lacking ammunition themselves, Kottman and his men briefly retreated into an apartment. They seized a large footstool and threw it down the stairs, following it quickly to the bottom, where they found the hallway empty of people. They were able to exit the building only after another charge by the Zouaves outside once more cleared the door. After this they helped to evacuate the wounded to the place de la Brèche, where an ambulance was stationed.

The final multiple murder of the day took place just around the corner on the rue Béraud in a business owned by two brothers, Maurice and Gilbert Dadoun. The rue Béraud, where the watchmaker Jacob Bentata had also been murdered that morning, was a tiny street that linked the rue Abdallah Bey (where the Halimi and Zerdoun families were murdered) and the rue des Zouaves (where the members of the Attali and Attal families were killed). The Dadoun brothers were killed in their office along with their secretary, Blanche Guedj. All three had their throats cut.[48] These killings probably occurred just before the Attali and Attal murders, but it is impossible to know the exact timing, as there were no survivors, and their bodies were not discovered until later.[49] Lucien Dadoun, the son of Maurice Dadoun, later stated that the family had heard a warning about the possibility of further violence while attending the synagogue the day before. "What can the Arabs do to me?" Maurice Dadoun had replied. "They are all my friends."[50]

The close proximity of the Dadoun murders to the Halimi and Attali apartments and to Jacob Bentata's watch shop led the police to suspect initially that a single group of killers had been responsible for the attacks on Jacob Bentata at 11:00, the Halimi family at 11:30, the Attali family at 1:00, and on the Dadoun brothers' office, which seems to have happened just before that of the Attali family.[51] To this list, they might reasonably have added the murders of Abraham Bedoucha at 9:00 a.m. in the rue Rouaud, and Lucien Chemla at 10:30 a.m. in the rue Germon. All these streets were close to one another, and all the victims were murdered in exactly the same way, by having their throats cut. It would have been possible for members of a relatively small group to commit all these murders in succession as the fighting went on in the surrounding streets.[52] If this is indeed true, it would mean that as many as nineteen of the twenty-five Jews who were killed on August 5 in and around Constantine were killed by the same group of people in the same fashion. If we were to add to this list Henri Guedj, found steps away by Commissioner Jean Besse on the rue Nationale, with his throat slit, the total is twenty out of twenty-five.[53]

While these attacks were taking place, however, there were other deaths that could not be attributed to a possible group operating in the area of the rue Béraud, the rue Nationale, the rue des Zouaves, and the rue Abdallah Bey. At about noon, an autobus was crossing the place Lamorcière as it prepared to leave for Sétif. A crowd of people in the square identified one of its passengers as a Jew. Elie Guedj, an accountant who worked for the bus company, was sitting near the driver. People on the street shattered the windshield with stones, and the driver, blinded by the web of broken glass in front of him, was forced to slow down and then stop as a group of men jumped on the platform. Guedj was stabbed multiple times before eventually being pulled from the bus by his feet and clubbed as he lay dying on the ground.[54]

What information exists about the composition of the crowd during the riots of August 3 and 5? Eyewitness accounts, such as that of Commissioner Miquel, emphasized a large number of very young people in the crowd, as if it was composed mainly of adolescents and young men in their early twenties.[55] Photographs taken that day also show that many young people were present. A list of thirty-two Muslims injured during the fighting who were admitted to the civil hospital over the weekend indicates that the average age of the crowd may have been older than Miquel's impressions would imply. The average age of the seventeen people identified as members of the crowd and admitted to the hospital on August 5 was just over twenty-nine years old, with a range extending from ages fifteen to forty-seven.[56] By comparison, a similar list of injured Jews contained twenty-nine names, with an average age of thirty-eight, in a range from ages three to eighty. Of course, these lists were far from complete—one must assume that the vast majority of people injured in the riots did not seek medical help. Some police reports also emphasized that police did not recognize the men in the crowd, as if they had come from somewhere else. This too appears to have been a misperception, or at least an exaggeration. Later reports broke down the origins of a group of 162 people who were sentenced for petty crimes committed during the weekend of August 3–5 and found that of the 111 people whose origins were known, 80 had been living in Constantine for a long time.[57]

Given the fact that such violence had been anticipated for some time, the passivity of the police and military was especially surprising. In addition to the city's several dozen police officers (106 employees on August 5, of which 60 were trained for duty in the street), the Prefecture of Constantine had approximately one thousand troops at its disposal, but they were divided into roughly three hundred "French" soldiers and seven hundred *tirailleurs algériens* who served under French officers. The military commanders made clear in their later reports that they were unwilling to use the *tirailleurs algériens* in a dispute between Muslims and Jews for fear that the troops would take sides against the city's Jewish population.[58] The number of available troops was limited further by Secretary-General Landel's refusal of reinforcements from Algiers on Saturday following the Friday night disturbances at the mosque. At 5:00 a.m. on Sunday, before the riot began, the local military command believed that there were only 240 soldiers available to be stationed throughout the city. Landel called in reinforcements that morning from Philippeville, bringing the total number of troops to 540 by 8:00 a.m.[59] The nearly seven hundred *tirailleurs algériens*, meanwhile, remained confined to their barracks. The order to put them into the streets was not made until 12:30 p.m., after the bulk of the murders had already taken place.[60]

Early in the day, police agents and soldiers were dispersed throughout the city, and when the first disputes occurred at the market in the place des Galettes, the police at first intervened, but then withdrew after the crowd protested the actions of several Jewish officers. The reports of Miquel, Fusero, and Besse show these officers to have been active largely as individuals, leading at most small groups of police officers against pillagers in the area around the rue Nationale, while nearby the murders in the Halimi and Attali apartments were taking place.[61] It is striking, too, that although the police reports are very precise about the timing of their actions at the beginning of the riots, they became notably vague about where they were and what they were doing during the crucial period between 11:00 a.m. and 1:00 p.m., when the majority of the murders took place. During these hours, Miquel's report does not mention any specific times, though he had given hourly updates on what he had been doing at 7:30, 8:30, and 9:30 in his report. Speaking generally about his actions on the rue Nationale after 9:45, Miquel simply recounts a long series of events, culminating in a description of the police's attempts to control several of the fires in the area, stopping to note that "during this time, we were informed of the murders committed in the Halimi and Attali households." By "during this time" he must have meant a moment sometime after 1:00 p.m., when police agent Said Djemaa and the soldiers led by Kottman interrupted the murders as they were taking place in the Attali apartment. In any case, at 1:00 p.m. Miquel was informed that Mayor Morinaud had returned from his country residence, at which time Miquel immediately joined a meeting in the mayor's office with Morinaud, Secretary-General Landel, and General Kieffer.

The difficulties of the police during these hours stemmed from the fact that the city's small force was neither equipped nor expected to handle a crisis of this nature, which was really the domain of the military and the gendarmerie. The hesitation of the military authorities to act more forcefully as the fighting began may have been rooted in a fear that the presence of armed troops might provoke the crowd to further violence. The highest-ranking army officer in Constantine, General Kieffer, had asked as early as 3:00 p.m. on Saturday that the troops be provided with ammunition, but Secretary-General Landel at the prefecture refused. Landel brought up the issue on the phone with Paul Souchier, secretary-general of the Office of the Governor-General in Algiers, at 6 p.m. on Saturday, and Souchier made Governor-General Carde's position clear: the authorities in Constantine were formally forbidden by their superiors to provide the troops with cartridges.[62] This order was not changed until 2:00 p.m. on Sunday, after Morinaud's return to Constantine and his meeting with Miquel, Landel, and Kieffer. At that point the orders were quickly transmitted, and the population was made aware that troops would open fire when faced with resistance or in cases of murder and looting.[63] After this moment, the police had more success in defending homes that continued to be besieged by rioters, and Miquel's report gives an account of his efforts to move a group of Jewish families numbering near twenty people from the avenue du 11 Novembre to a more secure area in the old Jewish quarter.[64] Only after 4:00 p.m. did the soldiers and police begin to report that they had reestablished their authority in the streets.[65] After 7:00 p.m., two companies of *tirailleurs* arrived from Philippeville, the units this time being composed of West African colonial troops. A network of military posts was set up throughout the city, and soon after an additional company of Foreign Legionnaires arrived from Telergma.[66]

It is also puzzling that the police and military did not act more aggressively to isolate the areas of pillaging and looting—especially the place des Galettes, where the disturbances began—from the rest of the city. The police had been well aware of mounting tensions in the city over the preceding years, and in the summer of 1933, as we have seen, they did not hesitate to lock down the central neighborhoods in response to rumors of planned violence. In 1933, this action was enough to prevent a similar disturbance. The incident at the mosque on August 3, 1934, was certainly warning enough, and the police and military should have been able to implement a similar plan on August 4 and 5. Landel possibly considered such an action on Saturday and dismissed it for the same reason that he apparently rejected distributing ammunition: a fear of inflaming tensions and transforming a conflict between Muslims and Jews into a conflict between the majority population of colonial subjects and the French state. Given the timing of the decision to release cartridges to the troops, and the failure to implement any restrictions on movement on August 5, it is difficult to avoid the conclusion that Landel made a calculated decision to allow the disturbance to burn itself out through attacks on Jews and Jewish businesses because he feared that a more muscular intervention would lead to attacks on the European population in general.

Police Chief Miquel later claimed that as soon as the crowd began to break into Jewish-owned businesses, he ordered military-style armored cars to take up position at strategic points within the city.[67] According to the testimony of most witnesses, this would have placed the order to call out the armored cars at approximately 10:00 a.m., for it was at about this time that the first shops were attacked on the place des Galettes. Based on the chronology of a gendarme report on troop deployments that morning, however, it is clear that the order was not given until later. Captain Gouadain reported that he had arrived on the rue de France with his men around 10:45 a.m. after hearing erroneous reports that a gendarme had been killed. Instead, he found one of his men wounded in the face by a stone. By this time, he noted, the pillaging of Jewish stores "was happening everywhere [*était général*] in the entire neighborhood between the rue de France and the rue Nationale." He then went on to recount several more incidents in his report—the efforts of him and his men to extinguish fires on the rue Rabier and the place des Galettes, efforts of the gendarmes to push "one thousand natives" back toward the place Lamorcière and beyond to the newer quarters of Saint-Jean and Bienfait outside the old city's walls, efforts to protect the Guedj family house on the place Molière from being invaded by rioters. After this recitation, Gouadain noted that he encountered Miquel on the rue Nationale, where they cooperated with other troops in trying to drive the crowd back before they could reach the place de la Brèche. By then, there were three or four large fires burning in the center of the city, and the first reports of murders were coming in. Only at that point did Gouadain state that Miquel called out the armored cars. Depending on which murders were being reported, this would place his order for the armored cars sometime around 11:00, after the riot had been well under way for at least an hour.[68] In any case, the armored cars were stationed in the street by 11:30, but without ammunition, and they seem to have done little beyond driving the angry crowds into the adjacent streets. They did, however, give the police more mobility. Shortly after 3:00 p.m., as the military took more aggressive measures to stop the looting in the old city, Fusero and Miquel drove across the gorge to the faubourg d'el Kantara with three armored cars to disperse a crowd of 150 people who were besieging a villa owned by the Elbaz family before an audience of curious Europeans. Miquel reported that when Madame Elbaz came out of her house to thank her rescuers, she kissed the commissioner's hand while the European onlookers shouted "Hou-Hou!"[69]

This curious incident points to the fact that the riot was also a spectacle, with the European population often passively watching attacks on Jews without intervening. That many Europeans thought that the Jews of Constantine had earned their comeuppance was never said openly once the extent of the violence was widely known, but there is evidence that the rioters felt themselves to be undertaking a patriotic act in attacking the Jews. Such an attitude would not have been surprising, given the very public expressions of anti-Jewish sentiment that were common in the preceding months. Many people recounted later that the people attacking Jewish stores cried "Vive la France!" ("Long live France!") as they broke windows and doors. The most extraordinary sign of this sentiment was observed at about 5 p.m. on August 5, when Mayor Morinaud conducted an inspection tour of the city in the immediate aftermath of the violence, accompanied by General Kieffer, Police Chief Miquel, Prosecutor Raymond Cura, and Joseph Landel of the prefecture. When this group arrived at the Sidi Rached Bridge they encountered several cars covered with fluttering ribbons of cloth. At the opposite side of the bridge a crowd of one hundred men was stopping the vehicles that crossed the bridge and decorating them after determining that nobody inside was Jewish. The group of officials could see a banner that said "Vive la France!" suspended above the bridge.[70] Sentiments like this may have reinforced the soldiers' passivity throughout the day, and this effect was apparently magnified by the evident care that the rioters took not to disturb the soldiers or police and to avoid attacking any establishment that was not owned by Jews. These expressions of loyalty among those most closely involved in the violence were almost never recalled publicly in the aftermath of the violence.[71]

Whatever the reasons, it is clear that between 9:00 a.m., when the fighting began on the place des Galettes, and 2:00 p.m., when the order to distribute cartridges went out, the authorities effectively lost control of the city. Aside from isolated attempts to help the injured, much of the police action was limited to very localized efforts to control the movement of groups as they ran through the streets and to helping firefighters evacuate burning buildings. In the days and weeks that followed there were multiple reports of police and military having refused to intervene as the violence and pillaging spread from the city center into the adjacent faubourgs of Saint-Jean and El Kantara.[72]

The same rumors and information that provoked the violence in Constantine—the story of the mosque profaned by Khalifa, the rumor of Bendjelloul's assassination, stories of Jews firing on Muslim crowds—spread rapidly throughout the region by midday on Sunday. In the surrounding countryside, too, the resulting violence led to murder. Albert Halimi, a hairdresser visiting from Mila, was pulled from a bus on the road headed toward Constantine and shot in the heart. In Bizot (Didouche Mourad), a farm owned by a Jewish family was besieged by its neighbors. Michel Attal, the father, was attacked by a crowd as the family tried to flee. He died after his skull was fractured from a blow to the head. An elderly Muslim neighbor hid members of Attal's family, rescuing them from the attackers, but only the young Robert survived without physical injury.[73] In Hamma-Plaisance (Hamma Bouziane), Salomon Guedj's broken body was found eight hundred meters from his farm. In the nearby town of Aïn Beïda, angry crowds pillaged Jewish-owned businesses and threw the merchandise into the streets. In Jemmapes, demonstrators attacked a post of gendarmes. Other disturbances took place in Aïn-Smara, Châteaudun-du-Rhumel, Khenchela, and Oued Atmenia.[74] In the following days, other attacks on Jews occurred elsewhere in the surrounding region, and Jews from smaller towns were evacuated to Constantine on August 6–7.[75]

In the course of the street fighting in Aïn Beïda, a twelve-year-old Muslim boy, Athmane Saidi, was shot in the stomach and transported to the hospital in Constantine on Monday, August 6. He died the next day. The same hospital admitted fourteen other Muslim men with bullet wounds on August 5 and 6, ranging in age from fifteen to forty-seven.[76] After the deaths of Belkacem Boutarane and Lachemi Akkacha, the death of Athmane Saidi on August 7 brought the number of Muslims killed in this weekend to three. In all, twenty-eight people died from the violence of August 3–5, 1934, in Constantine and the surrounding areas—twenty-five Jews and three Muslims. The last to die was René Nabet, a twenty-three-year-old Jewish man, who was clubbed and stabbed on August 5 in Constantine and died later of his wounds, according to historian Robert Attal.[77]

By early evening on Sunday, August 5, an observer in the streets may have assumed that no Jewish-owned business in Constantine had been spared. More than two hundred had been pillaged. Their windows were shattered, their doors broken, their furniture destroyed. Their stock had been pulled out and dragged into the street, covering the pavement with bolts of soiled and torn cloth and other broken goods. Multiple fires continued to smolder in different neighborhoods, above all along the central arteries of the old city. Police and soldiers arrested looters—247 arrests were made between August 3 to 5—dispersed the remaining members of the crowd, helped firefighters put out the most dangerous fires, and brought the injured to makeshift first aid stations and the clinic of Dr. Pierre Guedj on the rue Nationale near the madrasa.[78]

While this was going on, telegrams began flying to the governor-general's office in Algiers and the Ministry of the Interior in Paris, containing the first reports from the prefect and the police, and eyewitness accounts from local officials. Among these many telegrams was a letter of resignation addressed to Governor-General Carde and the prefect from Constantine's Jewish municipal councilors, signed by Henri Lellouche, Émile Barkatz, Adolphe Sultan, Maurice Laloum, Benjamin Zaoui, and Martin Levy.

CONSTANTINE. . . . . . 18H10 WE REGRET TO INFORM YOU MAINTENANCE OF ORDER ABSOLUTELY INSUFFICIENT FROM 10:00AM UNTIL 2:00PM NUMEROUS ATTACKS AGAINST PERSONS MURDERS STORES PILLAGED ALL PERPETRATED UNDER INDIFFERENT EYE OF TROOPS AND POLICE STOP STORES BURNED IMPUNITY BE ASSURED INCREDIBLE SCENES VANDALISM NO ARRESTS MADE STOP BEFORE SUCH SPECTACLE WE SUBMIT THIS VERY DAY RESIGNATION— LELLOUCHE CONSEILLER GENERAL BARKATZ ADJOINT MAIRE SULTAN LALOUM ZAOUI LEVY CONSEILLERS MUNICIPAUX.[79]

By the end of the day, as order was reestablished in the streets, and the surviving family members of the victims were being treated for their wounds in the hospital alongside several dozen injured protesters, the riot was quickly turning into something quite different: a political crisis.

CHAPTER 10

Shock and Containment

On Monday, August 6, firefighters called in from neighboring towns struggled to contain the fires that continued to burn, including one behind the Hotel Cirta that was not extinguished until 8 p.m.[1] Throughout the day, large gatherings of people led many to think that violence might begin again. News of the agony of Belkacem Boutarane in the Hôpital Civil, where he had lain since he was shot in the stomach on Friday evening, spread throughout the city, reinforcing these fears. The military took no chances. The largest gathering, at the Sidi Rached bridge, was the target of a charge by a unit of *tirailleurs* that dispersed the assembled people.

The soldiers had been reinforced since the afternoon of August 5 with the arrival of West African troops and a *battalion mixte*—a unit containing both French and sub-Saharan African colonial troops—from Algiers.[2] The military expressed its satisfaction at the presence of these West African soldiers, because officers believed they bore a grudge against North Africans due to the history of the slave trade. Military commanders in Constantine used a parallel logic to justify their decision to keep Algerian Muslim troops in the city confined to their barracks, fearing that they would join in on the side of the crowd in the streets. In the days that followed, however, the prefecture faced questions about Joseph Landel's decision to refuse the governor-general's offer of reinforcements on August 4 when it might have made a difference. In the meantime, gendarmes moved throughout the department where smaller communities of Jews lived, evacuating some of them to Constantine. This was ostensibly to prevent further incidents, but some antisemitic local officials may have tried to rid their towns of an unwanted Jewish population by encouraging their departure for safety reasons.[3] In this way, the logic of security reinforced the regional lines of racial division.

As Constantine's residents began the task of clearing the streets and returning to their daily routines, they struggled to understand both the extent of the violence and its immediate consequences for their lives. Some Jewish witnesses recounted seeing their European neighbors surveying the wreckage of Jewish homes and businesses with satisfied expressions. "It was laughter, joyous exclamations, one would have thought that we were back in the Middle Ages."[4] The shock was most profound among the surviving members of Jewish families whose relatives had been murdered. The most poignant recorded reaction came from the printer Makhlouf Attali, whose children, Alexandre and Ausélia, were killed in their home in front of their parents on August 5. Speaking from his hospital bed where he was recovering from his wounds, he declared, "I am suffering, I have seen too much blood around me, I have heard too many cries of agony. But I have no hatred, no rancor against true Muslims."[5] These words were widely reported in the French-language press.

The Attali family pointedly indicated where they believed at least a portion of responsibility for the violence lay: they sent a funeral announcement for Alexandre and Ausélia to the office of Governor-General Carde, unaccompanied by a letter. A thick black border surrounded the text:

The extended family and friends [of Makhlouf Attali and his wife] have the immense pain to inform you of the tragic death of

> Mademoiselle Ausélia Attali
> midwife, aged 24 years
> and of
> Monsieur Alexandre-France Attali
> aged 14 years

their children, their sister and brother, their brother-in-law and sister-in-law, their aunt and uncle, their niece and nephew, their cousins, their family members, their allies, and their friends, cowardly assassinated in Constantine during the riot of 5 August 1934.[6]

The governor-general's office staff dutifully went through the death announcement with the blue and red wax pencils of the French administration, highlighting the key points for Carde's perusal—the names of the families, marked in blue in the margins, and a bold red stroke next to the phrase "cowardly assassinated." The blunt simplicity of the death notice, its concise language, and the absence of an accompanying letter stood as an accusation: the Attali family believed Governor-General Carde to be complicit with the murderers of their children. Amid the stilted and repetitive bureaucratic language of the police and prefectural reports that surround it in the file, the funeral announcement was itself a kind of provocation, a statement of the family's outrage at the inability—or unwillingness—of the colonial government to protect its own citizens.

Meanwhile, public officials in Constantine began to write reports for their superiors on what they had seen. Within the bureaucracy these reports followed the chain of command, but for elected officials the preferred avenue was to express themselves directly to the governor-general. The August 6 letter from Eugène Vallet, an ally of Mayor Morinaud and a member of both the *délégations financières* and the Conseil général, was typical of those who saw the riot as the logical outcome of the reforms that had allowed Muslim colonial subjects such as Bendjelloul to run for office.[7] Although Bendjelloul was not mentioned by name in Vallet's letter to Carde, he asserted that the initial dispute at the mosque on Friday evening was "amplified" by a "command post [*état-major*] which aimed to create difficulties everywhere for the authorities with the goal of total emancipation, as announced by the meetings in Paris."[8] Vallet's reference to a Paris connection was an attempt to link the violence in Constantine to the campaign led by Maurice Viollette to offer citizenship and parliamentary representation to Algerian colonial subjects. He warned that on August 5, the unnamed instigators "took great care to make clear that the 'French' should not be attacked" but that "tomorrow, after the punishments that Justice will be obliged to take against the murderers and the authors of this aggression, they will say to the natives [*indigènes*] that the French defended the Jews, and they will lead, in France, a 'pathetic campaign' about the unhappy fate of the autochthonous Algerians."[9] Vallet called for an investigation that would lead to the arrest of these "leaders [*meneurs*], however highly placed they may be in the native world." These figures, he stated, "proclaim in the Metropole their attachment to a 'generous and immortal' France, while they prepare for riots in Algeria."

If some were quick to blame Bendjelloul and his colleagues at the FEMC, there were other recriminations as well directed in particular at the passivity of the military. On August 8 General Kieffer filed an official protest with the prefecture about a report in *La Dépêche de Constantine* that criticized the behavior of the military during the riots. The article stated that the families had been murdered while "nearby, soldiers mounted an illusory guard."[10] *La Dépêche algérienne*, another daily, drove the point further with a long eyewitness account that stated "I will pass in silence the scenes of massacre, of women, of children calling from the height of their balconies to the police and soldiers who watched, powerless to help, because they had not received the order to intervene!"[11] Kieffer, incensed, demanded that the prefecture make it known to the population that their office had refused the distribution of cartridges to the troops.

Resentment within the military was palpable. Lieutenant Gondal of the Third Zouaves Regiment posted multiple copies of a typed message on thoroughfares both in and outside the walled city on August 8:

Discipline and Nobility

The Army in its noble serenity never expected
that a town of DUNCES would praise them.
Duty alone, fulfilled with the greatest order
And the most exact discipline, is sufficient.

GONDAL[12]

Gondal posted the message on the rue Rohault de Fleury, a street that led from the place de la Brèche to the newer European neighborhoods outside the old city wall. He was congratulated by "a large number of readers," to whom he responded, "I have only just begun!" Passersby recommended that he set a watch to make sure that the posters were not defaced. Gondal's regiment, the Third Zouaves, was also that of Elie Khalifa, who had started the weekend of troubles by insulting the men at the mosque on Friday evening.

On August 8, twenty-four Jewish victims from Constantine were buried in a collective ceremony at the city's Jewish cemetery on the other side of the gorge across the El Kantara bridge. Inevitably, the occasion highlighted the contrast between political posturing and the mourning of families in grief. The number of victims meant that the crowd had to wait silently in the heat as each coffin was brought in one by one and lined up along a low wall that ran alongside one of the cemetery's principal alleys. Leaders of Constantine's Jewish community were present, as were officials from the municipal and prefectural administration, the military, and police. Secretary-General Joseph Landel of the prefecture was there—the target of criticism for his failure to distribute cartridges to the troops or to call for reinforcements after the disturbances of Friday the third. René Miquel, the central commissioner of police, was also present. Before the riot, Miquel had complained of the number of Jewish and Muslim police officers on the city's payroll, and he had successfully resisted efforts by Jewish members of the municipal council to have him removed from office.

Mayor Morinaud, the erstwhile ally of Constantine's Jewish municipal councilors whose political career had begun in the 1890s on an anti-Jewish platform, spoke at length at the funeral, expressing his horror at the murders:

> Whatever race or religion one belongs to, one can only blush with shame for humanity in the face of such monstrosity. Under the French flag, no more painful events have ever bloodied the ground of our city. That in 1934, 104 years after the arrival in Algeria of our noble and generous France, such revolting crimes could still be possible, that there are still people who might commit them, or excuse them—there is in this fact enough to confound the spirit of even the most insensitive of men. I distinguish clearly between these infamous assassins and those peaceful and honest men that make up the mass of our native population. They will do themselves honor by helping justice to punish these attacks on unfortunate people who were minding their own business and who have done nothing to deserve this horrible fate.[13]

Morinaud's public astonishment about a violence that "could still be possible" after 104 years of French presence in Algeria made clear that the riot should only be seen as the eruption of a monstrous, atavistic, and specifically Algerian past. It is important to recognize the work involved in declaring this to be true. For Morinaud, it had to remain unthinkable that such events could occur "under the flag" of a "noble and generous France," though of course they did. His attempt to distinguish between "infamous assassins" and the "peaceful and honest men that make up the mass of our native population" was equally awkward, since he had long worked to prevent this mass of peaceful and honest men from possessing the rights of full citizenship. It was also convenient for Morinaud that the perpetrators would be judged in French courts, after an investigation by French police, because the circumstances made it easier to demand, as he did, that the Muslim population demonstrate their loyalty by helping the French administration punish them.

Nowhere in Morinaud's speech did he mention that the victims of the riot were Jewish. The mayor was clearly anxious to avoid appearing as a defender of Constantine's Jews, even at their moment of greatest vulnerability. Given the increasing visibility of the local section of the Croix de feu and the relentless antisemitism of an ever-larger portion of the electorate, Morinaud's alliance with Jewish municipal councilors was paying fewer and fewer political dividends. His outrage, therefore, was expressed in the language of universals, without forgetting that certain kinds of difference still mattered enough to be mentioned obliquely. As he put it: "Whatever race or religion one belongs to, one can only blush with shame for humanity." The message was clear enough: we live in a world of fixed differences; conflict between them is embarrassing. Between the lines, however, was a more subtle message: the violence was a byproduct of ageless hatreds and should in no way be interpreted as an indictment of French colonial rule in Algeria.

Henri Lellouche—president of the Jewish Consistory in Constantine and an elected official—also spoke, saying out loud many things that were inconvenient. Although the newspaper accounts do not mention Lellouche's demeanor, one can easily imagine his voice shaking with anger as he expressed his outrage at the events of the previous Sunday:

> In the presence of police and troops who watched the carnage and pillage without intervening, the throats of children were slashed, their parents mutilated, and homes that all knew to be inhabited were set afire; for eight consecutive hours, in the middle of the European center of the city and in plain daylight, these deeds were accomplished before the indifferent eye of the representatives of the military who had received no orders to intervene. Apparently one needs orders in order to stop murderers and arsonists. . . . For a long time, we will return to this alley of martyrs to collect ourselves and to find in your suffering and your sacrifices the strength that is required for French citizens that are guilty of being Jewish, to continue to deeply love France, the avant-garde of civilization.[14]

Up until this point, Lellouche had been a vocal and earnest patriot whose political views tended toward the conservative, even nationalist, side of the French political spectrum. His angry words at the Jewish cemetery nevertheless revealed a deep uncertainty about the place of Jews in the French Republic. Although he would soon go much further in his criticism of other political figures in Constantine, his wording here—emphasizing the "strength" required for Jews to express their love of France—could only be heard as an acknowledgment that the previous weekend's violence threatened not only the Jews of Algeria but also the integrity of the Republic itself.[15] His insistence on naming the areas of Constantine where the murders took place—the streets lined with Jewish businesses within the walls of the old city—as "the European center of the city" was his way of emphasizing the success of Algerian Jewish assimilation since the Crémieux decree of 1870. Official reports from the governor-general's office, for example, were more likely to identify the sites of the murders as the "Jewish quarter"—even though the rue Abdallah Bey and the rue des Zouaves, where the Halimi and Attali apartments were located, or the rue Béraud and the rue Germon, where Jacob Bentata, the Dadoun brothers, and Lucien Ichoua Chemla were murdered, were not in the traditional Jewish quarter at all, but rather in a neighborhood that more prosperous Jews had moved into after several large streets penetrated the old city in the colonial period. The most important of these, the rue Nationale (officially renamed rue Georges Clémenceau after the First World War), ran diagonally from the place de la Brèche to the place Molière by the madrasa, and from there along the gorge to the bridge of El Kantara. Lellouche's insistence on invoking the term "European" to refer to these neighborhoods was also a direct challenge to the violent rhetoric of the antisemitic right that sought to overturn the Crémieux decree and render Algerian Jews "native" once more.

There was an additional awkwardness in Lellouche's words at the funeral: just as Morinaud did not mention that the victims were Jewish, Lellouche did not mention that the rioting crowds that had concealed the murderers of twenty-five Jews consisted largely of Algerian Muslims. Lellouche mentioned the "assassins," "executioners," and "arsonists" but did not allude to the ways that popular anger against Constantine's Jews had been fed by local political rivalries couched in ethno-religious terms. His anger at the funeral was focused above all on the authorities in Constantine, especially the police and the military, who had failed to protect Jews when they most needed it. Their guilt was to have failed to live up to the Republic's promise to Algerian Jews. In private, however, Lellouche drew a very different conclusion from Mayor Morinaud, who had implied that the violence proved that Algerians were still incapable of "civilized" behavior. In a conversation with an inspector from the French judiciary just after the riots, Lellouche confided his urgent and emotional wish that the government speed up the pace of reform: "Make them into French citizens so that such things never happen again!"[16]

Bendjelloul and the other Muslim elected officials of the FEMC agreed to stay away from the funeral in order to avoid any incident, but they published a letter in the local press denouncing the violence and those who sought to use the situation for political ends. The letter was released on August 13 after the Muslim elected officials had met with the new prefect, Jean-Marie Laban. The FEMC repudiated the violence of the riots and blamed the murders on an "instinct of bestiality" that had been awakened in "a tiny group of individuals." The acts of these people, the statement insisted, were thoroughly opposed by "the quasi-unanimity of the Muslim population which was committed to a pure Islamism and an elevated humanism." The public letter also proclaimed their loyalty to France and the prefect's authority, as well as their willingness to cooperate in the task of governing the department of Constantine, "the largest French Department, and the most difficult to administer because of its diversity and the clash of interests which collide there." The letter concluded by saying to the prefect that "you have in us French Muslims who want nothing more than to live in peace and union with all the inhabitants of this land under the authority of France. Our unique concern is to contribute to the development of our great Algeria . . . and to make it into an entirely French land."[17]

In the following days, an extraordinary number of reports and letters from officials and local notables surged through the administration's information channels. At the same time, rapidly circulating rumors magnified the uncertainty felt by Constantine's residents. No whispered story was too outlandish to be ruled out, and the shocked population felt no incentive to disbelieve the worst. In the department's rural areas rumors circulated that the riots had begun because Jews had slit the throats of Muslim women and children.[18] Many officials pointed to the recent history of antagonism between Jews and Muslims in the city, and the "exasperation" felt by Muslims at "the arrogance of the israelites."[19]

The most inflammatory claims had to do with evidence that the violence had been organized ahead of time. On this issue, there was a convergence between local officials who were quick to sound the alarm on any perceived threat to social stability and Jewish residents of the city who could not believe that such an event could have happened without considerable planning. The speculation began immediately. A telegram sent by Joseph Landel of the prefecture to the governor-general's office on Monday, August 6, concluded its summary of the weekend's events by stating cautiously, "Am tempted to think that extremist elements support indirectly the movement."[20] In his report from Algiers to the minister of the interior in Paris, Secretary-General Paul Souchier was even more blunt: "The minor nature of the pretext that led to such a serious disturbance, reveals a veritable method in the attack, leading one quite naturally to suppose that we are dealing with a carefully organized operation."[21] Neither Landel nor Souchier named the people that they believed to be responsible, but their targets could only have been Mohamed Bendjelloul or 'Abd al-Hamid Ben Badis, the two most prominent local leaders of movements with a largely Muslim following. Note, too, that Souchier and Landel were the two figures most closely associated with the decision not to distribute cartridges to the troops in the street on August 4–5. Claiming an undetected conspiracy may have been preferable to admitting that this decision was an error.

On August 7 an administrator from nearby Khroub (El Khroub) wrote to the governor-general that the disturbances in their community did not begin until two men came from Constantine in a truck to tell them that Bendjel-loul had been assassinated.[22] On the same day, the *Écho d'Alger* wrote that the Friday "brawl" on August 3 was spontaneous but that the riot on Sunday, August 5, was a "pogrom" that had been organized beforehand. The paper also repeated the rumor that some houses in the Jewish quarter had been marked beforehand with the identifying label "Christian House."[23] By the end of the week, rumors and speculation took a more developed form. Adolphe Sultan, a Jewish member of the municipal council and the president of the local chapter of the League of the Rights of Man, asserted on August 9 that the murders had been planned ahead of time and carefully organized. The rioters had been infiltrated by "teams of technicians" with specific goals and tasks. First, there were "teams of blacksmiths and metalworkers" whose job was to break down doors and dismantle the metal curtains that shop owners used to protect their establishments. They were followed by "teams of butchers," trained in the techniques of the slaughterhouse, and other groups trained to seek out account books, property deeds, stock certificates, and legal papers. All this was accomplished under the protection of crowds armed with clubs and metal bars who waited for a signal to begin their attacks. Sultan concluded his note with an indictment of the police, who he claimed had arrested nobody—this was not true, in fact—and who had given the rioters "complete and absolute liberty to pillage, to sack, and to murder." The riots in Constantine were "a veritable pogrom" made possible by a simple fact, stated forcefully: "France was absent in Constantine, from 9:00 a.m. until 5 p.m." on Sunday, August 5.[24] Sultan's phrase—that France was absent in Constantine on August 5—would be repeated by many in the days and weeks to come. As a rhetorical formula, it was a powerful indictment of the local French authorities and their failure to prevent murder. As an analysis of what had happened on August 5, however, Sultan's phrase was incorrect. The events of that day had everything to do with France.

Other disturbing reports followed. On August 11, an anonymous letter from "A group of JEWS" arrived at the office of the local magistrate (*juge d'instruction*) reporting that "the Israelite population of Constantine was convinced" that the "massacre" of August 5 was "a premeditated crime." The author or authors of the letter saw the riots and murders as the endpoint of an "anti-French campaign" of long standing led by "agitators who are perhaps already known to the Prefectural Administration." The people responsible, it continued, were those who "had made the people who shared their faith [*coreligionnaires*] into fanatics by preaching 'HOLY WAR.'" Proof of this premeditation, according to the letter, came in several reported facts: (1) a Muslim tobacconist in the rue de France had emptied his store of merchandise on Wednesday, August 1, in order to limit his losses in case of a disturbance; (2) the mayor of Robertville, a neighboring village, reported that numerous *indigènes* returning home from Constantine after August 5 said that "Bendjelloul had ordered them to sack the stores but not to steal anything"; (3) a woman had reported that the "Arab butchers" in the rue Combes had announced the coming trouble eight days before the riots.[25] The mayor of Gastonville, a certain M. Chavannes, reported similar statements from individuals in his community. Men who had returned to Gastonville after being in Constantine on August 5 reported that "Bendjelloul told us to go and pillage, to kill the Jews. Don't touch a hair on the head of the French. Nobody will say anything. The troops have no cartridges. The Administration itself wants to teach the Jews a lesson."[26]

The most developed arguments that accused Bendjelloul and his associates of being responsible for the violence came from two visitors to Constantine from Jewish organizations based elsewhere, who visited Constantine at roughly the same time in the second week of August. Albert Confino, the representative of the Alliance Israélite in Algiers, arrived in Constantine on August 9. Joseph Fisher, an investigator sent by the Comité des délégations juives (the Geneva-based organization that was a predecessor of the World Jewish Congress), arrived in Constantine on August 10. The two of them stayed for five or six days, collecting testimony from the city's Jewish leaders, including Henri Lellouche, Adolphe Sultan, and André Bakouche, the president of the Ligue contre l'antisémitisme. Both Confino and Fisher prepared separate reports for their respective organizations, and a few copies of each one circulated to officials in both Algeria and France, but neither report was published at the time.[27]

Seeking to counter the impression left by the Parisian newspapers that the riots were "a purely local incident" produced by hatred "which has always existed between the two Algerian races," Fisher's report asserted (as did Confino's) that Jews and Muslims had always lived on good terms in Constantine, but that Muslims had been manipulated in recent years by politicians who used an anti-Jewish platform to encourage "anti-French" agitation. Confino blamed Bendjelloul for contributing to political tensions, saying that he was the "soul" in Constantine of a "pan-Islamist movement that stretched from Morocco to India" and that the violence against the Jews was his revenge for having been refused an audience with the interior minister, Camille Chautemps, the previous year. Fisher's report duplicated many of Lellouche and Sultan's assertions and added more direct accusations than Jewish leaders had yet to make public: that the "pogrom" had been organized by members of Bendjelloul's organization; that it had been abetted by the European right, including the Action française, and others who sought to abrogate the Crémieux decree. Both Confino and Fisher argued that the local authorities were complicit because of their passivity and their loose talk about a lack of reinforcements in front of the assembled Muslim elected officials on the afternoon of Saturday, August 4.

Claims that the riots and murders had been organized ahead of time seemed to be confirmed on August 12, while Fisher and Confino were still in Constantine. A witness identified a young Muslim man who worked at a butcher's shop of having participated in the murders of the Halimi and Zerdoun families. His arrest and interrogation quickly led to the arrest of five more individuals—several of them butchers' employees—and for several weeks, the local press was filled with startling stories about the "gang of throat slitters" that was responsible for the multiple deaths on August 5. The police eventually backed away from this story of the butcher boys' conspiracy, but the very public nature of these accusations exacerbated the sense of horror that surrounded these events, and reinforced the emerging consensus that the riots were premeditated and carefully organized.[28]

The rush to condemn the arrested young men resulted from the enormous pressure on the police to produce a coherent explanation for the murders. At the same time, however, stories of conspiracy worked against Mayor Morinaud's contention that the riot was rooted in the religious fanaticism of the entire Muslim population. The mayor's explanation provided a quick justification for repressive measures against Muslim organizations such as the FEMC that had long been viewed as potentially subversive. Blaming the riots on the vestiges of precolonial barbarism also comforted officials who could not explain how they lost control of the city on August 5. Adolphe Sultan would have been deeply troubled had he realized it, but his formulation—that "France was absent in Constantine" on August 5—became an important part of the way that the authorities deflected responsibility away from themselves and toward the whole population of Algerian Muslims.

Claiming that the riots were the result of primitive hatreds may have worked to excuse the failures of the colonial regime, but it also ran counter to the pressing legal need to produce individuals who could be charged with specific crimes. Producing perpetrators who could be punished by the criminal justice system meant investigating individuals whose identity and political allegiances were unpredictable. Anti-Jewish sentiment was widespread in many sectors of Constantine society, in the local military, in the police department, among middle-class supporters of the Croix de feu, and in the small groups of right-wing extremists who rallied around figures such as Henri Lautier. Given this complex situation, the need to assign clear responsibility posed a potential problem for the authorities, because there was always a danger that the investigation might implicate somebody other than Muslim leaders and the FEMC. From the administration's point of view, the idea that somebody else may have been involved could only destabilize an already uncertain political atmosphere in dangerous ways.

The official investigations of the riots by different parts of the colonial bureaucracy reflected this tension. While the local police in Constantine began their search for witnesses and suspects in the murders of August 5, the governor-general's decree of August 10 announced an official commission that would conduct its own investigation.[29] The commission was chaired by Jean Vigouroux, an official who soon attracted criticism from some Jewish residents for past antisemitic comments.[30] The bulk of the commission's work was conducted by experienced administrators, especially the indefatigable Augustin Berque, who headed the Bureau of Native Affairs in Algiers. In two months, Vigouroux's commission interviewed and took depositions from 128 people, including 30 officials in civil government, 43 members of the military, and 55 "local personalities and diverse witnesses."[31] The Vigouroux commission collected hundreds of pages of reports and testimony, in some cases going back many years, and fielded a voluminous correspondence with officials and private individuals with information to share or political views to express. Though they also sought to keep tabs on the police investigation, the commissioners' goal was not merely to describe the circumstances of individual crimes—they sought a different kind of understanding, one that aimed for a broader view over a longer time span. They looked at possible economic causes, local precedents for religious and ethnic violence, the role of organized political groups, and searched for connections with movements in other parts of the world. The Vigouroux commission submitted its report to the governor-general on October 7, 1934, but it was never released to the public.[32]

What is remarkable about the early statements and testimony assembled by the Vigouroux commission is how universal were the claims about conspiracy and preplanning in the first weeks of their investigation. These claims came not only from Jewish leaders but also from pillars of the colonial establishment, including Gustave Mercier and Eugène Vallet. Nevertheless, the commission examined the claims about conspiracy and preplanning in the riots of August 5—and refuted them all. The report sided with Mayor Morinaud in blaming the riots on religious fanaticism alone and discredited stories of conspiracy by labeling them collectively as the "Jewish explanation." Such claims, the commission implied, were merely the disordered emotional reactions of the riot's traumatized victims who could not accept their own role in the events.

Like Morinaud, Vigouroux's report portrayed the Jews and Muslims of Constantine as two hostile communities whose mutual antipathy was unrelated to the French colonial presence. The "Arab town," with its "narrow streets and tortuous alleys," was juxtaposed to the "Ghetto"—a multitude of "little streets, hardly larger than that of the Arab quarter," constituting the "sensitive nerve [*point névralgique*] where the first incident broke out, and where the struggle was the most intense on Sunday morning."[33] As we have seen, this was not really true. Although the first fighting broke out on the place des Galettes near the traditional Jewish quarter, the majority of the killings took place in the streets off the rue Nationale in an area of mixed residences and commercial establishments that connected the public squares of the European administrative quarter with the older neighborhoods along the gorge.

In describing the topography of the city, the report managed to mention the Remblai, the area just outside the old wall where the poorest Muslim colonial subjects lived, in connection with the difficulties that the French had had in conquering the city in 1836–1837, as if the urban landscape was permanently inscribed with resistance to French rule. Only later did the report admit that the Remblai was a relatively new neighborhood, a product of the colonial situation where recent migrants from an increasingly impoverished countryside made their homes. The inhabitants of this quarter were described as a "lazy and primitive proletariat, with a rude and aggressive temperament" constituting a "permanent danger" for the city.[34]

The report's section titled *"Renseignements démographiques"* (demographic information) completed the picture of an irrevocably divided population. As was customary in Algeria, the census contained three categories: "Europeans," "Israelites," and "Natives" [*Indigènes*].[35] The population figures were listed as follows:

Table 10.1 Population of Constantine, 1911–1931

YEAR	EUROPEANS	ISRAELITES	NATIVES	TOTAL
1911	20,877	9,230	35,066	65,173
1921	23,141	9,889	45,190	78,220
1926	35,050	10,483	48,214	93,747
1931	36,092	12,058	51,445	99,595

Source: Commission Report, p. 4. ANOM: ALG GGA 9/H/53.

Although Constantine had grown by half between 1911 and 1931, to about one hundred thousand total inhabitants, the city remained about one-third "European," slightly less than one-sixth Jewish, and a little more than one-half "native." The report seemed to acknowledge the peculiarity of treating Jews and Europeans separately in the census but justified the practice with what was essentially a political explanation:

Following the Crémieux decree (October 24, 1870), the Israelites are French citizens, but whereas those who are of French origin are voluntarily independent, and disperse their votes, the [Algerian] Israelites form a strongly disciplined collectivity, obeying orders from above, and constituting a powerful electoral mass; hence the tendency on the part of elected officials to cultivate them and privilege them, even at times to the detriment of the indigenous who are far from having the same electoral strength.[36]

The report's acknowledgment of the overrepresentation of the Jewish population in the electorate was thus cast to make it seem as if the Jews themselves were responsible for this situation. It was certainly true that Jews constituted 25 percent of the voting population, in spite of the fact that they were only 12 percent of the population as a whole, but this was because the Third Republic excluded half the city's population—Muslim colonial subjects—from full citizenship rights. It is hard not to read the Vigouroux report's assertions about Jewish citizenship and Jewish political behavior as a reminder of the "indigenous" origins of Algerian Jews and their essentially North African personality.

Rather than acknowledging that the atmosphere of tension between *Israélites* and *indigènes* might have had something to do with the political arrangements made by the colonial regime, the report preferred references to an atavistic antisemitism on the part of the Muslim population inflamed by the Jews' apparent ability to manipulate the colonial order for their benefit. The resentment arose, the report said, because Constantine's Jews had been too successful in winning for themselves the jobs of public functionaries, particularly in the police force and the post office. This conclusion was in fact a simplification from the commission's own documentation from Police Commissioner Miquel, which made clear that the overrepresentation of Jews in public employment resulted from a shortage of European candidates combined with relentless discrimination against Muslim applicants.[37] The report also emphasized the role played by Jews in banking and moneylending, especially to Muslims, "whose lack of thrift and ignorance in these matters is well known."[38] Here, too, the assertions of the official report went considerably beyond the evidence of their own investigation. In fact, moneylending and the extension of credit to Muslim colonial subjects had expanded during the period of relative prosperity that followed the end of the First World War, but Jews had not been overrepresented in this activity. In fact, so many European settlers had lent money to Muslims during the 1920s that it drew the attention of administrators as a potential source of trouble after the economic crisis of 1929, when many borrowers found themselves unable to pay.[39]

Although the Vigouroux commission appeared to blame both Jews and Muslims for contributing to the circumstances that led to the violence, it nonetheless judged the city's Jewish population more harshly when it came to the public discussion that followed the riots. In a separate discussion of public claims made after the riots, the report addressed two opposing explanations: the "Jewish thesis" (la thèse israélite) and the "native thesis" (la thèse indigène). The Jewish thesis, according to the report, asserted that the riots had been planned ahead of time, and that the violence had been widely anticipated by Muslims, who did not show up for work or closed their businesses early. The native thesis, on the other hand, argued that the dispute was a local disturbance unrelated to politics, and that the spark was provided at each crucial moment by the actions of Jews: on Friday night at the mosque when Elie Khalifa insulted the men preparing for their prayers, and on Sunday morning at the place des Galettes when a group of Jewish men fired pistols in the direction of a crowd at the market. Proceeding as if the only possibility was to adjudicate between these two explanations, the report's conclusion took clear sides: "The facts unfolded as indicated by the native thesis." The "Jewish thesis does not survive a critical examination of the facts."[40]

The structure of the commission's report—a narrative account followed by two contradictory interpretations bearing labels associated with the parties to the conflict—was a clear response to attempts by Muslim and Jewish community leaders to influence the investigation. Adolphe Sultan published his accusations of Muslim conspiracy in La Lumière on August 18. Henri Lellouche published his own charges in two installments of Le Réveil Juif on August 17 and 24. Joseph Fisher, we have seen, presented similar accusations to the Comité des délégations juives in Geneva on August 20. Together, these reports bitterly denounced the city's mismanagement of the crisis, blamed the mayor and the prefecture in equal measure, and bluntly charged that cynical Muslim politicians had organized the violence from the outset to fuel their own political ambitions. They accused the press of inflaming the situation on Saturday, August 4, by printing the false rumor that Elie Khalifa had penetrated the interior of the mosque the night before during the original altercation. They suggested that Muslim shopkeepers had known about the violence of August 5 beforehand and had closed their doors ahead of time, and that rioters were instructed which houses and storefronts to attack by chalk marks that were visible from the street. Finally, they suggested that the city's officials were complicit. They had committed a "fatal imprudence" on August 4 by speaking openly in front of the Muslim elected officials about the small number of soldiers that were available to keep order in the event of further violence. In his account of August 5, Lellouche said that he and his colleagues learned of an imminent attack on the rue des Zouaves and the rue Abdallah Bey (where the Attali and Halimi families lived) as early as 11:30 a.m., only to have their warnings ignored by the overburdened police. Lellouche's report was triply provocative—accusing the rioters of premeditation, the Muslim leadership of the city of abetting the perpetrators of murder, and the colonial administration of criminal negligence.[41]

One by one, the Vigouroux report refuted the evidence for conspiracy put forth by Adolphe Sultan, Henri Lellouche, Joseph Fisher, and other Jewish commentators. The commission interviewed the tobacconist who had emptied his kiosk the morning of August 5 and concluded that he had merely been preparing to renovate his establishment. Vigouroux's report noted the chalk marks that had been placed on buildings during the riot and discovered that they had been made by the police and gendarmes as they searched for looters and victims. The report described the activities of Bendjelloul and other members of the FEMC and found that they had tried to prevent the violence from spreading on the place des Galettes. This refutation of "the Jewish thesis"—circulated by the governor-general to the prefecture—gave permission to local administrators to set aside the more dramatic claims put forth by Lellouche and the other Jewish members of the municipal government, who as a result found their influence waning after the riots. Lellouche and Sultan became the target of antisemites in the settler population, and Mayor Morinaud's commitment to his long alliance with the Jewish municipal councilors became increasingly tenuous.

Bendjelloul's strategy for dealing with the Vigouroux commission after the riots was quite different from the direct confrontation sought by Lellouche, Sultan, and Joseph Fisher. First, he and his FEMC colleagues on the municipal council, twelve names in all, publicly deplored the violence of August 5 with a campaign of signed posters placed on the walls of the city in both French and Arabic: "Without insisting on the true cause of the deplorable and absolutely unexpected and unpredictable events, consisting of the profanation of a Mosque and multiple subsequent provocations, not to mention prior individual exasperations, the Muslim Elected Officials and the healthy population of Constantine unanimously and profoundly deplore the riot and its monstrous excesses."[42] At the same time, Bendjelloul prepared a careful dossier of dozens of personal witness testimonies and submitted it directly to the commission. Bendjelloul's dossier did not seek to synthesize these individual testimonies into a coherent narrative. Most were quite short—several paragraphs at most, typed carefully in French on individual sheets under a heading that included the incident being described and the name, age, and address of the witness. No fewer than sixteen Muslim witnesses described the initial encounter at the Sidi Lakhdar Mosque. These witnesses reported Khalifa's insults in detail and such acts as spitting, urinating, and provocatively displaying his penis. It did not seem to matter if the accounts did not exactly correspond; their cumulative effect was to outweigh the account given by Khalifa himself, who portrayed himself as equally outraged at the men's nonchalant display of their naked bodies in front of his family. Bendjelloul's chosen strategy—to give voice to individual Muslims who were on the streets during the weekend of August 3–5—contrasted with Lellouche's blanket condemnation of the city's authorities, and thus dovetailed perfectly with the administration's desire to portray Constantine's Jews as an essentially tribal community within the city, responsible for their own persecution.

Bendjelloul's insistence that individual Muslim voices be heard may have shaped the Vigouroux commission's conclusions, but the report itself contained little that might be called "testimony." In fact, the report's very structure seemed to militate against the relevance of any individual voices from the city's various populations. The only individuals who emerged as distinct voices in the account were public officials—the police agents on the streets, the staff of the prefecture, and the military decision makers who organized the defense of the city by calling in reinforcements from nearby garrisons. What emerged most clearly from the commission's synthesis of these reports was a vision of urban space permeated with interlocking civil and military jurisdictions, a kind of bureaucratic topography in which the city was rendered visible to the colonial administration only through its own institutions, and the population was visible only in so far as its members conformed to the categories of *indigènes*, *Israélites*, and Europeans. Those spaces that had been appropriated by others for their own uses (such as the Remblai or Les Pins) and those that were vestiges of a precolonial order (the "Ghetto") were the grains of sand in this well-oiled mechanism, spaces that did not conform to the colonial administration's normative distinctions of public and private, urban and rural, European and indigenous.

The report's reductive portrait of Constantine's three populations as having minimal points of contact and predisposed to conflict had very little to do with the reality of social life in the city before the riot. The conflicts of the late 1920s and early 1930s had taken place against the background of a dense network of ongoing social and political relationships. Henri Lellouche had emphasized this history of good relations between Jews and Muslims in his report, and Joseph Fisher made the same assertion. After the riots, however, relations between Muslims and Jews began to resemble more clearly the reductive portrait depicted in the official report. The Vigouroux commission's depiction of three populations divided by mistrust and fear resonated with both Muslim and Jewish residents who felt the strain in the days and weeks that followed the killings in the city. This, of course, was the logical outcome of a situation in which definitions of public order and community relations were shaped by the persistent threat of provocation. The violence of August 5, after it happened, produced the very divisions that the city's residents later determined to be its primary causes. What is the opposite of a self-fulfilling prophecy? A consequence that arrives dressed as a point of departure. This is what people mean when they say that two groups are caught up in a "cycle of violence"—they are talking about a perpetual-motion machine fueled by its own tautologies.

PART 4

Making the Riot Algerian

CHAPTER 11

Empire of Fright

The atmosphere in Constantine and the surrounding region remained volatile for many weeks. The arrest of the alleged "gang of throat slitters"—Muslim butchers' employees—for involvement in the multiple murders led to a rash of disturbing articles in La Dépêche de Constantine in August.[1] These and other equally frightening stories circulated rapidly, and the police sifted nervously through them, struggling to make sense of threats that came from all directions and threatened to spread to other cities in Algeria. The administration perceived three kinds of danger. First, the police highlighted the possibility that rumors, café and market disputes, or schoolboy fights might once more escalate into something bigger. Second, the police feared that individuals might intentionally provoke further violence against Jews. Finally, the administration worried that organized political movements—especially the Federation of Muslim Elected Officials (FEMC), but also the Communist Party, the growing Algerian nationalist movement in metropolitan France, and right-wing groups such as the Croix de feu—would take advantage of the situation to rally their supporters and destabilize political life in the region. The fact that Mohamed Bendjelloul would soon face charges for striking Inspector Gassab on the night of August 3 weighed heavily on the administration, and they monitored him and his political allies closely in the run-up to his trial. Even before August, Bendjelloul had been laying the groundwork for the next elections to the *délégations financières*, scheduled for January 1935. The administration understood that the riot would shape the upcoming political season, but remained deeply uncertain about what would happen next.

Most obviously, the city's Jewish residents were forced to confront the extent of their vulnerability. Their dependence on the police and the military for protection had been obvious for some time, but the riots seemed to demonstrate that the colonial administration was either unable or unwilling to guarantee their safety. Above all, Jewish political leaders in Constantine were more isolated than before. In the first weeks of September, Ernest Lanxade used the pages of his anti-Jewish weekly, *Le Tam Tam*, to stir up anger against Henri Lellouche and Adolphe (Abraham) Sultan for their outspoken criticism of local authorities in the riot's aftermath. *Le Tam Tam* defended General Kieffer, Police Commissioner Miquel, Joseph Landel of the prefecture, and Bendjelloul himself against Jewish attacks. Lanxade blamed the riots on Morinaud's Jewish deputy mayor Émile Barkatz, and called for Lellouche and Sultan to be brought up on charges of spreading hatred and lies.[2] A week later, *Le Tam Tam* repeated Lanxade's attacks on Lellouche and Sultan, while also demanding that Mayor Morinaud resign for having nominated the two Jewish city councilors for the Legion of Honor.[3] Jewish residents feared that Lanxade's attacks would drive Morinaud to reevaluate his long-standing strategic association with Jewish municipal councilors in a political environment increasingly poisoned by antisemitism. They were right to fear this, as this was exactly what Morinaud did.

Bendjelloul, no less than the local Jewish leadership, found himself politically isolated and on the defensive after the riots. The FEMC already faced hostility from the Algerian political establishment, even before the summer of 1934, and the violence of August 3–5 discredited Bendjelloul's constituency in the eyes of his few allies in France, such as Senator Maurice Viollette. Bendjelloul's interest in preserving these relationships make it unlikely that he himself was actively involved in provoking anti-Jewish violence before August 3. After August 5, however, he was all the more dependent on local support from the population of Muslim colonial subjects. His political ambitions required that he maintain his position as their most vocal leader, even though they were now tainted by association with a violent attack on Constantine's Jews.

In fact, anger among the Muslim population at large had many targets in the weeks after the riots. Many still felt a stinging resentment at the memory of Elie Khalifa's profanation of the mosque on August 3. Others remained convinced that Muslim deaths during the riots had been discounted or covered up by an administration that had seemed to condone the violence against Jews during the riots of August 5. It was not true that many Muslims had died, but it was well known that over a dozen Muslim men had been hospitalized with gunshot wounds, and Lachemi Akkacha had been killed before hundreds of onlookers in the place Molière. This context—in which rumor and disinformation formed a toxic mix with older fears and resentments—fostered expressions of anti-Jewish feeling that Bendjelloul, as the most visible political leader of Constantine's Muslim population, would have keenly followed. He would have noticed, for example, that Henri Lautier's anti-Jewish newspaper, *L'Éclair*, found more Muslim buyers in Constantine in the latter weeks of August than it had ever achieved before. This surge of interest in the antisemitic newspaper infuriated Jews who were still in mourning, but it would have been impossible for Bendjelloul to ignore.[4] Unsurprisingly, local Muslim leaders were very cautious about their public statements. 'Abd al-Hamid Ben Badis privately called on his followers to avoid any expressions of anti-Jewish feelings, because more violence would discredit his leadership at a moment when he was being watched closely by the government.[5]

Ben Badis was not wrong that the authorities were looking for any evidence that could be used to discredit local Muslim leaders. His call to abstain from public expressions of antisemitism came at a moment when Algerian nationalists in Paris were trying to attach the unrest in Constantine to their anticolonial struggle by accusing Algeria's Jews of being the facilitators and beneficiaries of French colonialism. Members of the Étoile Nord-Africaine (ENA), a growing but still relatively small organization that had yet to find a mass following in Algeria, sent tracts to Muslims in Constantine declaring their "solidarity with Muslim Algerians who have been the victim of repression in Constantine." The tract repeated the arguments commonly made in the French anti-Jewish press, that the patience of the Algerian population had been sorely tested by the "insatiable cupidity of Jewish financiers, the arrogance of the newly rich, [and] their incomparable and ancient talent for picking our pockets and ruining us." At the same time, however, the tract criticized the hypocrisy of Émile Morinaud, the "old crook . . . who pretends to forget that he began his career as a political adventurer by wetting his parliamentary sash in the blood of the Jew." The actions of the anti-Jewish rioters in Constantine, said the tract, were "legitimate self-defense."[6] The publication of such views could only have driven Constantine's Jews to despair, finding themselves caught between antisemitic defenders of the colonial order who despised them for being too close to North African *"indigènes,"* while anticolonial Algerian nationalists hated them for being too close to the French. The political ramifications of the ENA's tract, meanwhile, further restricted the FEMC's room for maneuver, as Bendjelloul and his colleagues sought both to remain in touch with their embittered and angered Muslim constituency, while also struggling to maintain their position as a loyal opposition that wanted only to reform Algeria's restrictive electoral laws.[7]

Bendjelloul's difficult political position in the aftermath of the riots also helps to explain his surprising decision to begin a quiet conversation in mid-August with Mayor Morinaud about his political future. The mayor apparently assured him of a light sentence in his court case in exchange for a promise that he would abandon his plans to run for a seat on the *délégations financières* in January 1935. If this is true—and several documents seem to indicate that these conversations were taking place in mid-August—it seems to indicate that Bendjelloul sought to repair his relations with local power-brokers in the run-up to his trial date in mid-September.[8] In his dealings with the mayor's office and with representatives of the prefecture, he expressed regrets for having struck the police officer, his hopes that he might avoid jail time, and his readiness to pay a fine.[9]

The only clear beneficiaries of the situation after August 5, in other words, were the rabble-rousers like Ernest Lanxade and Henri Lautier, who found an expanded audience for their anti-Jewish papers in the wake of the violence. Also anxious to take advantage of the unrest were the right-wing leagues such as the Croix de feu, whose antisemitism was central to their growing appeal to Constantine's middle-class constituency. Members of the Croix de feu approved of the attacks on Jews, and some of their members had tried to provoke this violence before. They also welcomed the opportunity to crow about the weaknesses of the government and the need for a muscular response to preserve order. The riots gave the local Croix de feu a club with which to beat Morinaud for his failures during his long tenure as mayor, and an opportunity to challenge him by campaigning for offices on the local municipal council, the departmental assembly, and on the Algeria-wide *délégations financières*.

In the meantime, the pervasive sense that a resumption of violence was imminent helps to explain the extraordinary volume of police reports that surged through the administration's information channels. No detail was too small to be recorded. On August 24, Clothilde Bott, a fifty-seven-year-old woman known in her Constantine neighborhood as "dame Marchika," reported that while she took her morning bath, she overheard through the window two Arabic-speaking neighbors washing themselves in the courtyard. One of the women said to the other: "It will start again, and this time, it will be without any distinction of race." Dame Marchika's testimony was not taken seriously by Constantine's police chief, René Miquel. "Dame Marchika," he wrote, "is an unbalanced woman who acts under the empire of fright."[10] He nevertheless devoted an entire report to the incident and sent it to the Vigouroux commission, which was investigating the causes of the riots.

"Empire of fright" was an inadvertently appropriate phrase for the situation in Constantine in the late summer of 1934. Only a few days before Dame Marchika's statement, the cafés in the rue de France had hastily closed after a story circulated that a Jewish man had been struck in the face on the street. The customers of the cafés and shops rushed to their homes, while the Muslim vegetable sellers in the place de Galettes ran off "in a single movement" to the safety of their own neighborhood. A few moments later on the rue Vieux, a large group of Muslim men arrived bearing clubs, but they were stopped by West African troops who blocked the streets and prevented Jews and Muslims from confronting one another directly.[11] The reestablishment of daily routines inevitably brought differing peoples back together, but sudden contagious flashes of fear showed how easy it was for boundaries to reconstitute themselves brutally in response to a whispered story, a sudden noise, or a shout of alarm.

Incidents of this sort occurred frequently that August, leaving behind echoes of rumor and misinformation that prolonged the collective anguish and guaranteed that the coming days would be just as volatile as those before. On August 31, the news that a young unmarried Jewish woman had gone missing from a Jewish neighborhood led to anxious meetings and to stories that she had been kidnapped by a band of Muslim men. In fact, she had merely gone to Algiers to be with her lover.[12] The police, demonstrating an all-too-predictable professional commitment to insensitivity, ordered her family to spread the news of their dishonor to their neighbors in order to counter the earlier rumor's effects.

Many of the letters from local officials collected by Jean Vigouroux's investigating commission gave evidence—direct and indirect—of conspiracy and organized behavior during the riots. Gustave Mercier repeated the testimony of local Muslims that they had been given orders to "destroy and burn, but not steal" the goods in Jewish stores, and had witnessed organized bands controlling access to the city along the principal thoroughfares.[13] The mayor of El Khroub, twelve kilometers to the southwest of Constantine, provided a story about provocateurs inciting people to join the riots. On the morning of August 5, two men driving a truck appeared in El Khroub's central place and announced that Mohamed Bendjelloul had been killed or injured by the Jews of Constantine. The men went "from group to group peddling this news, exhorting the numerous natives, who had been calm up to this moment, but who seemed to be waiting for a hidden word of command, to go and avenge their Chief, Bendjelloul." Having succeeded in assembling a crowd of over a thousand people, the two men got back in their truck and resumed their journey toward the communes of Ouled Rahmoun and Aïn Abid, which lay further to the south and west. Later that afternoon, "all the cars" coming from Constantine were filled with "large pieces of partly burned cloth." In the meantime, the mayor, escorted and assisted by two cooperative local Muslim leaders, succeeded in protecting the local Jewish population in El Khroub.[14]

El Khroub turned up again in police reports in early September, this time in connection with anti-Jewish provocation organized by Europeans. An administrator in Haut-Sebaou in Kabylia claimed that a "European" of unidentified nationality had sold two million francs worth of rifles and revolvers to "two [Algerian Muslim] landowners" (gros fellah) who deposited them in a warehouse in El Khroub. They planned to mask the true source of the weapons by placing them where they could be seized by local groups at a moment of general disorder. The informant said this transaction happened before August, and that the conspirators were waiting to hear the results of the criminal trials from the riots before using the weapons. The same report claimed that a German boat had recently docked in Bougie and that the crew had distributed Nazi propaganda, including ten-centime pieces engraved with the slogan "Down with the Jews" (À bas les Juifs).[15] After investigation, the prefect of Constantine dismissed these stories as "a fantasy that should be urgently repudiated."[16]

Of particular interest, however, is the ambiguously identified "European" who seems to have been part of the alleged plot reported by the administrator of Haut-Sebaou. References to Europeans come up frequently in police reports of rumors and provocation, but they were rarely addressed in public statements made by officials in the wake of the riots. Henri Coquelin, director of the prefecture's office of departmental security in Constantine, took a statement on September 7, 1934, about a conversation at a dentist's office. The source was a Jewish man from Constantine, Joseph Attali, who had heard it from a woman in Bône who visited the dentist after the riots. This elongated chain of reported speech was typical of rumor reports. The unnamed woman from Bône had been in the dentist's waiting room with a working-class "European" woman and a woman "from the upper levels of Muslim society." They exchanged their views on the riots, and the working-class European woman said that "what happened to the Jews was well done. They occupy the most important places everywhere and their arrogance has no limits. It's not a movement of the native population against the Jews, it's a Franco-Arab movement against them. And the proof is that three young

French people disguised themselves as Arabs at my brother's house and four more at the house of a neighbor!"[17]

No statement about the riot could have been more troubling. The idea that among the rioters of August 5 were Europeans disguised as Arabs was potentially explosive. Aside from the political implications, the story contained too many taboos of colonial society: that the distinction between French and Algerian was not fixed, that changing one's clothes allowed you to assume a new identity, and that anti-Jewish sentiment was the glue for a new kind of Franco-Arab solidarity. For these reasons the prefecture devoted considerable effort to investigating this story. They identified the dentist in question, Natal Camilleri, and found his practice in the rue Bugeaud. They had more trouble finding the women in the waiting room. Camilleri was uneasy about being connected with the investigation, and he stated that he never recorded the names of his "native customers." He also did not allow indigènes to sit in the waiting room—he preferred to place them in an office where they would not meet his European customers. He eventually admitted that the description matched a certain "Madame Karezi" who had visited his office during the weeks in question. When the police interviewed her, however, she said that she had met no one because she had been ushered into the dentist's separate office. It thus proved impossible to identify the woman who had reported seeing French men disguise themselves as Arabs on the day of the riots. No follow-up on these initial reports was saved in the dossier.[18]

Nevertheless, this story reveals so much about the hierarchies of Algerian colonial society that it is impossible not to dwell on its permutations. There is the underlying skepticism of the police toward the testimony of a Jewish man, Joseph Attali, who was clearly disturbed at the idea that the rioters on August 5 may not all have been "Arabs" at all, but rather European antisemites in Arab dress. The police took his report seriously enough to investigate, but were hindered by dentist's commitment to the racial segregation of his clientele, and his lack of concern with any record-keeping for his "native" patients, even those, like the prosperous Madame Karezi, who had appeared at his office with her servant. It is impossible to know if the story was true, but in some sense it does not matter. What is important is that the woman from Bône took it seriously enough to repeat it to Joseph Attali, and that he was disturbed enough to tell the police. Madame Karezi may have realized that the story was troubling and that pretending the conversation never happened was the only safe recourse. The power of such provocative stories depended on this condition of underlying possibility. No matter how unlikely it might seem, simply saying it out loud seemed to give it a kind of plausibility, an explanatory power that was no more or no less credible than many of the other things that people were saying in the aftermath of the violence. Once reported and logged in the police files, the story carried its perverse logic even further: because it could not be disproven, it could not be denied altogether.

Other reports noted a "Franco-Arab" dynamic to the region's anti-Jewish violence in 1934. Among the most suggestive was a report from Birkadem, just south of Algiers, about anonymous threats slid under the door of a Jewish shop at the end of August. The first was a note written in pencil, and in French, on the squared notepaper common to schoolrooms in France. The threats in the note were composed in the familiar language of the antisemitic gutter press, with a dose of adolescent sexual aggression:

> Down with the Jews
> It's going to be the moment to get rid
> of you. Bunch of faggots bunch of thieves
> down with the Jews bunch of bastards it's your skin we'll
> ask for
> Get out of the village at once if not your skin
> Long live the Arabs[19]

The message was accompanied by a strange piece of paper, trimmed and decorated in the shape of an unfinished fleur-de-lys—a symbol commonly used by French royalists and nationalists in the interwar years—with the phrase "Down with the Jews Long Live the Arabs" rendered phonetically in a misspelled representation of colloquial French, written in blue and red-orange wax crayon: "AMBA LiJUIFE ViVE LiZARABE." The range of meanings that emerged from this combination of French nationalist symbolism, the red-white-and-blue color scheme, and the anti-Jewish slogan was compounded by the images on the other side of the paper. It showed that the paper was trimmed from an orange soda advertisement in such a way that a fragment of the ad's slogan, a cartoon illustration of a man with an orange for a head sipping soda from a long straw, and the name of the soda—Orange Ora—were partially visible. The advertising slogan was printed in a three-dimensional blue-and-orange typeface, clearly the inspiration for the lettering of the anti-Jewish slogan on the other side. Underneath the advertising slogan was a crude drawing of a human head wearing a soft cap, also drawn in blue and orange crayon. This drawing imitated the printed illustration of the orange-headed man just above it, though a lit cigarette was substituted for the drinking straw. The drawing was positioned on the paper in such a way that when it was folded along the crease, it formed the top of the

fleur-de-lys on the other side, so that the man in the cap smoking the cigarette became the "flower" at the top of the royalist symbol.

It is not at all clear that this drawing with its provocative caption was really
written by a young Muslim. Provocations by European antisemites that pur-
ported to be by Muslims were well known to the police already during these
months.[20] Particularly suspicious is the crude reproduction of an uneducated
person's spoken dialect, which was similar to the caricatural language that
one might find in satirical newspapers of the time. One assumes that a person who had learned the Latin alphabet and the rudiments of written French
would know how to render the plural definite article "les" with an "s" rather
than a "z," which is less often encountered in French, except in cruel parodies
of foreign accents.

In any case, even if it was a counterfeit, it is worth pausing to think how
it might have worked as propaganda. The celebration of "LiZARABE" (the
Arabs) merged with the careful and detailed rendering of the fleur-de-lys,
by far the most carefully drawn portion of the imagery on this tattered bit
of paper. The confusing juxtaposition of nationalist cliché and advertising
hucksterism contained a cacophony of messages about what it might mean
for a young Algerian adolescent to imagine the consequences of "Frenchness" during these years—to be able to smoke, to drink sugared fruit soda,
to participate in a consumer economy, to wear the soft cap of the European
worker, to embrace the patriotic fervor of both a French and an Arab nationalism simultaneously, and to seal the deal by proclaiming hatred of Jews. The
image points to the possibility that for some, expressions of antisemitism
were also a way of embracing a certain idea of Frenchness, and that Algerian
Muslims were being invited to think that this was the case. Being anti-Jewish
was one way of showing that you were on the side of the French tricolor
flag—and it didn't preclude being on the side of "LiZARABE" either.

Provocateurs such as Lanxade, Lautier, and even Morinaud himself were
perfectly willing to use antisemitism as a lever to manipulate the loyalties
of the Muslim population. The settler political establishment nevertheless
sought to prevent Bendjelloul and the FEMC from using the unrest to their
own advantage. In particular, the mayor, the prefect, and the governor-
general were determined to use the crisis to derail Bendjelloul's political ambitions. The fact that he had to be charged for striking a police officer was
inconvenient, because it required confronting him in a way that could only
enhance his claim to represent the disenfranchised Muslim population as a
whole. Jewish political leaders in Constantine were still blaming Bendjelloul
for the riots and insisting on a harsh prison sentence, while his colleagues
in the FEMC argued that a light fine would be sufficient.[21] Hoping that the

passage of time would relieve some of the tension surrounding the case, the administration postponed Bendjelloul's court date, initially set for August 22, to September 19. This clumsy attempt at delay only made the situation worse, however, because the new date coincided with Yom Kippur, the most sacred day on the Jewish religious calendar, the Day of Atonement. In the meantime, a new development made it unlikely that a delay of a few weeks would improve the atmosphere.

In late August it became clear that many Muslims were no longer buying goods from Jewish-owned businesses. The central police commissioner, René Miquel, stationed special officers in commercial neighborhoods to collect information on the boycott. During the riot, the majority of Jewish-owned shops and businesses had been pillaged, their stocks and furniture thrown into the street. The city's textile merchants had been particularly hard hit, but grocers, butchers, sellers of household goods, and professional offices were also damaged. The prefecture established a committee to assess the extent of the damages after each business submitted an inventory. The inventory process took more than two weeks, and almost all Jewish-owned businesses remained closed. When they reopened at the end of August, many of their Muslim customers did not return, perhaps fearing that they would not be well received.[22] After the first week, when this reticence persisted, people began to speak of an ongoing boycott of Jewish retailers by Constantine's Muslims.

Some Jews immediately suspected Bendjelloul of organizing the boycott, but it is possible that he was simply following a course of events that were not completely under his control. After the violence, his political movement had lost much of its leverage with the local population. Many of his constituents still felt justified in their anger at their Jewish neighbors, and he had been seen on the street on August 5 trying to stop the violence. Faced with limited options, Bendjelloul may have felt that he had no choice but to double down and shore up his base of support with a boycott. From the perspective of the authorities, Bendjelloul's postponed court date on September 19 fell at an especially inopportune moment—after the boycott's effects had begun to create more tension and hostility on the streets but before the police were able to determine who may have been involved in organizing it. Faced with the prospect of renewed violence, the police went so far as to inquire about the possibility having the Jews of Constantine emigrate to France for good.[23] Under these circumstances, reports that people from the surrounding region would be coming to voice their support for Bendjelloul before the Palais de Justice in Constantine on the day of his court date raised considerable alarm.[24]

An incident two days before the trial put everybody on edge. Two young musicians were drinking together, a young Jewish man named Raymond Leyris and a Muslim man, Mohamed ben Abdelmoumène Amri. Leyris, at the time only twenty-two, would later become a beloved figure in Algeria under the name Cheikh Raymond because of his sensitive performances of songs in the Malouf tradition, the local variant of the classical music of Muslim Andalusia.[25] On this day, however, he was still a relative unknown, and was drinking with a friend and musical colleague at a café on the rue de France owned by a member of the politically well-connected and influential Aouizerate family. Leyris was concerned about the situation in the city, and he told his Muslim friend to remain inside for the next few days because, he was reported to have said, "the French are going to shoot and machine-gun the Arabs."[26] Unfortunately, Amri reacted badly to Leyris's expression of concern, and instead of returning quietly to his apartment after finishing his drinks, he began shouting on the street corner that "Dr. Bendjelloul had summoned all natives to the place des Galettes"—that is, the public market adjacent to the Jewish quarter.[27] Amri's disturbance caused a panic in the neighborhood that dissipated only after he was arrested and taken to the police station. The next day Bendjelloul asked that charges be brought against Amri for "publication of false information and disturbance of public peace."[28]

That afternoon, only one day before Bendjelloul's trial, Muslim elected officials placed posters on walls throughout the city:

Declaration

Fantastical and odious rumors are circulating in the city and suburbs of Constantine. Muslim elected officials and notables are accused of having made incendiary anti-French statements regarding the trial of Dr. Bendjelloul.

These unreasonable statements have astonished and profoundly wounded the Muslim elected officials, who feel that it is their duty to address the entire population directly in order to formally deny these false rumors and to call on everyone to defend themselves against all alarming news.

Since the deplorable events of August 5, the Muslim elected officials have demonstrated many times over their calm and restraint.

They are departing now from their reserve only to oppose those who seek to take advantage of our troubles, to stigmatize the professional agitators, and to provide a solemn denial to their lies and calumnies.

> These elected officeholders once again assure the population that they continue and will continue to call for calm and to work toward the pacification of the city.
>
> No matter what the verdict, the trial of Dr. Bendjelloul will have no influence over their desire for peace. They consider that Dr. Bendjelloul is subject to the authority of the court [*un justiciable*] and as such must submit to French law and regulations.
>
> Confident in French justice and in the impartiality of judges, the Muslim elected officials repudiate all efforts to pressure anyone. They demand that all people of goodwill cooperate in reestablishing as soon as possible peace and the normal life that everybody desires.[29]

This public statement captured the double-bind defined by a discourse of provocation and counter-provocation. For Muslim elected officials, to speak out loud was to "depart from their reserve"—to run the risk of appearing provocative. At a minimum, speaking out only drew attention to the very rumors that they wished to deny. The stridency of their protests underlined the extent to which they opened themselves to a charge of double-speak, calling for calm when so many believed that they would only benefit from more disorder. Their statement conceded that Bendjelloul, as an elected official, should be subject to French law, but its careful tone pointed to the difficulty they faced: a moment when the FEMC's supporters were outraged at the administration's treatment of their most popular leader became yet another occasion where the Muslim elected officials felt obligated to demonstrate their loyalty to France. That the poster was in French, and that its intended audience was clearly the administration and the city's French-speaking population rather than their own constituents, also drew attention to their awkward political position.

After all the buildup, the trial itself was anticlimactic. Bendjelloul appeared before the judge at 7:30 in the morning on September 19 and recognized the facts as they were laid out by the prosecutor. He did not deny that he had struck Inspector Gassab on the evening of August 3. He explained that at the moment of the confrontation he was exhausted after a long day of free medical consultations and strenuous attempts to halt the violence. The prosecutor asked only for a substantial fine and did not call for prison time. When the judges returned from their consultation, they announced their decision: a suspended sentence of one month in prison and a one hundred franc fine. Bendjelloul's sympathizers gathered outside had expected a further delay and were surprised by the severity of the sentence. The police laconically reported that the members of the crowd "did not dare to demonstrate their unhappiness because of the measures taken."[30]

Caught between the criticism coming from the authorities and the anger of their constituents, FEMC officials and their allies debated among themselves how to respond. When they held a public meeting on September 28 to commemorate the three Muslims who died because of the riots, seventy-one hundred people came to the ceremony at Constantine's Muslim cemetery.[31] The event provided an occasion for Bendjelloul and 'Abd al-Hamid Ben Badis to appear together, but relations between the two men had become strained, in part because Bendjelloul's candidacy for the *délégations financières* put him in competition with Ben Badis's father, an incumbent member from Constantine.[32] Throughout these weeks, anger among the Muslim population remained at a very high level, not least because Bendjelloul's conviction was immediately followed by the convictions on September 21 and 25 of twenty-seven men on looting and weapons charges related to the riots. The procedures were hastily organized, and the accused were given little chance to respond to the charges made against them. Dozens more convictions followed every week until the end of October.[33]

Rabah Zenati, editor and publisher of *La Voix indigène*, called for a parliamentary commission to investigate the demands of Algeria's Muslim population in the aftermath of the riots, but the FEMC had little faith in the goodwill of the French parliament. Zenati and several other FEMC members were in favor of appealing Bendjelloul's conviction to the higher court in Algiers, but the majority of the local members were convinced that a confrontational approach would only hurt their efforts to restore their credibility. In the end, the Fédération accepted the tribunal's judgment and respected the sentence imposed on their leader. The ongoing boycott, however, made it difficult for the FEMC and their supporters to pursue their cautious policy of reestablishing their reputation for loyalty. Zenati himself was now facing a boycott of *La Voix indigène* by some of his Muslim subscribers because he continued to use the print works owned by Makhlouf Attali, whose family members had been murdered on August 5.[34]

Henri Lautier, the fascist sympathizer and editor of the anti-Jewish paper *L'Éclair*, explicitly encouraged the boycott movement by posting multicolored stickers on walls throughout the city on the night of October 3–4 with the slogan "To be done with the Jew, not a penny to the Jew." Following Lautier's campaign, the boycott became more organized. The police received complaints about men standing outside Jewish-owned businesses and discouraging Muslim customers from entering, and the police noted that the movement focused above all on Jewish textile retailers.[35] The police assigned officers to keep track of five different locations in the old city where they believed disturbances between boycotters and Jewish business owners were likely to develop: the rue des Zouaves, the place des Galettes, the place Jules Fabre, and two locations on the rue Combes.

The police concluded that the primary beneficiaries of the migration of buyers to other textile retailers were a group of Muslim-owned businesses from the M'Zab, a region to the southwest of Constantine with a distinctive culture and particular religious beliefs. M'Zabite merchants were active throughout Algeria and had long been associated with trade routes that linked sub-Saharan Africa to Algeria's coastal networks on the Mediterranean. Their businesses were among the main competitors of Jewish merchants in Constantine, especially in the textile trade. Police reports from the fall of 1934 suggest that retail textile businesses owned by M'Zabites in Constantine enjoyed "a kind of monopoly" after the riots, allowing them to raise prices.[36] They also concluded that a few M'Zabite business owners were helping to organize the boycott.

In mid-October, Mayor Morinaud asked the prefect to meet with the president of the M'Zabite *jamma'a* (council) to demand that he and his colleagues use their influence to put a halt to the boycott.[37] The president of the M'Zabite *jamma'a* declared his loyalty to the government and said that he had no part in the boycott, and the meeting had no effect. The prefect then convened an unusual meeting on October 31 that brought together a representative group of leading personalities from the city, including, in his words, "French, *Israélites*, and natives." This meeting, too, was not a success. Maurice Laloum, a Jewish member of the municipal council, appealed to the "sentiments of humanity and fraternity" of the Muslims present, but the Muslim officials, led by Bendjelloul, remained silent. The prefect concluded that the boycott was only the most visible sign of the "hostile sentiments that Muslims feel toward the Jews that the troubles of the month of August have only exacerbated."[38] At the same time, he pointed out that "the *Israélites* have done nothing to avoid this result." No Muslim was hired during the period of cleanup and reconstruction in the city after the riots, and during the same period a group of Jews met at the synagogue to organize a Jewish boycott of Muslim businesses. The police concluded that the Muslim political leadership had decided it was not in their interest to take a public position against the boycott of Jewish businesses, and that there was no reason to hope for any improvement until after the elections to Algeria's *délégations financières* in January 1935. In fact, the boycott was already much diminished by the end of October, and by early December it appeared to be over.[39]

In late October, however, while the boycott was still going on, Morinaud and his allies on the Conseil général did their best to take advantage of Bendjelloul's difficult position. They proposed a declaration on the August events that Bendjelloul and his allies could not reject without appearing to contradict their professions of loyalty to France. The declaration was worded in such a way as to maximize the discomfiture of Bendjelloul and his allies before their constituents. Declaring their pride in the "benevolent work of protection" that the "French population" had accomplished in Algeria, and their indignation at the "extreme volatility of character" that the "mass of natives" had exhibited during the riots, the "representatives of French origin" on the Conseil général demanded a "necessary gesture of solidarity" from their Muslim colleagues:

- to condemn with the same energy the recent crimes that have dishonored Algerian soil and diminished the prestige of France;
- to combat, in the interest of the Muslim population, the anti-French politics that now are infiltrating North Africa;
- to denounce the guilty, wherever they are found and whatever their situation;
- to seek with all the means they have the pacification of a public opinion that has been overexcited by the recent events;
- to affirm out loud that they will stand in opposition to all those who try to trouble the French Peace in this land.[40]

The declaration was signed by Morinaud and thirty-three other members of the Conseil, including the lawyer Étienne Muracciole, the Croix de feu leader Jules Valle, and Paul Cuttoli, and placed before the Conseil for a vote.

For Bendjelloul and the FEMC members on the Conseil général, the declaration was a bitter pill—they were being asked to assume responsibility for the rioters of August 5, as if the murderers were representative of Muslim opinion as a whole, and of their voting constituency in particular. Particularly damning was the implication that their own political activities were "anti-French" and that the Fédération's work to expand Muslim voting rights may have been a contributing cause of the riots. Ben Khellaf of Djidjelli insisted that there was nothing anti-French about what had happened, saying that "it was only a local event that took on very regrettable proportions."[41] Ferhat Abbas was more explicit in his defense of the FEMC, asserting strongly that he and his colleagues "remain an element of peace and concord," and if "one day a wave overwhelms and inundates our country, be assured that even if it will not spare you, we will be among the first victims."[42]

Étienne Muracciole clearly relished the opportunity to put Bendjelloul and the FEMC in difficulty. Muracciole, a lawyer, was a prominent ally of Mayor Morinaud, an elected member of the Conseil général, and a leading member of the Constantine bar. He would later play a leading role in the trials of those charged with murder during the riots of August 5. He expressed his "surprise" when the members of the FEMC resisted the demand that they sign the declaration put forth by the majority on the Conseil général. "Our native colleagues are like newborn infants in political life," he stated, "and they are experiencing reactions which only demonstrate their inflexibility."[43] When Muracciole finished speaking, Bendjelloul announced that he would not support the declaration. He said he would never question French sovereignty in Algeria, but there were things in the declaration that he could not support. He reiterated his arguments about the causes of the violence— the profanation of the mosque and the gunshots fired by Jews during the unrest—and forcefully described all that he had done to prevent its outbreak. Abbas then followed with a speech declaring that he could not tolerate that he or his constituency should be labeled "anti-French." Recounting the story of his origins, of his schooling, and his education, he said that he had debts to France, to his comrades in the army and at the university, but also to the *"masse indigène"* of his village. "France belongs here to everyone, and I claim my part of it."[44]

Bendjelloul took a different tack in the weeks that followed—he was walking a finer line with an eye toward the elections for the *délégations financières* in January 1935. With his trial over and the mocking words of Muracciole still ringing in his ears, Bendjelloul made it clear that his earlier promise to Morinaud for a more conciliatory position after the riots would not stand. He would challenge the administration more directly, but he would do so with a page from their own playbook, by running against Constantine's Jewish population. Already in the week after his trial on September 19, Bendjelloul had declared in a public meeting before his supporters in El Milia that he was "struggling against 'the enemies.'" The administrator who witnessed this speech was unsure whom Bendjelloul was referring to, but the report made clear that the audience obviously understood Bendjelloul to be referring to Jews.[45] Any remaining ambiguity in Bendjelloul's attitude on this question was soon resolved. On November 22, the sub-prefect in Philippeville reported that Bendjelloul had given financial support to Ernest Lanxade, the editor of the anti-Jewish tabloid, *Le Tam Tam*, and that they had been seeing making inquiries about the purchase of a printing machine.[46] The sub-prefect's reports suggested that Bendjelloul and Lanxade were considering producing a new newspaper together. That same week, while still in Philippeville, Bendjelloul officially announced his candidacy for the *délégations financières*, after appearing openly with Lanxade at a theatrical performance with a political theme.[47]

Bendjelloul's arrangement with Lanxade led to a rift with his longtime ally Rabah Zenati, the editor of *La Voix indigène* who had supported Bendjelloul's earlier campaigns and come to his defense in his September trial. Zenati was a teacher, and his assimilationist program embraced the opportunity offered by the Third Republic's educational system and its naturalization procedures. Zenati was upset to see that the subventions that had formerly come to *La Voix indigène* were now going to Lanxade's *Le Tam Tam*.[48] Bendjelloul made no effort to reconcile with his former colleague. Instead, the president of the FEMC moved toward a different expression of what French patriotism could mean: one that combined his claim to represent the interest of Algerian Muslims with attacks on the place of Jews in North African society. In the aftermath of the August riots, there was more than one way to claim allegiance to the tricolor flag. Frenchness was a still a moving target, and for Bendjelloul at least there was a potential advantage to imitating the language of the anti-Jewish right.

Bendjelloul's calculations, though cynical, proved correct. He campaigned hard, and the vote was widely seen as a referendum on his leadership of the FEMC. The administration backed his rival, the moderate lawyer Hadj Said Mokhtar, and spread rumors that Bendjelloul did not support Viollette's proposal to give Algerian colonial subjects parliamentary representation. In late January 1935 Bendjelloul's campaign paid off, and he won his seat on the highest elective assembly in Algeria. The days before the vote were tense, and the director of the Sûreté départementale de Constantine, Henri Coquelin, warned of the danger of "serious brawls between Muslims and *Israélites*" if Bendjelloul's partisans gathered in large numbers during the voting.[49] In the end, Bendjelloul's margin of victory was overwhelming—the official tally gave him 8,514 votes out of 11,560 cast.[50] His success was not matched by other FEMC-backed candidates, however: of the four others sponsored by the Fédération, only the one in Bône was elected. In Akbou, Aïn Beïda, and Oued Amizour the incumbents survived the FEMC's challenge.

Bendjelloul's victory was overshadowed by the new political dynamic created by the riots of August 5. Just over a week after the elections, on February 7, *tirailleurs algériens* in the nearby town of Sétif rioted after a member of their unit was shot and killed following a dispute with a local police agent in front of a brothel.[51] The soldiers attacked a police station, killing a police officer and injuring two others. The original reports claimed that the soldiers believed that the police agent was Jewish, and this was offered as an explanation for the unrest.[52] The francophone press quickly drew a more dramatic conclusion, arguing that the sudden outbreak of violence in Sétif was a sign of insubordination among the entire Muslim population. A historian and journalist, André Servier, wrote in *L'Écho de l'Est* that the Sétif riot could not be explained away as a banal example of antisemitism, and he blamed Bendjelloul. The president of the FEMC, Servier argued, had begun with legitimate claims but had gone too far in his confrontation with the established order, and the violence of the Algerian riflemen should be laid at the feet of the Fédération: "Haven't they played with fire in chasing after their least evolved coreligionists with a propaganda that seems not to have been understood by its targets, since it has resulted only in an unhealthy excitation? Perhaps without intending it, they have only reanimated the old seeds of discord; they have encouraged the worst instincts."[53] Servier's critique of Bendjelloul combined a contempt for his constituency (the "least evolved coreligionists") with a refusal to see that Bendjelloul's move was in fact a successful act of assimilation, though of a novel kind. The president of the FEMC had become a politician very much like his rivals Morinaud and Muracciole on the Conseil général, willing to use exactly the same anti-Jewish tactics and exploit the very same vulnerabilities in order to claim political power within French Algeria's electoral system.

Morinaud was more succinct in his appraisal of Bendjelloul's victory. In a handwritten note to the prefect on the evening of the election, he wrote: "Native elections. Wasn't I right? (Our program should be this: let the natives elect whomever they want and talk to the winners). . . . But we don't want to listen anymore . . . to the other ones!"[54] The reference to "the other ones" was ambiguous. Did he mean his former Jewish allies on the municipal council, or the other candidates of the FEMC who had failed to win their seats? To all appearances, it does not matter what he meant, because Morinaud had clearly decided it was not necessary to listen to either group. The mix of condescension and complacency in Morinaud's note betrays his sense of having managed to survive the crisis created by the riots of the previous August. Bendjelloul had been elected, but most of his colleagues in the Fédération had been defeated and could now be ignored. French Algeria's institutions had survived the crisis, and Morinaud himself was now free of his troublesome attachment to Jewish politicians. Bendjelloul's political success, on the other hand, came at the cost of openly soliciting the help of the nationalist and anti-Jewish right, and his constituents were tainted with the stain of fanaticism. The riots had produced new political possibilities that Morinaud was fully willing to exploit.

CHAPTER 12

The Police Investigation

The task of investigating the August 5 killings in Constantine fell to the city's Police Mobile, while the gendarmerie took responsibility for police operations in the nearby countryside. By August 8, gendarmes arrested 189 people related to disturbances in towns and villages throughout the region. Given the scale of these operations, and the fact that they occurred only three days after the riots, one can only conclude that the gendarmes conducted the most cursory of investigations. Arrests in communities outside the city were largely a performance designed to show the administration's energetic response in the face of a challenge to its authority. In Constantine, on the other hand, public scrutiny was unprecedented. The Police Mobile faced enormous pressure to discover those responsible for the sensational murders of August 5.

The Police Mobile was a small investigating unit with both "European" and "native" officers. Unlike the Municipal Police or the gendarmes, they did not wear uniforms while on active duty but dressed *en bourgeois*—in street clothes. Many had been present during the fighting on August 5, and they took charge of identifying witnesses and taking statements afterward. The chief of the Police Mobile, responsible for the initial murder investigations, was Jacques Cauro, who worked closely with Inspector Marius Gaillard.[1]

Cauro and Gaillard's investigation took a dramatic turn after only one week. On Sunday, August 12, a domestic servant who survived the attack on the Halimi family in the rue Abdallah Bey identified one of the murderers. Waiting in line in a Jewish-owned butcher's shop in the rue de France, the Boucherie Taïeb, Rosette Benisti recognized a young man behind the counter. She believed him to be one of the group that invaded the Halimi apartment and chased the family up the back stairs to the attic where the murders took place. The *Dépêche de Constantine*'s breathless account could not resist a dramatic re-creation: "Imagine her surprise in seeing, a knife in his hand, one of the attackers of her employers."[2] The young man, Tayeb ben Saïd Benamira, was a twenty-year-old employee of the butcher, originally from the *commune mixte* of Tahir, and known to the neighborhood as "Santo." Benisti immediately went and told the police, who arrested him and took him to the Office of Departmental Security for interrogation.

There can be little doubt that the police physically abused Benamira and other suspects during their interrogations. Abuse and beatings were common in Algerian police stations. During the trials in February 1936 where Benamira and other defendants in the Halimi-Zerdoun case eventually faced their accusers in court, every defendant claimed to have been beaten, and they all stated that their confessions were the result of torture. From the testimony at the trials, it appears that the interrogators focused their attentions on their suspects' hands and feet. One defendant even produced a signed medical statement saying that the scars from his injuries were consistent with such mistreatment.[3] These circumstances make it very difficult to assess the confessions extracted by the police.

The police leaked Rosette Benisti's identification of Benamira to the press immediately.[4] The first newspaper article resulting from her tip-off appeared in the *Dépêche de Constantine* on Tuesday, August 14, and was picked up the next day by the *Écho d'Alger*. The press reports exploited the story's most theatrical aspects, and the details could only have come directly from the police. The articles described dramatic confrontations between witnesses and suspects and recounted ruthless interrogations with relish. In Benamira's first questioning, on the evening of Sunday, August 12, he denied all of Benisti's claims. On Monday morning, he admitted that he had been among the rioters, but continued to deny that he had been present at the murders. He did, however, name another butcher's employee, Saïd ben Abdallah Benhamama, as having played an active role in the murders on the rue Béraud (of the watchmaker Jacob Bentata, as well as that of the Dadoun brothers and their employee, Blanche Guedj), on the rue Abdallah Bey (the Halimi and Zerdoun families), and the rue des Zouaves (the Attali and Attal families). Following this lead, the police quickly arrested Benhamama, also from

Tahir, who worked at another butcher shop in the Constantine suburb of Saint-Jean.

Benhamama produced an alibi for August 5—he said he had been at a *café maure* with a third butcher, Mohamed ben Amar Takouk. Soon, however, Benhamama went further and formally accused "Santo" Benamira of murder. Benhamama told the police that Benamira had showed up at the café at midday with a bloody knife and told them "I just cut the throats of some Jews." The police arrested Mohamed Takouk, who confirmed Benhamama's story. When confronted with his accusers, Benamira, in the *Dépêche's* account, "lowered his head and confessed to his crime."[5]

Surprisingly, the crime that Benamira confessed to was not the murders of the Halimi and Zerdoun family members in the rue Abdallah Bey where Rosette Benisti claimed to have seen him. Instead, he confessed to the murder of Joseph Salomon Attal, the downstairs neighbor of Makhlouf Attali, in the rue des Zouaves. Benamira said that he had been with Benhamama among the rioters in front of the Attali apartment when the latter invited him to enter the building. He encountered Attal on the first landing and clubbed him until he fell to the ground "and stopped moving."[6] The police took Benamira to the Attalis' building in the rue des Zouaves, and, according to their report, he willingly indicated the place where he had struck Attal with the blows that killed him. He took them into the Attali apartment and indicated where the family members fell, claiming all the while that he had been armed only with a club. Taken to the Halimi apartment, Benamira continued to deny that he had been present at their murders. The *Écho d'Alger*, having already decided on Benamira's guilt, reproduced his response to the inspector's questions about the murder of the Halimis: " 'No!' answered the murderer, 'no, I swear it!' "[7] Benamira was charged with murder and held in prison, and the police announced that other arrests were imminent.

The next day's newspapers brought a new revelation: the arrest of three more young men who confessed to the murders of Lucien Chemla and Abraham Bedoucha. The *Dépêche de Constantine* reported that this "sinister gang" of "throat slitters" was composed "almost exclusively of butchers' employees."[8] The police determined, after further interrogation, that Saïd Benhamama and his friend, Mohamed Takouk, the third butcher, had participated along with Benamira in the murder of Chemla in the rue Germon. They also named two more young butcher's employees as participants in Chemla's murder.[9] Rabah ben Salah Hachiche was arrested on the evening of August 13 attempting to leave Constantine on a bus. After a "long interrogation," Hachiche confessed to helping murder Chemla and named a further accomplice, Mohamed ben Mohamed Alliche, known as Cherif.[10] Alliche, arrested in turn, "was interrogated, and did not hesitate to make a complete confession." He had been passing through the rue Nationale when he saw a group attacking Chemla's business on the rue Germon. Joining the group, he arrived just in time to see Chemla struck down with a club. The news account saw fit to put the event into his own words: "Because he was still moving," said Cherif, "I slit his throat as others held him down and then I took off."[11]

The same article described the arrest of a suspect in the murder of Abraham Bedoucha, killed at 9:00 a.m. on August 5 on the rue Rouaud. After "Santo" Benamira had accused Saïd Benhamama of being involved in the murders, the police held Benhamama overnight for questioning on Monday, August 13. His father, Abdallah Benhamama, became concerned and went to the police station to find out what had happened to him. According to the *Dépêche de Constantine*, the elder Benhamama arrived at the station just as Rosette Benisti, the domestic who worked for the Halimi family, was leaving after giving her testimony against Benamira. In a curious repetition of the scene the day before, Benisti now claimed to recognize Abdallah Benhamama from the day of the murders. The journalist used the same rhetorical language to describe the encounter: "Imagine her surprise in recognizing in the man who crossed her path one of the rioters who, she said, had invaded the Halimi apartment."[12] Abdallah Benhamama took flight quickly after being identified by Benisti, but was arrested several hours later and brought to the station. Under interrogation, the elder Benhamama denied having killed anybody in the Halimi household, but he confessed to Bedoucha's murder in the rue Rouaud. After stabbing him, the elder Benhamama told the police, he entered an adjacent house, where he encountered Benamira on the second floor. According to the account in the *Dépêche de Constantine*, Benamira told Abdallah Benhamama that he had finished Bedoucha off. "Thus, 'Santo' [Benamira] found himself one more time implicated in a murder."[13] The *Écho d'Alger*, meanwhile, reported that Abdallah Benhamama nevertheless recanted his confession when he appeared the next day before the investigating magistrate.[14]

The sensational nature of these press accounts, their rush to judgment, and the fact that they attempted to tie Benamira and the other men first to four, and then five, different murder sites—the Halimi apartment, the Attali apartment, the Chemla and Bedoucha murders (they would add Jacob Bentata to the list by the end of the week)—indicates that the Police Mobile and their superiors at the prefecture were hoping for a quick end to the investigation. They wanted to present the murders as the work of a small gang of killers. Both the press and police reports of that week spoke as though the murderers had acted in concert. An article in the *Dépêche de Constantine* on August 15 emphasized that all the crimes were committed in the same fashion, and they spoke of the slashed throats of the victims as a "bloody signature." This story seemed to confirm the charge made by Adolphe Sultan and Henri Lellouche that the conspirators had been divided into specialized groups—metalworkers to dismantle the iron grills protecting businesses, locksmiths to break down doors, and butcher boys to do the bloody work of killing.

It was also clear, however, that the interrogations produced confusing contradictions as well as confessions. Benisti identified Benamira as having been present at the Halimi murders on the rue Abdallah Bey, but he had confessed to killing Joseph Salomon Attal in the rue des Zouaves. Benamira had accused Saïd Benhamama of having been involved in unnamed murders in the rue Béraud (which included those of Bentata and the Dadoun brothers and their secretary), as well as the deaths of the Attali family, but Saïd Benhamama had only confessed to participating in the Chemla killing in the rue Germon. Benhamama's father, who was apparently recognized by Benisti as having been present at the Halimi home, confessed only to killing Abraham Bedoucha and then quickly recanted. Given these inconsistencies, the police were remarkably confident, especially since the arrests all stemmed from the testimony of a single panicked eyewitness who had glimpsed the attackers in a dark stairway and had hid while the murders in the Halimi attic took place. In no case was there any attempt to ask why this group—if they were indeed the killers—had behaved differently from the majority of people who participated in the riot. On this issue, at least, the rush to condemn Benamira and the other butcher boys was supported by the general tendency to blame the Muslim population as a whole for the violence. Motive was made irrelevant by the general assumption of "fanaticism."

The speed with which the police announced their progress publicly was also remarkable. Benamira had been identified and arrested on Sunday, August 12. He did not admit to anything until Monday morning, and yet the police must have leaked his identification to the press by later that day in order to have the article published in the *Dépêche de Constantine* by Tuesday, August 14. Saïd Benhamama, his father, Takouk, Hachiche, and Alliche were all arrested by late Monday, and articles about their confessions appeared in the press on Wednesday—with photos of inspectors and the accused—indicating an almost seamless transition from interrogation of suspects to meetings with journalists. It is impossible to know who authorized these leaks to the newspapers, but it is likely that it originated with the Police

Mobile, who were closest to the events and perhaps felt the most pressure to bring the case to a rapid conclusion.

The cascade of confusing press articles produced by these interrogations nevertheless appears to have disturbed officials higher up the chain of command. A sudden outpouring of five police reports on August 17–18 indicates that the Police Mobile either felt obligated or had been instructed to bring their superiors up to speed about the progress of their investigation. Unusually, each of these murder reports contained an addendum stating that copies had been forwarded to the governor-general, the director of general security for Algeria, and to the prefect of Constantine. After two weeks of leaking to the press, the Constantine police were now on a short leash. It was to get shorter still.

The five police reports from August 17–18 reproduced the general outlines of the stories that had already been leaked to the press, with a few more incriminating details about the testimony that linked individuals suspects with specific acts of murder. Only one of these reports, from August 17, contained information that had not already been leaked. In this report, Jacques Cauro stated that he and his men had solved the murder of Lachemi Akkacha, the Muslim man who was shot on the rue Nationale at the place Molière between 11:30 and 12:00 on August 5, approximately at the same time that the Halimi household was invaded. The Jewish man who fired the shot, a hairdresser named Jacob Levy, had fled to Guelma in the riot's aftermath; but upon his return to Constantine several days later, he admitted readily to what had happened. The shooting of Akkacha was judged to be self-defense, and Levy remained at provisional liberty before a trial date could be set.[15]

The four other reports, all dated August 18 and consecutively numbered, dealt with the murder of Jews on August 5: one each for the murders of Jacob Bentata, the Halimi family, Lucien Chemla, and Abraham Bedoucha. In the leaks over the previous days, the press had alluded to Bentata's case only in passing, as it recounted Benamira's accusations that Saïd ben Abdallah Benhamama had been involved in the murders on the rue Béraud where Bentata had been killed. Instead, the police report described the circumstances that had led to a different suspect, Saâd ben Ferhat Djebali. The report was vague on how Djebali had come to the attention of the police, saying only that "in the course of their investigation, the personnel of the Police Mobile collected precise information that directed their suspicions to a native known as 'Lakhdar,'" and that this individual had proved to be Djebali.[16] Given the timing, Djebali's name possibly came from either Benamira or Benhamama's interrogation, but neither butcher boy's names appear in the report. Instead, the police recounted how Djebali had showed up at a brothel between 11:00 and 11:30 a.m. with two watches that had been taken from Bentata's shop. He had given the watches to a relative for safekeeping. After being confronted with his relative's testimony, Djebali was interrogated further, and ultimately confessed to murdering Bentata by clubbing him and slashing his throat.

Gaillard's and Cauro's report of August 18 on Rosette Benisti's identification of Benamira, on the other hand, contained less information than the earlier press reports. Benamira's denial of having been present at the Halimi household, and his eventual confession to the murder of Joseph Attal in the hallway outside the Attali apartment, were recounted in matter-of-fact terms without any mention of the multiple interrogations that had been leaked to the press. Even stranger, Saïd Benhamama's name did not appear in this report, though according to the press accounts it was Benamira's testimony about Benhamama's involvement, and the latter's countercharges of Benamira's culpability, that had led to Benamira's confession to the murder of Joseph Attal.[17] This report's lack of detail and its bare-bones style seem to betray some retroactive embarrassment over the inconsistencies that had already appeared in the press. It is hard to avoid the impression that the authors of this report had already been severely chastised by their superiors.

The police report on Chemla's murder, on the other hand, was filled with new details, as though its authors were anxious to regain the trust of their handlers. Whereas the press reports had simply noted that successive interrogations had led the police to charge five individuals with participation in the murder, the police report gave a more substantive account. First, the report made clear that a group of butchers' employees consisting of Tayeb "Santo" Benamira, Saïd Benhamama, Mohamed Takouk, Mohamed Alliche, Rabah Hachiche, and Ahmed Hamireche had been "at the head of the rioters" on the rue Germon outside Chemla's car messenger office on the morning of August 5.[18] Hearing that a Jewish man had locked himself in, they broke down the door and found Chemla hiding in the back. Takouk and Alliche both testified that they had stretched the victim out on the ground under orders from Benamira, and that Benamira had cut his throat. Alliche confessed to delivering a second blow with his knife in the same place on Chemla's body. Benhamama and Hachiche, meanwhile, admitted to having helped to restrain the victim.

In order to put this confusing story into a more easily understood narrative, Jacques Cauro prepared a detailed seven-page report one week later that summarized the Police Mobile's findings on the entire weekend of August 3–5.[19] The report concluded with a list of seven separate incidents of murder, listing the arrests of people charged in each case.[20] Cauro's report was determined to push the story that had already been leaked to the press—that the murders had been committed by a "sinister gang" of "throat slitter" butcher boys who were responsible for nearly all the killings on August 5. Cauro's report recounted how "under the empire of an ever greater excitation, this gang of furious fanatics, drunk with blood, rendered more ferocious by shots fired from Jewish buildings, invaded the homes to coldly and savagely slit the throats of the occupants, the elderly, the women, and children."[21] Tayeb "Santo" Benamira was portrayed as the ringleader, accused of participating in murders at four different sites: the Attali family in the rue des Zouaves (five victims), the Halimi family in the rue Abdallah Bey (eight victims), the murder of Abraham Bedoucha in the rue Béraud, and the murder of Lucien Chemla in the rue Germon. In all, Cauro's report suggested that fifteen of the twenty-five Jews killed on August 5 were killed by the butcher boys. Cauro was also keen to portray the local police and the prefectural authorities as having been beyond reproach both during the riot and the subsequent investigation.[22]

Cauro's synthesis was not flawless—Belkacem Boutarane, the man who was shot in the stomach on August 3, was misidentified as "Lachemi Acacha," a reference to the man killed on the place Molière two days later. Abraham Bedoucha was listed as having been killed on the rue Béraud, when his body had been found on the other side of the rue Nationale. The murders of the Dadoun brothers and their secretary, Blanche Guedj, were left off the list, presumably because the police had no witnesses to their deaths. Cauro's report nevertheless was the first attempt to construct a coherent narrative from the bits and pieces that had previously been released to the press and compiled in fragmentary police reports.

The report made no effort to establish a definitive chronology of the events, despite the precise times mentioned by multiple eyewitnesses. Instead, Cauro's description moved haphazardly from one event to another, using vague phrases such as "at the same moment" when describing the murders in the rue Abdallah Bey and the rue des Zouaves. A similar vagueness characterized Cauro's laudatory description of his officers' investigation. The Police Mobile, he wrote, "worked night and day, without relief . . . to arrive at the identification and the arrest of pillagers and assassins. . . . Every clue collected was immediately checked and verified, and after long and minute research [the Police Mobile] had the satisfaction of seeing its efforts crowned with success by the arrest of the presumed authors, all of them butchers, and many of whom have confessed to having committed these crimes."[23] Cauro's report made no mention of the information that had been leaked to the press about Rosette Benisti's testimony or of the swirl of charges and countercharges provided by many interrogated suspects, and did not acknowledge the many contradictions that had emerged from the strange assemblage of accusations and confessions produced by his service's interrogations. More to the point, the only substantiating facts mentioned in the report were the discovery of several knives in the suspects' possession. The charges depended above all on confessions produced through presumably coercive interrogations with little corroborating evidence.

At this point, Governor-General Jules Carde's office appears to have directly intervened to clean up an investigation that was becoming an embarrassment. On September 4, Carde's staff drew up a memo about the influence he could legally exercise over an ongoing police investigation. The memo noted that the governor-general in Algeria had less authority over local police than did government ministers in metropolitan France.[24] In Algeria, only two controllers-general had the authority to inspect the Police Mobile, and these inspectors had "administrative" authority and not "active" authority over investigations. In metropolitan France, on the other hand, a much larger staff of sixty-four commissioners, inspectors, and communications specialists were free to intervene actively in ongoing investigations throughout French territory. This structure, the report noted, allowed a minister "to monitor and to control the information coming from the Prefects or from the special Police, and to manage, *with or without the cooperation of local police* [emphasis added], certain affairs whose character is strictly confidential." The report concluded: "It appears to me necessary that we create such an office in Algeria."

No records in the archives document the exact exchange that took place between the governor-general's office and the police authorities in Constantine in the last week of August and the first week of September. Nevertheless, the memo about Carde's authority to intervene in local police work was filed with papers documenting the governor-general's handling of the August riots. This leaves little doubt that Carde was looking for ways to take charge of the narrative that was emerging from the Police Mobile's investigation. Why would he seek to do this? There are several plausible reasons: first, the Police Mobile's initial theory—that they could pin many of the murders on a small group of people associated with Benamira—ran counter to the desire of the authorities to blame the murders on "religious fanaticism" in Constantine's Muslim population. Second, the Police Mobile's attempts to pin the murders on this small gang supported the public statements being made at the same moment by Jewish community leaders Adolphe Sultan and Henri Lellouche, as well as by Albert Confino and Joseph Fisher, the investigators sent by the Alliance israélite and the Geneva-based Comité des délégations juives. These four men all prepared reports between August 9 and August 20 that attributed the riots to an organized conspiracy, and they pointed to Mohamed Bendjelloul and members of the Federation of Muslim Elected Officials of Constantine as the likely masterminds.[25] In the run-up to Bendjelloul's trial for striking Inspector Gassab on September 19, the governor-general would have hesitated before responding publicly to these accusations. Above all, he may have sought to avoid adding further turmoil to an already delicate local situation by seeming to side with the popular Muslim leader's Jewish accusers.

Finally, it seems clear that the investigation of the "gang of throat slitters" had turned up lines of investigation that Carde and the police authorities themselves preferred to keep under wraps. Many of the details in Sultan's, Lellouche's, Confino's, and Fisher's accounts were reinforced during the last two weeks of August by an independent investigation carried out by Ruben Halimi, the brother of Alphonse Halimi, who was murdered with his family on August 5.[26] After the riots, Ruben Halimi approached the police and the Vigouroux commission with shocking eyewitness testimony that confirmed the most inflammatory charges of conspiracy, paid provocateurs, and police inaction on August 5. When the police refused to respond to his evidence, he went over their heads—approaching the general prosecutor in Constantine, Raymond Cura, and writing to Jean Vigouroux, the president of the governor-general's investigating commission. The timing of Halimi's accusations—and his status as a relative of many of the victims—must have been deeply troubling for the governor-general's office, because taking them seriously would have made it difficult to avoid a review of police behavior both before and after the riots. They also implied a demand to push the investigation far beyond the small circle of butcher boys who had already been arrested.

Ruben Halimi's formal testimony came in the form of a seventeen-page letter he sent to the Vigouroux commission in early September. The letter alluded to previous conversations he had had with Jean Vigouroux and the inspectors from the Police Mobile.[27] Halimi recounted how on August 5 he was returning from Narboni's funeral to his home on the rue Cahoreau in central Constantine just as the fighting spread along the rue Nationale. Unable to pass through the crowd, he implored the police to help him get to his home, where his wife was alone and unprotected. He encountered Police Commissioner René Miquel, who refused to help, stating that he had orders "not to enter the streets that cross the rue Nationale"—that is, the streets where the majority of the murders took place. Helpless, Halimi took refuge until 3 p.m., when a Muslim friend helped him to get through the streets to rescue his wife just before their apartment was invaded and pillaged. Later that day, Halimi described seeing a Muslim man hiding what appeared to be jewelry under the roof tiles of his building, and when he reported this to a police inspector, François Pisani, the inspector appeared to pocket the jewelry for himself.

Continuing his letter, Halimi recounted how Marius Gaillard of the Police Mobile called him to the station to give a statement on August 15. By chance, Halimi was present at the moment that Inspector Pisani brought in the accused murderer of Jacob Bentata, Saâd Djebali. Halimi heard Djebali say to the inspectors that he had been in the place Molière on August 5 "when a Muslim leader whose name he mentioned said 'Go all of you! Pillage, sack, burn and kill but put nothing in your pockets!'" Following these instructions, Djebali said that he proceeded to Bentata's shop in the rue Béraud and killed him. Halimi was surprised later to read a very different story in the *Dépêche de Constantine*; the paper reported that Djebali had been passing by the shop when Bentata opened fire on him with a pistol and that he had killed the Jewish watchmaker in self-defense.

Halimi's account continued: on August 17, he was visited by "Mr. and Mrs. Pochelu" and their daughter, who told him that they had been in their apartment in the rue Sidi-Lakdar at 3 p.m. on August 5 when they saw the hairdresser across the street with three accomplices washing their bloody hands in a sink while dividing up a considerable sum of money. In the room with them was a large bladed weapon spotted with blood. When the four men saw that they were being observed, the hairdresser stepped to the door of his shop and made a sign indicating that they would cut their throats if they spoke of what they saw. Pochelu and his wife decided to leave Constantine for Philippeville, but before they left they spoke to agents of the Police Mobile, who refused to follow up on their account. Incensed at the Pochelus' story, Halimi went straight to the office of the general prosecutor, Raymond Cura, who insisted that the police invite the family to make a statement. Immediately thereafter, said Halimi, the hairdresser and his companions were arrested. The hairdresser admitted nothing, but one of his associates confessed and brought the police to Gambetta Square, where he had hidden the weapon along with stolen cash and jewelry.[28] Finally, Halimi recounted that when he was allowed back in his house on August 7 to survey the damage caused by looters, he found three razors, two daggers, and a sickle in one of the bedrooms. He described these to a relative, Joseph Allouche, who told him that the sickle had come from a large group distributed by the proprietor of a *café maure* on the rue Nationale across from the Allouche's apartment. Halimi demanded that the police investigate the *café maure*, but they refused to do so.

Halimi's explosive letter to the Vigouroux commission was written after nearly three weeks of communication with the police and the prosecutor's office—these were the same weeks that the Police Mobile was leaking stories about the "gang of throat slitters" to the *Dépêche de Constantine*. Lellouche and Sultan had published their claims of conspiracy during the same period, and Sultan had sent a copy of his report to at least one member of parliament, Henri Guernut, a figure on the left noted for his engagement on behalf of the League of the Rights of Man.[29] While Ruben Halimi pursued his accusations in Constantine through private channels, Albert Confino was in touch with both the Alliance israélite and the Central Consistory in Paris, and Joseph Fisher was in Geneva presenting similar arguments to the Comité des délégations juives. Fisher's report, in particular, contained the same critique of local authorities, the same claims of premeditation, but added a direct accusation against Muslim political figures in Mohamed Bendjelloul's entourage. Fisher was dumbfounded, however, when the Comité's executive board refused to allow him to present his findings during their meeting on August 20. The board confiscated all copies of Fisher's report after one of its members complained that the report was "anti-French." Fisher identified this person only as "MRB," indicating that he was the director of a financial newspaper in Paris with strong connections to the French government. Fisher was apparently referring to Robert Ballack, the publisher of *L'Agence économique et financière* (*L'Agefi*) and a member of the executive board of the Comité des délégations juives. In the end, Fisher managed to keep only two copies of his report for himself: the first was confiscated by the Gestapo in 1940 after he went into hiding during the occupation, and the second he sent to a colleague in Palestine, where he found it nearly three decades later in the Zionist Archives in Jerusalem.[30] Unknown to Fisher, however, the Ministry of the Interior came to possess a third copy, presumably given to them by Ballack.[31]

It seems clear from these interlocking stories that Governor-General Carde and the Ministry of the Interior were being hit with disturbing news from several sides—from Lellouche, Sultan, and Ruben Halimi in Constantine, from Jewish organizations and members of parliament in Paris, and on the international front from Joseph Fisher's investigation. There is no way of knowing if Halimi's and Fisher's direct accusations played a role in Carde's decision to intervene in the Police Mobile investigation, but the timing is suggestive, especially since all of their efforts appear to have hit brick walls at precisely the same moment. The Vigouroux commission made no attempt to deal with Halimi's explosive claims in its final report and simply ignored his letter. Adolphe Sultan was stonewalled on every front, despite a letter-writing campaign to government officials in Paris and the League of the Rights of Man that continued for almost two years.[32] Fisher was prevented from publicizing his findings by the very organization that had sent him to Algeria, apparently because a member of the board used his authority to suppress and confiscate nearly all the existing copies of his report. There is little mystery as to why the Vigouroux commission avoided following up on Halimi's allegations—the potential damage to the colonial authorities' reputation was too great, and the political atmosphere was too volatile to tolerate a public airing. A similar logic seems to have dictated the governor-general's decision to intervene in the police investigation. Simultaneously, the executive board of the Comité des délégations juives appears to have decided that a cautious approach that avoided provoking a political crisis with direct accusations against local authorities and elected officials such as Bendjelloul was the best strategy, given the continued vulnerability of Constantine's Jewish population in August and September 1934. It is also plausible to think that the Comité decided it could not afford to antagonize the French government at the precise moment that the Comité was organizing the first World Jewish Congress to meet the overwhelming threat to Europe's Jews posed by Nazi Germany.[33] The decision was so sensitive that nobody explained to Fisher why his report was suppressed.

Whatever the reasons for the governor-general's intervention in the police investigation, there is strong evidence that it was successful. Up until August 24, the Police Mobile continued to insist that the eight butcher boys were responsible for as many as fifteen of the twenty-five deaths on August 5, and that Tayeb "Santo" Benamira, in particular, had been involved in multiple murders. After the governor-general's staff produced the memo about how to take charge of a local police investigation on September 4, however, an entire week elapsed before the police again began to produce investigatory reports. After this week of silence, the inspectors stopped writing about the "gang of throat slitters." Instead, the inspectors began treating each murder site as a separate investigation, and they assigned a separate and distinct list of suspects to each site. Most remarkable, between August 29 and September 10, the police investigation took an abrupt turn with the arrest of eleven new suspects. Three of the new suspects were charged with involvement in the Halimi-Zerdoun killings, the other eight with involvement in the murders of the Attali and Attal family members.

More arrests were made on August 28, 31, and September 10. In each case, the suspects were not presented as belonging to a gang, and no mention of any connection to Benamira or the butcher's apprentices appeared in subsequent press reports. No acknowledgment was given of the claims made by Ruben Halimi or the Pochelu family. On August 28, Lakhal ben Larbi Ziad, a twenty-eight-year-old cart driver, and Tayeb ben Fergani Boulkraa, a gardener in his forties, both confessed under interrogation to participating in the Halimi-Zerdoun murders. They were charged and imprisoned in spite of the fact that the Halimi family's employee, Rosette Benisti, did not recognize them when they were brought before her.[34] Two days later, the press announced another "veritable theatrical coup": the arrest of no fewer than eight suspects, all of whom had apparently confessed to participating in the murders in the Attali household.[35] The article recounted how the first suspect had come to the attention of the police because of careless words uttered at his workplace. Soon interrogated, he named the others, also employees of the Société d'entreprises éléctriques. This produced more confessions, including to the murder of Ausélia Attali—recounted once more in voyeuristic detail—but they recanted their confessions before the investigating magistrate. All were nevertheless charged and held in prison. Finally, on September 10, the Police Mobile reported the arrest of another suspect in the Halimi-Zerdoun killings, Mohamed ben Salah Chelghoum, an eighteen-year-old brothel employee who had apparently come to their attention because of a visible injury to his left arm that he had received on August 5. He too confessed under interrogation. In spite of the details he offered about the scene of the murder, Chelghoum never mentioned any of the butcher boys who had been accused of participating in the Halimi murders, and he appeared to have no connection with Benamira.[36]

The best indication that the governor-general's intervention in the Police Mobile's investigation succeeded is the list of individuals who were eventually tried for the murders. The first trials took place in July 1935, and a second series of trials—including the most sensational trials of the massacres at the Halimi and Attali apartments—occurred in February 1936. During these trials, there was no talk of a "gang of throat slitters." "Santo" Benamira was tried and convicted of participating in the murders of the Halimi family, alongside Ziad and Boulkraa, arrested on August 29, and Mohamed Chelghoum, arrested on September 10. Remarkably, Benamira's name did not come up in any of the other cases—even the murder of Joseph Salomon Attal, to which he had confessed in his original interrogation. Four of the "butcher boys" arrested by the Police Mobile in August 1934 were tried for the murder of Lucien Ichoua Chemla in July 1935—Saïd Benhamama, Mohamed Takouk, Rabah Hachiche, and Ahmed Hamireche—but they were all acquitted because the medical examiner's statement did not conform with the details enumerated in the charges against them. The fifth butcher's apprentice, who had confessed to delivering the second blow to Chemla's throat, Mohamed Alliche, never stood trial at all. It seems as well that Abdallah Benhamama never stood trial for the murder of Abraham Bedoucha, in spite of newspaper reports that he had confessed under interrogation.[37] In all, only two of the eight suspects initially accused by the Police Mobile of participating in the "gang of throat slitters" were eventually convicted of murder: Tayeb "Santo" Benamira, convicted in February 1936 of participating in the Halimi murders, and Saâd Djebali, who was convicted in July 1935 of the murder of the watchmaker Jacob Bentata.

Many of the other individuals who were eventually convicted of these crimes were arrested later, after the governor-general's office decided to intervene in the Police Mobile's investigation. Unfortunately for historians, after Jacques Cauro's summary report of August 24, the detailed leaks to the press stopped, and the archive contains fewer records of the investigation after that point. Most of the police reports that we have come from the files of the special administrative commission headed by Jean Vigouroux, which completed its work in the last weeks of September and sent its report to Governor-General Carde on October 7, refuting all charges of conspiracy. It is difficult to know what twists and turns the investigations may have taken after this point, but one thing is certain. After Carde's office expressed its concern about its ability to control the information coming from the Police Mobile's investigation in early September, the police and the press stopped talking about a small "gang of throat slitters," and the list of accused individuals who appeared in the successive trials in 1935 and 1936 underwent significant revision. Each individual site of murder was treated separately, and the legal machinery was allowed to run its course in the absence of any public discussion of the evidence for conspiracy, coordination, or provocation. There is compelling evidence, however, that the police believed something quite different from what was made public during the investigation and the subsequent trials.

CHAPTER 13

The Agitator

In January 1938, a police inspector in Paris, Robert de Escarrega, was investigating a political murder. French right-wing extremists had assassinated two Italian antifascists, Carlo and Nello Rosselli, in Normandy in June 1937. De Escarrega had connected the murders to two individuals, one of whom was from the department of Constantine. Seeking information about these men, he wrote to the governor-general's office in Algiers asking for help. Here is the note in full:

> Said person FILIOL, Jean Paul Robert, born May 12, 1909 at BERGERAC (Dordogne), object of an arrest warrant dated January 22, 1938, from the investigating magistrate at DOMFRONT, indicted for murder (ROSSELLI affair), may have taken refuge in Morocco, where he has possibly acquired property (no details known).
>
> This individual, identified as very dangerous, was put in relation with said person, EL MAADI Mohamed Lakdar, born July 1902 at Aïc Ketone [*sic*] (Constantine) by the intermediary of Mister MURRACIOLI [*sic*], son of a lawyer in Constantine.
>
> EL MAADI is held to be one of the agitators who provoked the "pogroms" of Constantine and is known to be on the payroll of MURRACIOLI.

It would be of great interest to collect any useful information about those named above, whether in Constantine or in Morocco, where said FILIOL may be looked for.

Photographs of EL MAADI and FILIOL JEAN attached.

Inspector of the Police Mobile

Signed:

DE ESCARREGA[1]

The information in this brief note is extremely suggestive. It connects the Constantine riots of 1934 with two notorious figures, Jean Filiol and Mohamed El Maadi, and links El Maadi with a third, Étienne Muracciole, a lawyer and elected official in Constantine who was an ally of Mayor Émile Morinaud. Jean Filiol (1909–1975?) was well known to the police as a ruthless, violent, and capable organizer for multiple right-wing extremist groups in the 1930s. In 1936–1937, he assembled a group of conspirators to create a shadowy terrorist organization known as the Cagoule, which briefly threatened an insurrection in metropolitan France in late 1937. The murder of the Rosselli brothers was only one of several political assassinations carried out by Filiol and his team. Filiol would later collaborate enthusiastically with the Germans during the Second World War. By 1944, he had joined the Milice, France's own fascist paramilitary police force, and participated in the torture and murder of members of the French Resistance.[2]

Mohamed El Maadi (1902–1954?)—named in de Escarrega's note as "one of the agitators who provoked the 'pogroms' of Constantine"—moved in the same circles. El Maadi was a veteran of the French army who served in Morocco and Algeria until early 1937. In the spring of that year, Filiol recruited El Maadi to his Cagoule network. When the police arrested the clandestine group's leadership in November 1937, they also arrested El Maadi. He was detained for nearly nine months before being released and reinstated in the army. In the years that followed, El Maadi became the most prominent of a small number of Algerian Muslims who followed a path from right-wing nationalist militancy to collaboration with the Germans and a full embrace of fascism.[3] Both his fascism and his antisemitism were rooted in his engagement with the most extreme elements of right-wing French nationalism and converged with Nazism during the Second World War.[4]

El Maadi's association with the Cagoule in 1937–1938 first brought him to the attention of the French intelligence services and the press—but historians have been more interested in his subsequent wartime activities. After the German occupation of France in 1940, El Maadi supported the Vichy

government's anti-Jewish policies and collaborated actively with the oc-
cupation authorities. With funding from German military intelligence, El
Maadi published a journal in both French and Arabic, *Er Rachid* (The Rightly
Guided), which aimed to turn the North African population living in France
against the British and the United States. Beginning in 1943, El Maadi re-
cruited over three hundred young Algerian men living in Paris to form a
North African Brigade that fought alongside the Germans against the French
Resistance in 1944. By the end of the war, he was a captain in the German
SS, and his evolution from right-wing French nationalist to National Socialist
foot soldier was complete.

On their own, these well-known facts about El Maadi's later career prove
nothing about his connection with the Constantine riots of 1934. Nevertheless, the fact that in January 1938 Inspector de Escarrega named El Maadi
as "one of the agitators who provoked the 'pogroms' of Constantine" adds
a new chapter to what is already known about this unusual figure and has
the potential to transform our understanding of the riots. De Escarrega's
note proves that by January 1938, the police in Paris were confident that the
violence of August 5, 1934, had been the result of purposeful agitation, con-
tradicting the official report produced by the investigating commission. De
Escarrega knew the name of at least one of the agitators, and he knew that
Mohamed El Maadi had been in the French army when the riots took place.
Most explosively, de Escarrega had reason to believe that El Maadi was connected to the son of Étienne Muracciole, a prominent member of Constantine's settler political establishment, a lawyer who had been a *batonnier* of the
Constantine bar and an ally of Émile Morinaud on the department's Conseil
général. Étienne Muracciole played a key role in the murder trials related to
the Constantine riots, helping to shape the narrative that emerged from the
public proceedings. De Escarrega's brief note shines a light on pieces of a
story that have long been hidden from view.

A single note, however suggestive, is a thin reed on which to hang a revised explanation of the 1934 riots. Fortunately, de Escarrega's note is not the
only source that connects El Maadi to the events of August 5. Multiple documents in the archives place El Maadi at the site of the most notorious crimes
that occurred on that day. When the riots broke out, he was in the streets as
an adjutant in the French army, serving in the Third Zouaves Regiment based
in Constantine. (Elie Khalifa, whose outburst sparked the riot on Friday, August 3, was also a reserve soldier in the Third Zouaves.) El Maadi's military
service record confirms that he was assigned to the second company of the
Third Zouaves in Constantine on August 1, 1934, only days before the riots,
and that on August 5 he was stationed at a blockade on the rue Nationale.

The military file also notes that immediately after the riot his commanding officer granted him an exceptional six-month leave for a "hydro-mineral and physical therapy treatment" in Barèges, a thermal spa in the Pyrénées, where he was treated for a broken humerus that he had suffered from a fall off a horse during his service in Morocco in 1927. Because of his absence from Constantine in the weeks after the riots, El Maadi never filed a report about what he saw on August 5, though other soldiers who were present provided detailed testimony to the Vigouroux commission. He did not return to active duty until February 27, 1935, but while he was away he was awarded a medal, the Ordre de la Division, by his commanding officer for his "sang-froid, energy, and uncommon courage" in "coming to the assistance of a besieged Israelite family" on August 5 and "his success in saving several of them before they could be finished off" by their attackers.[5] His six-month absence—during which the Police Mobile prepared their list of people to be charged with murder and the governor-general's investigating commission completed its report—removed him from the scene during the most sensitive moments after the riots.

There is more. El Maadi's name appears on a list of soldiers who were injured in the riot. This list gives the date and time of injury, placing him directly at 6 rue des Zouaves, the home of Makhlouf Attali, at 1 p.m. on Sunday, August 5.[6] At that moment, five people from the Attali, Zerbib, and Attal families were being killed, including Makhlouf Attali's two children, Ausélia and Alexandre. Several of the surviving accounts by military and police personnel present at the scene also mention El Maadi by name. One—that of Inspector Alliche of the Constantine municipal police—states that "under the command of Adjutant El-Mahdi [sic]" the Zouaves were able to "hold off the Natives [Indigènes] and then to drive them back into their quarter."[7] These documents do not accuse El Maadi of being involved in the murders, but they demonstrate that he was there. They also prove that the local police were aware of his presence and had taken the time to praise him for his efforts during the riots.

Finally, Mohamed El Maadi's presence as a unit commander at the site of the rue des Zouaves killings is confirmed by the press accounts of the Attali murder trial that took place in Orléansville (Chlef) in February 1936. In these accounts, a witness described as a soldier named "Maadi" gave crucial testimony, confirming the details of the scene offered by the surviving family members, and allowing the prosecutors to establish the exact time of the murders. "Maadi" was presented by the prosecutors as a hero, as one of the first soldiers through the door at the moment that the murders were taking place, and as the man who prevented the surviving members of the Attali and Attal families from having their throats cut. The survivors had their own lawyer as well, who spoke eloquently about the Attali family's pain at the loss of their children, and who played a key role in obtaining convictions for the accused murderers. This lawyer was none other than Étienne Muracciole, whose son Roger was later implicated by the Paris police as the man who introduced Mohamed El Maadi to the Cagoule assassin Jean Filiol.

This strange web of connections between a French-Algerian soldier with a sulfurous and violent future, a lethal group of right-wing French provocateurs and assassins, and the family of a prominent lawyer and elected official in Constantine raises many difficult questions for a historian. There is first of all a question about the narrative: what kind of story is this? Terms such as "conspiracy" do not usually lend themselves easily to sober historical accounts. Almost by definition, the evidence for conspiracy is circumstantial rather than definitive. Most historians would agree that skepticism is the most reliable guide when it comes to accounts of shadowy manipulators who hide behind the curtain to influence what we can and cannot see about a particular event. Such skepticism is certainly warranted in this case, for although there is ample evidence that many people sought to manipulate the events of August 3–5, 1934, for their own political ends, it is also clear that there were limits to what manipulation could accomplish. Thousands of people were on the streets on that August weekend in Constantine. The ability of any particular individual or small group of conspirators to change the outcome once the riots were under way was probably minimal—with one notable exception. Murders committed while the riots were under way would dramatically increase the intensity and the political consequences of the disturbance in the streets without requiring a large number of people to be party to the conspiracy.

At the very least, de Escarrega's note naming Mohamed El Maadi as an "agitator" poses challenging questions about the place of the murders within the events of that day, and the way local actors shaped the meaning of these deaths and their consequences. In the first days after the riots, as we have seen, local officials and Jewish leaders all drew attention to what they saw as evidence for conspiracy and preplanning, and they placed responsibility on Mohamed Bendjelloul and the members of the Federation of Muslim Elected Officials. These claims appeared to be supported by the Police Mobile when they announced the arrest and interrogation of a "gang of throat-slitters." By mid-September, however, the official position had changed, and the authorities in Algeria stood solidly behind the view defended by the Vigouroux commission's report of October 1934, that the riots resulted from a kind of spontaneous combustion. The Police Mobile never challenged the commission's findings, but by 1938 were speaking freely among themselves of "the agitators who provoked the 'pogroms' of Constantine" as if this was a known fact. If nothing else, de Escarrega's note proves that the police in Constantine and elsewhere knew more about the riot's origins than they ever revealed to the public. Did the authorities remain silent because they did not want to undermine the official story that blamed the riots on religious fanaticism? Did the possible involvement of a French soldier, Mohamed El Maadi, make it necessary to insist on the spontaneity of the crowd?

Given the evidence that now lies before us, it is possible to say that the initial assessment of the Police Mobile and the Jewish community leaders was at least partially correct. The riots of August 1934 were *both* spontaneous *and* exacerbated by the activities of a small group. The evidence suggests that the riots may have originated in a banal dispute that began on Friday, August 3. On Sunday, August 5, however, a group of provocateurs sought to dramatically escalate the dispute's destructive consequences by provoking more unrest and committing sensational acts of murder during the ensuing disorder. The Jewish leaders' accusations against Bendjelloul for organizing the violence seem to have been misplaced, however. All the evidence seems to indicate that Bendjelloul was on the streets on August 5 trying to prevent the violence from taking place. Was Mohamed El Maadi responsible for the provocations and violence on that day? This seems at least possible, since the documentary evidence places him close to the scene. Inspector de Escarrega's note from Paris to the governor-general's office about El Maadi and Filiol indicates that the police themselves had come to this conclusion.

To clarify this confusing set of possibilities, we need to do three things. First, we need to revisit the events of August 5, 1934, in order to examine Mohamed El Maadi's possible role. Second, we need to examine the circumstances that produced de Escarrega's note to the governor-general's office in January 1938. It is surprising, to say the least, that a relatively low-level inspector of the Police Mobile in Paris, one of the foot soldiers of the Rosselli murder investigation, should have been so well informed about El Maadi's activities in 1934 and his connections to a prominent lawyer in the distant city of Constantine. If we cannot determine how such information came to de Escarrega's attention, we have little standing to claim that the information is true. Finally, the fact that El Maadi's subsequent career is relatively well documented provides an opportunity to ask questions about his motives. Nothing about El Maadi's later activities can be said to "prove" his involvement in 1934. Once we have accepted that this involvement was likely, or at least possible, however, a close look at his political engagements between 1936 and 1945 might help us better understand the meaning of his apparent actions.

Mohamed El Maadi was born in 1902 in the village of Aïn-Ketone, in the *commune mixte* of La Séfia, a region in the department of Constantine between the town of Guelma and the Tunisian border.[8] His family had close relations with the French, and both his mother's and his father's sides of the family were well assimilated to French culture by the standards of the day. His paternal grandfather, Abdallah ben Messaoud El Maadi ('Abdallah bin Mas'ud al-Ma'adi), a naturalized French citizen, had been a lieutenant in a French cavalry unit, the Spahis, and married a Frenchwoman, Marie Madeleine Thérèse Lacave. Mohamed El Maadi's maternal grandfather, Mohamed Lakhdar ben Messaoud El Maadi (Muhammad al-Akhdar bin Mas'ud al-Ma'adi) was also a naturalized French citizen and had worked for the colonial administration as an *adjoint indigène* (native assistant). Mohamed El Maadi's two grandfathers were, in fact, brothers—his father, Mahfoud El Maadi, married his first cousin, Melouka El Maadi, and both of El Maadi's parents were thus French citizens by filiation. The official records of births, deaths, and marriages in the El Maadi family bear witness to the extent of their assimilation and exposure to French culture. In these documents, only Mohamed El Maadi's great-grandfather, Messaoud El Maadi (b. 1815) signed his name in Arabic. The men in his grandparents' and parents' generation signed their names in the elegant and flowing cursive script that was a sign of a French education.[9]

Mohamed El Maadi was therefore an unusual figure in colonial French Algeria—he was a Muslim man who possessed French citizenship by birth. Both his parents, both his grandfathers, and his paternal grandmother were all French citizens.[10] Toward the end of his life, El Maadi reportedly told people that his parents were a "mixed couple."[11] This was slightly misleading, as the phrase was more commonly used to indicate a marriage between a Muslim man and a woman of European origin. In a strictly legal sense, they were not "mixed" at all—they were both French citizens by birth. What made them "mixed" was the fact that they were also Muslim, and they moved easily between Algerian and French cultures.

El Maadi's upbringing appears to have followed a pattern typical of Algerian landowning elites with ties to the administration, including study in French schools. After a period at the Sorbonne in 1922, El Maadi joined the French army and served for over a decade in Morocco, becoming an officer in the Rif War (1920–1926). This service is probably where El Maadi first came into contact with right-wing political militancy. No documentation of El Maadi's early political engagement appears in his military record, but historians have noted his presence in the Paris riots of February 6, 1934.[12] During this unrest, French right-wing groups battled with police in central Paris, leading some to fear that a fascist coup was imminent. El Maadi's presence in Paris at this moment—when he was still on active duty—shows the extent to which he had enthusiastically embraced the cause of the antirepublican right in the months leading up to the Constantine riots, possibly with the support of his superiors who had allowed him leave to make his way to the capital. El Maadi had been assigned to the Third Zouaves Regiment based in Constantine in May 1933 but was away from Algeria in early 1934 and did not return to Constantine until February 28. On August 1, two days before the Constantine riots, El Maadi was assigned to the second company of the Third Zouaves.[13]

No document has been found that links El Maadi with the initial dispute between Elie Khalifa and the men at the mosque on the evening of Friday, August 3. The arrival of several police officers was enough at first to quiet the anger of the people who responded to Khalifa's insults, and the streets were clear for more than an hour. Sometime between ten and eleven, however, a much larger crowd of nearly two thousand people arrived, armed with clubs, knives, and stones. Even in a town as tense as Constantine in 1934, it is difficult to imagine that such a crowd could be produced spontaneously, without some individuals acting as leaders to provoke the community's anger and spread stories about their grievance against a Jewish man who had insulted Muslims preparing for their prayers. Soldiers from Khalifa's and El Maadi's unit, the Third Zouaves, first arrived on the scene after midnight on the night of August 3–4 when the fighting was at its worst. No evidence connects El Maadi specifically with the arrival of troops from his regiment, but it is noteworthy that their arrival provoked the anti-Jewish protesters in the street to shout "Vive La France!" for the first time. Some of the protesters, at least, believed that their grievance against Khalifa and the Jews of Constantine would resonate with soldiers in French uniform who shared their anti-Jewish resentment. It was soon after this chaotic moment that Belkacem Boutarane was shot in the stomach, and his unconscious body was found on the street, probably by Ernest Lanxade, the anti-Jewish troublemaker, and the photographer Roger Lauffenberger.

Clearer circumstantial evidence of organized agitation and premeditation exists for the morning of Sunday, August 5, when most of the murders took place. The police reports recount at least three separate events that one could cite as possible or even likely intentional provocations early that day. First,

Reine (Rose) Atlan and another Jewish woman were clubbed in the face at the place des Galettes market shortly before 9:00 a.m., precipitating the outbreak of prolonged street fighting that would eventually engulf the entire city. Second, two individuals ran toward the crowd returning from Les Pins across the El Kantara bridge shortly after 9:00 a.m. with the false message that Bendjelloul had been assassinated by Jews. Finally, at 10:15 a.m., police agent Selim Benmoussa reported that he was in the rue Sidi Nemdil when he heard a group of men pass by shouting the following words: "Run! Doctor Bendjelloul has been killed by the Jews. Arm yourselves! We have to be done with them, it's the last day, it's a Holy War."[14]

Benmoussa, who was familiar with the people in this neighborhood, reported that the shouting group of men were all strangers to the city and that they joined up with other groups armed with clubs and knives. When Benmoussa saw the armed men, Abraham Bedoucha had already been killed near the intersection of the rue Rouaud and the rue Humbert—a short walk just on the other side of the rue Nationale. Perhaps fifteen minutes later, at about 10:30 a.m., only steps away on the nearby rue Germon (connected to the rue Sidi Nemdil via the rue Ben Cheikh Lefgoun), a group of men broke into the office of the car messenger service and cut the throat of Lucien Ichoua Chemla. From the rue Germon to the rue Abdallah Bey, where the Halimi family was murdered between 11:00 and 12:00, was another short walk; from the Halimi household on the rue Abdallah Bey to the Attali home on the rue des Zouaves, attacked around 1:00 p.m., one would only have to traverse a short passage between the two streets. Finally, the murders of the Dadoun brothers, Maurice and Gilbert, and their secretary, Blanche Guedj, took place in the rue Béraud, also an adjacent street, though the time of these murders is not known. It is entirely possible—even likely—that the group of men Benmoussa saw spreading the rumor of Bendjelloul's death at 10:15 were responsible for inciting or actually carrying out most or even all of the murders in this neighborhood between 9 a.m. and 1 p.m. Even if they were only responsible for inciting the murders that took place in invasions of homes or businesses, that would still make them responsible for the deaths of eighteen out of the twenty-five Jews who died: eight people in the Halimi household, five in the Attali apartment, three in the Dadoun brothers' office, Lucien Chemla, and the watchmaker Jacob Bentata. If one includes the two additional men who were murdered in the adjacent streets roughly during the same period—Abraham Bedoucha and Henri Guèdj—then twenty out of a total of twenty-five Jews who died that day in Constantine may have been killed by the same group working in this small neighborhood alone. These twenty murders occurred in a concentrated area that was both distinct from the traditional Jewish quarter and also separated from the places where the disturbances began that morning. The attacks began simultaneously with the first violence on the place des Galettes at about 9 a.m. and followed one another in close sequence thereafter, ending with the deaths at the Attali apartment after 1 p.m., where we know that Mohamed El Maadi was present.

Selim Benmoussa's testimony on the group of men he saw on the morning of the fifth in the rue Sidi Nemdil was filed away in a dossier kept by the prefect's Office of Departmental Security, but it does not appear to have been included in the papers examined by the governor-general's investigating commission led by Jean Vigouroux. Neither did Benmoussa's name appear as a witness in the press accounts of the trials that took place in 1935 and 1936. Benmoussa's compelling testimony about a group of armed men from out of town was possibly forgotten, ignored, or purposely kept out of the official report.

A similar fate seems to have befallen the two most detailed accounts of the murders at the Attali household—the one location where we have proof of El Maadi's participation in the events. The first is the report from the Muslim police officer, Said Djemaa, who was the only representative of the police or military to enter the Attali apartment on the rue des Zouaves while the murders were taking place. Djemaa threatened the killers with his revolver and was able to rescue the three-year-old daughter of Moise and Zaïra Zerbib.[15] The second report of the Attali murders that was apparently ignored by the Vigouroux commission came from Corporal Émile Kottman of the Third Zouaves, who saw the Attali family attacked on the balcony of their building and who several minutes later succeeded in breaking through the crowd at the door and found the bodies upstairs. Kottman testified that when he was able to gain access to the entry hall—after three tries—he met several soldiers already in the building. They accompanied him upstairs, but no explanation was given as to how they had gained entry, after it had taken Kottman so long to get inside, or how long they had been there. Copies of Djemaa's and Kottman's testimonies were included in the papers assembled by the Vigouroux commission, but none of the information that they recounted made its way into the final report or was mentioned by any other subsequent police reports preserved in the archives. Nobody appears to have pursued any questions about what this group of soldiers was doing at the bottom of the stairs while the Attali family and their friends were under attack in the apartment above.

Remarkably, given the elaborate detail of their statements, neither Said Djemaa nor Émile Kottman was called to give testimony at the 1936 trial of the young men charged with the murders in the Attali apartment. Instead, the prosecutors called Mohamed El Maadi to testify about the actions of his regiment on the rue des Zouaves that day and the appearance of the Attali apartment when the soldiers arrived. Many aspects of El Maadi's story sounded a great deal like Kottman's: he recounted how he succeeded in clearing the Attali family house only "after a third charge."[16] Asked to be precise about the time, he responded that it was "about 12h45." It was a curious answer, because it placed him inside the building either before or during the time when the killings were taking place—both Kottman and Djemaa said they entered the building at around 1:00 p.m., while attackers and looters were still in the apartment.

El Maadi's statement at the trial about entering the apartment at 12:45 also contradicted the account that he gave his commanding officer in the midst of the struggle that morning. His superior officer, Lieutenant Carbonnel of the Third Zouaves, told the Vigouroux commission that he was on a barricade in the rue Nationale not far from the Attali house "between 1:00 and 1:30 p.m." when he heard a "sudden burst of gunfire [*une vive fusillade*]." One of his men approached him and said that calls for help were coming from the balcony of a house only forty meters away in the rue des Zouaves. Carbonnel arrived at the house in time to see the fighting on the balcony while furniture and bedding were being thrown from the windows onto the agitated crowd below. At that moment, Carbonnel got a report from an officer from his unit whom he identified as "l'Adjutant-Chef El-Maadi." El Maadi told him that he had tried to enter the house with several men, but they had been stopped by "numerous gunshots, one of which had grazed his hand."[17] El Maadi made a point of showing his injury to his superior officer—this is the injury mentioned later in the document that places him at the scene, and it is the only gunshot wound suffered by a French soldier on August 5 in Constantine. Is it possible that El Maadi had already been in the building prior to speaking to Carbonnel and had exited sometime before or after Kottman had entered with his men? It is impossible to know for sure, but El Maadi himself later testified at the trial that he had entered the apartment. In the end, it was Lieutenant Carbonnel who organized the final assault, with fixed bayonets, on the Attali family's building. Although they were met by more gunshots, they managed to clear the entrance. Kottman and his men, who were already inside, were finally able to exit and arrange for a medical team to tend to the wounded members of the Attali and Attal families.

The evidence linking El Maadi to the murders of the Attali family is thus largely circumstantial.[18] It suggests that he was in a position to incite others to murder, and one must assume that it was this fact that drew the attention of the police investigators who eventually concluded that he was one of the riot's primary instigators. El Maadi told his superior officer that he had been prevented from entering the building by gunfire, but nobody fired on Kottman and his men during their multiple attempts to pass through the crowd. It is curious that, after struggling through the crowd, Kottman came upon a group of soldiers standing inside in the stairwell at the moment of the murders. Yet there is no conclusive evidence linking these soldiers to acts of provocation, except for their unexplained presence in the building at the very moment that shots were being fired from the balcony and furniture was being thrown down on the crowd below. Finally, no police or military document clearly identifies El Maadi as one of the soldiers who entered the building. The fact remains, however, that it was El Maadi, among all the soldiers present that day, who was chosen to give testimony at the 1936 trial about how the soldiers stopped the murders in the Attali apartment.

Even if the evidence about El Maadi does nothing more than confirm his presence, the elements of the story that emerge from these multiple testimonies indicate that unnamed individuals were intentionally provoking the crowd in the rue des Zouaves. Makhlouf Attali and other family members denied possessing a revolver or firing down on the crowd—and this was confirmed by their neighbor, Eugène Delaporte, who watched from his apartment across the street. Nevertheless, Kottman reported seeing an unidentified person firing from the balcony on the crowd when there were already rioters in the apartment. Other witnesses spoke of seeing people in the apartment throwing furniture and bedding onto the crowd below, but none of the Attali or Attal members described doing this themselves. The behavior of the rioters who entered the building seems to indicate a level of organization—some attacked the people they found, others rushed to the balcony, fired their weapons, and threw whatever was at hand down on the people below, creating more chaos on the streets.

Regardless of how one interprets this evidence, the possibility that these killings were encouraged by the actions of an organized group seems to be reinforced by the close proximity of the Attali family murders to the other places in this neighborhood where people were killed. These murders did not, as Henri Lellouche and Joseph Fisher pointed out, take place in the traditional Jewish quarter in the northeast corner of the old city, but rather in a mixed commercial and residential neighborhood off the rue Nationale closer to Constantine's administrative center. The rioters may have been afraid of invading homes in the Jewish quarter because they believed they would likely encounter more armed Jewish men there than elsewhere in the city. If a small group of provocateurs was responsible, their choice of neighborhood would have emerged from a nuanced calculation of circumstance, proximity, and vulnerability, and the results would have looked very much like what happened on August 5.

It is impossible for the historian to be certain about much of this story. Knowing that the long interrogations that produced confessions during those weeks in August 1934 were almost certainly accompanied by violent coercion and torture, it is difficult to evaluate the guilt or innocence of the young men caught up in the investigation and subsequently brought to trial. Given the circumstances of the murders, their timing, and the close proximity of the places where they occurred, however, one can also understand why the Police Mobile pushed the thesis of a small group acting with some form of coordination. Knowing, too, that the police hierarchy in Paris eventually concluded that there was provocation and incitement on August 5, and that they believed Mohamed El Maadi to have been an active instigator of the riot, one might ask whether the police in Constantine connected a figure like El Maadi to a possible conspiracy in the course of their investigation. The documents in the archives that demonstrate El Maadi's presence at the site of the massacre of the Attali and Attal family members were part of the police files. Anything that we now claim to know or suspect on the basis of these documents was also available to investigators at the time—except of course the knowledge of El Maadi's future as a right-wing militant and violent anti-Jewish supporter of the Nazi occupation after 1940. One might ask if the police in their investigation heard something that may have led them to suspect that a soldier was helping to coordinate attacks on Jewish families. If El Maadi was at the Attali apartment building at 1:00 p.m. on August 5—and by his own and others' testimony we know that he was—that meant that he was also not far from the site where the Halimi and Zerdoun families were killed in the previous hour, and equally close to the sites where Jacob Bentata, Abraham Bedoucha, Lucien Ichoua Chemla, Blanche Guedj, and the Dadoun brothers were killed earlier in the day. Even if the police did not know El Maadi's identity until later, they may have asked the same questions that we did reading Émile Kottman's account of his arrival in the Attali family's building in the heat of the struggle, only to find a group of soldiers—possibly including El Maadi—inexplicably standing idle at the bottom of the stairs while the killing was going on upstairs. Why was this group of soldiers there? And why did they wait until Kottman and his men arrived to take action?

It does not take much imagination to speculate that the police investigators thought this as well. If they articulated these suspicions to their superiors, we can also imagine the reaction of their superiors to the possibility that a conspiracy involving uniformed soldiers may have been behind at least some of the attacks on Jews. These suspicions would have become even more disturbing when they collided with Ruben Halimi's explosive allegations about men with bloodied hands dividing up large amounts of money. We cannot know if these questions were, in fact, asked. But we can be certain that one obvious response to such a possibility would be to do exactly what Governor-General Carde apparently did: prevent any more stories about conspiracy from circulating in public, hammer home a more general narrative that blamed the riot and the killings on "Muslim fanaticism," and ensure that each murder was treated in separate trials, with a separate list of the accused for each, and no connections made between them in the course of the proceedings. The alternative—to speculate publicly about the involvement of anti-Jewish elements within the French military and connections between the military and the extreme right—would have been something that the authorities would have gone to great lengths to avoid.

For the sake of argument, then, let's assume that Adjutant El Maadi was in fact involved in the murders, and that the investigation of Constantine's Police Mobile in September 1934 uncovered more than they wrote down in their official reports. The precipitous actions of the governor-general's office in shutting down the Police Mobile investigation makes even more sense, as it would have been alarmed at the possibility that a soldier in French uniform could have been implicated in the murders. Assuming that the police knew of El Maadi's involvement also helps to explain why the authorities were reluctant to feed speculation on the riot's causes by releasing publicly the Vigouroux commission's official report. Finally, this assumption also helps to explain the curious differences between the story of the "gang of throat slitters" that had first been leaked to the press and the narratives of the riot that determined the guilt of the individuals who were brought to trial in July 1935 and February 1936. The account of the riots that appeared in the trials is the subject of the next chapter. For all of this to make sense, however, we still have to ascertain how Inspector de Escarrega knew about El Maadi's involvement when he wrote the note requesting information about El Maadi and Jean Filiol in January 1938. To answer that question we need follow the thread of Mohamed El Maadi's subsequent career. This will also help us to understand his motives.

Mohamed El Maadi left the army in May 1936 when the Popular Front coalition won a parliamentary majority and Léon Blum became the first Socialist—and the first Jewish—prime minister in French history. El Maadi resigned his commission, he apparently claimed, "so as to avoid owing his promotion to Léon Blum."[19] In fact, he remained on the active service list until April 1937, when he was awarded a pension for "30 percent invalidity" due to his 1927 injury in Morocco. He was already in Paris in February 1937, living in the eighteenth arrondissement, when he came into the orbit of the violent right-wing extremists led by Jean Filiol. Filiol, born in 1909, was a dissident member of the royalist and antisemitic Action française, the most enduring of the right-wing leagues that originated in the anti-Jewish agitation of the Dreyfus affair in the 1890s. As a young man, Filiol had been a section leader in Paris for the Camelots du roi, a group of street toughs who distributed the Action française's newspaper. The Camelots also acted as a protection service for Action française when they marched in street rallies and brawled with counterprotesters from the French Communist Party. After the Paris riots of February 6, 1934, failed to produce the right-wing coup that they hoped for, Filiol and others from his section of the Camelots grew frustrated with the leadership of the Action française. In December 1935 they left to create a political party that was more oriented toward direct action, calling it the Parti national révolutionnaire (PNR). The PNR drew its membership from the most embittered of the right-wing leaguers, including antisemites, dissident Catholic monarchists, and diehard opponents of the Republic, who were all convinced that the government of France was in the hands of corrupt Jews and Freemasons. In February 1936, Filiol helped to organize an infamous attack by the Camelots du roi on Léon Blum during the Popular Front campaign that would make Blum prime minister later that spring. Blum was pulled from his car and beaten so severely that he had to be hospitalized. Filiol stole Blum's hat and later left it in the offices of the Action française in an apparent attempt to incriminate some of his former colleagues. The government did not wait to find it, however—the Action française was banned that very evening, though its members had nothing to do with this particular crime.

While working with the PNR, Filiol began a close collaboration with Eugène Deloncle, a military veteran and engineer known for his anticommunist militancy and his connections with wealthy French industrialists. In June 1936, after the Popular Front victory, Deloncle and Filiol dissolved the PNR in favor of a clandestine group that they called the Organisme spécial d'action régulatrice nationale (OSARN). Later they referred to it as the Comité secret d'action révolutionnaire (CSAR)—and it was only after the group was broken up by the police that the press dubbed it the "Cagoule." Directed by Deloncle, the CSAR dedicated itself to sensational terrorist acts that its leaders hoped would destabilize the republic and create the conditions for a military coup. Agents of the CSAR established arms caches throughout

France, recruited fellow travelers in the military and police hierarchy, and established an independent intelligence network whose lists of Communist Party members rivaled those maintained by France's security services. The group received financial support from a cross-section of French business elite, including Eugène Schueller, the founder of the L'Oréal cosmetics company, as well as from André Michelin, the tire manufacturer, and Louis Renault, the automobile maker.[20] Its very existence was proof of the extraordinary anxiety that leading figures of France's business establishment felt about the left-wing Popular Front government that had come to power in May 1936. For its paymasters, the CSAR was an instrument of national defense. For its most violent militants, like Filiol, the CSAR was a vehicle for planning remorseless attacks on people they identified as their enemies.

According to his own testimony to the police after his subsequent arrest, Mohamed El Maadi met Jean Filiol in Paris in either March or April 1937 in a café in the place Pereire. De Escarrega's note of January 1938 suggests that Roger Muracciole, the son of Étienne Muracciole of Constantine, was the intermediary that put the two men in contact with one another. Filiol engaged El Maadi in conversation, and the latter told him that he was from Algeria and that he was looking for a position in Paris. Filiol responded that he was a *"garçon sympathique"* (agreeable boy) and came to see him several times in the weeks that followed. Filiol eventually gave El Maadi 4,000 francs to help him as he looked for a job. He did not ask for receipts but asked that El Maadi pledge his loyalty to the CSAR. In a café not far from the place de l'Opéra, El Maadi placed his hand on a box of red, white, and blue matches and swore allegiance to "Fidelity, Obedience, and Discipline."[21] It seems plausible that Filiol was aware of El Maadi's involvement with the riots, perhaps through his connection with Roger Muracciole. El Maadi in turn clearly understood the nature of the organization that he was joining. During his later interrogation, he seemed to understand that his declaration of allegiance to Filiol's organization was potentially incriminating, and after recounting his dealings with Filiol, El Maadi exclaimed, "I love France very much, and ask only to serve her."[22]

At the moment Filiol recruited El Maadi in the spring of 1937, the Cagoule leader was dividing his time between several dangerous assignments. Already in January 1937, he and a group of Cagoule assassins had murdered Dimitri Navachine, the director of the Paris branch of the Soviet State Bank.[23] During the months that followed, Eugène Deloncle, François Métenier, and Filiol traveled several times to Italy, where they contracted with Mussolini's secret service to kill the Italian antifascist Carlo Rosselli. On May 16, either Filiol or an Italian accomplice murdered one of the Cagoule's own recruits,

Laetitia Toureaux, on the Paris metro, probably because they feared that she was about to tell the police about the plan to assassinate Rosselli.[24] Filiol and his gang murdered Carlo Rosselli and his brother Nello on June 9, 1937. On September 10, Filiol and other Cagoulards helped an engineer from the Michelin company to prepare two bombs that were detonated that night at two adjacent trade associations near the place de l'Étoile in Paris, the Confédération générale du patronat français and the Groupe des industries métallurgiques et mécaniques. Two police officers were killed—the press was outraged, and the right blamed the Communists for the attack.

During these same months, Filiol put together a group of front organizations that were designed to pump out anti-leftist propaganda to aid in recruiting for the Cagoule's planned insurrection. One front organization was a royalist journal, Le Courrier royal, published by Pierre Longone. (Then only twenty-six years old, Longone would later become the founding editor of France's preeminent postwar demography journal, Population et sociétés, published by the Institut national des études démographiques.) When the police working the Cagoule case searched Longone's office at Le Courrier royal in November 1937, they found documents related to a different association, Algérie française, also a part of Filiol's network.[25] Longone told the police that Filiol provided funds for Algérie française but did not want to deal with the association directly. Instead, he used the publisher of Le Courrier royal as the intermediary in most of his dealings with the group. On the rare occasions that Longone and the leading members of Algérie française met with Filiol, he was always referred to as "Monsieur Philippe."[26]

Filiol had established Algérie française the previous year as a charitable organization to help Algerian Muslims working in France. The organization's original director, an Algerian named Amar Hamouni, used the funds given to him by Filiol to pay for dinners for indigent workers and to assist them in finding housing. Such political soup kitchens were a common recruiting tactic on the right during these years of economic dislocation, as they competed with the left for support among the working classes and the unemployed.[27] On September 11, 1937—the day after the Cagoule's bombing of the trade associations at the place de l'Étoile—Filiol replaced Hamouni with Mohamed El Maadi, tasking him with transforming the now well-established organization into a combat group for the Cagoule, while at the same time maintaining the association's cover as a social assistance and support program for Algerians working in Paris. Algérie française's treasurer was Jean Berger-Buchy, a journalist later known primarily for the humorous cartoons that he published in the French press—and another cut-out for Filiol that allowed him to hide the source of funding. El Maadi was assisted in recruiting North Africans to the organization by another Algerian, Faci Kaddour, who was responsible for writing articles in Arabic. To disseminate the documents published by Algérie française, Filiol put El Maadi in touch with Fernand Jakubiez, another conspirator in the Cagoule who had been active in arms smuggling.

El Maadi's propaganda role was key, so much so that when he was arrested in November 1937 he listed his profession as "publicist." In addition to using the organization as a cover to recruit Algerian Muslims to their cause, Filiol and El Maadi's explicit goal was to counter the propaganda of the Algerian nationalist organization, the Étoile Nord-Africaine, which had long had connections with the French Communist Party. Under El Maadi's leadership, Algérie française planned to publish a journal, *L'Algérien*, to promote both French authority in Algeria and good relations between Algerian Muslims and militants on the French extreme right. El Maadi also rewrote Algérie française's statutes to emphasize this goal and to make clear who their targets were. Previously, article 2 of the statutes had read:

> To unite all individuals with the goal of strengthening the links of solidarity and fraternity *between French and Algerian members*, without distinction of politics [*tendance*] or religion and to provide its members its material and moral support in all circumstances [emphasis added].

El Maadi's new version substituted the following sentences:

> To unite all individuals with the goal of tightening the links of solidarity and fraternity *of all Algerian Muslims* without distinction of politics [*tendance*] and to provide its members its material and moral support in all circumstances [emphasis added].
>
> It is of course understood that, under no title and in no circumstance, the association cannot admit candidates of Jewish origin, even if they are naturalized French citizens.[28]

El Maadi also deleted the article that stated that members of Algérie française were not allowed to engage in politics, adding the following list of goals:

> To group all Muslim Algerians of the Paris region outside of all political parties and obtain for them the same rights as the French.
>
> To combat the Jews, the Freemasons, the Parties of the Popular Front and the organizations that are attached to them, including the CGT [the Communist-linked trade union federation], Messali Hadj's Party of the Algerian People, and the Ulémas.[29]

This statement of enemies revealed El Maadi and Filiol's true goals—their anti-Jewish, anti-Masonic, and anti–Popular Front postures were a given for the right-wing leagues in the 1930s—but Filiol needed a person like El Maadi to fight against Messali Hadj and the growing presence of Algerian national-ists in Paris, as well as the influence of 'Abd al-Hamid Ben Badis's religious group, the Association des ulémas algériens. When El Maadi himself was arrested and interrogated by the police in November 1937, he told them that Filiol had instructed him to find unemployed Algerians on the streets of Paris. El Maadi had replied that if Filiol could find them jobs, he would bring him three thousand men a month. Filiol responded, "I don't need 3000. 350 who are determined are enough for me."[30] He wanted shock troops for what he saw as an imminent civil war with the left in all its dimensions: Jews, Ma-sons, Popular Front, and Algerian nationalists.

This plan was derailed when the police finally moved against the Cagoule in earnest in November 1937 after the September bombing attacks on the place de l'Étoile. The police had in fact been keeping the group under surveil-lance since February 1937 when their arms-smuggling operations had first come to the authorities' attention.[31] Once the police decided to act, it did not take them long to round up the leaders. The case was supervised by Pierre Béteille, a politically minded magistrate who understood that his task was to dismantle the Cagoule's leadership structure while minimizing the publicity that would be generated by exposing the military and police officials who knew about the group's activities. When Fernand Jakubiez was caught trans-porting a shipment of machine-gun ammunition for the Cagoule from Swit-zerland on October 22, 1937, he was found to be carrying notes of payments to El Maadi, Hamouni, and Kaddour, the three Algerians who ran Algérie française. It was this discovery that led the three men to be arrested along with the leaders of the Cagoule.[32] Béteille's investigators eventually arrested and held 105 conspirators, including Deloncle, the retired general Édouard Duseigneur, and the former Croix de feu leader Joseph Pozzo di Borgo. During the investigation the police seized 34 machine guns, 135 German automatic rifles, 95 Beretta automatic rifles from Italy, 149 military rifles, 300,000 cartridges, and 7,740 grenades. Such arms caches had been estab-lished throughout France. At the largest in Paris, on the rue Jean Beausire just off the place de la Bastille, Algérie française documents were found among the weaponry. As a result, El Maadi spent more than eight months in prison before Béteille dismissed all charges and released him in August 1938.[33]

Béteille's investigation produced the documentation that has allowed us a deeper view of Mohamed El Maadi's political engagements during these years: patriotic, conspiratorial, deeply anti-Jewish, and associated with the most violent elements of the French right. The investigation also produced the crucial note by Inspector Robert de Escarrega that has allowed us to connect El Maadi to the Constantine riots of 1934. If we are to fully believe de Escarrega's claim that El Maadi was "one of the agitators who provoked the 'pogroms' of Constantine," however, we must have a plausible explanation of how this low-level police inspector in Paris could have come by such specific information about Mohamed El Maadi and his connections to the Muracciole family of Constantine. How did de Escarrega know this? Whom did he talk to? El Maadi's own testimony to the police after his arrest is no help here—at least in the version that the police recorded on paper. He gave only a minimal amount of information about his contacts with Filiol and the Algérie française group, essentially confirming what the police already knew but offering little else. Who else did de Escarrega talk to who could have provided him with this information?

Additional documents from the Cagoule investigation of 1937–1938 provide a possible answer. To understand these documents, we need to return to the murders of Carlo and Nello Rosselli by Filiol and other Cagoulard militants on June 9, 1937. During the investigation of those murders, a set of fortuitous circumstances led de Escarrega to contact the Police Mobile in Constantine. This connection provides the only plausible avenue for the information that de Escarrega had about El Maadi's role in the Constantine riots and his connection to the Muracciole family. How did this come about?

Benito Mussolini's secret service contracted in the spring of 1937 with François Métenier of the Cagoule to assassinate Carlo Rosselli in exchange for a shipment of arms.[34] Rosselli had escaped from prison in Italy and developed an active antifascist network from his exile in Paris. The Italian dictator found Rosselli's support for the Republicans in the Spanish Civil War intolerable, as Mussolini was allied with their opponents, the nationalist forces of General Francisco Franco. Rosselli had fought in Spain on the Republican side, returning to France in the spring of 1937 to recuperate from his wounds. In May, Eugène Deloncle confided the assassination plans to Filiol, who immediately put Rosselli under surveillance at his apartment on the rue Notre Dame des Champs in Paris.

Filiol organized the surveillance in his customary hands-off fashion, relying on recruits from the young men active in the Action française and the Camelots du roi, often brought to him by André Tenaille, one of those responsible for maintaining the Cagoule's arms caches in the Paris region. Among Tenaille's recruits was a twenty-year-old member of the Action française named Jean-Marie Bouvyer. Tenaille had been put in touch with Bouvyer by another Cagoulard from the Action française, Robert Puireux, whose family lived near Bouvyer's in Paris's wealthy sixteenth arrondissement.[35] Tenaille introduced Bouvyer to two other conspirators, Louis Huguet, a petty crook and sometime boxer who was another member of Filiol's circle, and Jacques Fauran, whom Bouvyer recognized from school. Filiol himself completed the recruitment by bringing in François Baillet and Fernand Jakubiez, both of whom were already deeply immersed in Cagoule operations.

When Rosselli and his English wife, Marion Cave, left for a recuperative vacation at the Normandy spa town of Bagnolles-de-l'Orne at the end of the month, Filiol put his plan and his group of conspirators into action. Bouvyer, Fauran, and Huguet traveled back and forth several times from Paris to Bagnolles-de-l'Orne to keep an eye on Rosselli's movements, and Filiol used Bouvyer to identify him on each occasion because of his experience watching the Rosselli apartment in Paris. By the time Filiol had gathered the team—along with his mistress Alice Lamy—in Bagnolles-de-l'Orne on June 9, Nello Rosselli had arrived from Italy to join his brother, unwittingly sealing his own fate. Bouvyer once more identified the brothers in the lobby of their hotel to Filiol's gang. After lunch, Carlo and Nello Rosselli dropped Marion Cave at the train station and proceeded back to Paris, with the Cagoule hit squad following behind in two cars. Puireux drove the first car, along with Filiol, Baillet, and Jakubiez, tailing the Rossellis' Ford closely. Fauran drove the second car, following at some distance with Bouvyer and Alice Lamy as passengers.

Just before a point where the road narrowed considerably, Filiol's car accelerated quickly, overtook the Rossellis, and then stopped suddenly at a diagonal, obstructing the way forward. Carlo Rosselli stopped the Ford, and Nello stepped out of the car to see what was wrong. Filiol fired his automatic pistol immediately. Carlo, behind the wheel of the car, died from the first shot that struck him, but Nello was still alive, and the group finished him off by stabbing him twenty-one times. While the killings were taking place, Fauran's car approached from behind before making a half turn and accelerating toward Paris. The remaining conspirators moved the bodies to a more secluded spot and placed a bomb in the Ford to destroy any evidence, but the fuse went out, and the bomb did not go off. Filiol had distributed daggers to each member of the group before the murders, and they left one with an Italian inscription at the scene in a clumsy attempt to implicate an Italian antifascist group.

After the murder of the Rosselli brothers, the group split up. Filiol returned to Paris and installed El Maadi at the head of Algérie française in September 1937. When the police went after the Cagoule leadership in November, Filiol fled to Morocco and later found refuge in Spain along with Alice Lamy and François Baillet. Fernand Jakubiez was arrested at the Swiss border on October 22, as we have seen, leading to the arrest of El Maadi and the other North Africans in the network, and the police soon connected El Maadi to Filiol. In the multiple interrogations of Cagoulards that followed, Bouvyer turned out to be the weak link. He had been noticed by the hotel employees while staking out the Rossellis in Bagnolles-de-l'Orne in June and was apparently so brazen that a journalist picked up on the story, leading to an article in *Paris-Soir* identifying him as the mysterious "dark-haired man" who been hanging about the hotel just before the murders.[36] Bouvyer deflected attention temporarily by saying that he had been at the hotel because of a "intimate and personal appointment," but when the police got an anonymous tip on December 2 that he had boasted of participating in the murders, they began to put the pieces together. Apprehending Bouvyer turned out to be a problem, however, because he had entered the army in October with a commission in the Second Regiment of the Chasseurs d'Afrique. When the anonymous tip came in incriminating him in the Rosselli murders, he was at the Instruction Center for Reserve Officers in Constantine, Algeria.

Bouvyer's presence in Constantine put Inspector de Escarrega's team in Paris in touch with the city's Police Mobile. It took them several weeks to gather the necessary evidence before they asked the authorities in Constantine to arrest Bouvyer. André Tenaille, who had recruited Bouvyer to Filiol's team, was arrested on December 3—the day after the anonymous tip—and François Métenier, who handled the Cagoule's relations with the Italian secret services that had put the contract on Carlo Rosselli, was arrested on December 10. On January 12, the Police Mobile in Constantine arrested Bouvyer at his barracks and took his statement on the Rosselli killings. It was filled with half-truths—Bouvyer claimed that he was there simply to identify Carlo Rosselli and did not know that the brothers were going to be murdered.[37] He nevertheless led the police to Robert Puireux and Jacques Fauran, who were arrested in Paris the next day.

For our purposes, however, what is important is that the police officer who interrogated Bouvyer and provided the report on his testimony to the Paris police was Inspector Marius Gaillard of the Police Mobile in Constantine. Gaillard had worked closely with Jacques Cauro on the Police Mobile's investigation of the Constantine riots in 1934. He had been a part of the original team of investigators that had made the first arrests, interrogated the first suspects, and leaked stories to the press about the conspiracy of the "gang of throat slitters." He had also helped to write the reports that changed the story after the intervention by the governor-general's office. Gaillard, in other words, was in a position to know everything that the local police in Constantine believed about the riots of 1934. He would also have understood the reasons for any discrepancy between what they discovered in the course of their investigations and the official account put out by Jean Vigouroux's investigating commission. One assumes that the coordination of Bouvyer's arrest and interrogation in January 1938 required multiple telephone calls and telegrams between the police in Paris and in Constantine. They would have exchanged the information they had about the Rosselli murders, about Jean Filiol and Jean-Marie Bouvyer—and about Mohamed El Maadi, who was then in prison and talking to the police and who was from the department of Constantine. Eleven days after Gaillard sent the report on Bouvyer's testimony to Paris, the judge in Normandy issued an arrest warrant for Filiol. Shortly after that, de Escarrega wrote his note to the governor-general's office in Algiers asking for information about Mohamed El Maadi, accusing him of being "one of the agitators who provoked the 'pogroms' of Constantine" and of being "on the payroll" of Muracciole, the son of the Constantine lawyer. The timing of these events, and the communication between Marius Gaillard in Constantine and Robert de Escarrega's team in Paris, is the only plausible explanation for how the police in Paris could have known about El Maadi's role in the Constantine riots.

How shall we read the complicated story of Mohamed El Maadi's evolution across the 1930s, and how should we think about the connections between his possible involvement in the murder of Jews in Constantine in 1934 and his engagement as an enthusiastic fascist in the Second World War? What were his motives during these years? His affiliation with right-wing terrorism did not prevent El Maadi from reenlisting in the French army in 1939 or from receiving the Croix de Guerre for his service during the German invasion in 1940.[38] After the fall of France, he was reunited with his former colleagues from the Cagoule who, under Eugène Deloncle's direction, had created a new group, the Mouvement Social Révolutionnaire (MSR).[39] The MSR was initially affiliated with Marcel Déat's "neo-socialist" Rassemblement national populaire (RNP), a group that enthusiastically supported Pierre Laval in his efforts to cement a closer relationship between Philippe Pétain's Vichy government and Hitler's Germany and that openly endorsed Vichy's anti-Jewish policies. During these same months El Maadi and several MSR members attempted to occupy a Jewish-owned building in Paris without going through the proper channels. This episode led the police to arrest El Maadi in 1941, though he was quickly released following a verification of his identity.[40] By that November, he had been hired by Vichy's Commissariat général aux questions juives, directed by Xavier Vallat, the office responsible for organizing

the legal exclusion of French Jews from citizenship, the seizure of their property, and their elimination from political and economic life.[41]

In June 1941, El Maadi created a new organization, the Comité Nord-
Africain, agitating in speeches and in print for a French alliance with Hitler
and the expulsion of Jews from North Africa. The early months of the Comité's activities coincided with a break between Deloncle's MSR and Déat's
RNP—and El Maadi's loyalty always remained with Deloncle, whom he described as "the only director of a French political movement who really understood the situation of [North Africans], who wants to improve them, and
who wants to place them at the level of all civilized men."[42] Under El Maadi's
direction, and with the assistance of Faci Kaddour, who had also worked with
him in Algérie française, the Comité published the intermittent monthly journal *Er Rachid* from January to December 1943. Beginning in January 1944,
with an infusion of cash from the German Abwehr (military intelligence), *Er
Rachid* became a large-format weekly journal that was published most weeks
until August 1944. At its peak, *Er Rachid's* print run was as large as twenty-five
thousand copies. Historians differ as to the actual size of its audience—Ethan
Katz suggests that it reached a substantial number of the Algerians living in
metropolitan France under the occupation, whereas Patrice Rolli suggests
that as much as 60–90 percent of each edition went unsold.[43]

Er Rachid's articles combined German and French racial theories with anti-
Jewish political commentary and references to Islamic history in an attempt
to rally support among North Africans for the fascist cause.[44] El Maadi was
particularly incensed at the intervention of the British and the United States
in North Africa after November 1942, and he used the pages of *Er Rachid* to
promote a French-led Mediterranean federation that would encompass all
of France, Morocco, Algeria, and Tunisia. He endorsed equality between
non-Jewish North Africans and French citizens within this federation and
called for the creation of an autonomous North African army within the
French military—a position that led the French police to conclude that the
Comité musulman de l'Afrique du Nord "was oriented toward North African
nationalism."[45]

El Maadi's endorsement of a French–North African federation was in fact
an outgrowth of his increasingly embittered sense of French nationalism.
Paradoxically it was both this bitterness and the sincerity of his devotion
to a particular vision of France that drove him further and further into collaboration with Germany. By late 1943, he was working with the notorious and brutal Henri Lafont, the chief of the French section of the Gestapo
in Paris, on the rue Lauriston. It was during these months that El Maadi

recruited several hundred men from the population of Algerians living in Paris to create a North African Brigade that would fight for the fascist cause in the waning months of the war.[46] El Maadi's energy and enthusiasm for this task earned him the nickname "SS Mohamed."[47] In the spring of 1944, the North African Brigade took part in bloody repressive actions with Wehrmacht security division forces in the Limousin, the Dordogne, Périgord, and the Franche-Comté. The goal was to wipe out French Resistance units, but it was the civilian population that bore the brunt of their violence. Thousands were arrested, many were tortured and deported to concentration camps, and hundreds were killed, including many Jews. In July 1944, a month after the D-Day invasion, the brigade was dissolved, and El Maadi fled east to Berlin, where he became a part of the small circle around the controversial figure of Hajj Amin al-Husayni, the former mufti of Jerusalem, who worked to forge an alliance between Arab anticolonial nationalism and Hitler's Germany during the war years. By that time, the French state that Mohamed El Maadi served had deported 75,721 Jews to concentration camps in the east. Of these, 2,567 survived. In 1945, the Cour d'Appel in Paris issued a warrant for El Maadi's arrest under charges of "conspiracy to change the form of the government" and "conspiracy to incite a civil war," but he was never found.[48] He is believed to have died in Egypt in late 1953 or early 1954.

El Maadi's political evolution from fervent French nationalist to enthusiastic foot soldier for a last-ditch Franco-German fascist alliance at the end of the war appears to have been driven by a consistent set of political aspirations rooted in a strongly ideological vision of North African history. In May 1943, six months after Algeria had been occupied by Allied troops and more than a year before the D-Day invasion, El Maadi published a political pamphlet in Paris, *L'Afrique du nord, terre d'histoire*, that summed up the position that he also defended in *Er Rachid*. Part historical lesson and part political manifesto, this short book announced his hopes for a "Eurafrican" partnership between a fascist France and the "Arabo-Berber" people of North Africa. In a broad summary of North African history since the Roman conquest, he declared that the "Arabo-Berbers" that had occupied the Iberian peninsula for centuries were "without contestation, the origin of modern European civilization."[49] In his reading of this history, the North African conquerors had been generous and tolerant rulers in the past, and he contrasted this with the "hatred, constraint and inhuman exploitation" that their descendants experienced in the present. When it came to the history of French colonialism in Algeria, however, El Maadi refused to blame the troubles of North Africa on "metropolitan France." Instead he criticized the "Jewish IIIrd Republic" for the abuses of empire. "The majority of the French are innocent in relation

to our long unhappiness," he wrote.[50] By blaming Jews for Algeria's misfor-
tunes, El Maadi's pamphlet managed to reconcile his detailed critique of
colonialism's many injustices with a deeply felt loyalty to France. This link
between French patriotism and antisemitism is the continuous thread in El
Maadi's political engagement.

The possible involvement of Mohamed El Maadi in organizing the violence in Constantine in 1934 is not, therefore, evidence of a connection
between these murders and an emergent Algerian nationalism. On the contrary, all the evidence indicates that he acted as a member of the French
military who was gravitating toward the most extreme edge of French right-
wing politics. The most sensational murders on Sunday, August 5, in other
words, may have been organized by an agitator acting in the name of France.
This may well have been the message that the governor-general's office did
not want made public when it shut down the investigation of the Police Mobile. If this were true, it was not a truth that could not be spoken out loud.

Perhaps the most telling statement about the way that the authorities—
and many subsequent historians—have misread the meaning of the riots in
the eyes of the perpetrators comes from the published words of Mohamed
El Maadi himself. In the 1943 manifesto that he published defending his
hopes for a Eurafrican fascist alliance, he expressed his bitter disappointment
that the Vichy regime and the defenders of the French empire had never fully
taken advantage of the support they could have received from the "Arabo-
Berber" people of North Africa. Instead, the French had insisted on seeing
North Africans as their inferiors and as their enemy. El Maadi had come to
this conclusion reluctantly and late in life, after spending decades trying to
prove his loyalty to an extremist version of French nationalism. In a chilling
passage, El Maadi's despair at being rejected by the French comes through,
his resentment at the consequences of colonialism melding with the injured
loyalty of an obedient soldier. The passage reached its extraordinary climax
in an invocation of the Constantine riots, held up nine years later as an example of a misunderstood act of patriotic devotion:

> The beneficiaries [of colonization in Algeria] and its privileges are sur-
> prised to see before them men possessing the same intellectual capaci-
> ties. Humiliated by the sense that they are less and less the masters who
> dispose of everything, angered by the destruction of their prerogatives,
> and the abandonment of inequalities. . . [the settlers] desperately cling
> to their privileges, thinking that by bad faith and material advantage
> they can delay the date when they must face the settling of scores.
>
> In this way, they conjure up the specter of pan-Islamism, pan-
> arabism, or bolshevism, or call on foreign armies for help. From this it

is only a small step to calling us dangerous agitators and hateful anti-Europeans. Once the threat to their interests becomes clear they take this step. For them, everything is a pretext. The events of Constantine—August 5, 1934—those of Sétif—February 1, 1935—provoked by the abuses and the insolence of the Jews, will be deformed and presented to public opinion as an infringement on French sovereignty, even though these pogroms were carried out to the accompaniment of cries of "Vive la France!"[51]

"The events of Constantine . . . were carried out to the accompaniment of 'Vive la France!'" These anguished words, in light of what we now know, sound like a confession. Resorting to the first person and a coincidental near-quotation of de Escarrega's note on his Cagoule connections—"calling us dangerous agitators"—El Maadi plaintively argued that the violence of Constantine was *both* the fault of the Jews *and* a patriotic act. It seems almost too easy to analyze this statement from a psychological point of view. In making the Jews responsible for the violence that caused their deaths, was he exhibiting a need to deflect the guilt he felt at having participated in multiple murders? If so, it was a guilt that was inseparable from his anger at the French "beneficiaries of colonialism" for not having realized the true meaning of this violence. In his mind, the anti-Jewish animus that he shared with other French patriots was proof of his allegiance to France and to France's African empire. These acts of murder were misunderstood expressions of love.

CHAPTER 14

The Trials

The trials of those charged for the murders committed on August 5, 1934, took place in two phases—July 1935 and February 1936—against the background of an uncertain and bitter political season. Émile Morinaud's political dominance in Constantine was weakened by the riots, his coalition of convenience with Jewish officials on the municipal council irrevocably broken. This became visible to all when he lost his bid for reelection in the municipal elections of May 1935, ending his thirty-seven-year run as Constantine's mayor. He still had his seat in parliament, however, and to maintain it he took a hard swerve to the antisemitic right, hoping to replace the votes he had lost from Constantine's Jewish voters with those from the Croix de feu and its supporters. The campaign leading up to the legislative elections of May 1936 was bitter, and members of the local Constantine establishment struggled to deal with the fallout of Morinaud's scorched-earth tactics.

The first group of murder trials took place in Constantine in July 1935 just as the local community was struggling to make sense of the sudden void at the center of the city's political life opened by Morinaud's defeat. The new mayor (and former first deputy mayor), Pierre Liagre, created a new political party devoted to the suitably vague principle of "French supremacy." He sought to bring together disparate and seemingly incompatible parts of Constantine's fragmenting political spectrum, including several members of the Croix de feu and a coalition of Jewish political activists who called themselves the Parti jeune juif. This was less odd than it seemed. The Parti jeune juif seems to have been an ephemeral vehicle for a few Jewish political activists who had grown tired of the older generation of Jewish officials led by Henri Lellouche and Maurice Laloum. This older generation must have found it painful to explain to their own constituents their long association with Morinaud's electoral machine in the 1920s and early 1930s. The Parti jeune juif attracted few followers, and most Jewish voters looked toward the antifascist coalition of center and left-wing parties known as the Popular Front, led by Léon Blum.

In France as a whole, the legislative campaign leading up to May 1936 was seen largely through the lens of an ideological conflict between the leftist politics of the Popular Front coalition and the conservative nationalists who railed against what they saw as the threat of an imminent Communist coup. In Constantine, on the other hand, the fractured political situation was murkier. At one point in January 1936, a group of local elites comprising supporters of Pierre Liagre, a few Jewish elected officials led by Henri Lellouche, Colonel Gros of the Croix de feu, and Louis Morel, the publisher of *La Dépêche de Constantine*, went so far as to form a "secret committee" dedicated to convincing Morinaud to bow out of his campaign for parliament in favor of Gratien Faure, a wealthy landowner who had recently been elected to the *délégations financières*. In the end, Morinaud outmaneuvered them all and managed to hold on to his parliamentary seat in spite of the loss of his municipal base in Constantine. The elections of May 1936 thus came at the end of a bitterly turbulent political campaign that brought the leftist Popular Front to power in Paris, while simultaneously demonstrating the power of the antisemitic right in French Algeria.[1]

The second series of murder trials took place in Orléansville in February 1936, only a few weeks after the secret committee began its ultimately futile campaign to prevent Morinaud from continuing to represent Constantine in parliament. Even if we do not assume that members of this committee had any knowledge of the complicated circumstances of the murders on August 5—or of the involvement of a figure like Mohamed El Maadi, a soldier in French uniform—it is not difficult to imagine local political leaders dreading the prospect of a public airing of the causes of the riots in open court. Each individual case covered a separate site where murders took place, and each case required a rehearsal of the events of that day, with a shifting cast of many characters. Every trial was a potentially dangerous public spectacle, an adversarial judicial process, where the voices of Jewish victims and alleged Muslim perpetrators would be projected through their legal representatives to a local audience and to representatives of the French and Algerian press. The stakes could not have been higher.

The trials also pose challenging interpretive questions for the historian. As we have seen, the police investigators routinely beat and tortured suspects and paraded them before the press with sensational stories about "a gang of throat slitters." With little explanation, they then abandoned this theory and replaced their earlier list of suspects with other alleged perpetrators conveniently arrested at the same moment. Given such circumstances, how are we to evaluate the accounts of the riots that came out in the trials? There are also questions about the significance of the El Maadi–Muracciole connection, the fact that the police apparently understood that a person they considered to be an "agitator" who provoked the riots—Mohammed El Maadi—was "on the payroll" of a member of the Muracciole family. It was not surprising that the lawyer Étienne Muracciole was closely involved in the murder trials—he had been president of the Constantine bar and was arguably the most prominent lawyer in town. But is there any evidence to confirm that either his son Roger or he was in any way involved in planning the conspiracy to provoke the riots? In the absence of more evidence from the police files, the answer to this question must be no. Nothing found so far in the archives directly implicates any member of the Muracciole family in a conspiracy before the riots took place. The phrase used in the internal police memo from 1938—"on the payroll"—might lead one to assume that a dossier demonstrating this connection existed somewhere in the police files. Until more evidence surfaces, however, it is impossible to know when this relationship began or how long it lasted.

Even without such clear evidence, the fact that the police in Paris believed that a connection existed between the Muracciole family and El Maadi justifies closer attention to the role played by Étienne Muracciole in the murder trials. The two phases of the trials in 1935 and 1936 were extraordinarily sensitive. As the trial dates approached, the authorities became deeply concerned about the problem of public order and the very real danger that a public hearing about the events of August 3–5 would provoke another outburst of violence. They were also concerned about how the violence would be portrayed in the course of the proceedings, how the defendants would behave, and what arguments the defense lawyers would deploy. Not surprisingly, the prefecture in Constantine and the Office of the Governor-General in Algiers worked hard to prevent the proceedings from spinning out of control. It is impossible to say definitively that this close monitoring of the trials extended to attempts to engineer the outcome of specific cases, but it did succeed in preserving the general portrait of the riots as a spontaneous explosion of religious fanatics. At crucial moments—when it came to sentencing the accused who had been found guilty—this description was actually presented as "extenuating circumstances" that justified a lesser sentence.

Although I will argue that the trials had an important theatrical component, they were *not* mere formalities—prosecutors and defense lawyers called many witnesses, and there were dramatic moments of confrontation between survivors and the accused. With very few exceptions, however, the trials were over in a single day, and the broad outcomes were never in doubt. It seems possible that the lawyers on both sides may have tacitly agreed to basic ground rules about what was appropriate to bring up in the context of their arguments. The scope was wide—defense lawyers openly criticized the local authorities, protested that the official report of the Vigouroux commission had never been made public, and even attacked the Crémieux decree itself. Prosecutors, on the other hand, did not shy away from the most sensational and horrifying descriptions of the murder scenes, and they also seemed open to criticism of the local authorities. Clearly, it was not inflammatory language in itself that was out of bounds. Nevertheless, the most telling sign of possible collusion between the prosecution and the defense lawyers is the fact that nobody mentioned the theory about a gang of "throat slitters" that had been leaked to the press by the police in the immediate aftermath of the events. Neither the defense nor the prosecutors ever tried to link murders that had occurred in more than one location, even when it may have benefited their arguments. Instead, each trial focused on deaths that occurred in a single location, with a separate list of the accused for each site. In this way, the portrait of a spontaneous eruption of atavistic hatreds was preserved.

If each trial brought a new and different list of the accused, the cast of lawyers remained remarkably similar from day to day during both phases of the trials, and no lawyer from Constantine played a bigger role than Étienne Muracciole in framing the portrait of the riots that emerged from the proceedings. His role was complex—in different trials he defended both Jews and Muslims, and he was not above criticizing the authorities in their handling of the situation. In February 1935, he successfully defended Lieutenant Charles Zaoui, a French military officer and a Jew, along with his brothers and a Jewish police agent who were all charged with provocation on the morning of August 5 in the place des Galettes. Muracciole dismantled the testimony of witnesses and also severely criticized the Vigouroux report, which he claimed was responsible for the decision to charge the Jewish men with provocation. The public watched the trial closely, and the acquittal caused a great deal of unhappiness among Constantine's Muslim population, many of whom felt strongly that the city's Jews had precipitated the violence against themselves.[2]

On July 4, 1935, Muracciole played a significant role in the first murder trial when four men were tried for the murder of Elie Guedj, the man who had been killed on August 5 after being pulled from an autobus on the place Lamorcière. Each of the accused in the Guedj case had his own defense lawyer, and Muracciole's client was the only one of the four who was acquitted.[3] The other three, who were not named in the press accounts, were sentenced to long prison terms at hard labor. That same week, Muracciole represented two young Muslim men who had persuaded their Jewish employer to accompany them to Constantine on August 6, the day after the riots, telling him to disguise himself as "a native" (*indigène*). Once they arrived in the city, they exposed his identity to the crowd, shouting "Here is a Jew!" and struck him with a club and a knife. Muracciole succeeded in getting an acquittal for one of the men, but the second was sentenced to seven years forced labor.[4] Although these cases were closely watched by the public, their outcomes would not have been important to anybody concerned about evidence of conspiracy. Elie Guedj's death was not one of the murders that could have been committed by a small group active in the neighborhood around the rue Béraud, the rue Abdallah Bey, and the rue des Zouaves.

The first trial for a murder that had been originally linked to the alleged gang of throat slitters was the trial on July 10 of four men for the murder of Lucien Ichoua Chemla in the rue Germon at 10:30 in the morning on August 5. This murder had occurred only minutes after police agent Selim Benmoussa had seen a group of armed men run by on a nearby street shouting, "Run! Doctor Bendjelloul has been killed by the Jews. Arm yourselves! We have to be done with them, it's the last day, it's a Holy War." The Police Mobile's investigation had originally determined that Tayeb "Santo" Benamira— the young man identified by Rosette Benisti as having participated in the Halimi murders—had killed Chemla, with the help of Saïd Benhamama and three other butcher's apprentices, Mohamed Takouk, Rabah Hachiche, and Ahmed Hamireche. After subsequent interrogations, a sixth suspect, Mohamed Alliche, also confessed to delivering one of the fatal blows. These men had also been variously linked with the murders of Abraham Bedoucha, Jacob Bentata, Gilbert and Maurice Dadoun, Blanche Guedj, and the multiple murders in the Attali and Halimi apartments. After the apparent intervention in the Police Mobile's investigation by the governor-general's office at the end of August, however, Tayeb Benamira disappeared from the list of those accused of Chemla's murder, as did Alliche, in spite of his confession. Eventually, only four were formally charged—Benhamama, Takouk,

Hachiche, and Hamireche—even though their own testimony, as reported by the police, had made clear that they were following Benamira's orders in holding down Chemla so that Benamira could cut his throat. None of these inconsistencies were allowed to come out, however, because the case was dismissed before the opening statements could be made. The only reason given was that "the medical declarations [in the autopsy] were contrary to the facts of the accusation."[5] The lawyer representing Chemla's family—none other than Étienne Muracciole—gave his permission for the dismissal and did not insist on the trial moving forward. It is hard to avoid the suspicion that Muracciole was party to a silent agreement on the part of the authorities to prevent the details of this botched and tainted investigation from coming to light.

Muracciole also played a significant role in the equally politically sensitive trial that opened the next day, July 11. Here the question of the gang of throat slitters was not at issue—the case was that of Salomon Guedj, a Jewish man who had been murdered north of Constantine in the town of Hamma-Plaisance (Hamma Bouziane) on August 5. What made this case particularly charged, however, was the fact that the man charged with being the leader of the three accused murderers was a decorated veteran of a French colonial rifle regiment, a Muslim man named Aouchet. According to witnesses, Aouchet had led a group of men in the attack on Guedj, brandishing a revolver as he shouted, "France has given us the order to kill all the Jews! Anybody who moves or tries to stop us will be killed by me!" During the subsequent investigation, Aouchet had reportedly confessed to participating in the killing, but he recanted this confession later. His vocal expression of loyalty to France directly contradicted the official thesis about Muslim fanaticism, and his status as a veteran also made the authorities uneasy, as they knew that the verdict would be closely watched by Constantine's population of Muslim colonial subjects. If the authorities had discovered Adjutant Mohamed El Maadi's involvement by this point, one can only imagine their trepidation at seeing a veteran in the dock for the murder of Salomon Guedj.

The prosecutor accused Aouchet of failing in his duty and demanded the death penalty for him and two of his accomplices. Nobody in the court apparently expected any other outcome. Muracciole once again served as the lead defense lawyer in the case, and his electrifying closing speech was described in the press as a turning point in the trial. He convinced the jury that the crime had not been premeditated and begged them to be generous toward a loyal old soldier. In the end, the two accomplices were acquitted, and Aouchet was convicted of murder but sentenced to only five years without banishment. The surprisingly light sentence caused an uproar among the crowd gathered in the streets outside the tribunal—Jewish residents of Constantine felt betrayed by the judgment, while others debated whether or not the result was a repudiation of the government's case.

The next day brought an additional thunderclap—the newspapers reported that the long-awaited trial of the four men accused of invading the Halimi apartment and murdering eight people would not take place as planned. That morning, the Halimi trial had opened with the four accused on the bench and the victim's families in the gallery. Muracciole was again present as the representative of the Halimi family. When the young witness, Rosette Benisti, was brought to the tribunal, however, she was so paralyzed by fear that she had to be literally dragged into the courtroom. Queried by the judge, she revealed that she had received threats over a period of ten days and would testify only behind closed doors. The judge listened briefly and announced that he was postponing the trial. It would have to take place in another location in a different department, free from local pressures.[6]

The second phase of murder trials, therefore, did not take place until February 1936 in the colonial town of Orléansville in the department of Algiers, nearly six hundred kilometers to the west. Here, the trials unfolded under heavy military guard and the intense scrutiny of the press and members of the public. A familiar cast of lawyers from Constantine had made the journey to Orléansville. Étienne Muracciole was again present—in both the Halimi and Attali trials he represented the families of the victims. His colleague at the Constantine bar Albert Rédarès served as the lead defense lawyer in both the Halimi and Attali trials. Like Muracciole, Rédarès was a pillar of the local establishment, an ally of Mayor Morinaud who had served on the municipal council and alongside Muracciole on the Conseil général of the department of Constantine. One member of the defense team from Constantine, Hadj Driss, was the only Muslim lawyer present in either trial. Another Constantine lawyer, Simon Tubiana, also a member of the Conseil général, represented the surviving members of the Zerdoun family at the Halimi trial and was the only Jewish lawyer present. Léonce Déroulède, from the bar in Algiers, served as a defense lawyer in both the Halimi and Attali trials and was the only lawyer who played a significant role who was not from Constantine. Déroulède was a man of the left, known for his strong defense of civil rights. He was one of the few prominent lawyers in Algeria who regularly represented Muslim colonial subjects.

Again, no mention was made of the publicly announced conclusion of the initial police investigation—that the murders in the Halimi and Attali homes had all been committed by the same group of people. Tayeb Benamira, the butcher's assistant who had been identified by Rosette Benisti as a leader of the attackers of the Halimi family, had confessed after interrogation to murdering Joseph Attal in the Attali apartment. In spite of this confession, which had been widely reported in the press, Benamira's name came up only in the Halimi trial. In fact, the Police Mobile's investigation had publicly connected four men with the murders in the Halimi apartment: Tayeb Benamira, Saïd Benhamama, Mohamed Takouk, and Saïd Benhamama's father, Abdallah, who had also been identified by Benisti. This was the famous group of butcher boys that had led to sensational press claims during the week of August 14–17 about the gang of "throat slitters." After the governor-general's apparent intervention in the case, in the last week of August, the police announced new arrests in the Halimi murders. The only explanation given for this new list of suspects in the press was simply that they had been brought in for questioning after one had been heard uttering "imprudent words."[7]

The confessions and mutual incriminations of Mohamed Takouk, Saïd Benhamama, and his father Abdallah Benhamama therefore meant little when it came to the trial of the murderers of the Halimi-Zerdoun families. The three men who were tried in 1936 alongside Tayeb Benamira—Lakhal ben Larbi Ziad, Tayeb ben Fergani Boulkraa, and Mohamed Chelghoum— all protested their innocence at the first opportunity and stated that their confessions had come after beatings by the police. Benisti did not recognize them as having been among the group of men who invaded the Halimi household. Other witnesses gave incriminating testimony but only of a circumstantial nature. Tayeb Boulkraa had been seen leaving his village with a rifle that morning, and a cartridge casing was found in the Halimi apartment that "could well have been fired from the rifle that witnesses saw in the hands of Boulkraa."[8] The prosecutor produced a knife that he said Lakhal Ziad had used to attack the Halimi family, and Ziad, after not understanding what was being said at first, agreed only that the knife had been found in his house.

The last witness for the prosecution was none other than Marius Gaillard of the Police Mobile, the same agent who wrote up the report on Tayeb Benamira's forgotten confession to the murder of Joseph Salomon Attal at the Attali apartment—and who would be in touch with Robert de Escarrega in Paris two years later about Jean-Marie Bouvyer, Jean Filiol, and, we presume, Mohamed El Maadi.[9] Gaillard mentioned nothing of the confusing circumstances that had led his team to arrest and charge three other men alongside Benamira, before arriving much later at the charges against Ziad, Boulkraa, and Chelghoum. He did not explain why Tayeb Benamira's publicly reported confession of a different murder in a different location had not been mentioned in the trial. In fact, he didn't mention Benamira at all—presumably because Rosette Benisti's identification was enough to incriminate the young butcher's apprentice. Gaillard's role was to incriminate Ziad and Boulkraa: he claimed the two had spontaneously confessed to the murders in the Halimi home and that when brought to the scene of the crime they freely indicated where in the attic the murders had taken place. Ziad and Boulkraa energetically denied Gaillard's account and recanted their confessions, repeating their claims about the physical abuse that they had undergone in the offices of the Police Mobile.

The next day, Étienne Muracciole stood up to give a deposition to the court as the representative of the Halimi family. The later press accounts of this moment were somewhat breathless—the day was described as "a veritable tournament of eloquence" and a "fight without mercy" between the prosecutors and the defense lawyers. Muracciole's speech, delivered before a packed court, did not disappoint. He read aloud the names of each victim, repeating the phrase "throat slit" after almost every name. "In the gallery there was a shiver of horror." Muracciole's oration began with a clear statement about the challenge that the crimes of August 1934 posed to the nation itself: "No crime has ever provoked such horror on French soil, has ever bloodied it in this way." He accepted that the primary cause of the unrest was "racial adversity," but he did not condemn the Muslim population by name. Instead, he laid the blame squarely on the local authorities: "If France was absent on that day, it is because its administrators were incapable and they will perhaps pay the price someday." He specifically blamed the local police and military: "To the people who begged them to intervene, the soldiers and officers responded with these tragic words—'not my orders!' "[10] Strikingly, Muracciole's speech reproduced many of the rhetorical phrases put forth by Jewish observers—Adolphe Sultan, Henri Lellouche, and Joseph Fisher in particular—in the days immediately after the riots.

Albert Rédarès, the lead defense lawyer, rose in turn to give his own address, which was clearly designed—within the limits that were acceptable to the settler establishment—to channel the voice of Constantine's Muslim population, to represent "the Muslim thesis" about the riots. Rather than racial hatreds, he said, the riots had been "spontaneous" and were purely local in origin, caused by "the serious frictions that had been produced beforehand between the Muslim and Israelite populations." Rédarès reminded the court that the first victim of the riots was the Muslim man who had been shot on August 3 and asked why no investigation of that death had been undertaken. He attacked the testimony of Rosette Benisti, saying that there was not enough light in the darkened stairwell for her to have made a clear identification of the men who chased the family up to the roof. Finally, he challenged Muracciole's interpretation of the riots and complained that the report by Vigouroux's investigating commission had never been made available to the public. He returned to the thesis of Jewish provocation, citing the gunshots fired on the place des Galettes on Sunday morning, and saying that it was certain that Muslims and soldiers were wounded. (He did not, however, mention that the Zaoui brothers had been acquitted of provocation a year earlier, defended by Étienne Muracciole.) Rédarès cited the rumor of Bendjelloul's death as a mitigating factor in the violence of the crowd, explaining that this was why the crowd had been so angry. "That was the cause of the invasion of the Halimi and Attali homes," he concluded. Rédarès went even further—he read a long list of Muslims who were injured in the fighting and then referred obliquely to the uncounted number of Muslim "dead, who were mysteriously removed by their own."[11]

Rédarès's "eloquent" plea was in vain, however—in fact, it was never intended to be successful. Reading the account in the press, one is struck most by the stage-managed quality of the proceedings. As one might expect, a Jewish lawyer served on the side of the victim's families, and a Muslim lawyer served on the defense team. Each of these lawyers played a minor role, however, and the leading voices were reserved for the two dominant personalities from the Constantine bar, Muracciole and Rédarès. Whatever their political differences, they were both committed to the preservation of the colonial order, and one almost senses their enjoyment at the trial, sparring against one another in the name of the "Jewish" interpretation of the riots on the one hand, and the "Muslim" interpretation on the other. Neither version was meant to win on its own terms, of course—the accused were to be convicted, and neither Constantine's Jews nor the city's Muslims were in control of the image of their community that emerged from the trial. The most important goal of Muracciole and Rédarès's dueling performance was to fix in the minds of the public the vision of an eternal and irreconcilable conflict between Muslims and Jews that lay at the heart of the story. In that they were successful.

After their speeches, the court recessed at 11:30 p.m. for deliberation, and the crowd waited impatiently for the verdict. Rumors that the prosecutors had asked for two death sentences circulated quickly, and two hours passed before the court came back. One by one, the judges responded "yes" to all charges, declaring all four of the young men guilty, but admitting "attenuating circumstances." Benamira was sentenced to life imprisonment, Ziad to fifteen years at hard labor, Boulkraa to five years of the same punishment, and Chelghoum to two years in prison and 200 francs in fines. The Jews of Constantine emerged from the proceedings painted as both helpless victims and as active provocateurs, while the Muslims were tainted with the eternal stain of fanaticism and violent anger. The colonial order had won.

It would have been tidier for all concerned if the story could have ended there—tidier for Muracciole and Rédarès, who had served up the story of the riots in two such neat packages, one for a Jewish audience and one for a Muslim one. There was still one more trial, however—that of the men accused of participating in the murders at the home of Makhlouf Attali and his family at about 1:00 p.m. on Sunday, August 5. This trial was more challenging and posed more dangers for the lawyers from Constantine. Most obviously, there was the fact that Tayeb Benamira, tried and convicted the day before in the Halimi case, had once confessed to the murder of Joseph Attal in the Attali apartment building. If, as seems possible, the lawyers and the authorities knew something of Mohamed El Maadi's involvement in the agitation that led to the murders, this too was a problem, since his name had come up several times in the official reports.

The lawyers dealt with the Benamira question by simply not mentioning it. Nobody asked why he was not standing in the dock again for the second day in a row. In his place were three young men. Two of the three—Mohamed Abid and Mekki Behihou—energetically denied taking part in the attack. The third, Rabah Bencherif, had confessed under interrogation, but he recanted this confession on the stand, saying "I was beaten black and blue for six days, and the medical report states that I bear the scars." The presiding judge duly read from the medical report that described "the marks on the sole of the feet that could have been produced by blows with a whip."[12] Perhaps because nobody was surprised by this information, the trial moved quickly to the next stage, establishing the facts of the case.

As before, the outcome of the Attali trial was a nearly foregone conclusion—but there are indications that this was a more complicated case for the authorities. The first curiosity is the list of witnesses called by the prosecutors to describe the scene in the Attali home during the attacks. In the Halimi case, everything rested on the riveting testimony of Rosette Benisti, who had recognized Tayeb Benamira in the butcher shop after the riots. In the Attali case, there was no equivalently dramatic testimony to be had from a member of the household. Turkia Zaouche Attal, the injured wife of the murdered Joseph Attal, did point to Mekki Behinou during the proceedings, but defense lawyers noted that she had expressed uncertainty about his participation in the attack before the trial began. Her testimony was dramatic because her attackers had mutilated her body during the theft of her jewelry, but it left some uncertainty about the participation of the three accused. Other witnesses for the prosecution from the household also had little to say about the identity of the accused. Makhlouf Attali, the printer, restricted himself to a description of the events as they transpired during the attack, and did not incriminate any of the accused. Rosine Attal and her sister Marie Attal, who had been rescued by Said Djemaa, also described the scene during the attack but did not incriminate any individual attacker.

Given the challenges that the prosecution faced in connecting the accused to the murders, it is inexplicable that neither the police agent Said Djemaa or the corporal Émile Kottman was invited to testify. These two men were the authors of the most detailed reports about the events in the apartment on the rue des Zouaves. Djemaa's rescue of the surviving members of the Attali, Attal, and Zerbib families was even cited in open court by Marie Attal.[13] Djemaa had confronted the murderers directly and threatened them with a revolver. Kottman had burst into the room moments later and had seen where the bodies had fallen. In spite of this, neither Djemaa nor Kottman appeared as witnesses in the trial.

Instead, four soldiers were brought to the stand—Mohamed El Maadi, Louis Truchi, Jean Paray, and Henri Gantier. El Maadi gave the most complete testimony—in terms that sounded suspiciously similar to Kottman's report—but did not identify any of the accused. He was asked specifically what time he entered the apartment, and somewhat surprisingly his answer was "12:45"—a time *before* the murders began, though nobody noted this in court. Louis Truchi, also from El Maadi's Zouave regiment, said that he had seen one of the accused, Mohamed Abid, on the balcony from the street below, but under questioning he misidentified both the building (he called it the Halimi home) and the floor (he said it was on the second floor rather than the third). The testimony from the other soldiers was equally vague. The rest of the evidence against the accused was largely devoted to taking apart their alibis, and hearing statements from witnesses who saw incriminating behavior after the events—that Behihou bought an automobile after the riots, for example, that he had been seen later with a knife, and that he had been overheard boasting of killing Jews.

It seems likely that Djemaa and Kottman did not testify because they had seen too much, rather than too little. If, as seems possible, at least some the accused were simply looters who had been arrested later and saddled with murder charges, then Djemaa and Kottman were unlikely to identify them. The choice of El Maadi to replace them is particularly striking. El Maadi had told his commanding officer Lieutenant Carbonnel on the rue des Zouaves shortly after 1 p.m. that he had never made it into the apartment, and he had made a point of showing his injured hand where he had been grazed by a gunshot. In spite of this anomaly, prosecutors asked him to testify. This fact can only be explained if one assumes that the prosecutors understood very well what they were doing. They had spoken to the police and read the press reports. They knew there was evidence that suggested that a small group could have been involved with multiple murders. There is a good chance that they had seen many of the same reports used in this book to reconstruct the events of that day, including those from Émile Kottman and El Maadi's commanding officer, Lieutenant Carbonnel. These reports indicated that soldiers in uniform—and possibly El Maadi himself—were present in the building while the murders were taking place. In the face of these troubling circumstances, so pregnant with dangerous possibilities, it was imperative to construct a simpler story at the trial—namely that the police and soldiers had been unable to prevent the murders in spite of their best efforts. Having El Maadi be the one to deliver this simplistic story may well have been thought to be the safest move, since he had the most to lose should the story become undone. One assumes that the three other soldiers were coached in their testimony—and not very successfully, it turns out, given the mistakes in Truchi's statement—so as to provide additional incriminating identification of the accused.

The closing speeches in the Attali trial reproduced the same bifurcated vision of the riots that Muracciole and Rédarès had enacted the day before in the Halimi trial. Muracciole spoke at length of the nobility and honesty of Makhlouf Attali, and repeated his widely reported and moving words from his hospital bed the morning after the murders: "I am suffering, I have seen too much blood around me, I have heard too many furious cries. I am suffering, but I have no hatred, no rancor against true Muslims."[14] For ninety minutes, Muracciole walked the court through every step of the case, defended the identifications of Behihou and Abid that came from Turkia Attal and the soldier from the Third Zouaves, and summarized the holes in their alibis. "Attenuating circumstances?" he asked, "I have often asked for them. The death sentence? I am horrified by it. But can one hesitate before these men whose actions I have just described?" After Muracciole's speech, the prosecutor called for the death penalty for Abid and Behihou and life imprisonment for Bencherif.

The defense lawyer from Algiers, Léonce Déroulède, like Rédarès the day before, did his best to present a version of the "Muslim" view of the riots in his closing statement. He opened with a flourish of rhetorical questions: "Wasn't a mosque desecrated by a drunken Jew? . . . Wasn't an Arab killed soon after? . . . Didn't the arms dealers sell out their stocks the next day?" He criticized the government for not releasing the official investigating commission's report. The "Arabs" acted in a "moment of madness," and "the crime of these accused, if they are really guilty," he stated, was "excusable. It was the collective crime of delirious fanatics." He did not stop there—he criticized Governor-General Jules Carde and other representatives of the state who "having as their mission to make France more loved, end up by making the French administration more detested. That is the cause of the Constantine riots!"[15] He criticized the Crémieux decree of 1870 that gave Jews in Algeria French citizenship: "Wasn't this done prematurely? This decree was a mistake the moment it went into effect. . . . There are a multitude of facts, and a sequence of events that you cannot neglect, gentlemen. They have created a growing exasperation that produced on August 5 nothing but delirious dervishes [aissaouas en délire]." After Déroulède's impassioned speech, the remaining closing statements lasted until after midnight, and the judges deliberated afterward for two hours. At 2:15 a.m. the verdict was announced to a crowd that had noticeably diminished since the day before: Mekki Behihou and Mohamed Abid were found guilty but with unidentified "attenuating circumstances" and sentenced to forced labor for life. Rabah Bencherif, who had never been directly connected to the murders, was acquitted.

Just as they had done the day before, the court's judges and lawyers had threaded the needle. The possible story of agitation and provocation by a small group of murderers had been absorbed into a broader narrative about a cycle of violence between two irreconcilable communities. The Jewish families saw the young men named as their attackers convicted and sentenced. In the course of the trial, the surviving members of the Attali family heard their lawyers deliver an eloquent and horrific depiction of their torment and loss, but they had also been forced to sit through a speech that called the Crémieux decree a mistake that justified the anger of the rioting crowds. The Muslims in the audience, on the other hand, with little opportunity to contribute their own opinions, had heard "their" view delivered by a French lawyer who excused the violence of the murders by depicting it is an entirely unsurprising result of their essential fanaticism. From the point of view of the authorities, the dangers of the public trials had been largely avoided. The accused had been, for the most part, convicted. Nobody had been sentenced to death—which could have precipitated more unrest. No serious disturbances had accompanied the trials in spite of the large crowds, and yet the meaning of the August 1934 riots had been once again reduced to two incompatible narratives, one identified clearly with "Muslims" and the other with "Jews." When it came to the meaning of the riots, France was still absent.

Conclusion

Mohamed El Maadi died of throat cancer in Cairo, probably in late 1953 or early 1954. He ended up in Egypt after fleeing France to Berlin in 1945. Thanks to a memoir written by an Algerian nationalist, Nadir Bouzar, we have an idea of what his last days were like.[1] In the Egyptian capital, El Maadi mingled with a younger generation of Algerian political exiles who would go on to make the revolution that resulted in Algerian independence in 1962. There are reports that he tried to contact Algerian nationalists during his flight—the very same people that he had promised to subvert while working with Jean Filiol in 1937. It was through these contacts, presumably, that he met Nadir Bouzar in Cairo.[2]

In spite of his illness, El Maadi retained all his charisma. His throat was pierced with a tracheotomy, and part of his jaw was removed. He breathed through a tube that allowed him to communicate only with a hoarse croak. Bouzar and his friends gathered in El Maadi's apartment and listened with fascination to this "man of action" and the stories of his political struggles. They knew him by a nom de guerre—they called him Mustapha Bachir Meadi, one of the aliases he had used in the late 1930s while trying to infiltrate the Algerian nationalist movement. What these men actually knew of El Maadi's life is not completely clear, however, because much of what El Maadi told them about himself was apparently untrue. He told the Algerian militants that his mother was a European, and that his parents were a *"couple mixte."* This was not true—his mother was Melouka bint Mohamed El Maadi, daughter of a *qa'id* in Aïn Ketone, and it was his paternal grandmother who was a Frenchwoman. El Maadi boasted of his father's position in the French colonial administration. This was true, but El Maadi also told them that he had completed his legal studies in Paris, which was not. He told the young men that France had sentenced him to death in absentia in 1945. In reality he had been sentenced to life at hard labor "with extenuating circumstances."[3] He played up his contacts with the Algerian nationalists of Messali Hadj's Parti du peuple algérien to prove his own commitment to Algerian independence.[4]

The exaggerations and lies played to the political sensibilities of these revolutionaries. Bouzar and his friends were aware that El Maadi had been in the German army at the end of the Second World War, but they clearly saw this through the filter of their own bitter opposition to the postwar French government. After the Liberation, Charles de Gaulle's provisional regime consecrated the Allied victory of May 8, 1945—"VE Day"—with a brutal repression in the towns of Sétif and Guelma after a confrontation between the police and nationalist protesters. The police opened fire on demonstrators displaying the Algerian national flag in Sétif on May 8, and the nationalists responded by attacking and killing 102 "Europeans" in the surrounding streets and nearby countryside. In the repression that followed, the French military and citizen militias unleashed their revenge against the region's entire Algerian population, making no attempt to discriminate between those who had participated in the demonstrations and those who had not. Massacres, bombardment of villages, mass arrests, and summary executions followed, killing uncounted thousands.[5] The bitter event politicized a younger generation, including Nadir Bouzar, leading to the emergence of the National Liberation Front (FLN), a militant group that won independence for Algeria in 1962 after eight bitter years of war. In 1953, however, the war for independence had yet to begin. Bouzar and his friends in Cairo admired the dying El Maadi because he professed to be at war with the same regime they intended to fight, the postwar France that was doing everything it could to keep its vast empire. El Maadi clearly had not told the young Algerians in Cairo what he had said to the police interrogators when he was arrested in November 1937 for his Cagoule-related activities, that he "loved France very much" and asked "only to serve her."

Rejected by the France he loved, El Maadi failed in all of his political engagements. His commitment to right-wing French nationalism led to his imprisonment for nine months in 1937–1938. His bid for a "Eurafrican" fascism was funded by the Germans during the occupation, but his adoption of the

Nazi uniform, the final destination of his deeply held antisemitism, left him on the losing side at war's end. Even his aspirations for a literary career were disappointed. More than one novel—written in French—was left unfinished at his death. Bouzar marveled that El Maadi died "next to his typewriter." In his final conversations with the Algerian revolutionaries in Cairo, El Maadi apparently remade himself one last time—as an Algerian nationalist, a stance that was a betrayal of everything he had fought for in earlier years. What Bouzar could not have known, and what El Maadi could never tell him, was the extent to which "France was absent" in the stories he had told about his life—in spite of his talk of being the product of a *couple mixte*. When Bouzar, after a night's bedside vigil, heard El Maadi breathe his last breath, he and a friend proceeded to prepare the body for burial. As they did so, they disturbed the pillow, and several pieces of paper fell out. El Maadi had taken it upon himself to write out, "in proper schoolboy hand," several verses of the Quran. For Bouzar, the moment was filled with a poignant sadness: "Mustapha Bachir, Algerian nationalist militant and pioneer of the North African revolt, did not know Arabic."[6]

When historian Jacques Berque wrote about the Constantine riots in his canonical *French North Africa: The Maghrib between Two World Wars*—first published in French in 1962—he emphasized the difficulty of understanding this event. "An organized plot or an act of provocation, a spontaneous outburst or a deliberately created diversion: only the history of events, when its secret aspects are revealed, may perhaps shed light on the direct cause of these incidents some day."[7] This book has revealed some of these secrets.

We now know that the Constantine riots of August 3–5, 1934, had at least two dimensions. The first must be seen in terms of the long-term changes in social relations and civil status that accompanied the establishment of colonial rule in Algeria. These changes produced both the existential "homelessness" of the majority population of Algerian Muslims under French rule, and a fatal ambiguity at the heart of Jewish citizenship in Algeria, which connected them to the nation in ways that affirmed rather than overcame the markers of their difference. As members of a visible and vulnerable minority, local Jewish leaders were driven to seek protection from the very authorities who worked hard to exclude Muslims from full civil rights. This context did not make the outbreak of violence inevitable, but it colored the ways in which individuals at the local level experienced the ordinary disputes of daily life. Electoral reforms after the First World War created an opening for a new cohort of Muslim political leaders within the Third Republic, but this development threw the local political scene into a state of uncertainty, and the growing polarization of French politics in the early 1930s compounded the disequilibrium. This was the background for the apparently spontaneous dispute between a Jewish man and Muslim men preparing for their prayers on a Friday evening in early August 1934. When combined with the passivity of the authorities' initial response, this dynamic is enough to explain the outbreak of conflict at the mosque and may be sufficient to explain the motivations of many of the people who participated in the attacks on Jewish businesses in the city two days later.

If that were all that happened in Constantine on this weekend, this book would have been shorter. I have argued, however, that there was a second, more hidden dimension to these events. There is enough evidence of this darker story to be confident about its broad outlines. On the morning of August 5, a small group of conspirators appears to have succeeded in reigniting the tensions in the city through calculated acts of provocation. The police later came to believe that this group elevated the horror of the unrest by murdering Jews while stores and offices were being looted nearby, and they identified Mohamed El Maadi as an agitator who bore responsibility for organizing these crimes. Clear evidence shows that the Police Mobile in Constantine initially believed, during their investigations in August–September 1934, that a small group had committed many of the murders. Plausible evidence indicates that a police inspector from Constantine communicated this information to the Police Mobile in Paris in the course of the Cagoule investigation in 1938, and that El Maadi's name came up in this conversation, linked both to the riots and to the family of a lawyer and member of the local establishment, Étienne Muracciole. Persuasive evidence from August 1934 proves that El Maadi was present at the Attali apartment while the murders of the five people who were killed there were taking place, and this evidence also places him near four other sites close by where thirteen people were killed in home or business invasions: the Halimi household, the Dadoun brothers' office, Lucien Chemla's office, and the watchmaker's shop of Abraham Bedoucha. It also places him very close to the sites where two more bodies were found in the street. On the basis of location and timing, therefore, it is possible that as many as twenty out of the twenty-five Jewish deaths that day were the work of a single group. Even if one limits the total only to those killed in a home or business invasion in this neighborhood, eighteen of the twenty-five Jewish deaths may have been the work of this single group. These murders took place in relatively rapid succession in a tightly circumscribed neighborhood between 9 a.m. and the early afternoon of August 5.

This second dimension remained hidden from view for so long because people at several levels of French and Algerian society worked hard to prevent it from becoming public. Circumstantial evidence points to a cover-up of Mohamed El Maadi's participation that involved at least four separate levels or branches of authority: the military, the police, the local political establishment in Constantine, and the governor-general's office in Algiers. El Maadi's quick departure for a six-month leave to a spa immediately after the riots, during which he allegedly undertook a "hydro-mineral" cure for an injury resulting from a fall from a horse in 1927, suggests that his superior officers wanted him as far away from the city as possible during the investigation into the murders and the causes of the unrest. His service record avoided mentioning his actual injury, a bullet wound to the hand that occurred at the Attali family home while the murders were taking place. The fact that El Maadi never filed a report about what he had seen is surprising, especially since he was later decorated for his "heroic" actions in "rescuing" a Jewish family and was subsequently called to testify at the trial for the murders in the Attali apartment.

When the Police Mobile revealed through leaks to the press their intention to pin the murders on a "gang of throat slitters," the governor-general's office intervened to change the story. After this intervention, the police discarded their conspiracy theory and produced a separate list of perpetrators to be charged in separate trials for the murders at each site. These efforts to manage the public perception of the riots continued during the trials of July 1935 and February 1936. The trials reproduced the conclusions of the police investigation after the governor-general's intervention and refused to address earlier evidence about conspiracy or the presence of suspects at more than one murder site. Both the prosecution and defense's legal teams seemed to cooperate in order to ensure that the trials would be reduced to a contest between equally compromised versions of a disputed history, the "Jewish thesis" and a "Muslim thesis." The press accounts of the trials allowed each "side" to hear "their" version stated publicly, and the lawyers' speeches allowed the authorities to convict most of the young men who had been accused, but the prosecutors ignored evidence that tied murders at different sites together. The narratives that were allowed to emerge from the trials simply reproduced the basic outlines of the Vigouroux commission's unpublished report, which had blamed the riots—and the murders—on religious fanaticism alone.

This story of unrest, murder, and cover-up remains incomplete. The documents show that the police believed El Maadi to be one of those responsible for the violence of August 5, but they do not say how the police knew this. All I have been able to substantiate is that he was there, that he could have done it, and that his later career shows both motive and—possibly—a kind of confession. The archives do not provide a clear picture of who ordered this group to act. If El Maadi was responsible for inciting these deaths, it seems unlikely that a thirty-two-year-old adjutant in the Third Zouaves would have dreamed up this operation by himself. Who was he working for? De Escarrega's 1938 note stated that El Maadi was introduced to Jean Filiol by Roger Muracciole, the only son of Étienne Muracciole, and that El Maadi was "on the payroll" of the Muracciole family. Étienne Muracciole was perhaps the most important of the lawyers who helped to orchestrate the murder trials related to August 5. The thread of guilt by association is stretched rather taut at this point, but we also know that Étienne Muracciole was a reliable ally of Mayor Émile Morinaud as an elected member of Constantine's Conseil général, the departmental assembly. In 1930, Morinaud had risked a feud with the local Croix de feu section when he insisted that Étienne Muracciole be included among the local notables nominated for the Legion of Honor, in spite of the fact that he had not served in the First World War. Is this taut thread enough to connect Mohamed El Maadi to the political machinations of Émile Morinaud via their mutual association with Étienne Muracciole?

In fact, an independent and informal investigation by Maurice Eisenbeth, the grand rabbi of Algiers, did attempt to blame Émile Morinaud for the riots, although with much less evidence than I have presented here. Eisenbeth came to Constantine in late October 1934 to speak with Jewish leaders in the aftermath of the riots, and to participate in the official opening of a monument in memory of Constantine's Jews killed on August 5. The ceremony was combined with the official inauguration of the imposing monument to the dead from the First World War that had finally been completed the previous year. The timing for a ceremony of national unity could not have been worse. It took place on November 2, 1934, during the Muslim boycott of Jewish businesses in the city. Jewish families in the city were struggling to rebuild their lives after the destruction of their businesses and the death of their family members and neighbors. Mohamed Bendjelloul and the members of his Fédération were grappling with the fact that their Muslim constituency was now tarred with possessing a capacity for vengeful violence. Morinaud was preoccupied with the need to shore up his support from a "European" electorate that was increasingly attracted to the anti-Jewish and anti-Republican rhetoric of the Croix de feu.

Press accounts of the inauguration of the new memorials described an enormous crowd engaged in a "pious pilgrimage" up the many streets and paths that led to the Monument aux morts, which sat on the edge of a rocky bluff that looks out over the gorge. Arrived at the top, the people formed themselves into "a mass that was simultaneously contemplative and vibrating with emotion."[8] Taking front row seats were the local officials whose conduct during the riots had come under close scrutiny. Mayor Morinaud stood alongside Prefect Jean Laban. Both had distinguished themselves during the riots through their absence. The soon-to-be-replaced secretary-general of the prefecture, Joseph Landel, who had prevented the distribution of cartridges to soldiers on the day of the riots, was also there, as were the Jewish and Muslim members of the *délégations financières*, the departmental Conseil général, and the municipal council, including Mohamed Bendjelloul and the leading members of the FEMC. Étienne Muracciole was not mentioned in the press accounts, but Albert Rédarès, who would later play a large role alongside Muracciole in the trials of 1935 and 1936, was there as a member of the municipal council. Rabbi Eisenbeth himself stood in a group with other representatives of French Algeria's religious communities, including Roman Catholic archbishop Émile Thiénard, the mufti of Constantine Ben Mouloud, and Sidi Fredj Halimi, the grand rabbi of Constantine. Given the events of August 3–5, this spectacle of unity could not have been more fraught—or more pressing.

Élie Gozlan, a teacher of Arabic and French who after the riots embarked on a career as a journalist and a fierce opponent of racism, spoke first, giving an eloquent soliloquy that evoked the common history of Muslims and Jews in North Africa.[9] He shared the podium with Ali Derradji, the imam of the Grand Lycée in Algiers, who also spoke in Constantine's mosques of the need for "union between Jews and Muslims."[10] The words of these speakers were sincere, but their message was undercut by a bitter political undertow. Members of the Croix de feu had agreed to participate in the ceremony only under the condition that they be allowed to approve the list of speakers first, because they did not want to stand and listen to a speech by Henri Lellouche, whom they doubly despised as a Jew and as somebody they considered to be a *"combattant de l'arrière"*—a First World War veteran who had never served at the front.[11]

This was the background to Rabbi Eisenbeth's personal investigation of the riots, which he conducted in late October and early November. He came away convinced that Mohamed Bendjelloul was not responsible for the violence, though he suggested that Bendjelloul may have sought an understanding with Morinaud afterward. Instead, Eisenbeth decided that the violence of August 5 had been planned and ordered by Morinaud himself, and that the Muslims of the city had been manipulated by his agents. After his visit,

Eisenbeth summarized his accusations against the mayor in a private letter to the Paris Consistory.[12] Eisenbeth argued that provoking Muslim violence against Jews in Constantine served Morinaud's political interest in two ways. First, Morinaud wanted to teach the Jewish population a lesson about their own vulnerability, which would make it easier for him to convince Jewish voters that they continued to need his protection. He also sought to discredit Mohamed Bendjelloul's political movement with a public spectacle of Muslim violence, which would make it easier for him to pursue his divide-and-rule electoral strategy. To these arguments from motive, Eisenbeth added two observations. First, the rabbi found it inexplicable that Morinaud had contrived to be absent from Constantine on Sunday, August 5, since that was the day of the funeral of Elie Narboni, Morinaud's longtime ally and friend. Finally, Eisenbeth claimed that Morinaud had been seen in the central square of Djidjelli on the afternoon of Saturday, August 4, conversing with a local Muslim notable. According to Eisenbeth, Morinaud watched several trucks carrying Muslim men depart from Djidjelli for Constantine on that day, the eve of the murderous violence of August 5, and did not raise the alarm.[13] In Eisenbeth's view, these circumstances were enough to prove that the department of Constantine's Muslims had become the instruments of French antisemitism in the person of Émile Morinaud.

In the difficult months after the riots, Rabbi Eisenbeth did not immediately make his conclusions public, though his analysis appears to have been shared with some members of Constantine's Jewish community, as well with his correspondents in Paris at the Consistory and at the Alliance israélite universelle. The fact that Jewish leaders in Constantine—with the exception of Adolphe Sultan—toned down their demands for a public accounting of the behavior of police and other officials during the riots in August 1934 is curious, but a growing realization of Morinaud's possible complicity would have increased their sense of vulnerability while also reinforcing what was already a complete loss of faith in the local authorities. Under such circumstances, Jewish leaders may have been doubly cautious before instigating any open confrontation with a mayor who was still in power. The governor-general's office and the prefecture, for their part, had gotten wind of these theories in one version or another—through the published reports of Henri Lellouche and Adolphe Sultan, the communications of Ruben Halimi with the police and the Vigouroux commission, and the quietly circulated reports of Albert Confino and Joseph Fisher. The primary goal of the Vigouroux commission's report, completed only a few weeks before Eisenbeth's visit, was to diminish the power of these accusations by lumping them together under the discrediting label of "the Jewish thesis." Placed immediately in opposition to "the

Muslim thesis," the phrase made it seem as if the debate about the riot's causes was simply a seamless continuation of the conflict that had spread through the streets on August 5.

Is it possible that Mohamed El Maadi, through his apparent connection with the mayor's ally Étienne Muracciole, was working for Émile Morinaud? All I can say is that it is possible. No direct evidence that I have found connects El Maadi to Morinaud, and the only evidence that connects El Maadi to Muracciole is the single note from Robert de Escarrega of the Police Mobile in Paris that came out of the Rosselli murder investigation. El Maadi was almost certainly working for somebody else, but we need more direct evidence than I have at present to prove it definitively. What we can say is that El Maadi was never a lone wolf, neither as a military officer in the French army, a participant in the Cagoule in 1937–1938, nor as a fervent supporter of the Vichy regime in the Second World War. He always acted as part of a network. The broad participation of many individuals in the colonial administration, the police, and the military in containing and hiding the story of his involvement in the riots suggests that there were others who knew of his role and may have been involved in directing his activities both before and after the fact.

Paradoxically, however, Rabbi Eisenbeth's belief that Mayor Morinaud had engineered the riots for political reasons provided an opening for a different kind of relationship between Muslim and Jewish elected officials in Constantine, even though so much seemed to militate against such a possibility. In 1935, as we have seen, Morinaud failed in his bid for reelection as mayor, having lost the support both of Jewish voters and a significant portion of "European" citizens who were moving steadily to the right. Having no other place to go, Constantine's Jewish voters looked increasingly to the Popular Front coalition for allies. This made them more closely aligned with those elements in French politics who still supported an expansion of voting rights for Algeria's Muslim colonial subjects. Jewish leaders thus found themselves moving closer to certain members of the FEMC who were uncomfortable with Bendjelloul's attempt to align himself with openly anti-Jewish political figures such as Ernest Lanxade. Finding little to gain from the heavily racialized rhetoric on offer from extremists among the French settler population, FEMC leaders such as Ferhat Abbas sought to refocus their efforts on passage of the Viollette proposal and gaining parliamentary representation for Algeria's Muslims without resorting to anti-Jewish demagoguery.[14]

The Viollette proposal ultimately failed, blocked from even coming up for a vote by the settler lobby in parliament. In spite of this disappointment, however, a fragile and temporary alliance emerged from these circumstances that had its most immediate effects in the municipal elections of July 1938, when an unrepentant Morinaud once again tried to retake the mayor's seat. Morinaud's successor, Pierre Liagre, had died in office, and the July 1938 by-election to replace him became a test of wills between the increasingly vicious antisemitism of the local Croix de feu—reborn in 1936 as the Parti social français—and the supporters of the Popular Front. During the campaign, young Jewish voters marched through the streets chanting "Morinaud defeated!" while singing the "Internationale."[15] Morinaud's right-wing supporters retorted with their own demonstrations, shouting "Down with the Jews! Throw the kikes in the ravine!" Albert Rédarès, who had helped Étienne Muracciole stage-manage the spectacle of the murder trials in Orléansville in 1936, emerged as a leader of the hard right, a powerful voice pledging to "block the road taken by the Ghetto."[16] During the final ballot in July 1938, the candidate of the center-left, the radical-socialist Eugène Bourceret, was elected by a small majority after both the Communist and Socialist candidates bowed out in his favor. Morinaud had reportedly offered 50,000 francs to pay a vigilante group of Muslim men armed with clubs who would prevent Jews from voting. The prefecture credited Ferhat Abbas of the FEMC with preventing this ploy from succeeding, and Abbas pushed instead for a vote against Morinaud, whom he blamed for the failure of Maurice Viollette's plan to extend parliamentary representation to Algeria's Muslims.[17] In the end, Bourceret's majority was possible only because Constantine's Jewish and Muslim municipal councilors decided to vote together to prevent Morinaud from returning to the office that he had held for thirty-seven years. Henri Coquelin, the tireless director of departmental security at the prefecture, observed that "among the French population with nationalist tendencies, their faces were marked by sadness."[18] Here was a real debate about what the tricolor would mean in French Algeria.

This fragile alliance between Muslims and Jews in Constantine could not of course withstand the tsunami of events in the coming years. Eugène Bourceret, pilloried as the "mayor of the Ghetto," resigned in November 1938 as his waning support among the settler population eroded away. This precipitated another special election, which brought a different anti-Jewish candidate, Joseph Durieu de Leyritz, to the mayor's seat, comforting those who had been alarmed by the victory of the left the previous summer. With Durieu de Leyritz's accession to the town hall, the Popular Front's brief hold on municipal power in Constantine was over. Less than two years later, France fell to Nazi Germany's invading armies, and Algerian Jews lost their French citizenship under the Vichy regime's infamous Jewish Statutes. They got it back in 1943 after Allied troops landed in North Africa, but this reprieve was only temporary, and the vast majority of Algeria's Jews left for France at the end of the War for Algerian Independence in 1962. The fact the July 1938 electoral alliance between Muslims and Jews existed at all, however, shows that the historical circumstances that produced the Constantine riots contained within them something other than eternal conflict between Jews and Muslims. For a brief moment in July 1938, the last vestiges of a local Popular Front alliance allowed Muslims and Jews in Constantine to vote together to prevent the antisemite Émile Morinaud from retaking his seat as mayor of the city. In that moment, the perpetual-motion machine of provocation and counterreaction revealed its own essential contingency. Other futures were—and are—possible.

Appendix

Table A.1 Jewish deaths, August 3–5, 1934

NAME	CAUSE OF DEATH	TIME OF ATTACK	PLACE OF DEATH / PLACE OF ATTACK LEADING TO DEATH
Attal, Joseph Salomon 60 years old Jeweler in Constantine	Throat slit	Aug. 5, c. 1:00 p.m.	Attali apartment, 6 rue des Zouaves, Constantine
Attal, Michel 40 years old Farmer in Bizot	Fractured skull	Aug. 5, evening	Bizot (village outside Constantine)
Attali, Alexandre 14 years old	Fractured skull	Aug. 5, c. 1:00 p.m.	Attali apartment, 6 rue des Zouaves, Constantine
Attali, Ausélia 24 years old Midwife	Fractured skull, stabbed	Aug. 5, c. 1:00 p.m.	Attali apartment, 6 rue des Zouaves, Constantine
Bedoucha, Abraham 50 years old Tailor	Throat slit	Aug. 5, c. 9:00 a.m.	Intersection of rue Humbert / rue Rouaud, Constantine
Bentata, Jacob 40 years old Watchmaker	Throat slit	Aug. 5, c. 11:00 a.m.	Rue Béraud, Constantine
Chemla, Lucien Ichoua 30 years old Office worker	Throat slit	Aug. 5, c. 10:30 a.m.	Rue Germon, Constantine
Dadoun, Gilbert 25 years old Businessman	Throat slit	Aug. 5, time unknown	Rue Béraud, Constantine
Dadoun, Maurice 30 years old Businessman	Throat slit	Aug. 5, time unknown	Rue Béraud, Constantine
Guedj, Blanche 25 years old Office worker	Throat slit	Aug. 5, time unknown	Rue Béraud, Constantine

(continued)

NAME	CAUSE OF DEATH	TIME OF ATTACK	PLACE OF DEATH / PLACE OF ATTACK LEADING TO DEATH
Guedj, Elie 30 years old Accountant	Fractured skull, stabbed	Aug. 5, 12:00 noon	Place Lamorcière (autobus), Constantine
Guedj, Henri 60 years old	Throat slit (also reported as fractured skull)	Aug. 5, time unknown	Rue Nationale, near the madrasa, Constantine
Guedj, Salomon	Unknown	Aug. 5	Hamma (village outside Constantine)
Halimi, Albert 20 years old Hairdresser	Shot in the chest	Aug. 5	Autobus between Mila and Constantine
Halimi, Alphonse 35 years old Businessman	Throat slit	Aug. 5, 11:30 a.m.	Halimi apartment, 12 rue Abdallah Bey, Constantine
Halimi, Fortunée 40 years old	Throat slit	Aug. 5, 11:30 a.m.	Halimi apartment, 12 rue Abdallah Bey, Constantine
Halimi, Jeanine 6 years old	Throat slit	Aug. 5, 11:30 a.m.	Halimi apartment, 12 rue Abdallah Bey, Constantine
Halimi, Mady 9 years old	Stabbed	Aug. 5, 11:30 a.m.	Halimi apartment, 12 rue Abdallah Bey, Constantine
Nabet, Raymond (René) 23 years old	Fractured skull, stabbed in abdomen	Aug. 5; died later of wounds	Unknown
Zerbib, Moise 60 years old	Throat slit	Aug. 5, 11:30 a.m.	Attali apartment, 6 rue des Zouaves, Constantine
Zerbib, Zaïra 40 years old	Multiple wounds	Aug. 5, 11:30 a.m.; died of wounds on Aug. 8	Attali apartment, 6 rue des Zouaves, Constantine
Zerdoun, Huguette 3 years old	Throat slit	Aug. 5, 11:30 a.m.	Halimi apartment, 12 rue Abdallah Bey, Constantine
Zerdoun, Jacqueline 4 years old	Fractured skull	Aug. 5, 11:30 a.m.	Halimi apartment, 12 rue Abdallah Bey, Constantine
Zerdoun, Mouni 60 years old Concierge	Throat slit	Aug. 5, 11:30 a.m.	Halimi apartment, 12 rue Abdallah Bey, Constantine
Zerdoun, Rosa 40 years old	Throat slit	Aug. 5, 11:30 a.m.	Halimi apartment, 12 rue Abdallah Bey, Constantine

Note: Ages are estimates. Different sources give different ages for some of the victims.

Table A.2 Muslim deaths, August 3–5, 1934

NAME	CAUSE OF DEATH	TIME OF ATTACK	PLACE
Akkacha, Lachemi 22 years old Gardener	Shot	Aug. 5, between 11:30 and 12:00 noon.	Place Molière, Constantine
Boutarane, Belkacem 30 years old	Shot in the stomach	Friday, Aug. 3, evening; died Aug. 23	Rue Caraman, Constantine
Saidi, Athmane 12 years old	Shot in the stomach	Aug. 5 (died Aug. 7 in hospital)	Aïn Beïda

Note: Ages are estimates.

Notes

Abbreviations

The archival research for this project was conducted in France at the following sites. References to individual archival cartons are in the endnotes, according to the following abbreviations:

AAIU   *Archives de l'alliance israélite universelle, Paris*
AC   *Archives de la consistoire de France, Paris*
AN   *Archives nationales de France, Pierrefitte-sur-Seine*
ANOM   *Archives nationales d'outre mer, Aix-en-Provence*
             Fonds ministériels (FM)
             Algérie (ALG)
             Gouvernement général de l'Algérie (GGA)
             Département d'Alger (ALGER)
             Département de Constantine (CONST)
APP   *Archives de la préfecture de police de Paris, le Pré-Saint-Gervais*
BDIC   *Bibliothèque de documentation internationale contemporaine, Nanterre*
SHD   *Service historique de la Défense, Vincennes*

Introduction

1. On Ottoman Algeria and the French conquest see James McDougall, *A History of Algeria* (Cambridge: Cambridge University Press, 2017), 9–85. On the history of civil status in French Algeria see Kamel Kateb, *Européens, "indigènes" et juifs en Algérie (1830–1962): Représentations et réalités des populations* (Paris: Institut national d'études démographiques, 2001).

2. An early assessment of the riots is Charles-Robert Ageron, "Une émeute antijuive à Constantine (août 1934)," *Revue de l'Occident musulman et de la Méditerranée* 13, no. 1 (1973): 23–40. More recent accounts are Robert Attal, *Les émeutes de Constantine: 5 août 1934* (Paris: Éditions Romillat, 2002); Rochdi Ali Younsi, "Caught in a Colonial Triangle: Competing Loyalties within the Jewish Community of Algeria, 1842–1943" (PhD diss., University of Chicago, 2003), 142–92; Joshua Cole, "Antisémitisme et situation coloniale pendant l'entre-deux-guerres en Algérie: Les émeutes antijuives de Constantine (août 1934)," *Vingtième siècle*, no. 108 (October 1, 2010): 3–23; Ethan Katz, *The Burdens of Brotherhood: Jews and Muslims from North Africa to France* (Cambridge, MA: Harvard University Press, 2015), 85–94; Sophie Roberts, *Citizenship and Antisemitism in French Colonial Algeria, 1870–1962* (Cambridge: Cambridge University Press, 2017), 143–201. See also Geneviève Dermenjian, *Antijudaïsme et antisémitisme en Algérie coloniale, 1830–1962* (Paris: Presses universitaires de Provence, 2018), 181–202.

3. On the rupture between Algerian Jews and their North African heritage see Benjamin Stora, *Les trois exils: Juifs d'Algérie* (Paris: Stock, 2006).

4. Michael R. Marrus and Robert O. Paxton, *Vichy France and the Jews* (New York: Basic Books, 1981).

5. Jean-Louis Planche, *Sétif 1945: Histoire d'un massacre annoncé* (Paris: Perrin, 2006); Jean-Pierre Peyroulou, *Guelma, 1945: Une subversion française dans l'Algérie coloniale* (Paris: Découverte, 2009).

6. André Nouschi, *La naissance du nationalisme algérien* (Paris: Minuit, 1962); Mohammed Harbi, *Le F.L.N., mirage et réalité: Des origines à la prise du pouvoir (1945–1962)* (Paris: Éditions J. A., 1980); Mahfoud Kaddache, *Histoire du nationalisme algérien*, 2 vols. (Alger: Société Nationale d'Édition et de Diffusion, 1980); Gilbert Meynier, *Histoire intérieure du FLN, 1954–1962* (Paris: Fayard, 2002); James McDougall, *History and the Culture of Nationalism in Algeria* (Cambridge: Cambridge University Press, 2006).

7. Pierre-Jean Le Foll-Luciani, *Les juifs algériens dans la lutte anticoloniale: Trajectoires dissidentes (1954–1965)* (Rennes: Presses universitaires de Rennes, 2015).

8. Sung-Eun Choi, *Decolonization and the French of Algeria: Bringing the Settler Colony Home* (New York: Palgrave Macmillan, 2016).

9. Todd Shepard, *The Invention of Decolonization: The Algerian War and the Remaking of France* (Ithaca, NY: Cornell University Press, 2006), 169–82, 207–28; Sarah Abrevaya Stein, *Saharan Jews and the Fate of French Algeria* (Chicago: University of Chicago Press, 2014); Rebecca Wall, "Saharan Jews: The Jewish Community of Ghardaia, Algeria: 1945–1967" (PhD diss., University of Michigan, 2014); Katz, *Burdens of Brotherhood*, 201–41.

10. Yves-Claude Aouate, "Constantine 1934: Un pogrom 'classique,'" *Nouveaux cahiers—Alliance israélite universelle* 68 (1982): 49–56; Richard Ayoun, "À propos du pogrom de Constantine (août 1934)," *Revue des études juives* 154, no. 1–3 (1985): 181–86.

11. On El Maadi see Robert Soucy, *French Fascism: The Second Wave, 1933–1939* (New Haven, CT: Yale University Press, 1995), 47; Katz, *Burdens of Brotherhood*, 130–35. On the North African Brigade see Patrice Rolli, *La phalange nord-africaine en Dordogne: Histoire d'une alliance entre la pègre et la Gestapo, 15 mars–19 août 1944* (Boulazac: Histoire en partage, 2010); David Motadel, *Islam and Nazi Germany's War* (Cambridge, MA: Harvard University Press, 2014), 242.

12. ANOM: GGA 9 H 49 (36 H 4). See chapter 13.

13. Paul J. Kingston, *Antisemitism in France during the 1930s: Organisations, Personalities and Propaganda* (Hull: University of Hull, 1983); Ralph Schor, *L'antisémitisme en France pendant les années trentes: Prélude à Vichy* (Brussels: Éditions Complexe, 1992).

1. Constantine in North African History

1. Marc Côte, *Constantine: Cité antique et ville nouvelle* (Constantine: Média-Plus, 2006).

2. André Nouschi, "Constantine à la veille de la conquête française," *Les Cahiers de Tunisie* 3, no. 11 (1955): 379.

3. See Julia A. Clancy-Smith, *Mediterraneans: North Africa and Europe in an Age of Migration, c. 1800–1900* (Berkeley: University of California Press, 2010).

4. On the end of slavery in Algeria see Benjamin Claude Brower, "Rethinking Abolition in Algeria: Slavery and the 'Indigenous Question,'" *Cahiers d'études Africaines* 195, no. 3 (September 15, 2009): 805–28.

5. On slaves in Constantine see Isabelle Grangaud, *La ville imprenable: Une histoire sociale de Constantine au 18ᵉ siècle* (Paris: École des hautes études en sciences sociales, 2002), 66–71.

6. For an overview of this subject see Lucette Valensi, *Juifs et musulmans en Algérie, VIIᵉ–XXᵉ siècle* (Paris: Tallandier, 2016). See also Emily Benichou Gottreich and Daniel J. Schroeter, "Rethinking Jewish Culture and Society in North Africa," in *Jewish Culture and Society in North Africa*, ed. Gottreich and Schroeter (Bloomington: Indiana University Press, 2011), 3–23; Colette Zytnicki, *Les Juifs du Maghreb: Naissance d'une historiographie coloniale* (Paris: Presses de l'Université Paris-Sorbonne, 2011).

7. André Chouraqui, *Histoire des Juifs en Afrique du Nord*, 2 vols. (Monaco: Éditions du Rocher, 1998), 1:127–29.

8. On North Africa's two Jewish cultures—Iberian and Maghribi—see Haim Zeev Hirschberg, *A History of the Jews in North Africa* (Leiden: E. J. Brill, 1974), 13–15; Clancy-Smith, *Mediterraneans*, 40–42. See also Lucette Valensi, *On the Eve of Colonialism: North Africa before the French Conquest* (New York: Holmes & Meier, 1977), 9; Esther Benbassa and Aron Rodrigue, *Sephardi Jewry: A History of the Judeo-Spanish Community, 14th–20th Centuries* (Berkeley: University of California Press, 1999), lii–liii; Chouraqui, *Histoire des Juifs en Afrique du Nord*, 1:192–96.

9. See the figures from a document by *qa'id* Ibrahim, dated January 18, 1832, cited in Nouschi, "Constantine à la veille de la conquête française," 374.

10. Nouschi, 374–78.

11. Ernest Mercier, *Histoire de Constantine* (Constantine: J. Marle et F. Biron, 1903), 436–39; Nouschi, "Constantine à la veille de la conquête française"; Philip Brebner, "The Impact of Thomas-Robert Bugeaud and the Decree of 9 June 1844 on the Development of Constantine, Algeria," *Revue de l'Occident musulman et de la Méditerranée* 38, no. 1 (1984): 6–9.

12. Nouschi, "Constantine à la veille de la conquête française," 381.

13. Abdeljelil Temimi, *Le Beylik de Constantine et Ḥādj 'Aḥmed Bey, 1830–1837* (Tunis: Revue d'histoire maghrébine, 1978).

14. On the siege see Charles André Julien, *Histoire de l'Algérie contemporaine: La conquête et les débuts de la colonisation (1827–1871)* (Paris: Presses universitaires de France, 1964), 140–42. On cholera in 1837 see André Nouschi, *Enquête sur le niveau de vie des populations rurales constantinois de la conquête jusqu'en 1919* (Paris: Presses universitaires de France, 1961), 162. On the French military's capacity for violence see Benjamin Claude Brower, *A Desert Named Peace: The Violence of France's Empire in the Algerian Sahara, 1844–1902* (New York: Columbia University Press, 2009), 17.

15. Malek Bennabi, *Mémoires d'un témoin du siècle: L'enfant, l'étudiant, l'écrivain, les carnets* (Alger: Samar, 2006), 39.

16. On the ways that North Africans coped with the presence of the French see Julia A. Clancy-Smith, *Rebel and Saint: Muslim Notables, Populist Protest, Colonial Encounters* (Berkeley: University of California Press, 1997); Julia Clancy-Smith, "The Shaykh

and His Daughter: Coping in Colonial Algeria," in *Struggle and Survival in the Modern Middle East*, ed. Edmund Burke (Berkeley: University of California Press, 1993).

17. This event is recounted and analyzed in full in Grangaud, *La ville imprenable*, 29–33.

2. "Native," "Jewish," and "European"

1. John Ruedy, *Land Policy in Colonial Algeria: The Origins of the Rural Public Domain* (Berkeley: University of California Press, 1967); Jennifer E. Sessions, *By Sword and Plow: France and the Conquest of Algeria* (Ithaca, NY: Cornell University Press, 2011).

2. See Kamel Kateb, *Européens, "indigènes" et juifs en Algérie (1830–1962): Représentations et réalités des populations* (Paris: Institut national d'études démographiques, 2001), 46–47; Benjamin Claude Brower, *A Desert Named Peace: The Violence of France's Empire in the Algerian Sahara, 1844–1902* (New York: Columbia University Press, 2009), 47. Osama Abi-Mershed confirms these general figures in his account, suggesting that for the four decades between 1830 and 1870, the Muslim population of Algeria "declined by an aggregate 29 percent, which amounted to a net loss of some 866,000 lives." Osama Abi-Mershed, *Apostles of Modernity: Saint-Simonians and the Civilizing Mission in Algeria* (Stanford, CA: Stanford University Press, 2010), 65–67. These figures do not take into account those Algerians who died fighting on the side of the French, as was often the case, both during the conquest and in other wars that the French participated in, including the Crimean War of 1853–1856 and the Franco-Prussian War of 1870–1871.

3. The department is an administrative unit in the French state that lies between that of the commune and the national government. The highest executive office in the department is the prefect, who reports to the minister of the interior. For most of the colonial period, Algeria contained three departments: Algiers, Oran, and Constantine. The departments also have an elected assembly, known as the Conseil Général.

4. Philip Brebner, "The Impact of Thomas-Robert Bugeaud and the Decree of 9 June 1844 on the Development of Constantine, Algeria," *Revue de l'Occident musulman et de la Méditerranée* 38, no. 1 (1984): 9.

5. Brebner, 6, 9.

6. On the question of urban property in the early years of the conquest see Isabelle Grangaud, "Le droit colonial au service des spoliations à Alger dans les années 1830," in *Histoire de l'Algérie à la période coloniale (1830–1962)*, ed. Abderrahmane Bouchène et al. (Paris: La Découverte, 2012), 70–76.

7. André Nouschi, *Enquête sur le niveau de vie des populations rurales constantinois de la conquête jusqu'en 1919* (Saint-Denis: Éditions Bouchène), 740–49.

8. Johan Hendrix Meuleman, *Le Constantinois entre les deux guerres mondiales: L'évolution économique et sociale de la population rurale* (Assen: Van Gorcum, 1985).

9. David Prochaska, *Making Algeria French: Colonialism in Bône, 1870–1920* (Cambridge: Cambridge University Press, 2004), 65. On the sequestration of land see Sessions, *By Sword and Plow*, 208–63.

10. John Ruedy, *Modern Algeria: The Origins and Development of a Nation* (Bloomington: Indiana University Press, 1992).

11. Charles-André Julien, *Histoire de l'Algérie contemporaine: La conquête et les débuts de la colonisation (1827–1871)* (Paris: Presses universitaires de France, 1964), 255.

12. Julien, 475–95.

13. Nouschi, *Enquête sur le niveau de vie*, 337–78; Djilali Sari, *Le désastre démographique* (Alger: ENAG éditions, 2010), 91–102. See also Kateb, *Européens, "indigènes" et juifs en Algérie*, 67–68. On representations of the famine in the press see Bertrand Taithe, "La famine de 1866–1868: Anatomie d'une catastrophe et construction médiatique d'un événement," *Revue d'histoire du XIXe siècle* 41, no. 2 (2010): 113–27.

14. On the *ordonnance* of 1834 see Patrick Weil, "Le statut des musulmans en Algérie coloniale: Une nationalité française dénaturée," in *La justice en Algérie, 1830–1962* (Paris: La Documentation française, 2005), 95–109. On the significance of the 1834 *ordonnance* for the forms of colonial authority that developed in Algeria see Abi-Mershed, *Apostles of Modernity*, 63–64.

15. Laure Blévis pointed out that no law or decree from the period between 1830 and 1865 actually stated that Algerians possessed French nationality. Laure Blévis, "Sociologie d'un droit colonial: Citoyenneté et Nationalité en Algérie (1865–1947): Une exception républicaine?" (Institut d'études politiques, 2004), 67–69.

16. The distinction between Jewish citizens and Jewish colonial subjects predated the conquest of Algeria, because of the presence of small numbers of Jews elsewhere in the French Empire—in Martinique and Guadeloupe, or in West Africa, for example.

17. Pierre Birnbaum, "Between Social and Political Assimilation: Remarks on the History of Jews in France," in *Paths of Emancipation: Jews, States, and Citizenship*, ed. Pierre Birnbaum and Ira Katznelson (Princeton, NJ: Princeton University Press, 1995), 94–127.

18. Phyllis Cohen Albert, *The Modernization of French Jewry: Consistory and Community in the Nineteenth Century* (Hanover, NH: University Press of New England, for Brandeis University Press, 1977), xix–xxii, 45–55.

19. Valérie Assan, *Les consistoires israélites d'Algérie au XIXe siècle: L'alliance de la civilisation et de la religion* (Paris: Colin, 2012). On the establishment of Jewish consistories under Napoléon see Jay R. Berkovitz, *The Shaping of Jewish Identity in Nineteenth-Century France* (Detroit: Wayne State University Press, 1989).

20. Joshua Schreier, *Arabs of the Jewish Faith: The Civilizing Mission in Colonial Algeria* (New Brunswick, NJ: Rutgers University Press, 2010), 23–25.

21. Assan, *Les consistoires israélites*.

22. On the evolution of civil status see Kateb, *Européens, "indigènes" et juifs en Algérie*; Blévis, "Sociologie d'un droit colonial." On the importance of marital practices in Islamic and Jewish law for debates about citizenship in 1865 see Judith Surkis, "Propriété, polygamie et statut personnel en Algérie coloniale, 1830–1873," *Revue d'histoire du XIXe siècle: Société d'histoire de la révolution de 1848 et des révolutions du XIXe siècle*, no. 41 (2010): 27–48.

23. On the term "naturalization" to describe the accession to citizenship on the part of individuals who already possessed a form of French nationality see Laure Blévis, "La citoyenneté française au miroir de la colonisation," *Genèses* 53, no. 4 (2003): 25–47.

24. This figure for Muslim "naturalizations" between 1865 and 1945 comes from Ruedy, *Modern Algeria*, 76. On the question of Muslim "naturalization" see also Charles-Robert Ageron, *Les Algériens musulmans et la France, 1871–1919* (Saint-Denis: Éditions Bouchène, 2005), 1:343–51.

25. Ageron, *Les Algériens musulmans*, 1:14n2. Charles-André Julien cites a slightly higher figure for these same years, 398. See Julien, *Histoire de l'Algérie contemporaine*, 434.

26. On the Crémieux decree see Schreier, *Arabs of the Jewish Faith*, 143–76; Lisa Moses Leff, *Sacred Bonds of Solidarity: The Rise of Jewish Internationalism in Nineteenth-Century France* (Stanford, CA: Stanford University Press, 2006).

27. Cited by Kateb, *Européens, "indigènes" et juifs en Algérie*.

28. Joshua Schreier argues that support for French citizenship among Algerian Jews was by no means automatic. Schreier, *Arabs of the Jewish Faith*, 175.

29. The key text on the status of Muslims under the Third Republic remains Charles Ageron's monumental thesis, *Les Algériens musulmans*. See also Patrick Weil, *How to Be French: Nationality in the Making since 1789* (Durham, NC: Duke University Press, 2008), 214–16. On the *indigénat* see Isabelle Merle, "De la 'légalisation' de la violence en contexte colonial: Le régime de l'indigénat en question," *Politix* 17, no. 66 (2004): 137–62; Gregory Mann, "What Was the Indigénat? The 'Empire of Law' in French West Africa," *Journal of African History* 50, no. 3 (January 1, 2009): 331–53; Sylvie Thénault, *Violence ordinaire dans l'Algérie coloniale: Camps, internements, assignations à résidence* (Paris: Odile Jacob, 2012).

30. On the integration of new arrivals into Algerian settler society see Prochaska, *Making Algeria French*.

31. Patrick Weil, "Le statut des musulmans en Algérie coloniale," *Histoire de la justice* 16, no. 1 (2005): 93–109.

32. On the nationality law of 1889 see Paul Lagarde, *La nationalité française* (Paris: Dalloz, 1975), 27; Gérard Noiriel, *The French Melting Pot: Immigration, Citizenship, and National Identity* (Minneapolis: University of Minnesota Press, 1996), 54–56; Rogers Brubaker, *Citizenship and Nationhood in France and Germany* (Cambridge, MA: Harvard University Press, 1992), 87; Weil, *How to Be French*.

33. Blévis, "Sociologie d'un droit colonial," 87–94.

34. On North African cities during the colonial period see André Adam, *Histoire de Casablanca, des origines à 1914* (Gap: Éds. Ophrys, 1968); Kenneth L. Brown, *People of Salé: Tradition and Change in a Moroccan City, 1830–1930* (Manchester: Manchester University Press, 1976); Janet L. Abu-Lughod, *Rabat: Urban Apartheid in Morocco* (Princeton, NJ: Princeton University Press, 1980); Maria Sgroï-Dufresne, *Alger 1830–1984: Stratégies et enjeux urbains* (Paris: Éditions Recherche sur les civilisations, 1986); Zeynep Çelik, *Urban Forms and Colonial Confrontations: Algiers under French Rule* (Berkeley: University of California Press, 1997).

35. The *jamma'at* created in 1863 as part of the French administrative structure had little in common with the traditional *jamma'a*. Ageron, *Les Algériens musulmans*, 1:140–41.

36. The law of April 7, 1884, drastically reduced the narrow rights of the few Muslims who elected the few Muslim municipal councilors in the *communes de plein exercice*. The number of French municipal councilors was raised from sixteen to thirty-six, while the number of Muslim councilors was reduced from eight to six,

and their right to vote in the selection of mayors was taken away. Ageron, *Les Algéri-ens musulmans*, 2:1209. See also Charles-Robert Ageron, *Histoire de l'Algérie contempo-raine: De l'insurrection de 1871 au déclenchement de la guerre de libération (1954)* (Paris: Presses universitaires de France, 1979), 27.

37. These figures on taxation come from Ageron, *Histoire de l'Algérie contempo-raine*, 210–11. Ageron estimates that 90 percent of the Algerian population were Muslim colonial subjects in the first decade of the twentieth century. The *Annuaire statistique d'Algérie* gives a slightly lower figure—closer to 85 percent. In a retrospec-tive summary of the first three decades of the century, published in 1930, the *An-nuaire* gave the following figures for 1911: out of a total population of 5,563,828 in Algeria, 4,711,276 were "French subjects, arabs, kabyles, m'zabites and Jews of the M'Zab." *Annuaire statistique d'Algérie* (Alger: Direction des statistiques et de la compt-abilité nationale, 1930), 47.

3. The Crucible of Local Politics

1. Population figures are from John Ruedy, *Modern Algeria: The Origins and Devel-opment of a Nation* (Bloomington: Indiana University Press, 1992), 94.

2. Charles-Robert Ageron, *Histoire de l'Algérie contemporaine: De l'insurrection de 1871 au déclenchement de la guerre de libération (1954)* (Paris: Presses universitaires de France, 1979), 118–33.

3. Didier Guignard, *L'abus de pouvoir dans l'Algérie coloniale (1880–1914): Visibilité et singularité* (Nanterre: Presses universitaires de Paris Ouest, 2010), 416.

4. On the rivalry between Morinaud and Cuttoli see Jacques Bouveresse, *Un par-lement colonial: Les délégations financières algériennes, 1898–1945* (Mont-Saint-Aignan: Universités de Rouen et du Havre, 2008), 583–84.

5. The *délégations financières algériennes* was an elected assembly in existence between 1898 and 1945 whose primary responsibility was approval of the Alge-rian budget. The forty-eight members of the *délégations* were divided into two groups, representing the French citizens of Algeria and the "native" population. Further subdivisions ensured representation for settler landowners, members of the European urban population, as well as for Arabs and Kabyles among the so-called native population. For most of its existence, the number of representatives of the Muslim population was limited to twenty-one, of whom only fifteen were elected by a small number of electors. The remaining six were appointed by the governor-general.

6. Cited by Saddek Benkada, "La revendication des libertés publiques dans le discours politique du nationalisme algérien et de l'anticolonialisme français (1919–1954)," *Insaniyat / Revue algérienne d'anthropologie et de sciences sociales*, no. 25–26 (December 30, 2004): 182.

7. On the role of these clubs (*andia*, sing. *nadi*) in generating a new kind of so-cial and political sociability see Omar Carlier, *Entre nation et jihad: Histoire sociale des radicalismes algériens* (Paris: Presses de la Fondation nationale des sciences politiques, 1995), 43–46.

8. For the text of the 1912 Young Algerian Manifesto see Claude Collot and Jean-Robert Henry, *Le mouvement national algérien, textes 1912–1954* (Algiers: Office des publications universitaires, 1981), 23–24.

9. Charles-Robert Ageron, *Les Algériens musulmans et la France, 1871–1919* (Saint-Denis: Éditions Bouchène, 2005), 1:15.

10. Ageron, 585.

11. On the Dreyfus affair see Jean-Denis Bredin, *The Affair: The Case of Alfred Dreyfus* (New York: G. Braziller, 1986); Michael Burns, *Dreyfus: A Family Affair, 1789–1945* (New York: HarperCollins, 1991); Pierre Birnbaum, *The Anti-Semitic Moment: A Tour of France in 1898* (New York: Hill & Wang, 2003); Ruth Harris, *Dreyfus: Politics, Emotion, and the Scandal of the Century* (New York: Metropolitan Books, 2010).

12. See Nancy Fitch, "Mass Culture, Mass Parliamentary Politics, and Modern Anti-Semitism: The Dreyfus Affair in Rural France," *American Historical Review* 97, no. 1 (1992): 55–95.

13. For an account of the Action française that downplays the centrality of antisemitism to the leagues of the 1890s see Eugen Weber, *Action Française: Royalism and Reaction in Twentieth-Century France* (Stanford, CA: Stanford University Press, 1962). The historian most associated with claims of continuity between the antisemitism of the 1890s and the embrace of fascism under the Vichy regime is Zeev Sternhell. See Sternhell, *La droite révolutionnaire, 1885–1914: Les origines françaises du fascisme* (Paris: Éditions du Seuil, 1978); Zeev Sternhell, *Ni droite, ni gauche: L'idéologie fasciste en France* (Paris: Éditions du Seuil, 1983).

14. On anti-Jewish political movements and unrest in Algeria during the 1890s see especially Geneviève Dermenjian, *La crise anti-juive oranaise 1895–1905: L'antisémitisme dans l'Algérie coloniale* (Paris: L'Harmattan, 1986); Sophie Roberts, *Citizenship and Antisemitism in French Colonial Algeria, 1870–1962* (Cambridge: Cambridge University Press, 2017), 48–80. The anti-Jewish crisis of the 1890s in French Algeria is also summarized in Ageron, *Les Algériens musulmans*, 1:583–608; Stephen Wilson, "The Antisemitic Riots of 1898 in France," *Historical Journal* 16, no. 4 (1973): 789–806. For a contrasting view of the situation faced by Jews in the Southern Territories who remained "*indigène*" and under military authority see Sarah Abrevaya Stein, "Dreyfus in the Sahara: Jews, Trans-Saharan Commerce, and Southern Algeria under French Colonial Rule," in *French Mediterraneans: Transnational and Imperial Histories*, ed. Patricia M. Lorcin and Todd Shepard (Omaha: University of Nebraska Press, 2016), 265–92.

15. On the clientelism of Algerian municipalities and the corruption of Algerian elections see Guignard, *L'abus de pouvoir dans l'Algérie coloniale*, 170–92, 230–58.

16. Grégoire was the author of an antisemitic pamphlet that attempted to fuse a ruthless anti-Jewish politics to socialist and republican ideals. See Fernand Grégoire, *La juiverie algérienne* (Alger: Torrent, 1888).

17. Lizabeth Zack stresses the importance of this antisemitic moment in the development of a distinctive Algerian settler identity. See Zack, "French and Algerian Identity Formation in 1890s Algiers," *French Colonial History* 2, no. 1 (2002): 115–43.

18. Wilson, "Antisemitic Riots of 1898," 803–5.

19. Elie Narboni, a lawyer in Constantine, telegram to the Minister of Interior and Minister of Justice, date illegible [1896], ANOM: ALG CONST B/3/248.

20. On Morinaud's relationship with Narboni see Michel Abitbol, "Waiting for Vichy: Europeans and Jews in North Africa on the Eve of World War II," *Yad Vashem Studies* 14 (1981): 143.

21. Didier Guignard suggests that this cynical pragmatism was characteristic of all the anti-Jewish political figures in Algeria in the 1990s. Guignard, *L'abus de pouvoir dans l'Algérie coloniale*, 412.

22. For useful summaries on the relationship between the history of antisemitism in France and the Dreyfus affair see Michel Leymarie and Serge Berstein, *La postérité de l'affaire Dreyfus: Dix études, avec la bibliographie du centenaire* (Villeneuve-d'Ascq: Presses universitaires du Septentrion, 1998); Paula E. Hyman, "New Perspectives on the Dreyfus Affair," *Historical Reflections / Réflexions Historiques* 31, no. 3 (2005): 335–49.

23. Émile Morinaud, *Mes mémoires: Première campagne contre le décret Crémieux* (Algiers: Baconnier Frères, 1941), 92.

24. The tendency of Jews to vote as a block in Constantine in the 1890s was itself a reaction to the violence of settler antisemitism. Guignard, *L'abus de pouvoir dans l'Algérie coloniale*, 252.

25. Morinaud, *Mes mémoires*, 93.

26. On such incidents see Robert Attal, *Les communautés juives de l'est algérien de 1865 à 1906: À travers les correspondances du consistoire israélite de Constantine* (Paris: L'Harmattan, 2004), 52–58, 70–79.

27. Bennabi, *Mémoires d'un témoin du siècle: L'enfant, l'étudiant, l'écrivain, les carnets* (Alger: Samar, 2006), 40–41.

28. On the ambivalence of some North African Jews toward assimilation see Susan Gilson Miller, "Moise Nahon and the Invention of the Modern Maghrebi Jew," in Lorcin and Shepard, *French Mediterraneans*, 293–319. See also Benjamin Stora, *Les trois exils: Juifs d'Algérie* (Paris: Stock, 2006), 55–56.

4. The Postwar Moment

1. Richard Fogarty, *Race and War in France: Colonial Subjects in the French Army, 1914–1918* (Baltimore: Johns Hopkins University Press, 2008).

2. On the complicated issue of migrations to and from (and across) North Africa in the nineteenth century see especially Julia A. Clancy-Smith, *Mediterraneans: North Africa and Europe in an Age of Migration, c. 1800–1900* (Berkeley: University of California Press, 2010), 64–99.

3. Erez Manela, *The Wilsonian Moment: Self-Determination and the International Origins of Anticolonial Nationalism* (Oxford: Oxford University Press, 2007).

4. Michel Huber, *La population de la France pendant la guerre* (Paris: Presses universitaires de France, 1931), 76; B. Nogaro and Lucien Weil, *La main-d'oeuvre étrangère et coloniale pendant la guerre* (Paris: Presses universitaires de France, 1926).

5. Neil MacMaster, *Colonial Migrants and Racism: Algerians in France, 1900–62* (New York: St. Martin's, 1997), 7.

6. Gary S. Cross, *Immigrant Workers in Industrial France: The Making of a New Laboring Class* (Philadelphia: Temple University Press, 1983), 35.

7. Figures on colonial labor come from Tyler Stovall, "The Color Line behind the Lines: Racial Violence in France during the Great War," *American Historical Review* 103, no. 3 (1998): 741–42. See also Huber, *La population de la France pendant la guerre*, 102; Charles-Robert Ageron, *Histoire de l'Algérie contemporaine: De l'insurrection*

de 1871 au déclenchement de la guerre de libération (1954) (Paris: Presses universitaires de France, 1979), 260–62.

8. Cross, *Immigrant Workers in Industrial France*, 33–35.

9. Nogaro and Weil, *La main-d'oeuvre étrangère et coloniale*; Huber, *La population de la France*, 5.

10. These figures come from Huber, *La population de la France*, 102; Vincent Viet, *La France immigrée: Construction d'une politique, 1914–1997* (Paris: Fayard, 1998), 166.

11. See Fogarty, *Race and War in France*, 242–69; Ethan Katz, *The Burdens of Brotherhood: Jews and Muslims from North Africa to France* (Cambridge, MA: Harvard University Press, 2015), 26, 337–38. Fogarty confirms that Islam continued to mark Algerian soldiers as a kind of internal "foreigner" who could not be awarded full citizenship rights in spite of military service. Chapter 1 of Katz's book describes how the common experience of serving in the army brought both Muslim and Jewish North Africans into a different relationship to France—and to each other.

12. Charles-Robert Ageron, *Les Algériens musulmans et la France, 1871–1919* (Saint-Denis: Éditions Bouchène, 2005), 2:1193.

13. Minutes of the Conférence interministérielle de la main-d'oeuvre for March 3, 1917, AN: F14/11334.

14. Ageron, *Les Algériens musulmans*, 2:1190–93.

15. The League of the Rights of Man was not always a supporter of expanded rights for Algerian citizens. See William D. Irvine, *Between Justice and Politics: The Ligue des Droits de l'Homme, 1898–1945* (Stanford, CA: Stanford University Press, 2007), 144–45.

16. John Ruedy, *Modern Algeria: The Origins and Development of a Nation* (Bloomington: Indiana University Press, 1992), 112. See also the discussion of the law in Mahfoud Kaddache, *Histoire du nationalisme algérien*, 2 vols. (Alger: Société nationale d'édition et de diffusion, 1980), 1:33–34. On the application of the law see also Claude Collot, *Les institutions de l'Algérie durant la période coloniale (1830–1962)* (Paris: Édition du CNRS, 1987), 58–59.

17. The law had little effect on the small number of Muslims who applied for citizenship under the new rules of naturalization. Ageron, *Les Algériens musulmans*, 2:1221–23.

18. Rapport sur la situation politique et administrative des indigènes pendant le mois de mars 1919, ANOM: ALG GGA 11/H/47.

19. Gilbert Meynier, "Pouvoirs et résistance dans l'insurrection du Sud-Constantinois (1916–1917)," in *Actes des journées d'études* (Bendor, April 26–28, 1978: Cahiers de la Méditerranée, 1978), 211–23; Ageron, *Histoire de l'Algérie contemporaine*, 258–59.

20. Octave Depont, "Les troubles insurrectionnels de l'arrondissement de Batna en 1916," ANOM: ALG CONST 93/2523.

21. Gouvernement Général de l'Algérie, Direction des Affaires indigènes, Rapport mensuel sur la situation politique et administrative des indigènes durant le mois de septembre 1919, ANOM: ALG GGA 11/H/46.

22. On the debates about the Jonnart Law among Muslims and within the settler community see Ageron, *Histoire de l'Algérie contemporaine*, 276; Mahfoud Kaddache, *La vie politique à Alger de 1919–1939* (Alger: Société nationale d'édition et diffusion, 1970), 38–41; Ruedy, *Modern Algeria*, 129–31. Ageron argued that although the Jonnart Law of February 1919 looked like a step toward assimilation, it actually made full

assimilation of Muslim citizens less likely. The law assumed that all political activity of Muslim colonial subjects would be directed toward local Muslim-only assemblies, and take place largely in conversation among themselves. The new voters had no direct connection with national institutions. In this sense, the law may even have helped facilitate the development of a nationalist identity among Muslim elites.

23. On Khaled's career see Ahmed Koulakssis and Gilbert Meynier, *L'Emir Khaled: Premier za'im? Identité algérienne et colonialisme français* (Paris: L'Harmattan, 1987); Kaddache, *La vie politique à Alger de 1919–1939*; Kaddache, *Histoire du nationalisme algérien*, 1:71–118; Benjamin Stora, *Les sources du nationalisme algérien* (Paris: L'Harmattan, 1989); Lizabeth Zack, "Early Origins of Islamic Activism in Algeria: The Case of Khaled in Post–World War I Algiers," *Journal of North African Studies* 11, no. 2 (June 2006): 205–17.

24. Emir Khaled's program was summarized in an editorial in *L'Ikdam*, August 11, 1922. Republished in Claude Collot and Jean-Robert Henry, *Le mouvement national algérien, textes 1912–1954* (Algiers: Office des publications universitaires, 1981), 31.

25. On the growth of the Algerian press during these years see Peter Dunwoodie, *Francophone Writing in Transition: Algeria 1900–1945* (Oxford: P. Lang, 2005), 50–51. Dunwoodie suggests that few of the Algerian papers aiming for a readership among the population of colonial subjects had a print run of over one thousand, but it is probable that *L'Ikdam*'s circulation was larger than this. A Bureau of Native Affairs report from September 1919 suggests that *L'Ikdam* had two hundred subscribers in Mascara alone and more than that in Tlemcen. Similar numbers in a handful of Algerian cities would have put it well over one thousand copies per edition. Rapport mensuel sur la situation politique et administrative des indigènes durant le mois de septembre 1919, ANOM: ALG GGA 11/H/47.

26. Rapport sur la situation politique et administrative des indigènes pendant le mois de mars 1919, ANOM: ALG GGA 11/H/47.

27. Ruedy, *Modern Algeria*, 130.

28. Kaddache, *Histoire du nationalisme algérien*, 99–100; Nadya Bouzar Kasbadji, "L'Emir Khaled," in *La situation des musulmans d'Algérie*, by Emir Khaled (Alger: Office des Publications Universitaires, 1987), 5–19.

29. Zack, "Early Origins of Islamic Activism in Algeria."

30. Rapport mensuel sur la situation politique et administrative des indigènes pendant le mois d'avril 1919, ANOM: ALG GGA 11/H/46. In October 1919, the Bureau of Native Affairs reported that Kaddour Cherfaoui and Mardochéc Chaloum, a Jewish publisher of a socialist paper, were cooperating on an electoral list. See Rapport mensuel sur la situation politique et administrative des indigènes pendant le mois d'octobre 1919, ANOM: ALG GGA 11/H/46.

31. Kaddache, *La vie politique à Alger*, 39.

32. In July 1920, several Jewish shops were pillaged by Algerian colonial subjects in Sétif, a town one hundred kilometers from Constantine (Sous-Préfecture de Sétif, Rapport mensuel de l'administrateur-détaché à la sous-préfecture de Sétif sur la surveillance et l'administration des indigènes des communes de plein exercice de l'arrondissement, mois de juillet 1920, ANOM: ALG GGA 11/H/47). In August, the administrator in Perigotville (Ain El Kebira), twenty kilometers north of Sétif, reported he had asked Jewish merchants to refrain from attending the region's markets in order to avoid trouble (Département de Constantine, Arrondissement de

Sétif, Commune Mixte de Takitount, Rapport mensuel sur les faits ou circonstances de nature à appeler l'attention de l'administration, mois d'août 1920, ANOM: ALG GGA 11/H/47). In Constantine, a police report for July 1920 noted that following the incident in Sétif, a "rumor of probable brawls between natives [*indigènes*] and Jews [*israélites*] . . . circulated in town with a certain persistence" (Extrait du Rapport mensuel du Commissariat Central du mois de juillet 1920, ANOM: ALG GGA 9/H/53). These events contrasted with the decline in antisemitism in France as a whole between the Dreyfus affair of the 1890s and the 1930s. See Michael R. Marrus and Robert O. Paxton, *Vichy France and the Jews* (New York: Basic Books, 1981), 31–32.

33. Reports on the antisemitic campaign of *La Tribune*, and the subsequent violent events of June 11–14, 1921, were included among the papers of the governor-general's committee that investigated the causes of the riots of 1934 (ANOM: ALG GGA 9/H, cartons 52–56). Documents relating to meetings between the Jewish elected officials and the prefect during the *La Tribune* affair are in the archives of the Alliance universelle israélite (AIU) in Paris, Algérie 1C. The reports are from Albert Confino, a correspondent of the AIU based in Algiers, and from the lawyer Maurice Laloum, a correspondent of the AIU in Constantine.

34. The accounts of the violence on June 12 vary considerably. The Algerian correspondents of the Alliance universelle israélite claimed that the group that attacked the printers of *La Tribune* were simply excited young people who had managed to evade the efforts of local Jewish leaders to ensure a calm response to the vandalism against the gymnastics club (AAIU: Algérie 1 C). Several Parisian leftist papers also reported on the incident, but they asserted that the crowd was composed of "a large majority of combat veterans, some with serious injuries [*mutilés de guerre et anciens combattants*]." "Une vague d'antisémitisme . . . se brise," *L'Humanité*, June 14, 1921. See also "Les Juifs de Constantine savent se défendre," *L'Internationale*, June 13, 1921.

35. Dossier Antisémitisme, 1920–1933, Gouvernement Général de l'Algérie, Préfecture de Constantine, Sûreté Départementale, Troubles antisémites, Rapport, June 21, 1921, ANOM: ALG GGA 9/H/53. (This report is actually dated June 12, 1921, in what it is clearly a typographical error, since the contents of the report go through the events of June 20.)

36. Letter from Attal (member of the Conseil général); Narboni, Barkatz, Laloum, Lellouche, Nahon, Sultan (members of the Conseil Municipal); Elie Medioni and J. Attali, vice president and secretary of the Chamber of Commerce, undated (probably June 16 or 17, 1921), AAIU: Algérie 1C. This letter was sent to Morinaud.

37. Dossier Antisémitisme, 1920–1933, Gouvernement Général de l'Algérie, Préfecture de Constantine, Sûreté Départementale, Troubles antisémites, Rapport, June 21, 1921, ANOM: ALG GGA 9/H/53. The undated letter from the Jewish elected officials suggests that shots were fired first from the crowd that threatened the Jewish quarter.

38. "Une campagne antisémite provoque à Constantine de regrettables incidents, les explications de M. Morinaud, député," *Le Matin*, June 15, 1921.

39. "En Algérie, désordres antisémites à Constantine," *Le Temps*, June 16, 1921.

40. On cafés in nineteenth- and twentieth-century Algeria and the role that they played in the emergence of new kinds of sociability and, ultimately, a new kind of politics see Omar Carlier, "Le café maure: Sociabilité masculine et effervescence citoyenne (Algérie XVIIᵉ–XXᵉ siècles)," *Annales: Histoire, sciences sociales* 45, no. 4 (July 1, 1990): 975–1003.

41. Maurice Eisenbeth, *Le judaïsme nord-Africain: Études démographiques sur les Is-raélites de Constantine* (Constantine: Arno Natanson, 1931), 99–105.

42. Eisenbeth, 50–55.

43. In this sense, the Jews of Constantine faced a challenge similar to those of Jews elsewhere in France, as they attempted to understand the significance of the Third Republic's offer of citizenship for their continued sense of Jewish identity and feelings of solidarity with Jews elsewhere in the world. On this challenge see Paula Hyman, *From Dreyfus to Vichy: The Remaking of French Jewry, 1906–1939* (New York: Columbia University Press, 1979).

44. Jacob Katz, *From Prejudice to Destruction: Antisemitism, 1700–1933* (Cambridge, MA: Harvard University Press, 1980); Pierre Birnbaum, *Antisemitism in France: A Political History from Léon Blum to the Present* (Oxford: B. Blackwell, 1992).

45. Pierre Birnbaum, *The Jews of the Republic: A Political History of State Jews in France from Gambetta to Vichy* (Stanford, CA: Stanford University Press, 1996), 287–301.

46. Vicki Caron, "The Antisemitic Revival in France in the 1930s: The Socioeconomic Dimension Reconsidered," *Journal of Modern History* 70, no. 1 (March 1998): 24–73; Vicki Caron, *Uneasy Asylum: France and the Jewish Refugee Crisis, 1933–1942* (Stanford, CA: Stanford University Press, 1999); Ralph Schor, *L'antisémitisme en France pendant les années trente: Prélude à Vichy* (Bruxelles: Éd. Complexe, 1992).

47. Gérard Noiriel, *Le creuset français: Histoire de l'immigration, XIXᵉ–XXᵉ siècles* (Paris: Seuil, 1988), 337–38; Gérard Noiriel, *Immigration, antisémitisme et racisme en France, XIXᵉ–XXᵉ siècle: Discours publics, humiliations privées* (Paris: Fayard, 2007), 677–79.

48. Eugen Weber and Stephen Schuker, "Origins of the 'Jewish Problem' in the Third Republic," in *The Jews in Modern France*, ed. Frances Malino and Bernard Wasserstein (Hanover, NH: University Press of New England, 1985); Eugen Weber, *The Hollow Years: France in the 1930s* (New York: Norton, 1994).

5. French Algeria's Dual Fracture

1. Kevin Passmore, *The Right in France from the Third Republic to Vichy* (Oxford: Oxford University Press, 2013), 290.

2. Samuel Kalman, *The Extreme Right in Interwar France: The Faisceau and the Croix de Feu* (Burlington, VT: Ashgate, 2008).

3. Brian Jenkins and Chris Millington, *France and Fascism: February 1934 and the Dynamics of Political Crisis* (New York: Routledge, 2015).

4. Joseph Serda took the parliamentary seat for Bône in 1936, representing the Radical Republican Party that was a part of the Popular Front coalition. Émile Morinaud was reelected to his seat from Constantine from the independent center as a strong opponent of the Popular Front, and Stanislas Devaud won in the third *circonscription* in the southwest of the department, representing the right-wing extremists of the Croix de feu organization, of which he was a leading member.

5. One can get a good sense of the intense local rivalries that were at play in these negotiations in reading the pages of an ephemeral anti-Morinaud newspaper, *La Nausée*, the "organ of general disgust created for the defense and independence of universal suffrage" during the late 1920s by Paul Lefranc in Constantine. See the articles about the 1929 municipal elections in *La Nausée*, May 2, 1929.

6. See chapter 13.

7. On the Jewish consistories in Algeria see Valérie Assan, *Les consistoires israé-lites d'Algérie au XIXe siècle: L'alliance de la civilisation et de la religion* (Paris: Colin, 2012). On the French administration of organizations organized by Muslims in Algeria see James McDougall, "The Secular State's Islamic Empire: Muslim Spaces and Subjects of Jurisdiction in Paris and Algiers, 1905–1957," *Comparative Studies in Society and History* 52, no. 3 (2010).

8. Benjamin Zaoui was the grandfather of the noted historian Benjamin Stora. Adolphe Sultan was president of the local section of the League of the Rights of Man. Simon Tobiana was a prominent lawyer in Constantine who later became known during the war for Algerian independence for his vocal protests against the way that the French administration treated FLN prisoners accused of terrorism.

9. Charles-Robert Ageron, "Le Mouvement Jeune Algérien de 1900 à 1923," in *Études maghrébines: Mélanges Charles-André Julien* (Paris: Presses universitaires de France, 1964), 235.

10. Salah el Din el Zein el Tayeb, "The Europeanized Algerians and the Emancipation of Algeria," *Middle Eastern Studies* 22, no. 2 (April 1986): 207.

11. Rapports politiques périodiques, Gouverneur Général d'Algérie, Direction des Affaires Indigènes, Rapport sur la situation politique et administrative des indigènes de l'Algérie au 1er mai 1928, ANOM: ALG GGA 11/H/47 (47/1).

12. Tayeb, "Europeanized Algerians"; Julien Fromage, "Innovation politique et mobilisation de masse en 'situation coloniale': Un 'printemps algérien' des années 1930? L'expérience de la Fédération des Élus Musulmans du département de Constantine" (PhD diss., École des hautes études en sciences sociales, 2012).

13. See Saliha Belmessous, *Assimilation and Empire: Uniformity in French and British Colonies, 1541–1954* (Oxford: Oxford University Press, 2013), 175–78.

14. James McDougall, "The Secular State's Islamic Empire: Muslim Spaces and Subjects of Jurisdiction in Paris and Algiers, 1905–1957," *Comparative Studies in Society and History* 52, no. 3 (2010): 553–80, 562.

15. On this discussion see John Ruedy, "Chérif Benhabylès and Ferhat Abbas: Case Studies in the Contradictions of the 'Mission Civilisatrice,'" *Historical Reflections / Réflexions Historiques* 28, no. 2 (2002): 185–201. For reassessments of "assimilationist" politicians such as Bendjelloul see Malika Rahal, "L'Union démocratique du manifeste algérien (1946–1956): Histoire d'un parti politique" (Institut national des langues orientales, 2007); Fromage, "Innovation politique."

16. See for example the entry on Bendjelloul in Achour Cheurfi, *Dictionnaire encyclopédique de l'Algérie* (Éditions ANEP, 2007), 205.

17. Fromage, "Innovation politique," 327–58.

18. Early surveillance reports from the district administrator criticized Bendjelloul for his political activities, saying that they interfered with his professional responsibilities as a doctor. The implication of these reports was that *any* form of political activity by a professional like Bendjelloul was illegitimate and unacceptable, even within the parameters of the Jonnart Law. See the file on Bendjelloul in ANOM: ALG CONST 93/4298 Mohamed Salah Bendjelloul.

19. On Bendjelloul's relationship to the Ben Badis family see James McDougall, *A History of Algeria* (Cambridge: Cambridge University Press, 2017), 138–39.

20. On the Association of Algerian Muslim Ulama see especially Ali Merad, *Le réformisme musulman en Algérie de 1925 à 1940: Essai d'histoire religieuse et sociale* (Paris:

Mouton, 1967); James McDougall, *History and the Culture of Nationalism in Algeria* (Cambridge: Cambridge University Press, 2006).

21. James McDougall recounts how the wary cooperation between Bendjelloul and 'Abd al-Hamid Ben Badis in the early 1930s broke down in 1936 over the issue of how representatives of Muslim Algerians should respond to the opening offered by the Popular Front government that came to power that year. See McDougall, *History and the Culture of Nationalism in Algeria*, 129–37.

22. On the activities of CIAM see Pascal Le Pautremat, *La politique musulmane de la France au XXᵉ siècle: De l'hexagone aux terres d'Islam—espoirs, réussites, échecs* (Paris: Maisonneuve & Larose, 2003), 39–73.

23. The full text of Bendjelloul's telegram (sent on August 20, 1932) is reproduced in "Copie de télégramme chiffré," ANOM: ALG GGA 2/CAB 3. See also reports in ANOM: ALG GGA 3/CAB/40. Bendjelloul returned often to this community throughout the 1930s, and his activities there between 1932 and 1937 are documented in ANOM: ALG CONST 93/B/3/279.

24. The phrase "Béni-oui-oui" was often applied to the members of the Algerian Muslim elite who served the interests of the French by occupying the job of *qa'id*, *agha*, *bachagha*, or the religious offices of qadi, imam, and mufti. "Les Béni-Oui-Oui" was the title of a play performed by the musical troupe led by Mahieddine Bachetarzi throughout the department of Constantine in the spring of 1936. Joshua Cole, "À chacun son public: Politique et culture dans l'Algérie des années 1930," *Sociétés & représentations*, no. 38 (2014): 21–51.

25. Rapport, Sûreté Départementale de Constantine, no. 2459, December 9, 1930, ANOM: ALG CONST 93/B3/713.

26. André Nouschi, "Le sens de certains chiffres: Croissance urbaine et vie politique en Algérie (1926–1936)," in *Études maghrébines: Mélanges Charles-André Julien* (Paris: Presses universitaires de France, 1964), 208.

27. Samuel Kalman, *French Colonial Fascism: The Extreme Right in Algeria, 1919–1939* (New York: Palgrave Macmillan, 2013), 19–31.

28. Kalman, 42–47.

29. Population figures from *Répertoire statistique des communes de l'Algérie (recensement de la population algérienne au 8 mars 1931)* (Algiers: Victor Heintz, 1932).

30. Estimates of the Croix de feu's membership vary widely. There is little doubt, however, that the group went from being counted in the low thousands in 1929 to the hundreds of thousands in 1936. Jacques Nobécourt, *Le Colonel de La Rocque (1885–1946), ou, Les pièges du nationalisme chrétien* (Paris: Fayard, 1996), 139–42.

31. On this debate see William D. Irvine, "Fascism in France and the Strange Case of the Croix de Feu," *Journal of Modern History* 63, no. 2 (1991): 271–95; Kevin Passmore, "Boy Scouting for Grown-Ups? Paramilitarism in the Croix de Feu and the Parti Social Français," *French Historical Studies* 19, no. 2 (1995): 527; Sean Kennedy, "The End of Immunity? Recent Work on the Far Right in Interwar France," *Historical Reflections / Réflexions Historiques* 34, no. 2 (2008): 25–45; Sean Kennedy, *Reconciling France against Democracy: The Croix de Feu and the Parti Social Français, 1927–1945* (Montreal: McGill–Queen's University Press, 2007). Historians who downplay the connection between fascism and the Croix de feu include René Rémond, *La droite en France de la première Restauration à la Vᵉ République* (Paris: Aubier, Éditions Montaigne, 1968); Pierre Milza, *Fascisme français: Passé et présent* (Paris: Flammarion, 1987). For an opposing view see Kalman, *French Colonial Fascism;*

Robert Soucy, *French Fascism: The Second Wave, 1933–1939* (New Haven, CT: Yale University Press, 1995).

32. Caroline Campbell, *Political Belief in France, 1927–1945: Gender, Empire, and Fascism in the Croix de Feu and Parti Social Français* (Baton Rouge: LSU Press, 2015).

33. As Robert Paxton has pointed out, it is impossible to know what policies would be enacted by a movement that never came to power. The Croix de feu's fascism—if indeed it was fascist—remained largely aspirational. Robert O. Paxton, *The Anatomy of Fascism* (New York: Knopf, 2004), xii, 321.

34. Nobécourt, *Le Colonel de La Rocque*.

35. Thérèse Charles-Vallin, "La droite en Algérie (1934–1939)," thesis, l'Université de Paris X, 1974, 85.

36. Bensimon is mentioned as a member of the section's executive board (*conseil d'administration*) in "La présentation officielle du fanion à la Société des 'Croix de Feu,'" *La Dépêche de Constantine*, November 2, 1930. Bensimon's Jewishness did not preclude him from taking an active role in the organization between 1930 and 1934, though police reports of meetings where he attended noted that many in attendance stopped listening when he spoke. Lucien Bensimon persisted in participating in Constantine's Croix de feu activities until October 1934—after the Constantine riots—resigning at precisely the moment that the local section of the Croix de feu in Sétif entered into a cooperative agreement for the first time with members of Bendjelloul's Fédération des élus musulmans in order to win a majority on the municipal council and claim the mayor's seat. On Bensimon's participation in the Croix de feu during these years see ANOM: ALG CONST 93/B/3/522.

37. This "Mahdi" was probably not Mohamed El Maadi, whom the Constantine police later connected to the violence of August 5, 1934, in Constantine. In November 1930, when the reference to "Mahdi" as the treasurer of the local Croix de feu appeared in the newspaper, Mohamed El Maadi was still in the army in Morocco, according to his service record.

38. ANOM: ALG CONST 93/B/3/522. It appears as if this telegram was sent by Ernest Lanxade, the former editor of *La Tribune* who had led the anti-Jewish campaign in 1921.

39. Documents relating to the Croix de feu's dispute over Morinaud's nominations for the Legion of Honor are in ANOM: ALG CONST 93/B/3/707 and 93/B/3/522.

40. These figures come from Charles-Vallin, "La droite en Algérie," 86.

41. Soucy, *French Fascism*, 65–66. See also Danielle Tartakowsky, "Les morts des 6, 9, et février 1934," in *Autour des morts: Mémoire et identité*, ed. Olivier Dumoulin and Françoise Thelamon (Mont-Saint-Aignan: Université de Rouen, 2001), 190.

42. Soucy, *French Fascism*, 65–66.

43. These figures on the recruitment of Muslim Algerians to the Croix de feu are from Campbell, *Political Belief in France*, 159. One French historian (the daughter of a Croix de feu leader from Constantine) suggested that as many as 10 percent of the Croix de feu membership in Algeria were Muslims, which if true would make it truly exceptional among European political movements. This figure does not appear to be an accurate representation of the number attending monthly meetings, except perhaps in the city of Constantine during the tumultuous year of 1936. See Charles-Vallin, "La droite en Algérie," 86.

44. These police reports can be found in ANOM: ALG CONST 93/B/3/707. A report from January 29, 1933, mentions that Ali Bouakkaz Benbouzid, *qa'id* of the Douar Fekrina in Oum El Bouaghi, had joined the new Croix de feu section being created in Aïn Beïda.

6. Provocation, Difference, and Public Space

1. Sophie Roberts has emphasized the events in Palestine as an important part of the context that led to the Constantine riots. My interpretation of the evidence is different: I see the parallel tension between Muslims and Jews in Palestine as an element in the debate about the meaning of the Constantine riots after the fact, but less important as a cause of the events in French Algeria. See Roberts, *Citizenship and Antisemitism in French Colonial Algeria, 1870–1962* (Cambridge: Cambridge University Press, 2017), 154–63.

2. XIXᵉ Corps d'Armée, Division de Constantine, État-Major, no. 4274, Objet: Au sujet d'incidents survenue entre Tirailleurs et Israélites, Le Général Leguay, Commandant la Division de Constantine, à Monsieur le Préfet du Département de Constantine, February 20, 1914, ANOM: ALG CONST B/3/248.

3. The three men were Amor Ben Belkacem Hamel, an employee of the gasworks; Ali Ben Larbi Touati, a café employee; and Mostefa Ben Daoud, profession unidentified. They claimed that the beating had taken place in spite of the presence of local police, who were unable to intervene because of the presence of a crowd of up to twenty onlookers, many of whom had been drinking. Letter from Amor Ben Belkacem Hamel, Ali Ben Larbi Touati, and Mostefa Ben Daoud to the Prefect of the Department of Constantine, December 24, 1928, ANOM: ALG GGA 9/H/53.

4. ANOM: ALG GGA 9/H/53, dossier Antisémitisme.

5. For the police and prefecture's correspondence on incidents between Jews and Muslims in Constantine in 1929–1930 see Gouvernement Général d'Algérie, Direction de la Sécurité Générale, no. 27831, Le Gouverneur Général de l'Algérie à Monsieur le Préfet du département, Affaires Indigènes et Police Générale de Constantine, September 15, 1930, ANOM: ALG CONST 93/6740. See also the report from Police Commissioner René Miquel of Constantine, September 26, 1930, ANOM: ALG CONST 93/6740.

6. Affaires Indigènes, no. 554, Communication from the Prefect of Constantine to the Procureur de la République, January 11, 1929, ANOM: ALG CONST B/3/248.

7. Le Commissaire Central Aschbacher de la Ville de Constantine à Monsieur le Préfet du département Constantine, January 12, 1929, ANOM: ALG CONST B/3/248.

8. Mairie de Châteaudun, Interdiction du port de la matraque, du gourdin et du baton ferré, April 15, 1929, ANOM: ALG CONST B/3/248.

9. Sûreté Générale, Ville de Constantine, Cabinet du Commissaire Central de Police, no. 53, A. S. de violences exercées par un israëlite sur un indigène, April 30, 1929, ANOM: ALG CONST B/3/248.

10. Gouvernement Général de l'Algérie, Direction de la Sécurité Générale, no. 21074, Le Gouverneur Général de l'Algérie à Monsieur le Préfet du Département de Constantine, August 15, 1929, ANOM: ALG CONST B/3/248.

11. Copie du Rapport de M. le Commissaire Central p.i. [*sic*] de Constantine, en date du 6 août, no. 113, ANOM: ALG CONST B/3/248.

12. Affaires Indigènes, 2ᵉ Section, no. 16328, Letter from Secretary General of the Prefecture of Constantine to Deputy Mayor Émile Barkatz, August 9, 1929, ANOM: ALG CONST B/3/248.

13. Affaires Indigènes, 2ᵉ Section, Incidents entre Israélites et Indigènes, Le Gouverneur Général de l'Algérie (Direction de la Sécurité Générale), August 23, 1929, ANOM: ALG CONST B/3/248.

14. Belkacem Benhabylès, Avocat au Barreau, Constantine, Monsieur le Préfet du Département de Constantine, August 26, 1929, ANOM: ALG CONST B/3/248.

15. On the racism of the police and government officials in Algeria in the 1930s see Annie Rey-Goldzeiguer, *Aux origines de la guerre d'Algérie, 1940–1945: De Mers-el-Kébir aux massacres du nord-constantinois* (Paris: La Découverte, 2002), 19. For Miquel's report on the ethnic profile of the police force in Constantine see Ville de Constantine, Cabinet du Commissaire Central, no. 5209, August 21, 1934, ANOM: ALG GGA 9/H/52.

16. Préfecture de Constantine, Affaires indigènes, 2ᵉ section, September 16, 1930, Letter from Secretary General of the Department of Constantine to Grand Rabbi Maurice Eisenbeth, ANOM: ALG CONST 93/6740. The secretary-general wrote that "for some time I have recorded my deep regret at new acts of violence committed by Jews on natives [*indigènes*] who do not appear to have provoked them in any way."

17. The reports on the Aouizerat affair and the ensuing letter from the Jewish leadership to Morinaud are in ANOM: ALG CONST 9/H/53.

7. Rehearsals for Crisis

1. Maurice Viollette, *L'Algérie vivra-t-elle? Notes d'un ancien gouverneur général* (Paris: F. Alcan, 1931).

2. Bendjelloul became the president of the Cercle indigène de l'Union, a political club or *nadi*, and also the director of the Comité des meskines, a Muslim charitable organization. According to police reports, he played a significant role in the creation of a "Comité de défense de libertés indigènes" in March 1933, and a "Ligue des intellectuels musulmans" and a "Comité de défense des agriculteurs indigènes" soon followed. Gouvernement Général de l'Algérie, no. 14152 B, Note pour Monsieur le Gouverneur Général, June 10, 1933, ANOM: ALG GGA 2/CAB 3.

3. Telegram from Bendjelloul to "Président Conseil Ministre, Intérieur et Sénat Viollette," ANOM: ALG GGA 2/CAB/3. The telegram was also published in Algeria in *La Voix indigène*, a francophone paper with an educated Muslim audience. *La Voix indigène* was edited by Rabah Zenati, at that time a close collaborator of Bendjelloul.

4. Governor-General Jules Carde's exact words: "Il faut tout de même en finir avec les agissements de Bendjelloul." Préfecture de Constantine, Cabinet, no. 6665, Le Préfet du Département de Constantine à Monsieur Le Gouverneur Général de l'Algérie, September 8, 1932, ANOM: ALG GGA 3/CAB 40. For the governor-general's reaction see also subsequent note in the carton, "Lettre du Préfet de Constantine au sujet des agissements de M. le Docteur BENDJELLOUL, conseiller général. Annotation de Monsieur le Gouverneur General, signé: J. Carde," October 2, 1932.

5. Constantine was by no means unique in this regard, as anxiety about refugees was widespread throughout France during these months, leading to a significant increase in antisemitism throughout the country. Gary S. Cross, *Immigrant Workers in Industrial France: The Making of a New Laboring Class* (Philadelphia: Temple University Press, 1983); Vicki Caron, *Uneasy Asylum: France and the Jewish Refugee Crisis, 1933–1942* (Stanford, CA: Stanford University Press, 1999).

6. On March 31, 1933, Léon Assoun led a crowd of fifty young people, most in their mid-teens, through the streets of the old Jewish quarter. According to a summary police report written in May 1933, they shouted "Long Live War, Down with Hitler, Down with Germany, Long Live France." The author of the report, chief of departmental security Bourette, noted the negative reactions to the cries of "Long Live War" among the settler population who witnessed the demonstration, stating that they did not hide their "anti-Jewish sentiments." Sûreté Départementale de Constantine, no. 1336, Mouvement antisémite, May 30, 1933, ANOM: ALG GGA 9/H/53.

7. Sûreté Départementale de Constantine, no. 2871, October 27, 1933, ANOM: ALG CONST B/3/250.

8. Commissariat Central de Constantine, no. 6730, September 11, 1933, ANOM: ALG CONST B/3/249.

9. Sûreté Départementale de Constantine, no. 1948, Au sujet du journal antisémite "L'Éclair," July 27, 1933, ANOM: ALG CONST B/3/250. Other reports on antisemitic activity by settlers in the spring of 1933 in Constantine can be found in ANOM: ALG GGA 9/H/53, 9/H/45 (39), and Algérie, Département de Constantine, 93/B/3/687.

10. Pascal Le Pautremat, *La politique musulmane de la France au XXe siècle: De l'hexagone aux terres d'Islam—espoirs, réussites, échecs* (Paris: Maisonneuve & Larose, 2003), 50–53.

11. Gouvernement Général de l'Algérie, Direction de la Sécurité Générale, no. 14546 B, Note pour Monsieur le Gouverneur Général de l'Algérie, June 19, 1933, ANOM: ALG GGA 2/CAB/3.

12. Rapport, Sûreté Départementale de Constantine, no. 1295, Incidents antisémites, May 24, 1933, ANOM: ALG GGA 9/H/53.

13. Copie du Rapport Spécial no. 4200 adressé aux Autorités le 25 Mai 1933 [May 25, 1933], Commissariat Central de Constantine, Objet: Mouvement antisémite, ANOM: ALG GGA 9/H/53.

14. Le Commissaire Central de la Ville de Constantine, À Monsieur le Préfet, Cabinet Police Générale, no. 4279, May 29, 1933, ANOM: ALG GGA 9/H/53.

15. Rapport, L'Inspecteur-Chef Doutré, May 25, 1933, ANOM: ALG GGA 9/H/53. This crowd evidently meant the cry to be a reminder to the police that the police commissioner, René Miquel, shared their antisemitic views.

16. Sûreté Départementale de Constantine, no. 1336, Mouvement antisémite, Rapport, May 30, 1933, ANOM: ALG GGA 9/H/53.

17. ANOM: ALG GGA 3/CAB/40.

18. Gouvernement Général de l'Algérie, Direction de la Sécurité Générale, no. 14546 B, Note pour Monsieur le Gouverneur Général de l'Algérie, June 19, 1933, ANOM: ALG GGA 3/CAB/40.

19. Sûreté Départementale de Constantine, no. 1336, Mouvement antisémite, Rapport, May 30, 1933, ANOM: ALG GGA 9/H/53.

20. On the resignation of members of the FEC in Constantine see Sûreté Départementale de Constantine, no. 1669, Au sujet de la Délégation Musulmane, Rapport, July 2, 1933, ANOM: ALG CONST 93/B/3/263.

21. Sûreté Départementale de Constantine, no. 3051, Fédération des Élus Musulmans du Département de Constantine, Rapport, November 20, 1933, ANOM: ALG CONST 93/B/3/700.

22. The Departmental Security Bureau responded by noting that the doctor received his clients in an office at 8 rue Chabron, a building that also housed the editorial office of Rabah Zenati's francophone paper, *La Voix indigène* (the native voice). His patients, the report noted, were "principally *indigènes*." His medical practice was endorsed by the Ligue musulmane des familles nombreuses, and he devoted every Friday to the free treatment of the indigent, "without distinction of race." Sûreté Départementale, no. 2311, A/S du Dr. Bendjelloul, Le Chef de la Sûreté Départementale à Monsieur le Préfet (Cabinet) Constantine, September 1, 1933, ANOM: ALG CONST 93/B/3/700.

23. On the *café maure* see Omar Carlier, "Le café maure: Sociabilité masculine et effervescence citoyenne (Algérie XVIIᵉ–XXᵉ siècles)," *Annales: Histoire, sciences sociales* 45, no. 4 (July 1, 1990).

24. Département de Constantine, Sous-préfecture de Philippeville, no. 4283, Le Sous-Préfet de Philippeville à Monsieur le Préfet (Cabinet) Constantine, September 19, 1933; Commissariat Central de Philippeville, no. 233 D, Objet: Surveillance politique A/S. du Docteur Bendjelloul, Confidentiel, Le Commissaire Central à Monsieur le Sous-Préfet "Philippeville," September 14, 1933, ANOM: ALG CONST 93/B/3/700.

25. Sûreté Départementale de Constantine, no. 3223, Rapport, December 12, 1933, ANOM: ALG CONST 93/B/3/700. Letter signed "Le Chef de la Sûreté Départementale" and addressed to the prefect of Constantine and the governor-general in Algiers.

26. Sûreté Départementale de Constantine, no. 3361, A/s. du Dr. Bendjelloul, Rapport, December 19, 1933, ANOM: ALG CONST 93/B/3/700.

27. Préfecture de Constantine, Section des Affaires Indigènes, no. 3728, Réformes Indigènes, Constitution d'une Commission, Département de Constantine, Le Préfet du Département de Constantine à Monsieur Le Gouverneur Général de l'Algérie, March 12, 1934, ANOM: ALG CONST 93/B/3/700; see also Préfecture de Constantine, Section des Affaires Indigènes, no. 4475, Politique Indigène, Le Préfet du Département de Constantine à Monsieur Le Gouverneur Général de l'Algérie, March 21, 1934, ANOM: ALG CONST 93/B/3/700.

28. Telegram from Bendjelloul to "President Commission Algérie Colonies Chambre des Deputés Paris," March 19, 1933, ANOM: ALG CONST 93/B/3/700.

29. Sûreté Départementale de Constantine, no. 899, Mouvement politique Indigène, Rapport, March 20, 1934, ANOM: ALG CONST 93/B/3/700.

30. "M. Montigny précise les buts de son voyage à Alger," *La Dépêche de Constantine*, March 22, 1934.

31. Newspaper clipping, "À la Commission de l'Algérie et des Colonies," *La Dépêche de Constantine*, March 16, 1934, ANOM: ALG CONST 93/B/3/277.

32. Bendjelloul gave his own account of the events of this year in a meeting with FEMC members in April 1934. See Ville de Constantine, Cabinet du Commissaire

Central, no. 2465, Objet: Réunion publique organisée par la Fédération des élus indigènes [sic] du département de Constantine, April 30, 1934, ANOM: ALG CONST
93/B/3/700.

33. Fédération des Élus des Musulmans du Département de Constantine. A Monsieur le Préfet du Département de Constantine, April 3, 1934, ANOM: ALG CONST
93/B/3/277.

34. Police reports from throughout the region indicate that similar committees
were set up in other nearby towns as well in the following weeks: in Philippeville
(March 7, two hundred present at first meeting); in Souk-Ahras (March 7, four hundred people in attendance); in Batna (May 12, fifty people present, "majorité israélite"). See dossier on antifascist leagues in 1934, Ligues antifascistes, ANOM: ALG
CONST 93/B/3/707.

35. Sûreté départementale de Constantine, no. 2319, Mouvement communiste,
Rapport, September 2, 1933, Signed: Leymarie, Chef de la Sûreté Départementale,
ANOM: ALG GGA 9/H/19 1933.

36. Bendjelloul did not attend the public lecture at the Théâtre Municipal. The
police report indicated, however, that there were 150 "indigènes" in an audience
whose "major part" was "European." Sûreté Départementale, Commissariat Spécial
de Bône, no. 343, Surveillance politique des indigènes, A. S. Dr Bendjelloul et député
Moch, May 4, 1934, ANOM: ALG CONST 93/B/3/700.

37. The police were undecided as to the actual author of the telegram, suggesting that it was either Mohamed Zerkine, a municipal councilor, or Allaoua Bendjelloul, a pharmacist and brother of Mohamed Salah Bendjelloul.

38. Les Inspecteurs Alliche & Abbasi à Monsieur le Commissaire de Police du 2ᵉ
Arrondissement, ANOM: ALG GGA 9/H/53.

39. Sûreté Départementale de Constantine, no. L580, Mouvement indigène,
Réunion publique, Rapport, May 16, 1934, ANOM: ALG GGA 9/H/53. Commissioner Fusero gave a slightly lower estimate, between two thousand and twenty-
five hundred (see Copie d'un rapport adressé le 16 Mai 1934 aux autorités ci-après:
M. le Gouverneur Général, M. le Préfet, M. le Maire, Fusero, Commissaire de Police,
ANOM: ALG GGA 9/H/53). Inspectors Alliche and Abassi, who provided a transla-
tion of the Arabic speeches by Benbadis and Bendjelloul, gave eight thousand as the
figure, while the editor of La Voix indigène suggested ten thousand people were present. If this higher figure were true, it amounted to more than one-fifth of the entire
Muslim population of the city. (See La Voix indigène, May 18, 1934.)

40. This would, in fact, be one of the few moments in the 1930s in which Ben
Badis and Bendjelloul would appear together in a public forum. They would also
appear together on Saturday, August 4, 1934, after the initial dispute at the mosque
on August 3 when a Muslim man was shot, but before the riots of Sunday, August 5,
that took the lives of twenty-five Jews and two Muslims.

41. Les Inspecteurs Alliche & Abbasi à Monsieur le Commissaire de Police du 2ᵉ
Arrondissement, ANOM: ALG GGA 9/H/53.

8. Friday and Saturday, August 3–4, 1934

1. Gouvernement Général de l'Algérie, Département de Constantine, Sûreté
Générale, no. 2238, Constantine, Tentative de meurtre sur M. MIMOUN Léon, July 30,

1934, ANOM: ALG GGA 9/H/52. Jacques Cauro's report does not mention the Halimi family by name. A third brother, Ruben Robert Halimi, recounted the story of the July 24 shooting of Léon Mimoun in a letter to the commission investigating the riots in September 1934. À Monsieur Vigouroux, Président de la Commission d'Enquête "Événements du 5 Août" (copy of a letter from Ruben Robert Halimi to Jean Vigouroux from September 1934, no specific date given), ANOM: ALG GGA 9/H/52. The circumstances of Ruben Halimi's letter to Vigouroux are discussed in chapter 12.

2. 1930–1935, Croix de feu, Cabinet du Commissaire Central, no. 3847, Objet: Affiche, Croix de feu, Constantine, August 1, 1934, ANOM: ALG CONST 93/B/3/707.

3. The original documents used in compiling the official investigating commission's report are found in ANOM: ALG GGA 9/H/52, 9/H/53, 9/H/54, and 9/H/55. These documents were used by the police and the prefecture to reconstruct the major events of August 3–5, 1934. In addition to the official reports submitted by the local authorities (the mayor's office, the prefecture, the police, the military) there are several collections of documents put together by other interested parties, such as the 141-page dossier of witness statements from the Muslim population of Constantine submitted by Mohamed Salah Bendjelloul. A copy of this dossier is in 9/H/53.

4. This is the spelling of Khalifa's name that appears most often in the official documents. The copy of his marriage and birth certificates in the État Civil reads "Elie Khalifat." He was often referred to as "Eliaou Kalifa" by members of Constantine's Jewish community.

5. The État Civil for Algeria confirms Elie Khalifa's birth, the date of his parents' marriage, and his father's death. If Melki Oureida had a subsequent relationship with a Muslim man, it does not appear that they were married, as no marriage certificate under her name appears in the État Civil. The information on the Muslim members of Khalifa's extended family is repeated in the reports of two investigations by individuals commissioned by Jewish organizations: the report written by Albert Confino for the Alliance israélite universelle and the report written by Joseph Fisher (later Ariel) for the Comité des délégations juives (precursor to the World Jewish Congress). Both Fisher and Confino based their reports on conversations with leading members of Constantine's Jewish community in the days after the riots, and both repeated the story about Khalifa's family and his mother's relationship with a Muslim man. The Confino report is in AAIU Algérie 1C Antisémitisme 1, dated August 17, 1934. Fisher published his report later as Joseph Ariel (Fisher), "Un document inédit sur le pogrom à Constantine, 3–5 août 1934," *Das neue Israel* 17 (1964): 86–89, 193–203.

6. This is the language reported by Lucien Fusero of the Constantine Police. Fusero's version of the events are contained in two summary reports, both written on August 13, 1934. The first, comprising the events of August 3–4, is Rapport du Commissaire Fusero, Ville de Constantine, Commissariat de Police du 2e Arrondissement, no. 4345, Commissaire Central par interim sur les incidents du 3 août au 4 août, August 13, 1934, ANOM: ALG CONST 93/20020 (henceforth Fusero Report, August 3–4). The second, describing the events of August 5, is Rapport du Commissaire Fusero, Commissaire de Police du 2e Arrondissement, Journée du 5 Août, 1934, no. 4396, August 13, 1934, ANOM: ALG GGA 9/H/52 (henceforth Fusero Report, August 5).

7. The expression Khalifa used was *"sale bicot."* *Bicot* and *Arabicot* were derogatory terms for Arabs, commonly used during these years in the military. *Bicot* means young goat. The transcript of Khalifa's interrogation by the gendarmerie is Gendarmerie Nationale, Procès-verbal constatant l'audition de Khelifa [*sic*] Elie, inclupé d'ivresse manifeste et de tapage injurieux et nocturne, ANOM: ALG GGA 9/H/53 (henceforth Khalifa Statement).

8. Audition du Témoin Zerbib Binhas, Elie, ANOM: ALG GGA 9/H/53.

9. "Des Incidents," *La Dépêche de Constantine*, August 4, 1934.

10. Dossier remis par M. Bendjelloul, ANOM: ALG GGA 9/H/53 (henceforth Bendjelloul Dossier).

11. Bendjelloul Dossier, Incident de la Mosquée de Sidi Lakhdar du 3 août 1934. The language of Khalifa's insults varied according to different witnesses in the Bendjelloul dossier. Mohamed Ben Embareck Meziani reported it this way: "You cuckolds, sons of dogs, God curse your Prophet, your Saints, your prayer, I piss on you."

12. Dossier Kalifa, ANOM: ALG GGA 9/H/53. See also Fusero Report, August 3–4.

13. Bendjelloul Dossier. The witness was Rabah ben Messaoud Dhaou, *gargotier* (proprietor of a low-cost restaurant), who lived across the street from the Khalifa family's building.

14. Khalifa told the gendarmes on August 7 that when his wife went to the window she was confronted with a crowd of more than three thousand people. Given the descriptions from other witnesses, however, he was clearly conflating the numbers later that evening with the initial gathering shortly after the confrontation at the mosque. See Khalifa Statement.

15. The figure of 2000 comes from the Fusero Report, August 3–4.

16. *Tirailleurs algériens* (Algerian riflemen) were Muslim soldiers in the French army.

17. Many witnesses spoke of gunfire in the place des Galettes, which was separated from the mosque and Khalifa's apartment by only a few steps on the rue Combes. Captain Gouadain of the gendarmerie reported that gunfire was "exchanged," implying that shots were fired on both sides. See Rapport du Capitaine Gouadain Commandant la Section sur des troubles survenue à Constantine entre les éléments musulmans et israélites, Gendarmerie Nationale, no. 224/2, August 4, 1934, ANOM: ALG CONST 93/20020 (henceforth Gouadain Report, August 4). Maamar Maklouf, a watchman working for a private residence in the rue Combes, later reported that he saw "Jewish police agents shooting at natives [*indigènes*] in the rue Varna" (Bendjelloul Dossier, Maklouf Maamar). Another witness claimed that a police officer was wounded in the ear by gunshots, and that he attempted to clear the crowd by brandishing his own service revolver (Bendjelloul Dossier, Benmadjat Khoudir).

18. The events of August 3 are recounted in a number of reports. The Fusero Report, August 5, is the most detailed, but also the one most likely to highlight the courage and bravery of a small number of police officials. See also ANOM: ALG CONST 93/20019 for the report on August 3 from the director of the Sûreté Départementale, Henri Coquelin. Coquelin's report offered some speculation on the political consequences of the incident, fearing that it would cause a spike in Bendjelloul's

popularity as well as an explosion of Muslim antisemitism that would be "ably exploited by the nationalists" (by which he meant Bendjelloul and the members of the FEMC).

19. Fusero Report, August 5.

20. The police called for reinforcements from the gendarmes and the military as early as 11:30 p.m., and the larger squad of twenty-five soldiers from Khalifa's regiment, the Third Zouaves, arrived at 12:45 a.m. in response to Fusero's call. Figures for the number of soldiers on hand on August 3 come from Rapport sur les événements du 3 août et jours ultérieurs, le Général de Division Kieffer, Commandant d'Armes, August 20, 1934, ANOM: ALG CONST 93/20020 (henceforth Kieffer Report, August 20).

21. Commission d'enquête administrative sur les événements qui se sont déroulé du 3 au 8 août 1934 dans la Ville et le Département de Constantine, Rapport de la Commission, October 7, 1934, ANOM: ALG GGA 9/H/53 (henceforth Commission Report), 11.

22. Yves-Claude Aouate, "Constantine 1934: Un pogrom 'classique,'" Les Nouveaux cahiers—Alliance israélite universelle 68 (1982): 51.

23. The discovery of Boutarane by Lanxade and Lauffenberger is recounted in the official report produced by the commission appointed by the governor-general to investigate the origins of the riots (Commission Report, 13). The source of the information about Lanxade and Lauffenberger was a deposition from Hippolyte Massari, "rédacteur principal" (principal editor) at the prefecture in Constantine, given before the commission on August 29, 1934. Massari's testimony is missing from the dossier preserved by the commission in ALG GGA 9/H/53. It is interesting to note in this connection that on August 8, the prefect appointed Massari to a newly created office that supervised the examination and censorship of telegrams sent and received at the post office. In other words, Massari was directly involved in the prefecture's attempt to control the information that was emanating from the city in the aftermath of the riots. ANOM: ALG CONST 93/20020.

24. The Bendjelloul-Gassab-Halimi incident is reported briefly in the Fusero Report, August 5, and Gassab's own deposition is in ANOM: ALG GGA 9/H/53. The Bendjelloul Dossier gives additional details: one witness recounted that he saw Boudjema Gassab leaving the Café Tantonville in the rue Nationale at 12:30 a.m. on the night of August 3 and "arrest the native who had just struck a Jew. He seized him with his left hand and brandished his revolver with the right, threatening his prisoner and the natives who ran toward him saying 'You cuckolds and pimps, the first Muslim who approaches me I'll kill him like a pig, I'll kill you like flies'" (Bendjelloul Dossier, Mezhoud Bachir ben Mohammed). Ruben Robert Halimi's version of the story, which includes a narrative about his son's beating and the exchange in the police station, came in a letter that he later wrote to the investigating commission (Letter from Ruben Robert Halimi to Jean Vigouroux, September 6, 1934, ANOM: ALG GGA 9/H/52). The incident is also described in the testimony of the Muslim police officer, Alliche, in his deposition taken after the riot. Alliche stated that Bendjelloul waited outside the police station for the younger Halimi's assailant to be released so that he could persuade the crowd to disperse (Commission d'Enquête Administrative

sur les Événements de Constantine, Déposition de Monsieur Alliche, Inspecteur de la Police Municipale, September 12, 1934, ANOM: ALG GGA 9/H/53).

25. The number of people injured in the fighting on August 3 was certainly higher, as these figures include only those who sought medical assistance. Sûreté Départementale de Constantine, no. 2438, Rapport, Antisémitisme, Constantine, August 4, 1934, ANOM: ALG CONST 93/20019.

26. Boutarane was identified in a police report after August 5 (Émeutes du 3 au 5 août 1934, État nominatif des blessées indigènes admis en traitement à l'hôpital civil de Constantine, ANOM: ALG GGA 9/H/52). The same report listed two other Muslim men who were treated for gunshot wounds they received on the evening of August 3–4: Boubakeur Mechta, age twenty-one, shot in the arm, and Amar Bouchema, age seventeen, shot in the cheek.

27. The attack on Bensimon is recounted in the report from Henri Coquelin, the director of departmental security at the prefecture, August 4, 1934, ANOM: ALG GGA 9/H/52. Coquelin noted that Léonce Bensimon was also the brother of the previous editor in chief of Constantine's *Le Républicain* newspaper. More details on Bensimon's beating are given in the report of Jacques Cauro, head of Constantine's Police Mobile, no. 2474, August 24, 1934, ANOM: ALG GGA 9/H/52. Bensimon is referred to as "l'israélite frère avocat Bensimon" in a telegram from Paul Souchier to the GG in Paris (ANOM: ALG GGA 3/CAB/4).

28. Gouadain Report, August 4.

29. Fusero Report, August 3–4.

30. ANOM: ALG CONST B/3/250.

31. Fusero Report, August 3–4.

32. ANOM: ALG CONST B/3/250. These figures indicate the number that Landel believed to be stationed in the city on Saturday, August 4, and do not include a force of around seven hundred *tirailleurs algériens* under military command in the city.

33. ANOM: ALG CONST 93/20020. Both Commissioner Fusero of the second district and Commissioner Besse of the third district claim credit for arresting Khalifa in their subsequent reports. See Compte rendu sur les événements du 3 au 6 août par M. Besse, Commissaire de Police du 3ᵉ Arrondissement à Constantine, August 24, 1934, ANOM: ALG GGA 9/H/52 (henceforth Besse Report).

34. This sequence of meetings was described by Hamouda Ben Charad and Ammar Hammouche, whose statements were compiled by Bendjelloul after the riot. See Bendjelloul Dossier. Lellouche's meeting with the grand rabbi is mentioned in Ayoun, "À propos du pogrom de Constantine (août 1934)," 183.

35. Handwritten note from Secretary-General Joseph Landel of the Prefecture of Constantine, dated "samedi 4/8," ANOM: ALG CONST B/3/250.

36. A complete list of the attendees of this meeting, compiled by Police Commissioner René Miquel, is in ANOM: ALG GGA 9/H/52. Twenty-six people were in attendance, not including officials of the *mairie* or the prefecture. These included eight Muslim elected officials, the mufti, and eleven Muslim notables (an industrialist, several merchants, and 'Abd al-Hamid Ben Badis, listed as a "Professor of Arabic"). There were five Jewish elected officials in attendance, accompanied by Sidi Fredj Halimi, the grand rabbi.

37. ANOM: ALG CONST B/3/250.

38. Ben Badis's and Yhia Ouhamed's statements were recounted in the controversial report published later by Henri Lellouche, where he accused Ben Badis of "holding the Jewish elected officials hostage" for their inability to control the Jewish population and claimed that Ouhamed only wanted to disarm the Jews on Saturday, August 4, in order to pave the way for a massacre that was already planned for the next day. Rapport sur les événements tragiques du 5 août 1934, ANOM: ALG GGA 9/H/53 (henceforth Lellouche Report).

39. Lellouche Report.

40. Lellouche Report. Lellouche claimed in his report that "the native riflemen threatened to jump the walls in order to invade the Jewish neighborhood."

41. Kieffer Report. The *tirailleurs algériens* were not called up from barracks until after midday on Sunday, August 5, by which time the authorities had already lost control of the city. Souchier's own version of the conversation with Landel was given in a telegram to the governor-general, who was then in Paris. He reassured the governor, saying that Landel "appeared to master his calm and the situation." ANOM: ALG GGA 3/CAB/4.

42. Besse Report.

43. This detail comes from the deposition of the Service d'ordre, ANOM: ALG GGA 9/H/53.

44. Several different figures were given for the number of people at the central mosque on Saturday, August 4. Coquelin's report of August 5 gave a figure of three thousand (ANOM: ALG GGA 9/H/52). Fusero's Report of August 13, 1934 (no. 4396) gave a figure of one thousand (ANOM: ALG GGA 9/H/52). The Lellouche Report stated only that "several thousands" were present, but he was not himself an eyewitness, as he was attending the 6 p.m. meeting at the prefecture.

45. Ben Badis's words as reported in Coquelin Report of August 5, 1934 (ANOM: ALG GGA 9/H/52).

46. Commissioner Jean Besse's report of August 24 credits the announcement on Saturday afternoon about a Sunday morning meeting at Les Pins to Salah Améziane, a member of the municipal council close to Bendjelloul. See Besse Report.

47. A copy of this poster as well as a duplicate poster with the same text in Arabic is in ANOM: ALG GGA 9/H/55.

48. The Commission Report produced by the governor-general's investigating commission headed by Jean Vigouroux claimed that the text of this poster was agreed on by the assembled Muslim and Jewish leaders during the 11 a.m. meeting on Saturday, August 4. It is curious, however, that the only signature on the poster was from LICA, an organization that was detested by the right and associated with the Communist left. Commission Report, 17.

49. A similar poster produced by the Attali print shop is in ANOM: ALG CONST B/3/249.

9. Sunday, August 5, 1934

1. The Bendjelloul Dossier (ANOM: ALG GGA 9/H/53) asserts that "Muslim notables and elected officials" were in attendance at the Narboni funeral. Historian Richard Ayoun mentions Bendjelloul's presence at the funeral. Richard Ayoun, "À

propos du pogrom de Constantine (août 1934)," *Revue des études juives* 154, no. 1–3 (1985): 184.

2. Déposition du Général Kieffer, Commandant la Division Territoriale de Constantine, September 7, 1934, ANOM: ALG GGA 9/H/53.

3. The taxi driver's disturbance is reported in Rapport de Monsieur Miquel, Commissaire Central de Constantine sur les journées des 4 & 5 Août 1934, August 17, 1934 (henceforth Miquel Report). The archives contain at least two copies of this report. The first, preserved by the prefecture of Constantine, is in ANOM: ALG CONST 93/20020. The second, filed with the governor-general's office, is ANOM: ALG GGA 9/H/52.

4. Fusero Report, August 5.

5. René Miquel estimated the number of people at Les Pins to be seven to eight hundred (ANOM: ALG GGA 9/H/53), and the Bendjelloul Dossier contains a similar figure.

6. The figure of seven hundred to eight hundred comes from the Miquel Report (ANOM: ALG CONST 93/20020), and this figure is also given by witnesses in the Bendjelloul Dossier. The Sûreté Départementale's report of August 6, 1934, estimated two thousand (ANOM: ALG CONST 93/20019). Police agents Alliche and Abassi, on the other hand, said that the higher figures were much exaggerated. Abassi suggested that in reality there were fewer than two hundred, while Alliche said that there were only seventy people present when he arrived (ANOM: ALG GGA 9/H/53).

7. The Sûreté Départementale report of August 7 also emphasized the presence of Communist militants known to the police (ANOM: ALG GGA 9/H/52).

8. The time that the crowd began to file back over the bridge to the city of Constantine is given as 9 a.m. in a report from the Sûreté Départementale of August 7, 1934 (ANOM: ALG CONST 93/20019).

9. The false news of Bendjelloul's assassination is connected with the crowds returning from the aborted meeting at Les Pins in Charles-Robert Ageron, "Une émeute anti-juive à Constantine (août 1934)," *Revue de l'Occident musulman et de la Méditerranée* 13, no. 1 (1973): 26. Yves-Claude Aouate suggests that this rumor had already spread among those who waited for Bendjelloul at Les Pins, and that they found it confirmed by his absence.

10. Commissioner René Miquel's account of the scene after the Les Pins meeting on the morning of August 5 does not mention the men spreading the rumor of Bendjelloul's death. Miquel's report was filed nearly two weeks later, on August 17, at a moment when the higher reaches of the colonial administration were having second thoughts about press reports that sought to explain the riots in terms of a provocation led by a small group of conspirators (see chapter 12). Miquel Report (ANOM: ALG GGA 9/H/52).

11. Commission Report. Also cited in Mahfoud Kaddache, *Histoire du nationalisme algérien* (Paris/Alger: Éditions Paris-Méditerranée/Éditions EDIF 2000, 2003), vol. 2, 856–57. Ageron repeated this same suggestion in his 1973 article on the riots. Ageron, "Une émeute anti-juive à Constantine," 26.

12. Benmoussa's testimony is given in Gouvernement Général de l'Algérie, Préfecture de Constantine, Sûreté Départementale, Audition de Témoin, Procès-Verbal (no date, but in a file dated August 7, 1934, ANOM: ALG CONST 93/20019).

13. Police Commissioner Fusero later filed reports on the testimony of eight witnesses to the events that had immediately preceded the onset of violence on the place des Galettes on Sunday morning, August 5. The witness statements are included as addenda to Fusero's report of September 13, 1934 (ANOM: ALG GGA 9/H/53).

14. Reine Atlan statement to Lucien Fusero, August 23, 1934 (ANOM: ALG GGA 9/H/52).

15. Fusero's report of September 13, 1934 (ANOM: ALG GGA 9/H/53) identified Atlan as "Rose" and notes that a witness identified her as "la fille Tayeb." After the riot, a Muslim employee of the Jewish-owned Taïëb butcher shop in the rue de France was identified as having participated in the murders on August 5. See chapter 12.

16. Statement of Djohra Halimi taken by Lucien Fusero, August 23, 1934, ANOM: ALG GGA 9/H/52.

17. The files of the governor-general's investigating commission headed by Jean Vigouroux contained at least three different accounts of the gunshots on the place des Galettes on August 5. See Lucien Fusero's report on the Zaoui affair, Le Commissaire de Police du 2ᵉ Arrondissement à Monsieur le Président de la Commission d'enquête, Constantine, September 13, 1934 (Zaoui Dossier, ANOM: ALG GGA 9/H/53); the Miquel Report (ANOM: ALG GGA 9/H/52); and the Bendjelloul Dossier (ANOM: ALG GGA 9/H/53). The reports do not all coincide, indicating confusion and the possibility of multiple shooters. Miquel identified the house of Abraham Guedj; several of Bendjelloul's witnesses claimed that shots came from a house owned by a member of the Barkatz family. Other witnesses in Bendjelloul's dossier identified the origins of the gunshots as a hair salon owned by "Allouche," "the blinds on the window of the house above the café El Goufla," "the windows of the house of Dr Attal," "the Bitoun apartment," "women on the balcony of M. Attali and Halimi" who "threw projectiles and fired shots." Several witnesses in the Bendjelloul Dossier explicitly mentioned the Attali and Halimi residences, as if to provide some explanation of the murders of members of these families later in the day. These latter claims are not believable: the Attali and Halimi residences were not proximate to the place des Galettes, and the claims are contradicted by the testimony from a neighbor who witnessed the demonstrations unfolding in the street before the murders in the Attali home (see chapters 12 and 13 below).

18. Fusero's report of September 13, 1934, Zaoui Dossier, ANOM: ALG GGA 9/H/53.

19. Fusero's report of September 13 on the Zaoui affair does not mention Bendjelloul's presence, because it focuses on events before 9 a.m. Fusero's main report on the events of August 5 (see Fusero Report, August 5) contained more detail, including Bendjelloul's presence on the place exhorting the demonstrators to stop their attack on the police station. Concerning the events after 9 a.m., when the market disturbance turned into something much larger, Fusero's September 13 report became very general and contained little detail or specific times. The Bendjelloul Dossier puts the Muslim leader on the place des Galettes at 9:20 a.m.

20. Lucien Fusero (Fusero Report, August 5) described the crowd in deeply prejudicial and menacing terms: "Une foule d'indigènes au nombre de quinze cent à deux mille tous armés de matraques, cailloux, couteaux et même quelques uns de revolver, tous également furieux et surexcités, les faisant ressemblés à une herde de sauvages, se rouaient vers la rue de France par les rues Alcide Treille, Sidi-Lakdar et

rue Henri Namia." The Miquel Report repeated this figure of two thousand for the size of the crowd in the place des Galettes. If true, it would have been so crowded as to have made almost any movement impossible.

21. These details are from the Fusero Report, August 5.

22. Miquel Report.

23. Touam Chabane's statement, included in the Bendjelloul Dossier, is the most detailed account from a Muslim elected official. He recounted his efforts to prevent Jewish families from attempting to escape down the rue Nationale, directing them instead to an alternate route that brought them away from the fighting on the main thoroughfare. He also dissuaded a group of men from trying to set fire to a Jewish-owned business, "la firme Laloum." He succeeded by convincing them that the street was too narrow and that "they risked destroying a building owned by the French state and a *café maure.*" ANOM: ALG GGA 9/H/53.

24. Fusero Report, August 5.

25. General Kieffer testified that he received the first request for military reinforcements at 10:15 a.m. Déposition du Général Kieffer, Commandant la Division Territoriale de Constantine, September 7, 1934, ANOM: ALG GGA 9/H/53.

26. This scene is described in the deposition by Eugène Bourceret, member of the municipal council and delegate of the council to the police of Constantine, August 23, 1934, ANOM: ALG GGA 9/H/53.

27. Miquel Report.

28. Besse's testimony about Guedj's injury is in Commission Report, 44. The *Écho d'Alger* described Guedj's fatal injury as a skull fracture the following week. Historian Robert Attal appears to have relied on this later report in his book on the riots. Robert Attal, *Les émeutes de Constantine: 5 août 1934* (Paris: Éditions Romillat, 2002), 131.

29. The details of Abraham Bedoucha's murder are in Jacques Cauro, Rapport Spécial, no. 2408, August 18, 1934, ANOM: ALG GGA 9/H/52.

30. Lucien Ichoua Chemla's murder is recounted by Jacques Cauro of the Police Mobile, Rapport Spécial, no. 2407, August 18, 1934, ANOM: ALG GGA 9/H/52.

31. Two versions of Bentata's death are recounted in the police records. Jacques Cauro, Rapport Spécial, no. 2405, August 18, 1934, cited a claim by the accused, Said ben Ferhat Djabali, that Bentata fired on the protesters first (ANOM: ALG GGA 9/H/52). The second, reported in a letter from Ruben Robert Halimi to the Commission d'enquête, has the accused confessing to killing Bentata without any provocation (ANOM: ALG GGA 9/H/52). See discussion of the police investigation in chapter 12.

32. Miquel Report.

33. The Lucien Blanc procès-verbal from the Gendarmerie Nationale (no. 3805, August 23, 1934) contains a map of the scene. ANOM: ALG GGA 9/H/52.

34. Jacques Cauro, Rapport Spécial, no. 2391, Meurtre du nommé Akkacha Lachemi, August 17, 1934 (ANOM: ALG GGA 9/H/52). Cauro reported that Jacob Levy confessed to shooting Akkacha as he approached his store at number 72 rue Clémenceau (also referred to as the rue Nationale). Levy, a hairdresser, was later charged, but the shooting was ruled self-defense, and the case was dismissed. The Miquel Report identified the gunshots as coming from the Guedj family apartment, and this was repeated in an August 23 article published in *Le Républicain*, a newspaper

owned by Mayor Morinaud. Abraham Guedj formally protested in letters to Miquel and Jean Vigouroux, the president of the investigating commission (ANOM: ALG GGA 9/H/52).

35. Fusero's statement and these details come from Lucien Blanc, Procès-verbal constatant la mort d'un indigène au cours des émeutes du 5 août 1934, Victime: Akkacha (Lachemi), ANOM: ALG GGA 9/H/52.

36. Commission Report, 43.

37. Blanc's statement, among the most detailed, would place Akkacha's death between 11:30 and 12:00, or shortly thereafter. Lucien Fusero's statement to Lucien Blanc stated that the gunfire that killed Lachemi Akkacha "happened between noon and 1 p.m." Lucien Guedj, who was also in the Guedj family apartment, noted that he saw the men carrying Akkacha's body "between 11 a.m. and noon." Jacques Cauro's report on Akkacha's death (Rapport Spécial, no. 2391, August 17, 1934, ANOM: ALG GGA 9/H/52) does not mention a specific time at all, contenting itself with a vague reference to "the morning of August 5." Henri Coquelin, the director of departmental security, claimed to have seen a man shot on the rue Nationale at 10:15 a.m., and that this death was the cause of the frenzy that led the crowd to invade the homes and murder the Jewish families. Moving the time up to 10:15 made it easier to argue that everything that followed—the home invasions where thirteen people died—resulted from Jewish provocation and Muslim fanaticism, a conclusion that relieved local officials like himself of responsibility for the events. Henri Coquelin, Sûreté Départementale de Constantine, no. 2453, Antisémitisme, Rapport, August 8, 1934, ANOM: ALG GGA 9/H/52.

38. This issue came up in the trial in Orléansville in February 1936. Witnesses in the street testified about hearing gunfire. The family servants gave conflicting testimony: Turkia Benmerabet testified that Alphonse Halimi fired from the window at the rioters, while Rosette Benisti testified that Halimi did not fire his revolver until the door to the apartment gave way to the attackers. The surviving son, Roland Halimi, testified that his father could not have fired a gun because his revolver was old and did not work properly. See chapter 14. According to the list of injured Muslims prepared for the investigating commission by the civil hospital (État nominative des blessés indigènes admis en traitement à l'hôpital civil de Constantine, ANOM: ALG GGA 9/H/52), none of the fourteen men admitted with gunshot wounds on August 5 or 6 was shot on the rue Abdallah Bey.

39. The details of the Halimi-Zerdoun murders given here come from police reports, press accounts in the weeks that followed, press accounts of the trial in Orléansville in February 1936, and depositions of surviving family members given to the Commission d'enquête led by Jean Vigouroux. See Commission Report, Dépositions de M. Zerbib, Émile; M. Halimi, Roland; Mlle Benisti, Rosette, September 13, 1934.

40. Details on the family members present at the Attali home are from Armand Kessis, "Les cinq meurtres commis dans la maison Attali amènent 3 accusés devant la Cour Criminelle d'Orléansville," La Dépêche de Constantine, February 8, 1936. See also the deposition of Eugène Delaporte, Commission Report.

41. Armand Kessis, "La tragédie de la rue des Zouaves," La Dépêche de Constantine, February 8, 1936, 3.

42. Émile Kottman's statement was taken by Jacques Cauro, the chief of the Police Mobile. Audition du Témoin, Émile Kottman, August 11, 1934, ANOM: ALG GGA 9/H/52.

43. Commission Report, Deposition of Eugène Delaporte.

44. Déposition de Said Djemaa, Agent de Police, et de M. Delpla, Officier de Paix, Secrétaire du Commissariat Central, September 14, 1934, ANOM: ALG GGA 9/H/53.

45. Déposition de Said Djemaa, Agent de Police, et de M. Delpla, Officier de Paix, Secrétaire du Commissariat Central, September 14, 1934, 6, ANOM: ALG GGA 9/H/53.

46. "Les cinq meurtres commis dans la maison Attali amènent 3 accusés devant la Cour Criminelle d'Orléansville," *La Dépêche de Constantine*, February 8, 1936, 3.

47. Audition du Témoin, Émile Kottman, August 11, 1934, ANOM: ALG GGA 9/H/52.

48. Details of the Dadoun murders were not given in the initial police reports because their bodies were not found until later in the day, and there were no survivors to give an account of what happened. The information given here comes from Jacques Cauro, Rapport Spécial, no. 2474, Troubles de Constantine, August 24, 1934, ANOM: ALG GGA 9/H/52.

49. That the murders of Blanche Guedj and the Dadoun brothers in the rue Béraud occurred before the Attali family murders in the rue des Zouaves is supported by the testimony of Eugène Delaporte, who stated that the crowd of rioters that invaded the rue des Zouaves came from the rue Béraud. Commission Report, Deposition of Eugène Delaporte.

50. Attal, *Les émeutes de Constantine*, 294.

51. See Jacques Cauro, Chef de la Police Mobile de Constantine, Rapport Spécial, Sûreté Générale, Dépt. de Constantine, no. 2474 (ANOM: ALG GGA 9/H/52) for an assertion that many of these murders were all committed by the same small group of conspirators. See chapters 12 and 13 for an exploration of this investigation and the idea of conspiracy.

52. See accompanying map showing the proximity of the murder sites.

53. This figure of twenty out of twenty-five comes from adding up all the murders that occurred in this small neighborhood of the old city of Constantine between 9 a.m. and 1:30 p.m. It includes the eight people murdered in the Halimi apartment, the five people murdered in the Attali household, the three people murdered in the Dadoun brothers' office, and the murders of Lucien Ichoua Chemla, Abraham Bedoucha, Jacob Bentata, and Henri Guedj. The five deaths not attributable to any such small group are Elie Guedj (killed on the autobus on the place Lamorcière); Albert Halimi (killed on the autobus between Mila and Constantine); Michel Attal (killed in an attack on his farm in Bizot); Salomon Guedj (killed near his farm in Hamma-Plaisance); and René Nabet (clubbed and stabbed at an unknown location in Constantine on Sunday, August 5, and dying later from his wounds).

54. An account of the murder of Elie Guedj is in a report by Maurice (Marius) Gaillard, no. 2444, Homicide volontaire sur M. Guedj Elie, August 29, 1934 (ANOM: ALG GGA 9/H/52).

55. Miquel Report.

56. Émeutes du 3 au 5 août 1934, État nominative des blessés indigènes admis en traitement à l'hôpital civil de Constantine, ANOM: ALG GGA 9/H/52.

57. These figures come from a series of reports compiled by the prefect of Constantine on the basis of individual reports from administrators of nearby towns. See "État faisant ressortir la date d'arrivée à Constantine des Indigènes condamnés suivant la procédure des flagrants délits à la suite des Événements de Constantine," ANOM: ALG CONST 93/20020.

58. Kieffer Report.

59. Kieffer Report.

60. Kieffer Report.

61. This very point was made by Colonel Lavigne of the gendarmerie in his deposition to the Commission d'enquête on September 13, 1934. Lavigne criticized the military and police leadership for being too much in the heat of the action on the street and not coordinating the actions of their forces from above. Deposition of Colonel Lavigne, Commission d'Enquête Administrative sur les événements du département de Constantine, September 13, 1934, ANOM: ALG GGA 9/H/53.

62. Kieffer Report.

63. The timing of the distribution of cartridges was controversial. General Kieffer's report suggested that the order went out sometime after 2 p.m. Henri Coquelin, of the Sûreté Départementale, corroborated this, asserting that the crowds had quieted down by 3 p.m. after seeing the troops receiving ammunition. ANOM: ALG CONST 93/20019. Confino's report to the AIU in Paris claims that cartridges were not distributed until 5 p.m. This seems to have been a misperception. AAIU: Algérie 1C Antisémitisme 1.

64. Miquel Report.

65. Kieffer Report.

66. Kieffer Report.

67. General Kieffer claimed that the order to call up the *automitrailleuse* came from him, not from Commissioner Miquel (Kieffer Report).

68. Gouadain Report. This timing for the appearance of the armored cars on the street is confirmed by the deposition of the lawyer Lucien Bensimon to the Commission d'enquête, September 29, 1934 (ANOM: ALG GGA 9/H/53). Lucien Bensimon stated that he saw with his own eyes members of the crowd climbing on the armored cars and decorating them with textiles pillaged from Jewish businesses.

69. Fusero Report, August 5; Miquel Report.

70. See Commission Report, 55.

71. The incident of the "Vive la France!" banner was recounted publicly in a local newspaper at least once. Albert Rédarès was a prominent lawyer in Constantine and member of the political establishment, who served later as part of the defense team for the men charged with the Halimi-Zerdoun and Attali-Zerbib-Attal murders. By the end of the 1930s he was actively involved in the right-wing Parti social français, which emerged after the Croix de feu had been banned by the government. According to Rédarès, the banner read "Vive la France! Vive l'armée!" (Long live France! Long live the army!). Albert Rédarès, "Après la tourmente," *La Brèche*, August 18, 1934.

72. The reports from the Gendarmerie Nationale of August 6 suggest that the units stationed in Saint-Jean and Sidi-Mabrouk were quicker to react to pillaging in

these neighborhoods, and the damage there was much less extensive. ANOM: ALG GGA 9/H/52.

73. The events in Bizot are recounted in detail in Attal, *Les émeutes de Constantine*, 120–22. The author, Robert Attal, is the son of Michel Attal.

74. Information about these attacks in the region was summarized on August 6 in a telegram sent from the prefecture of Constantine to the office of the governor-general and the Direction of Native Affairs in Algiers. ANOM: ALG CONST 93/20020.

75. ANOM: ALG CONST 93/20019.

76. Athmane Saidi's death—with no accompanying name or circumstances—is mentioned in Attal, *Les émeutes de Constantine*, 132. Athmane Saidi's name, injury, and date of death are given in État nominative des blessés indigènes admis en traitement à l'hôpital civil de Constantine, Émeutes du 3 au 5 août 1934 (ANOM: ALG GGA 9/H/52). This list is also the source for the number of Muslim men admitted to the hospital with bullet wounds on August 5 and 6.

77. Robert Attal's list of victims, often reproduced elsewhere, includes "Raymond Nabet, 23 years old, died as a result of his wounds" ("Raymond Nabet, 23 ans, décédé des suites de ses blessures"). Attal, *Les émeutes de Constantine*, 131. The name "Raymond Nabet" does not appear on the lists of victims drawn up in the immediate aftermath of the riots by the police, but "René Nabet," age twenty-three, is listed in the hospital records preserved by the official investigating commission (État nominative des blessés israélites admis en traitement à l'hôpital civil de Constantine, ANOM: ALG GGA 9/H/52). René Nabet was admitted to the civil hospital in Constantine at 4:45 p.m. on August 5 with injuries to his skull and arm from being beaten with a club. An article in *L'Écho d'Alger* said that he had also been stabbed in the abdomen and that his medical status was "serious" ("Après les troubles sanglants de Constantine," *L'Écho d'Alger*, August 9, 1934, 3). According to the hospital record, René Nabet left the hospital "at his request" ("Sort sur sa dem.") on August 19. I have been unable to determine the date of his death.

78. Figures for the number of arrests and the number of stores pillaged come from the Commission Report, 62.

79. ANOM: ALG CONST B/3/250.

10. Shock and Containment

1. Rapport du Capitaine Sinibaldi, Commandant la Compagnie des Sapeurs-Pompiers, à Monsieur le Maire de Souk-Ahras, August 9, 1934, ANOM: ALG CONST B/3/250.

2. Rapport du Général de Division Kieffer, commandant la division de Constantine sur la participation de l'armée à la repression de trouble dans le département de Constantine, August 12, 1934, ANOM: ALG CONST 93/20020.

3. The mayor of Châteaudun ordered eighty-five Jews evacuated to Constantine on August 7. The Croix de feu chapter in Châteaudun was an active one, and it is difficult to avoid the conclusion that the mayor was using the riots as a pretext to encourage the departure of Jews from his town. The local military commander reported that the evacuation policy would be difficult to sustain because of the need to protect the empty houses of departed Jews, and also because any attempt by Jewish

families to return to their homes would produce more unrest. 19ᵉ Corps d'Armée, Gendarmerie Nationale, 19ᵉ Légion, 3ᵉ Compagnie, no. 228/2, Constantine, le 7 Août, 1934, Copie des messages téléphones ce jour à Monsieur le Gouverneur Général et au Général Commandant le 19ᵉ Corps d'Armée, relatifs aux événements survenus dans la journée, ANOM: ALG CONST 93/20019.

4. Cited in Robert Attal, "Un témoignage indédit sur le pogrom de Constantine (1934)," *Revue des études juives* 148, no. 1–2 (1989): 142.

5. Makhlouf Attali's words were reported in the press and also cited by Étienne Muracciole at the Orléansville trial of 1936. See, for example, Armand Kessis, "L'épilogue de la tuerie de la rue des Zouaves," *La Dépêche de Constantine*, February 9, 1936, 3.

6. ANOM: ALG GGA 2/CAB/5.

7. Eugène Vallet (1868–1950) was a former editor of Émile Morinaud's newspaper, *Le Républicain*, and a staunch defender of the colonial order.

8. Vallet, private letter to Governor-General Carde, dated August 6, 1934, ANOM: ALG GGA 2/CAB/4. Vallet later published his report and his letter to Carde, along with several other documents that blamed Algerian nationalists for the riots. Eugène Vallet, *Les événements de Constantine 5 août 1934 quelques documents* (Alger: Baconnier Frères, 1934).

9. Vallet, private letter to Governor-General Carde, dated August 6, 1934. ANOM: ALG GGA 2/CAB/4.

10. XIXᵐᵉ Corps d'Armée, Division Territoriale de Constantine, État-Major, no. TS/370, Objet: Incidents du 5 août, SECRET, Constantine, 8 août, 1934, ANOM: ALG CONST 93/20020.

11. "Les troubles antisémites de Constantine," *La Dépêche algérienne*, August 7, 1934, ANOM: ALG GGA 9/H/54.

12. Report by Henri Cocquelin, Sûreté Départementale de Constantine, no. 2466, Papillons, August 8, 1934, ANOM: ALG CONST 93/20019.

13. "Les événements de Constantine," *La Dépêche de Constantine*, August 9, 1934, 1.

14. "Les événements de Constantine," *La Dépêche de Constantine*, August 9, 1934, 1.

15. On the reactions to the riots in Constantine among Jews and Muslims in both Algeria and the metropole see Ethan Katz, "Between Emancipation and Persecution: Algerian Jewish Memory in the *Longue Durée* (1930–1970)," *Journal of North African Studies* 17, no. 5 (2012): 1–28.

16. Rapport du Contrôleur Général des Recherches Judiciaires, en mission spéciale à Constantine, sur les troubles survenus dans cette ville, ANOM: ALG GGA 9/H/52.

17. The statement, signed by twenty-two Muslim notables, including 'Abd el-Hamid Ben Badis and Mohamed Bendjelloul, is in ANOM: ALG CONST 93/20020.

18. See letter from Gustave Mercier, *délégué financier*, to Jean Vigouroux, president of the Commission d'enquête, August 21, 1934, ANOM: ALG GGA 9/H/53.

19. This was the language used by an investigator from the Ministry of Justice in the days after the riots. "Rapport du Contrôleur Général des Recherches Judiciaires, en mission spéciale de Constantine, sur les troubles survenus dans cette ville," August 9, 1934, ANOM: ALG GGA 9/H/52.

20. Telegram sent from prefecture of Constantine to the governor-general's office in Algiers, August 6, 1934, 15h00, ANOM: ALG CONST 93/20020.

21. ANOM: ALG GGA 2/CAB/4.

22. ANOM: ALG GGA 2/CAB/4.

23. "Des troubles à Constantine," *L'Écho d'Alger*, August 7, 1934.

24. Adolphe Sultan, Rapport de Monsieur Sultan, Avocat Conseiller Municipal à Constantine, August 9, 1934, ANOM: ALG GGA 9/H/53. A version of this report was published in *La Lumière*, August 18, 1934.

25. Letter no. 5466 sent to the *juge d'instruction* in Constantine, August 11, 1934, forwarded by the prefect to the commander of the gendarmerie, August 16, 1934, ANOM: ALG CONST B/3/250.

26. Letter from Pierre Cusin to Jean Vigouroux, president of the Commission d'enquête, August 19, 1934, ANOM: ALG GGA 9/H/53.

27. Albert Confino's report to the Alliance Israélite, dated August 15, 1934, is preserved in AAIU Algérie 1C Antisémitisme 1. Joseph Fisher (as Joseph Ariel) published his report later as "Un document inédit sur le pogrom à Constantine, 3–5 août 1934," *Das neue Israel* 17 (1964): 86–89, 193–203 (henceforth Fisher Report). For reasons that are explored in chapter 12, the executive board of the Comité des délégations juives refused to allow it to be made public at their August 20, 1934, meeting in Geneva. Fisher printed up to one hundred copies before the meeting, but the executive board refused to distribute them. Fisher kept two copies for himself: one was confiscated from his apartment by the Gestapo after he went into hiding in 1940, and the second he sent to Palestine. After the war he found this copy in the Zionist Archives in Jerusalem, and this was the version published in *Das neue Israel* in 1964 under the new name he adopted after the Second World War, Joseph Ariel.

28. The editors of *La Dépêche de Constantine* published an editorial on August 14 detailing the case for premeditation, concluding "To accept *a priori* and with closed eyes the easy thesis of spontaneous incidents is to voluntarily ignore the blinding truth." "Incidents spontanés," *La Dépêche de Constantine*, August 14, 1934. The police investigation of the "gang of throat slitters" is the subject of chapter 12.

29. ANOM: ALG GGA 2/CAB/4.

30. On Vigouroux's reputation as an antisemite see the Fisher Report and Yves-Claude Aouate, "Constantine 1934: Un pogrom 'classique,'" *Nouveaux cahiers—Alliance israélite universelle* 68 (1982): 52.

31. These figures are from the cover page of the commission's report. ANOM: ALG GGA 9/H/53.

32. An excerpt from the commission's report was published in the Constantine press in early January 1935. The full report is available in ANOM, and portions of it were published by historians later. See the portion published as an annex in Mahfoud Kaddache, *Histoire du nationalisme algérien*, 2 vols. (Alger: Société Nationale d'Édition et de Diffusion, 1980), 2:856–57

33. Commission Report, 3.

34. "Au Sud-Ouest et à l'Ouest, le Plateau du Koudiat, les avenues Bienfait et du 11 novembre ouvrent l'accès direct de la campagne par des routes à forte déclivité, tandis qu'à proximité du pont de Sidi Rached s'érige le 'Remblai' où grouillent 2 à 3,000 indigènes misérables. Cette topographie si spéciale évoque les difficultés qu'ont rencontrées nos troupes d'Afrique pour s'emparer de Constantine." Commission Report, 6.

35. For the history of these census categories in Algeria see Kamel Kateb, *Européens, "Indigènes," et Juifs en Algérie (1830–1962): Représentations et réalités des populations* (Paris: INED, 2001).

36. Commission Report, 5.

37. Le Commissaire Central de la Ville de Constantine à Monsieur le Préfet de Constantine, August 21, 1934, ANOM: ALG GGA 9/H/52.

38. Commission Report, 6.

39. See for example a report from the administrator of Takitount, a *commune mixte* near Sétif, October 13, 1937. Surveillances des Indigènes, Correspondances, ANOM: 9 H 18. Yves-Claude Aouate also refutes the arguments made at the time about Jews and usury. See Aouate, "Constantine 1934," 52.

40. Commission Report, 35. Historian Robert Attal also presented his narrative of August 5 in terms of "the Jewish thesis" and "the Muslim thesis." Attal, *Les émeutes de Constantine*, 78, 95.

41. Henri Lellouche, Rapport sur les événements tragiques du 5 août 1934, ANOM: ALG GGA 9/H/53.

42. Bendjelloul Dossier, "Proclamation."

11. Empire of Fright

1. These reports are explored in chapter 12.

2. *Le Tam Tam*, September 1, 1934, 1. Lanxade used Adolphe Abraham Sultan's Hebrew name to draw attention to his Jewishness. Official documents from the municipal council, where Sultan held a seat, invariably used his French name. Perhaps aware of the difficulty of sorting out the competing pressures that converged in his person, Sultan himself invariably signed his letters and published articles "A. Sultan."

3. *Le Tam Tam*, September 8, 1934, 1.

4. Sûreté Départementale de Constantine, no. 2705, Antisémitisme, Rapport, August 28, 1934, ANOM: ALG GGA 9/H/52. See also Sûreté Départementale de Constantine, no. 2716, Antisémitisme, Rapport, August 29, 1934, ANOM: ALG GGA 9/H/52.

5. Surveillance Consécutive aux Événements de Constantine, 1935, Sûreté Départementale d'Alger, no. 5077, September 5, 1934, ANOM: ALG ALGER 2/i/38. A bottle merchant from Algiers stated that Ben Badis had advised him "to abstain from any antisemitic expressions because if any such movement broke out in Algiers, [the authorities] would be quick to say that Muslims were obeying a command from above."

6. Comité d'action et de solidarité en faveur des musulmans algériens victimes de la répression à Constantine. Sûreté Départementale de Constantine, no. 2716, Antisémitisme, August 29, 1934. On the ENA and antisemitism at this moment see especially Ethan Katz, *The Burdens of Brotherhood: Jews and Muslims from North Africa to France* (Cambridge, MA: Harvard University Press, 2015), 87–90.

7. The ENA had already been banned in France and officially dissolved when this tract was sent, and the organization would be convicted in October 1934 of illegally resuming a banned association. Claude Collot and Jean-Robert Henry, *Le movement national algérien: Textes 1912–1954* (Paris: Harmattan, 1978), 49–53.

8. Sûreté Départementale de Constantine, no. 2551, Surveillance politique des indigènes, Rapport, August 16. 1934, ANOM: ALG GGA 2/CAB/5. The author of this report, Henri Coquelin, viewed with skepticism Bendjelloul's promise to curtail his political ambitions.

9. Sûreté Départementale de Constantine, no. 2655, Antisémitisme, Rapport, August 24, 1934, ANOM: ALG GGA 2 / CAB / 5.

10. "La dame Marchika est une déséquilibrée qui agit sous l'empire de la frayeur." Ville de Constantine, Cabinet du Commissaire Central, no. 5312, Constantine, le 25 Août 1934, Le Commissaire Central de la Ville de Constantine à Monsieur le Président de la commission d'enquête administrative, ANOM: ALG GGA 9 / H / 52. Two days earlier Miquel had downplayed a different report from a Jewish woman, Rosa Kalifa, who had claimed that a man threatened her with a knife as she crossed the Plateau du Coudiat the day before, saying that the facts recounted by Kalifa were "purely fantastical and imaginary."

11. Ville de Constantine, Cabinet du Commissaire Central, no. 5190, Constantine, le 21 août 1934, Le Commissaire Central de la Ville de Constantine à Monsieur le Président de la commission d'enquête administrative, ANOM: ALG GGA 9 / H / 52.

12. Le commissaire Central de la Ville de Constantine à Monsieur le Président de la Commission d'Enquête Administrative, August 31, 1934, ANOM: ALG GGA 9 / H / 52.

13. See for example the letter from Gustave Mercier to Jean Vigouroux, August 21, 1934, ANOM: ALG GGA 9 / H / 52.

14. Algérie, Département de Constantine, Commune du Khroub, Rapport Spécial, Le Maire de la Commune du Khroub à MM. le Gouverneur général de l'Algérie, le Préfet du Département de Constantine, August 7, 1934, ANOM: ALG GGA 2 / CAB / 4.

15. The administrator from Haut-Sebaou reported a stream of rumors to the governor-general's office from mid-August onward. See Événements de Constantine, 1934–1935, ANOM: ALG ALGER 2 / i / 38.

16. Préfecture de Constantine, Cabinet, no. 6429, Le Préfet du Département de Constantine à Monsieur le Préfet, Alger. Affaires Indigènes. September 28, 1934, ANOM: ALG ALGER 2 / i / 38, Événements de Constantine, 1934–1935.

17. Gouvernement Général de l'Algérie, Préfecture de Constantine, Sûreté Départementale, Procès-Verbal d'Audition, September 7, 1934, ANOM: ALG CONST B / 3 / 250.

18. In the accounts of Jewish witnesses to the riots, however, stories about Europeans in Arab clothing continued to circulate for years after the event. See for example the testimony of an unidentified Jewish eyewitness given in the form of marginal notes to the report on the riots published by Eugène Vallet. These notes were published in Robert Attal, "Un témoignage inédit sur le pogrom de Constantine (1934)," *Revue des études juives* 148, no. 1–2 (1989): 133.

19. Événements de Constantine 1934–1935, ANOM: ALG ALGER 2 / i / 38. This note appears attached to a report from the gendarmerie in Birkadem, dated August 28, 1934.

20. See for example the story of anti-Jewish stickers in Arabic distributed in July 1933 by Alexandre Toulon, a proprietor of a commercial garage in Khenchela, a provincial town to the south of Constantine. The stickers claimed that five centimes of every five francs spent in a Jewish shop went to buy arms for killing Arabs in Palestine. Toulon, who told the printer that the phrases in Arabic were verses from the Quran, distributed the stickers to encourage local members of Bendjelloul's Fédération to adopt an anti-Jewish platform. ANOM: ALG CONST B / 3 / 249.

21. See Sûreté Départementale de Constantine, no. 2619, Antisémitisme, Rapport, August 21, 1934, ANOM: ALG GGA 2/CAB/5.

22. Le Commissaire Central de la Ville de Constantine à Monsieur le Préfet, December 22, 1934, ANOM: ALG CONST 93/6740.

23. They concluded that the very rich would not leave because of their property interests. The very poor did not have the means to emigrate. Only the Jewish middle classes were in a position to migrate to metropolitan France. Sûreté Départementale de Constantine, no. 2634, Antisémitisme, Rapport, August 22, 1934, ANOM: ALG GGA 2/CAB/5.

24. The sources of these reports were disputed. The police interviewed Muslim leaders, who claimed that rumors of an invasion of the city by Muslims on the day of Bendjelloul's trial were being spread by Jews. Sûreté Départementale de Constantine, no. 2919, Antisémitisme, Rapport, September 13, 1934, ANOM: ALG GGA 2/CAB/5.

25. See the documents on this incident in ANOM: ALG GGA 2/CAB/5. Cheikh Raymond's assassination on June 22, 1961, precipitated the departure of Constantine's Jews from the city at the moment of Algerian independence. His death marked the end of the ideal that his career symbolized for many—the celebration of a common culture shared by Muslims and Jews in North Africa.

26. Sûreté Départementale de Constantine, Antisémitisme, Rapport, September 18, 1934, ANOM: ALG GGA 2/CAB/5.

27. The police report noted as well that Amri's sister was married to one of Bendjelloul's political adversaries. This relative by marriage was none other than Mohamed Ben Badis, member of the *délégations financières* and father of 'Abd al-Hamid Ben Badis of the Association des ulémas.

28. Sûreté Départementale de Constantine, Antisémitisme, Rapport, September 18, 1934, ANOM: ALG GGA 2/CAB/5.

29. Sûreté Départementale de Constantine, no. 3020, Affiches, September 18, 1934, ANOM: ALG GGA 2/CAB/5. The poster was signed by nine Muslim elected officials from Constantine, including Mohamed Ben Badis of the *délégations financières*, and eight members of the municipal council, including Salah Améziane and Allaoua Bendjelloul (the brother of Mohamed).

30. Sûreté Départementale de Constantine, no. 3031, Antisémitisme, Rapport, September 19, 1934, ANOM: ALG GGA 2/CAB/5.

31. Sûreté Départementale de Constantine, no. 3208, Surveillance politique des indigènes, September 29, 1934, ANOM: ALG CONST 93/B3/277.

32. Bendjelloul's FEMC, a political group, and Ben Badis's Association of Muslim Ulamas, which was devoted to religious and cultural work, had many common members, but the crisis after August 5 had opened up fissures between the two organizations. Bendjelloul, for example, sought to shore up his credibility with Muslim constituents by creating new educational associations, an area that the ulamas had traditionally seen as their own. On efforts to broker an agreement between the two men see Sûreté Départementale de Constantine, no. 3670, Surveillance politique des indigènes, October 27, 1934, ANOM: ALG CONST 93/B3/277.

33. See the reports on these trials in ANOM: ALG ALGER 2/i/38. By the end of October sixty-two more men were convicted in similar trials.

34. Sûreté Départementale de Constantine, no. 3069, Antisémitisme, Rapport, September 20, 1934, ANOM: ALG GGA 2/CAB/5.

35. Le Préfet du Département de Constantine à Monsieur le Gouverneur Général, October 18, 1934, ANOM: ALG CONST 93/6740.

36. Le Commissaire Central de la Ville de Constantine à Monsieur le Préfet, December 22, 1934, ANOM: ALG CONST 93/6740. The M'Zabite shopkeepers in the textile trade depended on very few wholesale merchants, including the Comptoir Textile de Cirta, the only European-owned wholesale textile firm, but also several Jewish-owned wholesalers. In order to prevent their continued business relationships with Jewish suppliers from becoming public knowledge, the M'Zabite businesses placed their orders by telephone and had the merchandise put in consignment at the central train station. This ruse was eventually discovered, and for a time the M'Zabite firms themselves were threatened with boycotts, but they continued to resupply their stocks from Jewish wholesale merchants.

37. Le Préfet du Département de Constantine à Monsieur le Gouverneur Général, October 18, 1934, ANOM: ALG CONST 93/6740. The report noted that there also seemed to be a movement to establish new Muslim-owned businesses to compete with Jewish textile merchants, and he cited a report by a notary who had attended a meeting at the home of Mohamed Bendjelloul to create a new textile wholesale company.

38. Le Préfet du Département de Constantine à Monsieur le Gouverneur Général, October 18, 1934, ANOM: ALG CONST 93/6740.

39. The police had little specific information on the boycott's origins. They reported that many in the city suspected the whole affair had been organized by the M'Zabite businessmen. Others—and this apparently included some Jewish retailers—suspected a collusion between M'Zabite retailers and Jewish wholesalers who had not wanted to extend credit to Jewish businesses severely weakened financially after the riot. The Jewish population as a whole continued to see the hand of Bendjelloul and the political leaders of the Muslim population in the boycott—and the police apparently accepted this possibility as well. It is possible that Bendjelloul may have encouraged the boycott once it was under way. It is also possible that the influence went the other way—that as the boycott continued, Bendjelloul began to see the potential arguments for catering to Muslim anger about their treatment after August 5. Le Commissaire Central de la Ville de Constantine à Monsieur le Préfet, December 22, 1934, ANOM: ALG CONST 93/6740.

40. Conseil général de Constantine, Politique indigène, Événements du 5 août 1934, Extrait du Procès-verbal de la séance du 28 Octobre 1934, ANOM: ALG CONST 93/B/3/277.

41. Conseil général de Constantine, Politique indigène, Événements du 5 août 1934, Extrait du Procès-verbal de la séance du 28 Octobre 1934.

42. Conseil général de Constantine, Politique indigène, Événements du 5 août 1934, Extrait du Procès-verbal de la séance du 28 Octobre 1934.

43. Conseil général de Constantine, Politique indigène, Événements du 5 août 1934, Extrait du Procès-verbal de la séance du 28 Octobre 1934.

44. Conseil général de Constantine, Politique indigène, Événements du 5 août 1934, Extrait du Procès-verbal de la séance du 28 Octobre 1934.

45. Département de Constantine, El-Milia, Commune Mixte, no. 6261, Objet: Dr. Bendjelloul, September 26, 1934, ANOM: ALG CONST 93/B3/277.

46. Sûreté Départementale de Constantine, no. 4053, November 23, 1934, ANOM: ALG CONST 93/B3/277.

47. The theater piece was Mahieddine Bachetarzi's *Phaqo* (Eyes opened!). Département de Constantine, Sous-préfecture de Philippeville, no. 7571, November 23, 1934, ANOM: ALG GGA 9/H/37.

48. Bendjelloul also refused to support Zenati's son, another candidate for a seat on the *délégations financières*. Zenati's son, like his father, was a naturalized French citizen, and Bendjelloul knew that his supporters were suspicious of candidates who were too close to French culture and society. See ANOM: ALG CONST 93/B3/277.

49. Sûreté Départementale de Constantine, no. 379, Surveillance politique des Indigènes, January 26, 1935, ANOM: ALG CONST 93/B/3/278.

50. The vote counts are given in Élections délégations financières, Sûreté Départementale de Constantine, no. 389, Résultat des élections aux Délégations financières, January 28, 1935, ANOM: ALG CONST 93/B/3/278. The suggestion that Hadj Said Mokhtar was the candidate of the administration is in Sûreté Départementale de Constantine, no. 188, January 15, 1935, ANOM: ALG CONST 93/B/3/278.

51. The governor-general's report on the riot of February 2, 1935, in Sétif is in Cabinet du Gouverneur Général de l'Algérie, no. 716, February 2, 1935, ANOM: ALG GGA 9/H/20.

52. A Jewish observer, Simon Bakhouche, suggested that the rioting riflemen knew that the policeman who shot their comrade was not Jewish. Their target was the French administration, not the Jews. Bakhouche also suggested that the FEMC had moved closer to the Jews after December 1934 because they had nothing to gain from "a racial struggle." Bakhouche's letter seems to confirm that Bendjelloul's increasingly open antisemitism in the fall of 1934 created divisions within the FEMC. Letter from Simon Bakhouche to Rabbi Maurice Eisenbeth, February 7, 1935, AAIU: 1C Antisémitisme. On settler antisemitism and Algerian Muslims see Emmanuel Debono, "Antisémites européens et musulmans en Algérie après le pogrom de Constantine (1934–1939)," *Revue d'histoire dela Shoah* 2, no. 187 (2007): 305–28.

53. "Après Constantine, Aïn-Beïda, et Jemmapes, voici le tour de Sétif," *L'Écho de l'Est*, February 7, 1935.

54. Copy of a letter from Émile Morinaud to the prefect of Constantine, January 28, 1935, ANOM: ALG CONST 93/B/3/278.

12. The Police Investigation

1. The police work of Cauro's team was overseen by three *juges d'instruction*: Pralus, Douvreleur, and Turin.

2. "Un des assassins de la famille ATTALI est arrêté. Le muertrier fait des aveux," *La Dépêche de Constantine*, August 14, 1934.

3. See chapter 14.

4. "Comment fut arrêté l'un des assassins de la famille Attali," *L'Écho d'Alger*, August 15, 1934.

5. "Un des assassins de la famille ATTALI est arrêté. Le muertrier fait des aveux," *La Dépêche de Constantine*, August 14, 1934. The same scene was described the next day in "Comment fut arrêté l'un des assassins de la famille Attali," *L'Écho d'Alger*, August 15, 1934.

6. "Comment fut arrêté l'un des assassins de la famille Attali," *L'Écho d'Alger*, August 15, 1934.

7. "Comment fut arrêté l'un des assassins de la famille Attali."

8. "Trois nouvelles arrestations. Les meurtriers de M. Chemla et du tailleur Bedoucha, arrêtés, font des aveux," *La Dépêche de Constantine*, August 15, 1934.

9. "Trois nouvelles arrestations," *La Dépêche de Constantine*, August 15, 1934.

10. The police report of August 18 makes clear that the police had already identified an additional person as being a suspect in the Chemla killing, Ahmed ben Mohamed Hamireche. Hamireche had fled Constantine, however, and it is probable that the police decided not to leak his name until he could be apprehended. By August 24 he had been caught, and his name appears in the report of that date. Sûreté Générale, no. 2407, Rapport Spécial, August 18, 1934, ANOM: ALG GGA 9/H/52.

11. "Trois nouvelles arrestations," *La Dépêche de Constantine*, August 15, 1934.

12. "Trois nouvelles arrestations," *La Dépêche de Constantine*, August 15, 1934.

13. "Trois nouvelles arrestations," *La Dépêche de Constantine*, August 15, 1934.

14. A slightly different story appeared in *L'Écho d'Alger* concerning the connection between Abdallah Benhamama and Abraham Bedoucha's murder. The Algiers paper simply implied that the arrest of Abdallah Benhamama's son had led to the father's arrest the next day, without mentioning Rosette Benisti. "Après les émeutes de Constantine. La Commission administrative a commencé hier son enquête," *L'Écho d'Alger*, August 15, 1934, 4.

15. Gouvernement Général de l'Algérie, Département de Constantine, Sûreté Générale, no. 2391, Rapport Special, August 17, 1934, ANOM: ALG GGA 9/H/52. In some later reports, Jacob Levy is identified as Gaston Levy.

16. Sûreté Générale, no. 2405, Rapport Spécial, August 18, 1934, ANOM: ALG GGA 9/H/52.

17. Sûreté Générale, no. 2406, Rapport Spécial, August 18, 1934, ANOM: ALG GGA 9/H/52.

18. Sûreté Générale, no. 2407, Rapport Spécial, August 18, 1934, ANOM: ALG GGA 9/H/52.

19. "Rapport Spécial, no. 2474, Troubles de Constantine (4, 5 et 6 Août 1934)," August 24, 1934, ANOM: ALG GGA 9/H/52.

20. The complete list of incidents and arrested individuals as of August 24 was as follows:

Rue des Zouaves: Attali, Attal, and Zerbib families. Two arrests:

TABTI Mohamed ben Ahmed

BENAMIRA Tayeb ben Saïd (aka "Santo")

Rue Abdallah Bey: Halimi and Zerdoun families. One arrest:

BENAMIRA Tayeb ben Saïd (aka "Santo")

Rue Béraud: Jacob Bentata. One arrest:

DJEBALI Saâd ben Ferhat

Rue Béraud: Abraham Bedoucha. Two arrests:

BENHAMAMA Abdallah ben Mohamed

BENAMIRA Tayeb ben Saïd (aka "Santo")

Rue Germon: Lucien Chemla. Five arrests:

BENAMIRA Tayeb ben Saïd (aka "Santo")
BENHAMAMA Saïd ben Youcef [sic]
HACHICHE Rabah ben Salah
TAKOUK Mohamed ben Amar
HAMIRECHE Ahmed ben Mohamed

Avenue Sétif: Elie Guedj. Five arrests:

KAHLALOU Mohamed ben Ahmed
LAID ben Said
BOUGHALOUT Hocine ben Nouar
HARBOUCHE Amar ben Tahar
DOULA Boudjemaâ ben Hamou

Rue Clémenceau (ex-rue Nationale): Lachemi Akacha. One arrest:

LEVY Gaston

Sûreté Générale, no. 2474, Rapport Spécial, August 24, 1934, ANOM: 9/H/52. Note that the Police Mobile made no attempt to charge anybody with the murders of the Dadoun brothers and their secretary Blanche Guedj. Their bodies had been found only later, and there were no witnesses. These murders were nevertheless also on the rue Béraud and were very close to the Halimi and Attali apartments.

21. Sûreté Générale, no. 2474, Rapport Spécial, August 24, 1934, ANOM: ALG GGA 9/H/52.

22. For example, Cauro described the meeting convened by Secretary-General Landel at the prefecture on Saturday, August 4—a meeting that included both Jewish and Muslim elected officials—as having "taken place in the best spirit of conciliation."

23. Sûreté Générale, no. 2474, Rapport Spécial, August 24, 1934, ANOM: ALG GGA 9/H/52.

24. Cabinet du Gouverneur Général de l'Algérie, NOTE, September 4, 1934. ANOM: ALG GGA 2/CAB/4.

25. See chapter 10.

26. Ruben Halimi was also the brother of Maurice Halimi, who was involved in the dispute that led to the shooting of Léon Minoum on July 24, and the father of Charles Halimi, whose beating on August 3 led to the confrontation between Inspector Gassab and Mohamed Bendjelloul (see chapter 8).

27. Halimi's letter to Vigouroux is dated only "September 1934," but its position in a chronological file of communications to the commission seems to indicate that it was written around September 6, 1934. See letter from Ruben Robert Halimi to Monsieur Vigouroux, Président de la Commission d'Enquête, September 1934, ANOM: ALG GGA 9/H/52.

28. It is possible that Halimi's intervention is what produced the additional arrests reported by Cauro later that month. Halimi's letter is the only account of these arrests I was able to find in the papers of the Vigouroux commission.

29. Albert Confino's letter of August 17, 1934, to the Central Consistory in Paris noted Sultan's correspondence with Henri Guernut, AAIU Algérie 1C Antisemitism 1.

30. These details are from Ariel (Fisher), Joseph, "Un document inédit sur le pogrom à Constantine, 3–5 août 1934," *Das neue Israel* 17 (1964): 86–89, 193–203.

31. A carbon copy of Joseph Fisher's report, retyped and unattributed to its author, is in ANOM: FM 81/F/864, in a collection of papers related to Interior Minister Marcel Régnier's visit to Algeria in 1935. Historian Sophie Roberts's account incorrectly attributes this copy of the Fisher report to Marcel Régnier himself and accepts its overall argument rather uncritically; see Roberts, *Citizenship and Antisemitism in French Colonial Algeria, 1870–1962* (Cambridge: Cambridge University Press, 2017), 189. There is much that is of value in Fisher's account, but it is important to recognize that his claim that people associated with Mohamed Bendjelloul were responsible for provoking the riot is only a reflection of what Jewish leaders in Constantine believed in the immediate aftermath of August 5. The evidence suggests that Jewish leaders in Constantine moved away from this initial belief in the weeks after Fisher's visit.

32. Sultan's correspondence can be found in the Fonds Ligue des droits de l'homme, BDIC F delta res 798 (169).

33. The circumstances of the August 20, 1934, meeting in Geneva are described in World Jewish Congress, *Unity in Dispersion: A History of the World Jewish Congress* (New York: World Jewish Congress, 1948), 36–39.

34. The arrests of Boulkraa and Ziad came after the police received tips about young men boasting of having killed Jews on August 5. "Les Événements de Constantine, À la recherche des coupables, Nouvelles arrestations," *La Dépêche de Constantine*, August 29, 1934. See also "Après les émeutes de Constantine. La Police arrête deux indigènes qui ont participé au massacre de la famille Halimi," *L'Écho d'Alger*, August 30, 1934.

35. "Les événements de Constantine. À la recherche des coupables. Un récit de la fin tragique de Mlle Ausélia Attali," *La Dépêche de Constantine*, August 31, 1934.

36. Sûreté Générale, no. 2606, Rapport Spécial, September 10, 1934, ANOM: ALG GGA 9/H/53.

37. The murder trials for the other victims are easily found by searching online newspaper databases such as Gallica under the names of the victims. I have been unable to find any evidence that a trial for the murder of Abraham Bedoucha ever took place.

13. The Agitator

1. The note is undated, but it must have been written in the days after January 22, 1938, shortly after the judge issued the arrest warrant for Jean Filiol mentioned in the text. ANOM: ALG GGA 9/H/49 (36/H/4).

2. Filiol's name is often spelled "Filliol." On Filiol's role in the Cagoule see Philippe Bourdrel, *La Cagoule: 30 ans de complots* (Paris: Albin Michel, 1970); Robert Soucy, *French Fascism: The Second Wave, 1933–1939* (New Haven, CT: Yale University Press, 1995), 46–53; Gayle K. Brunelle and S. Annette Finley-Croswhite, *Murder in the Métro: Laetitia Toureaux and the Cagoule in 1930s France* (Baton Rouge: LSU Press, 2010). On Filiol's activities in the Second World War see Brigitte Delluc and Gilles Delluc, *Jean Filliol, du Périgord à la Cagoule, de la Milice à Oradour* (Périgueux: Pilote 24, 2005). Jean Filiol never paid the price for his many crimes. He fled to Spain after the war, and Franco's nationalist government refused to extradite him back to France to face trial. He was condemned to death in absentia. He worked for the Spanish office of L'Oréal for many decades before his death.

3. For an account of the attractions of fascism among the Algerian population in the 1930s see Pascal Blanchard, "La vocation fasciste de l'Algérie coloniale dans les années 1930," in De l'Indochine à l'Algérie: La jeunesse en mouvements des deux côtés du miroir colonial, 1940–1962 (Paris: La Découverte, 2003), 177–94.

4. A useful summary of Mohamed El Maadi's career is in Ethan Katz, The Burdens of Brotherhood: Jews and Muslims from North Africa to France (Cambridge, MA: Harvard University Press, 2015), 133–37.

5. All these details on Mohamed El Maadi's military service are contained in the 156-page personnel file kept at the French military archives. The file contains several handwritten copies of his "Livret Matricule d'Officier," which give, among other things, his service record and dates of transfer. SHD: GR 8Y 128830.

6. Liste nominative des officiers, sous officiers et soldats blessés ou contusionnés au cours des événements qui se sont produits pendant les journées des 3; 4; et 5 août 1934, ANOM: ALG GGA 9/H/52.

7. Commission d'Enquête Administrative sur les Événements de Constantine, Déposition de Monsieur Alliche, Inspecteur de la Police Municipale, September 12, 1934, 9, ANOM: ALG GGA 9/H/53.

8. Séfia is now known as Mechroha.

9. El Maadi's French citizenship was often mentioned by police reporting on his activities in the 1930s. See for example Le Préfet de Police à Monsieur le Ministre de l'Intérieur, no. 40189, November 25, 1937. The note states: "Maadi, qui serait issu d'une famille de caïds algériens, serait français par ses parents." AN: 19920648/3.

10. The information on El Maadi's and his family members' citizenship comes from marriage, birth, and death certificates in the État Civil for French Algeria, available online from ANOM.

11. Abdellali Merdaci, Auteurs algériens de langue française de la période coloniale: Dictionnaire biographique (Paris: Harmattan, 2010), 116–17.

12. During the right-wing riots in Paris of February 6, 1934, El Maadi fought the police alongside marchers affiliated with Jean Renaud's Solidarité française. See Annie Rey-Goldzeiguer, Aux origines de la guerre d'Algérie: De Mers-El-Kébir aux massacres du nord-constantinois (Paris: Découverte, 2002), 50–51.

13. Military service record of Mohamed El Maadi, SHD: GR 8Y 128830.

14. Benmoussa's testimony is given in a procès-verbal that is part of a file dated August 7, 1934. ANOM: ALG CONST 93/20019. Benmoussa's report does not appear to have been included in the documents considered by the Vigouroux commission.

15. Djemaa's account is confirmed in its broadest outlines by the fact that his rescue of Moise and Zaïra Zerbib's three-year-old daughter was brought up at the trial in Orléansville on February 7, 1936. Armand Kessis, "Les cinq meurtres commis dans la maison Attali amènent 3 accusés devant la Cour Criminelle d'Orléansville," La Dépêche de Constantine, February 8, 1936, 3.

16. Kessis, "Les cinq meurtres commis dans la maison Attali."

17. Deposition of Lieutenant Carbonnel, ANOM: ALG GGA 9/H/53.

18. Two documents from August 1934 place Mohamed El Maadi by name at the Attali family's building at the moment the murders were taking place: (1) the injury report from his regiment, the Third Zouaves; and (2) the deposition of Lieutenant Carbonnel. Subsequent documents confirm his presence: (1) the citation for

his military medal awarded in December 1934; and (2) newspaper reports of his testimony at the trial of the alleged murderers of the Attali family that took place in February 1936. ALG GGA 9/H/52. El Maadi's injuries are described as "pistol shot wound of the hand, bruise on right thigh (blow from paving stone)." The time and place: "5 August 1934 . . . rue du 3ᵉ Zouaves entre 13 et 14 H." The deposition of Lieutenant Carbonnel is in ANOM: ALG GGA 9/H/53.

19. Roger Faligot and Rémi Kauffer, *Le croissant et la croix gammée: Les secrets de l'alliance entre l'Islam et le nazisme d'Hitler à nos jours* (Paris: Albin Michel, 1990), 123.

20. "Cagoule" means "hooded cloak." For a general history of the Cagoule see Philippe Bourdrel, *La Cagoule: Histoire d'une société secrète du Front populaire à la Vᵉ République* (Paris: Albin Michel, 1992). See also Robert Soucy, *French Fascism: The Second Wave, 1933–1939* (New Haven, CT: Yale University Press, 1995), 46–50. For an account of the Cagoule and the participation in the French Resistance of some of its members see Valerie Deacon, *The Extreme Right in the French Resistance: Members of the Cagoule and Corvignolles in the Second World War* (Baton Rouge: LSU Press, 2016).

21. Filiol's habit of having his recruits swear their loyalty in a ritual fashion is recounted in several witness accounts. Jean Berger-Buchy stated that Filiol remarked after his oath that "those who betray us will be found one day in the Seine." Interrogation of Jean Berger-Buchy by Pierre Béteille, September 10, 1937, AN: 19920648/3. See also, in the same carton, "Résumé Affaire 'l'Algérie française.'"

22. The police records documenting Mohamed El Maadi's interrogation after his arrest and his recruitment by Filiol are in AN: 19920648/3.

23. The murder of Dimitri Navachine is recounted in Brunelle and Finley-Croswhite, *Murder in the Métro*, 82–87. Prefecture of Police files on the Navachine murder are in APP: BA 1658.

24. The death of Toureaux is a central thread of Brunelle and Finley-Croswhite, *Murder in the Métro.*

25. AN: 19920648/3 contains separate dossiers on both *Le Courrier royal* and *L'Algérie française.*

26. Note, Résumé Affaire "l'Algérie française," AN: 19920648/3. Undated: prepared by an inspector of the Police Mobile.

27. See for example the description of the *soupes populaires* organized by the Croix de feu in Jacques Nobécourt, *Le Colonel de La Rocque (1885–1946), ou, Les pièges du nationalisme chrétien* (Paris: Fayard, 1996), 383.

28. Le Préfet de Police à Monsieur le Ministre de l'Intérieur, no. 40189, November 25, 1937, AN: 19920648/3.

29. Le Préfet de Police à Monsieur le Ministre de l'Intérieur, no. 40189, November 25, 1937.

30. This conversation took place during a meeting of Algérie française when Filiol was present. See Note, Résumé Affaire "l'Algérie française," AN: 19920648/3. El Maadi recounted the same exchange with slightly different wording in his interrogation by Pierre Béteille, November 10, 1937 (copy in the same carton).

31. The results of this long surveillance between February and September 1937 are summarized in a Report by Commissaire de Police Mobile Jobard to the Commissaire de Police, chef de la 2ᵉᵐᵉ Section de l'Inspection Générale des Services de Police Criminelle, September 8, 1937, AN: 19920648/1.

32. The circumstances of El Maadi's arrest are summarized in "Le Général Du-seigneur consigné à la disposition de la justice," *Le Figaro*, November 25, 1937, 1, 3. In fact, two lines of investigation led to him. In addition to the payment records found on Jakubiez, El Maadi's name had also come up in the investigation of Jean Filiol and Algérie française. There was nothing illegal about El Maadi's work as a "publi-cist." It was the connection with Jakubiez's arms smuggling and his closer connec-tion to Filiol that put El Maadi in jail for eight months. Faci and Hamouni were only briefly held before being released under "provisional liberty" while the investigation proceeded.

33. "Les 'cagoulards' sont renvoyés devant la chambre des mises en accusation," *Le Populaire*, July 7, 1939, 3. See also Patrice Rolli, *La phalange nord-africaine en Dordo-gne: Histoire d'une alliance entre la pègre et la Gestapo, 15 mars–19 août 1944* (Boulazac: Histoire en partage, 2010), 51. In spite of the work of the sprawling investigation, very few of the Cagoule's leaders were prosecuted before the war. A combination of a lack of evidence, uncertainty about what charges were most appropriate, and a desire to avoid public scandal on the eve of what many feared was the beginning of a war with Germany led Béteille to dismiss charges against most of those arrested in November 1937.

34. For a historical account of the Rosselli assassination see Stanislao G. Pugliese, "Death in Exile: The Assassination of Carlo Rosselli," *Journal of Contemporary History* 32, no. 3 (1997): 305–19. See also the version of the story in Brunelle and Finley-Croswhite, *Murder in the Métro*, 87–95.

35. Aficionados of French conspiracy theories will know that the Bouvyer family was also close with the family of François Mitterrand, the future leader of the French left and president of France from 1981 to 1995. After the Second World War, Jean-Marie Bouvyer was the lover of Mitterrand's sister, Marie-Josèphe Mitterrand, and some have claimed (probably erroneously) that Mitterrand himself was involved in the Cagoule. See for example Pierre Péan, *Une jeunesse française: François Mitterrand, 1934–1937* (Paris: Fayard, 1994).

36. "L'Homme brun proteste," *Paris-Soir*, June 16, 1937. Copy of article in AN: 19980411/7.

37. The record of Bouvyer's interrogation by Marius Gaillard is in AN: 19980411/7, dossier 1127-N, Affaire Rosselli. In fact, Bouvyer gave two accounts of the Rosselli murders: first after his arrest in 1938, and again in 1945 when the Cagoule case was reinvestigated after the Second World War.

38. An undated police report, probably from 1945, notes that El Maadi was a chevalier of the Legion of Honor and decorated with the Médaille Militaire and the Croix de Guerre for his service in the campaign of 1939–1940. APP: 1W 1752–102170. These decorations are confirmed in his military service record: SHD GR/8Y/128830.

39. El Maadi was one of several Algerians who rallied to the extreme right under Vichy and who expressed pro-Nazi sympathies. On the participation of Algerians in the movements that supported the Vichy regime see Pascal Ory, *Les Collaborateurs, 1940–1945* (Paris: Seuil, 1976), 174–76.

40. A police report of December 15, 1941, dates the attempt to occupy the Jewish-owned building as January 9, 1941. APP: 1W 1752–102170. A later undated report (probably from late 1944 or early 1945) dates El Maadi's arrest for the occupa-tion attempt to April 9, 1941.

41. Letter from the Commissaire Général aux Questions Juives to the Prefect of Police, November 4, 1941, APP: 1W 1752-102170. The letter is a simple request for information about El Maadi, who had apparently already been hired by the commissariat.

42. Letter from Mohamed El Maadi, as secretary-general of the Comité Nord-Africain, to a prospective member of the organization, October 11, 1941, APP: 1W 1752-102170.

43. Katz, *Burdens of Brotherhood*, 135. Rolli, *La phalange nord-africaine en Dordogne*, 50. El Maadi himself tended to overestimate the impact of *Er Rachid*. A police report from February 2, 1943, stated that El Maadi claimed that he would quickly assemble a list of thirty thousand subscribers for the journal. In point of fact, he had at that moment only three hundred subscribers, and the number was not increasing rapidly. APP: 1W 1752-102170.

44. These aspects of El Maadi's career are summarized in Katz, *Burdens of Brotherhood*, 133-35.

45. APP: 1W 1752-102170.

46. Robert Soucy suggests, almost certainly incorrectly, that El Maadi already had three hundred men under his command in 1937-1938. Since Filiol only placed El Maadi at the head of Algérie française in September 1937, and El Maadi was arrested in the Cagoule affair at the end of November, it seems unlikely that he had time to recruit and provide for a group of this number. The figure of three hundred is more often cited as the number of men recruited to the North African Brigade in 1943-1944, during its operations alongside the Wehrmacht. A more recent book by David Motadel gives a lower figure of 180 men in the brigade. David Motadel, *Islam and Nazi Germany's War* (Cambridge, MA: Harvard University Press, 2014), 242. The activities of the brigade in 1944, including its involvement in mass executions, are detailed in Rolli, *La phalange nord-africaine en Dordogne*.

47. A note from 1947 in a file at the prefecture of police indicates that in 1944, during the operations against the Resistance, El Maadi had the rank of captain in the SS. Préfecture de Police, Direction de la Police Judiciaire, Brigade des Notes, 9ème Section, 7431, Rapport, February 7, 1941, APP: JB 52.

48. Cour d'Appel de Paris, Extrait des minutes du greffe de la Cour d'Appel de Paris, November 3, 1945, APP: JB 52.

49. Mohamed El Maadi, *L'Afrique du Nord: Terre d'histoire* (Paris: Éditions France-Empire, 1943), 10.

50. El Maadi, 100-101.

51. El Maadi, 112-13.

14. The Trials

1. The existence of this "secret committee" is recorded in a single document, a report by Henri Coquelin, the director of Sûreté Départementale de Constantine, no. 652, February 23, 1936, ANOM: ALG CONST 93/B/3/522. The report cites the Croix de feu leader, Colonel Gros, as saying that Morinaud was "like money that no longer had value." Henri Lellouche, also present at the meeting, suggested that he could bring the Popular Front voters to support Gratien Faure, while Dominique Cianfrani, the leader in Constantine of the "neo-socialists," said that he would bow

out in favor of Faure if his own campaign appeared to benefit Morinaud. In the same meeting, Morel announced his intention to run against Stanislas Devaud, the Croix de feu candidate in the second *circonscription* of the department of Constantine. None of these efforts came to fruition: Morinaud and Devaud were both victorious in their campaign for parliament, and the failure of the so-called secret committee revealed the growing impotence of a once-powerful local establishment.

2. "Onze israélites inculpés de violences lors des troubles de Constantine ont été acquittés," *L'Écho d'Alger*, February 9, 1935. 3. See also Sûreté Départementale de Constantine, no. 560, February 8, 1935, ANOM: ALG CONST 93/B/3/700.

3. "Trois émeutiers de Constantine assassins de Guedj sont condamnés à 10 et 15 ans de bagne," *L'Écho d'Alger*, July 5, 1935.

4. "Deux émeutiers de Constantine sont condamnés à sept ans de bagne," *L'Écho d'Alger*, July 10, 1935.

5. "L'ancien tirailleur Aouchet, médaillé militaire, émeutier constantinois et assassin de M. Guedj, est condamné à cinq ans de réclusion," *L'Écho d'Alger*, July 12, 1935, 3. The facts of the Chemla trial were briefly summarized at the beginning of this article.

6. "Coup de théâtre à Constantine. La cour a renvoyé les affaires en instance l'atmosphère étant trop agitée après le jugement de l'émeutier Aouchet," *L'Écho d'Alger*, July 13, 1935, 1.

7. "La Police arrête deux indigènes qui ont participé au massacre de la famille Halimi," *L'Écho d'Alger*, August 30, 1934, 3.

8. Armand Kessis, "Les assassins présumés des familles Halimi et Zerdoun devant la Cour Criminelle d'Orléansville," *La Dépêche de Constantine*, 3. See also "Quatre indigènes accusés du massacre des familles Halimi et Zerdoun lors des émeutes de Constantine répondent de leur sauvage forfait," *L'Écho d'Alger*, February 6, 1936, 1, for the ages of the accused.

9. Gouvernement général de l'Algérie, Département de Constantine, Sûreté Générale, no. 2406, Homicide volontaire du Sieur Attal et des Membres de la famille Alphonse Halimi, Rapport Spécial, August 18, 1934, ANOM: ALG GGA 9/H/52.

10. Le Cour Criminelle d'Orléansville a jugé les assassins des familles Halimi et Zerdoun," *La Dépêche de Constantine*, February 7, 1936, 3.

11. Rédarès's closing speech was quoted and summarized by Armand Kessis in a subsequent article on the Attali trial the next day, "Les cinq meurtres commis dans la maison Attali amènent 3 accusés devant la Cour Criminelle d'Orléansville," *La Dépêche de Constantine*, February 8, 1936, 3.

12. "Les cinq meurtres commis dans la maison Attali amènent 3 accusés devant la Cour Criminelle d'Orléansville," *La Dépêche de Constantine*, February 8, 1936, 3.

13. "Les cinq meurtres commis dans la maison Attali amènent 3 accusés devant la Cour Criminelle d'Orléansville," *La Dépêche de Constantine*, February 8, 1936, 3.

14. Armand Kessis, "L'épilogue de la tuerie de la rue des Zouaves," *La Dépêche de Constantine*, February 9, 1936, 3.

15. Déroulède's desire to use the Constantine riots as part of a critique of Governor-General Carde is well documented in his correspondence with the League of the Rights of Man in the late summer of 1934. See BDIC F delta res 798 (169).

Conclusion

1. Nadir Bouzar, *L'odysée du Dina: Récit du premier transport d'armes de la Révolution Maghrébine* (Algiers: Bouchène—ENAL, 1993). Nadir Bouzar (1917–1975) was himself a veteran of the French army, a former official in the Moroccan Protectorate, and after 1953 a militant nationalist who helped arrange the first shipment of arms to the Algerian National Liberation Front (FLN) from abroad. He served as foreign minister of Algeria after independence. Among the revolutionaries that Bouzar knew in Cairo in 1953 were the Algerians Ahmed Ben Bella (future president of Algeria), Mohamed Khider, and the Moroccan nationalist Allal al-Fassi.

2. See Abdellali Merdaci, *Auteurs algériens de langue française de la période coloniale: Dictionnaire biographique* (Paris: L'Harmattan, 2010), 116–17.

3. Tried in absentia by a judge and a four-member jury after his flight from France, El Maadi was found guilty of "intelligence with the enemy" during the German occupation and sentenced in 1948 to life imprisonment at hard labor. The dossier noted that a majority of the jury also found "that there exist extenuating circumstances in favor of the accused," but these circumstances were not described. Cour d'Appel de Paris, dossier no. 5.015, July 29, 1948, AN: Z/6/593.

4. Historian Annie Rey-Goldzeiguer recounted how El Maadi had contacted Messali Hadj in 1941, while the nationalist leader was in prison, and offered him his freedom in exchange for open support of El Maadi's collaborationist Comité musulman nord-africain. Messali Hadj refused any cooperation with El Maadi. Rey-Goldzeiguer, *Aux origines de la guerre d'Algérie, 1940–1945: De Mers-el-Kébir aux massacres du nord-constantinois* (Paris: La Découverte, 2002), 51.

5. Jean-Louis Planche, *Sétif 1945: Histoire d'un massacre annoncé* (Paris: Perrin, 2006); Jean-Pierre Peyroulou, *Guelma, 1945: Une subversion française dans l'Algérie coloniale* (Paris: Découverte, 2009).

6. Bouzar, *L'odysée du Dina*, 21. This irony is perhaps not as surprising as it may have seemed, though Bouzar clearly thought it was significant. The educational opportunities for Algerian Muslims in the first half of the twentieth century ensured that even prominent members of the FLN leadership did not necessarily know how to read or write in Arabic in the 1950s.

7. Jacques Berque, *French North Africa: The Maghrib between Two World Wars* (London: Faber and Faber, 1967), 256.

8. The press accounts did not mention the monument to the Jewish dead, focusing instead on the Monument aux morts devoted to those who died in the war. "Une grandiose cérémonie a marqué l'inauguration officielle du Monument aux Morts de Constantine," *L'Écho d'Alger*, November 3, 1934. Reference to the smaller Jewish monument appears in prefectural reports, including Sûreté Départementale d'Alger, no. 5916, A. S. inauguration d'un monument aux morts israélites de Constantine, October 24, 1934, ANOM: ALG ALGER 2/i/38.

9. On Gozlan and other Jews active in the struggle against colonial racism see Pierre-Jean Le Foll-Luciani, *Les Juifs algériens dans la lute anticoloniale: Trajectoires dissidentes (1934–1965)* (Rennes: Presses universitaires de Rennes, 2015).

10. Sûreté Départementale d'Alger, no. 5916, A. S. inauguration d'un monument aux morts israélites de Constantine, ANOM: ALG ALG 2/i/38.

11. Sûreté Départementale de Constantine, no. 3610, "Croix de feu," October 24, 1934, ANOM: ALG CONST 93/B/3/707. Report by Henri Cocquelin to the prefect of Constantine.

12. Copies of this report exist both in the archives of the Central Consistory in Paris and in the archives of the Alliance israélite. See "Rapport sur le role de M. Morinaud dans les événements de Constantine, 21 November 1934," Archives de la Consistoire de Paris, carton B 130, and AAIU Algérie 1C Antisémitisme 1. On the evolution of Maurice Eisenbeth's theory of the riots see also the letter of November 6, 1934, from the Alliance israélite in Algiers to Sylvain Hallf, secretary-general of the Alliance israélite universelle in Paris, AAIU Algérie 1C Antisémitisme 2.

13. See Rochdi Ali Younsi's discussion of the Eisenbeth report in Younsi, "Caught in a Colonial Triangle: Competing Loyalties within the Jewish Community of Algeria, 1842–1943" (PhD diss., University of Chicago, 2003), 178–79. Younsi rightly emphasized that Eisenbeth's report represented a shift from earlier interpretations by Jewish leaders that had blamed Bendjelloul for the violence.

14. Abbas wrote an article in *La Dépêche Algérienne* in November 1935 that defended the members of the FEMC from the charge of antisemitism by distinguishing between the "Jewish proletariat," which deserved protection and sympathy, and the "Jewish bourgeoisie," which had both benefited from special treatment during the colonial period and cooperated with a political regime that continued to discriminate against Muslims. The article contained recognizable anti-Jewish tropes ("the kings of finance and politics" . . . "found everywhere after the war, in the freemasons' lodges, in the parties of the left, the League of the Rights of Man") but nevertheless was more open to a political movement that would not take religious allegiance as the primary marker of belonging. This alone marked a significant difference between Abbas and Bendjelloul's embrace of an openly ethno-religious and anti-Jewish political engagement in the months after the riots of 1934. Ferhat Abbas, "Juifs et Musulmans d'Algérie," *La Dépêche Algérienne*, November 10, 1935. On these positions of Abbas see also Ethan Katz, *The Burdens of Brotherhood: Jews and Muslims from North Africa to France* (Cambridge, MA: Harvard University Press, 2015), 100–101.

15. Police Spéciale Départementale de Constantine, no. 2217, Incidents, Rapport, Le Chef de la Police Spéciale Départementale, Henri Coquelin, June 27, 1938, ANOM: ALG CONST 93/6520.

16. Police Spéciale de Constantine, no. 2266, Parti Social Français, Source indicateur: bonne, Rapport, Le Chef de la Police Spéciale Départementale, Henri Coquelin, July 1, 1938, ANOM: ALG CONST 93/6520.

17. Police Spéciale Départementale de Constantine, no. 2243, Élections Municipales complémentaires, Rapport, Le Chef de la Police Spéciale Départementale, Henri Coquelin, June 30, 1938, ANOM: ALG CONST 93/6520.

18. ANOM: ALG CONST 93/6520.

INDEX

CPSIA information can be obtained
at www.ICGtesting.com
Printed in the USA
BVHW032304281020
591999BV00013BA/110/J

9 781501 739415